W9-BCK-619

JAMES FORD RHODES

The Man, the Historian, and his Work

James Ford Rhodes

The Man, the Historian, and his Work

With a Complete Bibliography of
the Writings of James Ford Rhodes

by ROBERT CRUDEN

GREENWOOD PRESS, PUBLISHERS
WESTPORT, CONNECTICUT

Library of Congress Cataloging in Publication Data

Cruden, Robert.
James Ford Rhodes : the man, the historian, and his work.

Reprint of the ed. published by Press of Western Reserve University, Cleveland, Ohio.
Bibliography: p.
Includes index.
1. Rhodes, James Ford, 1848-1927. 2. Historians--United States--Biography.
[E175.5.R45C78 1980] 973'.07'2024 [B]
ISBN 0-313-22255-X lib. bdg. 79-28196

Reprinted in 1980 by Greenwood Press,
a division of Congressional Information Service, Inc.
51 Riverside Avenue, Westport, Connecticut 06880

Printed in the United States of America

10 9 8 7 6 5 4 3 2 1

For

JANET

TABLE OF CONTENTS

ACKNOWLEDGEMENTS

Grateful acknowledgement is made to the following publishers for permission to cite from copyrighted works as follows:

Charles Scribner's Sons: H. A. Herbert, *The Abolition Crusade and Its Consequences;* Henry C. Lodge, *The Democracy of the Constitution;* Robert Grant, *The Chippendales.*

E. P. Dutton & Company, Inc.: Cleveland Amory, *The Proper Bostonians.*

Houghton Mifflin Company: W. R. Thayer, *Life and Letters of John Hay;* Charles F. Adams, *Autobiography;* Robert Grant, *Fourscore: An Autobiography;* and M. A. DeWolfe Howe, editor, *Later Years of the Saturday Club, 1870–1920.*

Harper and Brothers: Woodrow Wilson, *A History of the American People.*

Princeton University Press: Thomas J. Pressly, *Americans Interpret Their Civil War.*

Macmillan Company: James Ford Rhodes, *Lectures on the American Civil War* and *Historical Essays;* A. M. Schlesinger, Sr., *The Rise of the City, 1878–1898.*

Appleton-Century-Crofts, Inc.: M. A. DeWolfe Howe, *James Ford Rhodes: American Historian.*

University of Minnesota Press: Frank M. Anderson, *The Mystery of "A Public Man": A Historical Detective Story.*

Long's College Book Company: J. N. Larned, *The Literature of American History.*

The Viking Press, Inc.; A. T. Mason, *Brandeis: A Free Man's Life.*

Ohio Historical Society: John A. Garraty, editor, *The Barber and the Historian: the Correspondence of George A. Myers and James Ford Rhodes, 1910–1923.* Citations in this work are taken from the original articles as they appeared in the *Ohio Historical Quarterly* (*1955*).

University of Chicago Press: W. T. Hutchinson, editor, *The Marcus W. Jernegan Essays in American Historiography.*

INTRODUCTION

FIFTY YEARS ago the name of James Ford Rhodes was known and respected in the household of nearly every literate American. Rhodes held a unique position in public esteem, being regarded not only as a great historian but also as *the* historian whose fiat was final on all matters pertaining to the eventful years 1850 to 1877. His interpretations of the Civil War and Reconstruction, characterized on the one hand by a broad nationalism and on the other by an exclusive Anglo-Saxon racism, were accepted for years by laymen and scholars alike. Moreover, his judgments on a wide variety of subjects relating to morals, race, economics and politics found a warm response among the American public generally, a response which found echo among significant groups of Englishmen. In short, Rhodes exercised an influence upon his contemporaries equalled by few historians. That influence, although considerably diminished, has persisted down to our own day.

In view of Rhodes' importance, it is somewhat surprising that since his death in 1927 only one full-scale work has been devoted to him, Mark A. DeWolfe Howe's *James Ford Rhodes: American Historian*, an excellent source of valuable material, including correspondence, to which I am greatly indebted. Mr. Howe's volume, however, being biographical rather than historiographical, dealt only in passing with Rhodes' place in the history of American history.

The purpose of this work is to contribute to an understanding of that place. To understand Rhodes as historian, however, it is necessary to attempt an appreciation of Rhodes as a person and of his relation to the society of his day. This last is particularly revealing, for much of Rhodes' influence lay in his being so much a part of that society, so representative of its dominant currents of thought and attitude.

It is then possible to analyze Rhodes' historical work and his views on history and its functions, and on the role of the historian. Specific attention is given to Rhodes' use of sources and to his reputation for objectivity in the light of standards of historical criticism of our own day. In addition, the first exhaustive bibliography of Rhodes' works is supplied.

Every attempt has been made to explore all the sources; even so, there are some gaps, such as Rhodes' relations with Boston newspapers, but these are of minor importance in a study such as this. As to interpretation, it must be remembered that a hazard of biographical work is the unconscious growth of sympathy between writer and subject. I have striven for objectivity, conscious always that utter impartiality is impossible. My point of view will be readily apparent.

Responsibility for the work is my own, of course, but such merit as it may possess is due in large measure to the assistance of numerous individuals and institutions. I owe a deep debt of gratitude to Dr. Harvey Wish of Western Reserve University, who suggested the study, guided it through its gestation period as a doctoral dissertation and has continued to be a source of encouragement and stimulation. I am also under deep obligations to Mrs. Bertha H. Rhodes, Brookline, Mass., Rhodes' daughter-in-law, and Mrs. Lucia McBride, Cleveland, Ohio, Rhodes' niece, for interviews which shed much light on Rhodes' personality; the late Dr. Mark A. DeWolfe Howe, Boston, Mass., for a profitable discussion in which he suggested some productive areas of inquiry; Dr. Sidney B. Fay and Dr. Frederick Merk of Harvard University for reminiscences about Rhodes and his relations to Harvard; Mr. Stephen A. Riley, Director, Massachusetts Historical Society, for permission to work in the Rhodes Papers; Dr. Carl F. Wittke, Dean of the Graduate School, Western Reserve University, for generous encouragement and inspiration; and Dr. Fred E. Harris, Dean of Baldwin-Wallace College, whose active cooperation helped make possible final preparation of the manuscript.

I am grateful also to the Joseph and Feiss Fund, Western Reserve University, which helped to finance work in the documentary sources; and to the Faculty Development Fund, Baldwin-Wallace College, which aided in publication.

I may not complete this pleasant task without due acknowledgement of the assistance given by Dr. Walter M. Whitehill, Director, The Athenaeum, Boston, Mass.; Mr. Clyde Haselden, librarian, Lafayette College; Dr. John Hall Stewart, Western Reserve University; Dr. David Lindsey, Los Angeles State College; Dr. Louis Koren, M.D., Birmingham, Mich.; Dr. Carl Haessler, Highland Park, Mich.; Dr. C. D. Penner, Baldwin-Wallace College; Mrs. Helen Lamb, Cambridge, Mass.; the staff of the Western

Reserve Historical Society, particularly Miss Harriet Scofield, genealogist, and Mr. Joseph Nugent, who labored so faithfully to produce the files of necessary newspapers; and Mrs. Jean McCall, Baldwin-Wallace College, who, as typist, contributed no little to the work's publication. To Mr. Willis Thornton, Western Reserve University Press, is due a special note of thanks: his keen editorial eye and mellow scholarship have much improved the author's original work.

Chapter 1

THE NEW ENGLAND INHERITANCE

ON MAY DAY of that year of revolutions, 1848, there was born to the family of a prosperous businessman in Ohio City, the little town directly across the Cuyahoga River from Cleveland, a boy destined to leave his mark not only on the writing of American history but also on the beliefs of countless Americans who came to accept as holy writ both his interpretations of the Civil War and Reconstruction and the feelings and assumptions which colored those interpretations. In this way, he helped to influence in no small degree the attitudes of a considerable public on such issues as race, labor, immigration, the gold standard, the tariff and other major public concerns. The boy was James Ford Rhodes.

A typical product of the Western Reserve, James was the son of New Englanders, themselves descendants of New Englanders; and he grew up in a city the basic attitudes of which were cast in the Puritan mold—not the heroic mold which produced Garrison and Emerson, but the narrower pattern which shaped John D. Rockefeller and Mark Hanna.

His father, Daniel Pomeroy Rhodes, a cousin of Stephen A. Douglas, was one of those sons of impoverished Vermont who swarmed into the Western Reserve in the early decades of the 19th century. Daniel's destination was Franklin Mills, Ohio (now Kent). This small town, in 1835, the year of his arrival, was enjoying a boom based on the building of the Ohio and Pennsylvania Canal, which, traversing the town, would link Pittsburgh with the Ohio Canal. After a brief and apparently unsuccessful venture in a general store, Daniel entered into partnership with another Vermonter, William Pomeroy, operating a woolen factory, grist mill and sawmill. The enterprise did not survive the Panic of 1837, which struck Franklin Mills so hard that buildings in the center of town, deserted by their occupants, were used as shelters for cattle. The resourceful Daniel then turned to Democratic politics with some success, for in August, 1838, he was appointed postmaster.[1]

Thrifty and shrewd New Englander that he was, Daniel must have made something from his business and political exploits, for by 1840 he had sufficient capital to join two other enterprising young men in developing an iron furnace in Akron. With them (James Ford, after whom the historian was named, and David Tod, later the Civil War governor of Ohio) he went on to open up the Brier Hill coal mines near Youngstown. Since the coal produced was of a higher quality than that generally available in northern Ohio, output expanded to meet the demands of the steel industry in the Mahoning Valley and of varied interests in Cleveland.

The development of the Cleveland market was largely the work of Daniel, who labored assiduously to persuade home-owners, hotel-keepers and steamship operators that coal was more efficient than wood. The skeptical Yankees of the city were converted only "after much persuasion and experiment," as one commentator put it, but once the dam was breached, the flow was golden. Not only were the Brier Hill operations expanded, but the partners also bought extensive coal property in nearby Girard and in Wayne and Tuscarawas counties.[2]

So thriving was Daniel that in 1844 he was finally able to marry his long-courted sweetheart, Sophia Lord Russell, a Connecticut girl directly related to the Lords and Barbers, New England families of wealth and distinction who dominated the rather exclusive social circles of Ohio City. By 1848, when James was born, Daniel was already a figure of note in the business and society of northern Ohio.[3]

As we shall see, Daniel's influence upon his son was significant and long-lasting. To understand James, therefore, we must discover what manner of man was Daniel.

In business, he was a man of optimism, perseverance and aggressiveness—only such qualities could have carried him through the Panic of 1837 and the obduracy of Clevelanders wedded to wood as the only proper fuel. Some critics, noting Daniel's troubles as executor of the estate of his cousin, Stephen A. Douglas, have concluded that Daniel was somewhat insensitive to ethical considerations.[4] If so, it is difficult to understand why Douglas, himself no innocent in matters of business, named Daniel as executor. Nor does such a conclusion square with his reputation among the businessmen of Cleveland, indicated by the editorial comment of the Republican *Leader* on the occasion of Daniel's death: "We have known Mr. Rhodes for over a quarter of a century and we can sincerely say that we have never heard a word uttered disparagingly of him as a man of integrity and honor." [5] This was no mean tribute in view of the fact that Daniel had been a "stiff and uncompromising" Democrat in a business community overwhelmingly Republican.[6]

In family relationships, Daniel was jovial, generous, quick-witted, fond of his wife and family. He was a hospitable man, keeping open house not only for his own friends and relatives—Douglas, for example, was a frequent visitor—but also for those of his wife, who delighted in entertaining dignitaries of the Episcopalian Church, of which she was a conscientious member. In the words of Lucia McBride, a granddaughter who knew the family well, "Daniel was not much on religion, but he believed in letting his wife enjoy herself." [7] Like most men of his day Daniel enjoyed his liquor, and he likewise had a weakness for cards—failings which often vexed his wife, despite her Episcopalian tolerance in such matters.

Daniel never allowed the difference in outlook to disturb domestic tranquility. On one occasion when he reached home at 3 A.M. on a Sunday after a card session with James Ford, followed by an impromptu visit to a Fireman's Ball, he confronted an annoyed Mrs. Rhodes while Ford scuttled upstairs.

"Wherever have you been?" she demanded, "I haven't slept a wink all night."

"Neither have I," replied the imperturbable Daniel. "Let's go to bed and talk it over in the morning."

On another belated arrival he claimed to have reached home by midnight. That was impossible, said Mrs. Rhodes, for at that hour she had been on the stairs with a candle in her hand and had seen no one.

"Well, well," rejoined her husband, "we must have passed each other on the stairs." [8]

For all his joviality, however, Daniel was still the patriarchal father of Victorian days. When his elder daughter, Augusta, began keeping company with young Mark Hanna, Daniel flatly forbade her to see the "damned screecher for freedom," whose Republican doctrines he abhorred. Augusta defied him, but Daniel was far from beaten. He tried to make the young couple start housekeeping in his home, at first unsuccessfully. When business reverses forced the Hannas to yield, Daniel was openly exultant.[9] Daniel left religious training of the children to his wife, but their political education he took upon himself. James recalled later that his father thoroughly indoctrinated him in the Democratic faith, especially teaching the lad to revere his relative, Stephen A. Douglas.[10]

James' mother, Sophia, was as strong a character as her husband, and if her influence on the son was not so obvious as that of Daniel it was no less pervasive. Lucia McBride recalls her as a firm, kindly, gracious woman who "would dominate you—if you let her. She would be very nice about it—but she would dominate, nevertheless." [11] She was a paragon of the 19th century virtues: a good housekeeper, a good wife, devoted to her family and church—St. John's Episcopal Church, in which she was a leading spirit during her life.[12]

Together with her own mother, Mrs. A. G. Russell, she saw to it that the children received thorough religious training. Before he was twelve, James was as familiar with the Bible and the Episcopalian prayer-book as he was with Democratic politics.[13] Unlike many of her generation, Mrs. Rhodes was given to no narrow religiosity. Her son recalled her as a woman who loved to do good and enjoyed such pleasures as singing and playing the organ.[14]

Mrs. Rhodes was happy in her marriage and in her four children: C. Augusta, who married Mark Hanna; Robert Russell, who became a local millionaire; James Ford; and Fannie, the youngest, who married Philip McCurdy, a steel mill operator of Youngstown. With James, her relations were especially close. After his marriage, she was a frequent and welcome guest in his home, and she often accompanied the family on trips to Europe. When they were apart, James wrote to her so regularly that when, for any reason, the letter was delayed, she was certain that an accident had befallen him! [15]

Sophia passed on to James a passion for order and method, a rigid respect for the proprieties, and a firm belief in an absolute moral order which made such observance reasonable.[16] She also bestowed on him, as on the other children, the priceless boon of "family" in a community dominated by New Englanders. Sophia was born in Hebron, Connecticut, to Robert Russell and his wife, Abigail, a daughter of Josiah Barber. After Russell's death, the family in 1836 rejoined Barber in Ohio City, where he and his brother-in-law, Richard Lord, had established themselves as social, political and industrial leaders since their arrival from Connecticut in 1818. Not only did Barber and Lord own much of the real estate on the west bank of the Cuyahoga River, but they also led in establishing such enterprises as the Cuyahoga Steam Furnace Co., which manufactured steamship machinery and (later) railroad locomotives. At one time Barber had owned a distillery; he destroyed it when he felt it was harming the community. He had gained political prestige as mayor and judge and added to his reputation by helping his friend, Bishop Philander Chase, establish what is now Trinity Cathedral in Cleveland and St. John's Church in Ohio City. The social standing of the Barbers and Lords was impeccable.[17]

James Ford Rhodes, then, was born into a family of assured social and economic standing, and, perhaps of more significance to him as an individual, into a family enjoying marital felicity and emotional security. He was also born into a community about to shed its shell of comfortable, restricted mercantile enterprise to plunge into the inviting but turbulent waters of industrialism.

When James was born the shell had not yet been sloughed off; he drew his first breath in air unpolluted by smoke and fumes. Travelers found Cleveland's location dry and healthy, and commented favorably on the town's clear atmosphere, its numerous groves of elms and maples, and the taste displayed in the private houses, which helped make it "one of the most beautiful towns in the Union." The editor of the Cincinnati *Gazette* described it as "the most desirable town in the 'Great West' *to live in.*" [18]

Residents were not so certain. A local editor complained about the "long, lanky, lean cadaverous-looking hogs" that rooted through garbage in the streets and alleys.[19] Water supply and sewage disposal were private concerns; outbreaks of disease, especially smallpox and cholera, were frequent. Travel was hazardous at night or in bad weather, for the streets lacked lights, paving and sidewalks. Citizens found trying the virtual isolation of the town during the winter. With Lake Erie frozen over and the roads impassable, Clevelanders passed those months in "a sort of semi-life, analagous to that of a bear"—or so thought an editor trying to stir up interest in railroad building.[20]

Actually, in winter as in summer there were activities to interest and amuse the populace. Each Sunday they had their choice of divines to listen to: Presbyterian, Baptist, Methodist, Mormon, Episcopalian, African Methodist, Universalist, Wesleyan. On weekdays there were available lectures on such diverse topics as slavery, phrenology, the age of the earth, and moral conditions in Haiti. Concerts were provided by the noted Hutchinson family, combining Free Soil politics with music, and by non-political groups like the choir of the First Baptist Church. Booksellers offered a wide selection of reading material, ranging from George

Bancroft's *History of the United States* to *The Physiology of Woman.*[21]

Nor was amusement lacking. Theatres, although looked upon as "sinks of ungodliness," tried to make ends meet by offering double features, embracing such combinations as *Hamlet* and *A Kiss in the Dark.*[22] General Tom Thumb visited the city, as did the Great United States Circus, "the largest troupe ever organized." One could experiment with daguerrotypes at a new shop on Superior Street or try for prizes offered for the best planting of shade trees on the streets. Vulgar fellows enjoyed what an editor called "a nicely turned ankle" when the ladies, garbed in the newly-fashionable "short" dresses, made their way across the muddy streets.[23]

Many citizens, however, had matters on their minds other than pretty ankles. The election of 1848, coming after the conclusion of the controversial Mexican War, had upset the traditional two-party system. Anti-slavery Democrats and Whigs, deserting their party standard-bearers, rallied behind the free soil candidate, Martin Van Buren. The vexing issues of slavery and secession, which seemed to have been quieted in 1820 and 1832, now rose again to perplex men with a stake in things.[24]

More immediately, there was the problem of the city's future, symbolized by the organization of a Board of Trade in July, 1848. Cleveland had been a somnolent village until the opening of the Ohio and Erie Canals transformed it into the great *entrepot* between the industrial Northeast and the rural hinterland of Ohio. The growth of the city was indicated in the rise of population from 9,573 in 1845 to 17,034 in 1850.[25] The amount of goods moving through the city over the Ohio canal increased steadily, swelled by the new coal trade, which shipped nearly two million bushels in 1848 as compared with 893,806 bushels two years earlier.[26] Emigrants from Germany, Ireland, Scotland and Wales found employment in the infant industries, the first surge of a tide that was to carry the old New England stock to the commanding heights of industry, finance and commerce.[27]

Such growth was satisfying, but some leading citizens pointed out that Cleveland was doomed unless she speedily linked herself by rail with Cincinnati and the East. Others, unconvinced that railroads held profitable possibilities, promoted construction of plank roads to the nearby cities of Wooster, Warren, Ravenna and Chagrin Falls. A few mulled over, with some skepticism, the report of Dr. J. Lang Cassels, the Cleveland scientist, that there were iron ore deposits in the upper Lake Superior region which might be exploited with profit. They saw the potentialities for Cleveland of industry based on a union of iron ore and cheap coal; but being Yankees, they moved cautiously, wanting to make sure of success before embarking on new enterprise.[28]

However much they might quarrel over slavery, or differ over plank roads or railroads, men of Cleveland agreed on one thing: a man's success in life depended on himself, and himself alone. In the words of the *Daily True Democrat*, apropos of the rise to fortune of a local grocer: "What cannot a man accomplish, if he will but try?" [29]

This, then, was the city into which James Ford Rhodes was born: linked to the past through its New England inheritance, deeply imbued with the Puritan concepts of thrift, hard work and individualism, it was, however reluctantly, reaching out its hands for the manna of modern America: railroads, coal and iron ore. These, too, were to be the bread of life for the Rhodes family.

NOTES

1 Mrs. Lucia McBride, niece of James Ford Rhodes, in a typescript history of the Rhodes family in the Papers of James Ford Rhodes, Massachusetts Historical Society. The typescript is unsigned, but Mrs. McBride confirmed her authorship in an interview. See also *Cleveland, Past and Present; Its Representative Men: Comprising Biographical Sketches of Pioneer Settlers and Prominent Citizens, With a History of the City* (Cleveland, 1869), p. 330. *The Ohio Star* (Ravenna, Ohio), Jan. 21, March 31, May 12, and Sept. 1, 1836; Jan. 4 and Aug. 9, 1838. Karl Grismer, *The History of Kent: Historical and Biographical* (Kent, Ohio, 1932), pp. 21, 23, 29.

2 Col. Whittlesey in J. Wiggins & Co., *Directory of the City of Cleveland and Adjoining Towns, 1872–73* (Cleveland, 1872), pp. 27–30. Mark A. DeWolfe Howe, *James Ford Rhodes; American Historian* (New York, 1929), p. 16. Mrs. Lucia McBride, typescript, Rhodes Papers. *Cleveland, Past and Present*, p. 330.

3 Margaret M. Butler, *The Lakewood Story* (New York, 1949), p. 139. M. A. D. Howe, *Rhodes*, pp. 11–13.

4 Frank H. Hodder, "Propaganda as a Source of American History," *Mississippi Valley Historical Review*, IX (1922), 10. George Fort Milton, *The Eve of Conflict: Stephen A. Douglas and the Needless War* (Boston, 1934), pp. 145–146. See also the present work, Chapter III.

5 Cleveland *Leader*, Aug. 6, 1875; Cleveland *Daily Plain Dealer*, Aug. 6, 1875.

6 James Ford Rhodes to Sir George Otto Trevelyan, Aug. 18, 1920. Rhodes Papers.

7 Mrs. Lucia McBride, interview.

8 Characterization and anecdotes from interviews with Mrs. Lucia McBride and Mrs. Bertha H. Rhodes.

9 Herbert Croly, *Marcus Alonzo Hanna: His Life and Work* (New York, 1912), pp. 47, 49–50.

[10] M. A. D. Howe, *Rhodes*, pp. 18–19.

[11] Mrs. Lucia McBride, interview.

[12] *Ibid.;* Mrs. Bertha H. Rhodes, interview; *Cleveland Topics*, Nov. 5, 1927, p. 15.

[13] M. A. D. Howe, *Rhodes*, p. 18.

[14] *Ibid.*, pp. 15, 161–162; Mrs. Lucia McBride, interview.

[15] *Cleveland, Past and Present*, p. 332; Mrs. Lucia McBride, interview. Mrs. McBride is a daughter of Fannie Rhodes and Philip McCurdy.

[16] Mrs. Lucia McBride, interview.

[17] M. A. D. Howe, *Rhodes*, pp. 12–14; M. M. Butler, *The Lakewood Story*, p. 139; Elbert Jay Benton, *Cultural Story of an American City: Cleveland* (Cleveland, 1943–1946), II, 72.

[18] Travelers quoted in Samuel P. Orth, *A History of Cleveland, Ohio* (Chicago, 1910), I, 110, 131, 176; editor in E. J. Benton, *Cultural Story*, III, 7. Italics in original.

[19] Cleveland *Daily True Democrat*, Dec. 23, 1848.

[20] S. P. Orth, *History*, I, 127, 176, 196, 214; E. J. Benton, *Cultural Story*, II, 27, 70–71; *Daily True Democrat*, Nov. 2, 1848.

[21] *Daily True Democrat*, 1848, *passim.*

[22] Artemus Ward, quoted in E. J. Benton, *Cultural Story*, III, 32; *Daily True Democrat*, April 15 and Sept. 22, 1848.

[23] *Daily True Democrat*, May 16, June 28, July 24, Sept. 20, Dec. 5, Dec. 18, 1848.

[24] *Daily True Democrat*, Nov. 8, 9, 10, 1848. Cleveland voters preferred Lewis Cass, the Democratic candidate; Ohio City chose Van Buren.

[25] Cleveland *Weekly Leader*, Jan. 6, 1847; *Daily True Democrat*, July 7, 1848; S. P. Orth, *History*, I, 112.

[26] *Weekly Leader*, Jan. 6, 1847; *Daily True Democrat*, Aug. 8, 1849.

[27] E. J. Benton, *Cultural Story*, III, 24–25; S. P. Orth, *History*, I, 114–115.

[28] *Daily True Democrat*, March 24, 25, 31; April 22; Aug. 4; Nov. 6, 18, 29; Dec. 2, 12, 1848. James H. Kennedy, *A History of the City of Cleveland, 1796–1896* (Cleveland, 1896), p. 371.

[29] Oct. 25, 1848.

Chapter 2

"SERIOUS MINDED" YOUTH

JAMES spent his early years in a Cleveland beginning to realize on the promises held out in the '40's. By 1853 the city was linked by rail with Cincinnati, Buffalo and Toledo. Within another four years it tapped the coal fields of northeastern Ohio through the Cleveland & Mahoning railroad, assuring a year-round coal supply, not only for its own uses but also for shipment to Chicago and the West.[1] The first shipment of iron ore from the Lake Superior country arrived in 1852, and soon far-sighted businessmen were engaged in iron mining, shipping, and manufacture. Industrial expansion received additional stimulus from the Civil War. Population leaped from 43,000 to 65,000 between 1860 and 1865. The town whose "clear air" had charmed travelers in the 1840's was now proud of its two blast furnaces, six rolling mills and numerous forges, foundries and factories.[2]

James' father played a leading role in this transformation. In addition to expanding his coal operations in northeastern Ohio, he took an active part in promoting railroads to the coal fields, and to Toledo and Cincinnati. Within Cleveland he helped develop rail and street car connections to the West Side and Rocky River, areas in which he held extensive real estate. He was also an active figure in developing a gas works, a savings and loan association and an insurance company.[3] By 1868, Daniel's basic enterprise, the partnership of Rhodes and [Jonathan F.] Card, owned the largest docks on the waterfront.[4]

James, sharing in the family's growing prosperity, was influenced also by his father's energetic Democratic politics. An active partisan of Stephen A. Douglas, Daniel fought in state and national party conventions to advance the interests of his kinsman.[5] He held office as councilman in Ohio City; as a commissioner to effect the union of Ohio City and Cleveland; and as a member of the first elected board of education in Cleveland.[6]

Since politics was with him a matter of principle he did not hesitate to defy public opinion in a strongly abolitionist community. He served on the carefully selected jury which found Simeon Bushnell, a leading spirit in the Wellington-Oberlin Negro rescue incident, guilty of violating the fugitive slave law—a verdict which brought down torrents of abuse on those responsible.[7] During the Civil War, when many Democrats went over to the Union party, Daniel stayed staunchly with his party. In 1861 he ran for state senator on a platform condemning the use of force against the seceding states, and in 1863 he campaigned for Clement L. Vallandigham, the Democratic candidate for governor who was looked upon in the Western Reserve as a second Benedict Arnold. The Republicans promptly labeled Daniel a "copperhead"! [8]

Small wonder, then, that James' earliest memories were of politics: hearing a stump speech by Gen. Winfield Scott; marching in a torchlight procession for James Buchanan; listening to Daniel and Douglas trade views; reading the *Congressional Globe*. After Fort Sumter, James was swept off his feet by "the first flush of enthusiasm" but as the war went on he reverted to his father's views; in high school he argued against the Proclamation of Emancipation, and held that Vallandigham, far from being a traitor, had been outrageously treated.[9]

The freedom with which young James was allowed to criticize official government policy in wartime says a great deal about the public schools of that day, and helps explain his fond memories of his school days. A pupil in a private school before he was five years old, he was transferred to the public schools at seven, and remained in the public school system until his graduation from high school in 1865. In grade school, James recalled later, the emphasis was on teaching the students how to think. The teachers drew on their own backgrounds to enliven their presentations and were eager to encourage the students to investigate subjects in books other than textbooks.[10]

In high school, James benefited from an atmosphere in which free debate of public issues was actively stimulated through organized debate and encouragement of differences of opinion. One teacher he remembered with admiration, because, although an ardent Republican, the teacher permitted the few Democratic students "fair opportunity for free expression of their opinions." Teachers, in that day, were required also to impart moral and religious guidance; in Cleveland, it was inevitable that such guidance was distinctively Puritan. James, as an adult, thought that while it might have been narrow "it had a good side." [11]

Outside of school, there is little evidence that young James took part in such light-hearted boyish fun as Mark Twain described. There was a great lakefront to explore and the exciting new railroads around which to build adventures, but the boy, in the words of Mark A. DeWolfe Howe, was "serious minded, . . .

addicted rather to reading and thinking than to the more active pastimes of youth." [12] It is typical of the lad that one of his great pleasures was acting the part of clergyman in "playing church" at home after services on Sunday.[13]

In the fall of 1865 James entered the University of New York, now New York University, after spending the summer (at his father's behest) visiting the great cities of the East, during which he, in company with the widow of Douglas, paid a call upon President Andrew Johnson and listened sympathetically while the President inveighed against Thaddeus Stevens and Charles Sumner.[14]

James was, of course, a good student, and perhaps because of that he profited from rigorous training in the mastery of historical detail, vigorous class discussion and a wide range of reading, although, as he confessed, he was a slow reader, often having to read material two or three times before he mastered it.[15] His enthusiasm for history was kindled by two books in particular: Henry Thomas Buckle's *History of Civilization in England* and John William Draper's *History of the Intellectual Development of Modern Europe*. Draper, who served as a professor at the university, impressed James with his scientific spirit and his relentless pursuit of the truth. Buckle inspired in the youth a feeling that life held no higher pleasure than the writing of history; James resolved that he, too, would be a historian.[16]

Young James liked the school in New York City, but Daniel had other plans for him. Yielding to his father's "expressed desire," the youth transferred to the University of Chicago in the fall of 1866. The university (not to be confused with the present institution) had been built in 1857 on land donated by Douglas, which may explain Daniel's interest. If in New York the emphasis had been on science and history, in Chicago it was on metaphysics—not surprising, perhaps, in view of the fact that the president was Dr. John C. Burroughs, a Baptist clergyman, who taught a course in "Moral and Intellectual Philosophy."

James, who had been fascinated by the materialistic Buckle, now read the works of Sir William Hamilton, who sought to provide a psychological basis for belief in God. He also read a book which "had not been recommended by the faculty"—John Stuart Mill's Utilitarian *Examination of Sir W. Hamilton's Philosophy*. As an antidote to Mill, he read James McCosh, the president of Princeton who expounded Hamilton. James thought Mill had the better argument; from his study he came away with a profound and enduring respect for the English rationalist, diminished though it was later by Mill's espousal of the cause of women's rights.[17]

At Chicago, also, James developed a taste for English literature, wrote essays, became acquainted with Emerson for the first time, and began his lifelong addiction to *The Nation*, which, in his view, was the weekly journal "of civilization and good political morals," then edited by Edwin L. Godkin, "the gentleman and cultivated man of the world." *The Nation* exercised a significant influence on James for most of his adult life.[18]

Nor was his education confined to the classroom. In those days, if we are to believe James, most students "were eager to learn," and continued their learning through good talk about books and topics of the day and through the more formal channels of debating societies. James gained considerably from such intellectual activity, just as he did from a roommate, who introduced him to the teachings of Herbert Spencer. On Sundays, James listened faithfully to the sermons of Robert Collyer, the popular Unitarian preacher who expounded the mild social ethics of the liberal Christianity of the day. In this case, it would seem from James' later views that Spencer had the better of the argument.[19]

During this year he received a shock to one of the basic articles of his political faith. Taught by his father to revere Stephen A. Douglas, he was ill-prepared to cope with the *North American Review*, that ponderous but influential Bible of the mid-century intellectuals, when it savagely attacked the Little Giant. Identifying Douglas with President Andrew Johnson, to whose Reconstruction policies it was opposed, the *Review* set forth what later came to be an accepted interpretation of Douglas: He was an apostle of immorality in politics; driven by uncontrollable ambition, he sacrificed an enslaved race and the peace of his country to his lust for the Presidency; his doctrine of "popular sovereignty" was an insincere proposition designed to ensnare Southern votes; his support for the Union after Fort Sumter was revenge for the South's failure to support his political ambitions.[20]

The impact of such an indictment, coming from such a highly-respected source, must have been great. It "made a profound impression on me at the time," James wrote later.[21] That the impression endured is indicated by his treatment of Douglas in his *History*.[22]

The year at Chicago ended James' formal schooling. Daniel took him off to France, and while teaching the dazzled youth not to be deceived by the splendors of the Second Empire, persuaded him to give up his dream of a literary life in favor of a more solid career in business.[23] Daniel, gratified, returned to Cleveland, and James set off to Berlin, where he studied iron metallurgy at the School of Mines. This indoctrination in industry he followed up with extensive visits to mines and iron and steel works in Germany and Britain. When he was bored, which was often, he turned for relaxation to Goethe, Schiller and Auerbach in Germany; in England to the *Times* of London and the Tory *Saturday Review*. It is symptomatic of Rhodes' cast of thought that the *Review*, like *The Nation*, made a lasting impression on him.[24]

When James returned to Cleveland in the summer of 1868 he found that Daniel's business career had taken a new turn. Daniel was now concentrating on the production and financial aspects of his interests, having turned over the merchandising enterprise of Rhodes and Card to a firm made up of his son, Robert; his son-in-law, Mark Hanna; and an old business associate, George W. Warmington.[25] James apparently got his initiation in business as an assistant to his father, and Daniel thought highly enough of his acumen to dispatch him in 1869 to survey the possibilities of profitably exploiting coal and iron resources in Tennessee, Georgia and North Carolina.

The young man carried out the assignment with his usual conscientiousness, but he was much more interested in the process of Reconstruction. Already sympathetic with the policies of Andrew Johnson, and imbued with the Democratic outlook of his father, he returned North convinced that the Southern Democrats represented the forces of good government.[26]

NOTES

1 E. J. Benton, *Cultural Story*, III, 12–13; Herbert Croly, *Hanna*, pp. 55–56; James B. Whipple, "Cleveland in Conflict; A Study in Urban Adolescence, 1876–1900" (Unpublished Ph.D. dissertation, Western Reserve University, Cleveland, 1951), p. 12.

2 E. J. Benton, *Cultural Story*, III, 15, 57; J. H. Kennedy, *History of Cleveland*, p. 371; Thomas Beer, *Hanna* (New York, 1929), p. 27; *Cleveland, 1888; Its History and City Government* (Cleveland, n.d.), pp. 98, 102–103.

3 Daniel also acquired coal fields in Illinois and iron and steel interests in Tuscarawas County, Ohio. Mrs. Lucia McBride, typescript, Rhodes Papers. *Cleveland, Past and Present*, pp. 330–332; *History of Tuscarawas County, Ohio* (Chicago, 1894), pp. 543–544, 558; J. B. Whipple, "Cleveland in Conflict," p. 12; Cleveland *Leader*, Jan. 1, 1861; Jan. 15, 1867, June 4 and Dec. 28, 1868; March 4, 1869.

4 *Cleveland, Past and Present*, p. 332.

5 G. F. Milton, *Eve of Conflict*, pp. 225, 285, 310, 356, 377, 382.

Reports of Daniel's local political activities may be found in *Daily True Democrat*, Dec. 30, 1851; Jan. 10, 1852; Sept. 19, Oct. 6, and Oct. 7, 1853; Cleveland *Weekly Leader*, Dec. 22, 1857; Cleveland *Leader*, Dec. 2, 1859. See also *Cleveland, 1888*, p. 77; and Elroy McK. Avery, *A History of Cleveland and Its Environs: The Heart of the New Connecticut* (Chicago, 1918), I, 236.

[6] *Ibid.*, I, 216, 220, 357, 538; *Daily True Democrat*, March 4 and April 3, 1851; Cleveland *Leader*, April 10, 1854 and Oct. 11, 1859.

[7] James Ford Rhodes, *History of the United States from the Compromise of 1850 to the Final Restoration of Home Rule at the South in 1877* (New York, 1892–1906), II, 361–366; William C. Cochrane, *The Western Reserve and the Fugitive Slave Law: A Prelude to the Civil War* (Cleveland, 1920), p. 140. Cochrane to Rhodes, May 25, 1920, Rhodes Papers. Cleveland *Leader*, March 9, 1859.

[8] Cleveland *Plain Dealer*, Jan. 21 and Jan. 24, 1861; Cleveland *Morning Leader*, Jan. 25, 1861; Cleveland *Leader*, Sept. 23 and Oct. 10, 1861; April 4 and June 24, 1862; June 13, 25 and 26, 1863; June 24, 1864; April 5, 1865.

[9] M. A. D. Howe, *Rhodes*, pp. 18–20.

[10] *Ibid.*, pp. 17–18.

[11] *Ibid.*, pp. 18–20; J. F. Rhodes, *History*, III, 103 n.

[12] M. A. D. Howe, *Rhodes*, p. 31. Mrs. Lucia McBride confirmed this in an interview.

[13] M. A. D. Howe, *Rhodes*, pp. 30–31.

[14] *Ibid.*, p. 20; J. F. Rhodes, *History*, V, 534 n; Rhodes, quoted in Charles K. Bolton, *Notebook Kept by Charles K. Bolton, 1886–1914* (The Athenaeum, Boston, Mass.), p. 91 (Dec. 6, 1898).

[15] M. A. D. Howe, *Rhodes*, pp. 21, 35; James Ford Rhodes, *Historical Essays* (New York, 1909), p. 69.

[16] M. A. D. Howe, *Rhodes*, pp. 21–22. Draper also wrote a *History of the American Civil War* (3 vols., New York, 1867–1870), which while subscribing to the conspiracy theory, was remarkably free from the partisanship characteristic of the times. See Thomas J. Pressly, *Americans Interpret Their Civil War* (Princeton, N. J., 1954), pp. 34–37.

[17] M. A. D. Howe, *Rhodes*, pp. 22–23, 36–37. Rhodes to Sir George Otto Trevelyan, Aug. 29, 1915. Rhodes Papers.

[18] M. A. D. Howe, *Rhodes*, p. 23; J. F. Rhodes, *Historical Essays*, pp. 269, 280–282. Rhodes to Sir George Otto Trevelyan, Aug. 30, 1914. Rhodes Papers.

[19] M. A. D. Howe, *Rhodes*, p. 23; J. F. Rhodes, *Historical Essays*, p. 293; "Robert Collyer," *Encyclopaedia Britannica*, 11th ed., VI, 694–695.

[20] CCIII (1866), 511–515. Rhodes characterized the *Review* as "a monument of American scholarship and fair-minded criticism." *History*, I, 292.

[21] *History*, V, 620 n.

[22] *Ibid.*, I, 430, 431, 435, 494.

[23] M. A. D. Howe, *Rhodes*, p. 24.

[24] *Ibid.*, pp. 24–25; Rhodes to Sir George Otto Trevelyan, Aug. 29, 1915. Rhodes Papers.

[25] *Cleveland, Past and Present*, p. 332; *Cleveland Leader Annual City Directory, 1866–67* (Cleveland, 1866), p. 232; *Cleveland Leader Annual City Directory, 1869–70* (Cleveland, 1869), p. 248; Cleveland *Leader*, Jan. 15, and April 26, 1867; Sept. 24 and Dec. 28, 1868; March 4, 1869. William Ganson Rose, *Cleveland: The Making of a City* (Cleveland, 1950), p. 354.

[26] M. A. D. Howe, *Rhodes*, p. 25; J. F. Rhodes, *History*, VI, 300–301, 305, 310.

Chapter 3

THE RELUCTANT BUSINESSMAN

WHEN James dutifully entered the service of business, the omens were auspicious. America, rebounding from the brief post-war slump of 1866–1867, was flushed with the strain of transcontinental railroad building, the accompanying boom in iron and steel, and the exploitation of the riches of a virgin West.

Cleveland, center of a flourishing coal, iron and machine-building economy, metropolis of the new oil empire of John D. Rockefeller, shared in the national prosperity. Between 1860 and 1870 its population grew from 43,000 to nearly 91,000, and daily arrivals of immigrants gave ample indication that the fast tempo of development would continue. Land values rose until some farm land in the vicinity of the city sold for $1,000 an acre.[1] Official valuation of property in Cleveland, real and chattel, increased from $18,865,460 in 1860 to $57,841,746 in 1871.[2] James himself described the period as one in which "business was good in the quiet, satisfactory way of large sales at fair prices and moderate profits." So far as iron was concerned, "demand was active, profits were large." [3]

Daniel, having supervised James' apprenticeship, arranged a partnership for him with one Curtis S. Barrett, which made its appearance in 1870 as Rhodes and Barrett, dealers in coal and firebrick.[4] Apparently the firm shared in the prosperity of the time, for within two years James felt secure enough to marry Ann Card, daughter of his father's old partner, Jonathan. Those who knew her personally describe her as a witty, amiable, warm-hearted woman, who, despite the fact that for much of her life she was a semi-invalid, fulfilled the Victorian ideal of the wifely role: "to embellish the home, and to make happy the lives of the man and dear ones who dwell within it." [5] James, always chary of personal revelation, never referred to a honeymoon, but to judge from references in his work he and his bride went South, visiting New Orleans and Vicksburg—a trip which served to accentuate his feelings against Reconstruction.[6]

It is not surprising, then, that in the presidential campaign of 1872 James supported Horace Greeley, the choice of both Democrats and Liberal Republicans. In what appears to have been his sole excursion into active politics, he served as vice-president of a convention of those parties called to select a Congressional candidate for Cleveland on the Greeley ticket. He must have felt a quick pang of sympathy with Daniel, for the Republican *Leader* promptly labeled the venture "the Liberal-'Copperhead' party of this city." [7] Whether James, with his aversion to controversy, shrank from such rough-and-tumble politics, or whether he felt that dabbling in politics was too hazardous for a young man in business, is uncertain, but for the rest of the campaign he was silent. He was quiet, too, the following year, when his brother, Robert, and Mark Hanna led a successful fight to drive the local Republican "ring" from the City Hall.[8] When, in 1875, James deserted the Democrats because of their espousal of "soft money," he did so discreetly, with no flourish of trumpets.[9]

The firm of Rhodes and Barrett did not survive the Panic of 1873, but in the following year James made the connection which was to afford him the means of spending the latter part of his life as "gentleman historian": he became a partner in Rhodes and Company, in which Robert Rhodes was associated with Mark Hanna, the guiding genius of the firm. Under Hanna's shrewd management, the firm became the center of an economic empire which extended from the coal mines of northeastern Ohio to the iron ore country of Lake Superior.

The empire was integrated through the firm's own lake fleet and through an alliance with the Pennsylvania railroad, which not only transported the firm's coal and ore but also leased to Rhodes and Company its docks at Ashtabula, Ohio. The partnership sold not only its own coal and iron but also those of other producers, a lucrative position often attained through purchase by the individual partners of sufficient stock in producing companies to assure sales contracts going to Rhodes and Company. As a hedge against fluctuations in the raw materials market, the firm engaged in iron production at Dover, Ohio, and Sharpsville, Pennsylvania. As Herbert Croly put it: "[Rhodes and Company] could either sell the raw material or convert it according to the comparative opportunities for profit." [10]

Thus, for the ten years which James spent with the firm, he was at the center of a powerful and aggressive enterprise, intimately allied with one of the nation's great railroad systems, and exercising influence far beyond its own holdings. It brought him close to the seats of economic and political power—and it also confronted him with one of the major problems growing out of the new, impersonal industrial order.

The year in which James joined Rhodes and Company the coal operators of the Tuscarawas Valley, including his own firm, reduced coal miners' wages from ninety to seventy cents a ton. The ensuing strike was settled when the operators, at a meeting presided over by James, granted a wage of eighty cents a ton.[11] As business continued to decline, the operators, led this time by Rhodes and Company, slashed wages once more to seventy cents; a strike forced a concession of a seventy-five cent wage.[12] In March, 1876, wages were again reduced—to sixty-five cents a ton. The miners, trying to live on an average pay of five dollars a week, went on strike again.[13]

The strike was uneventful until, on April 11, Rhodes and Company sent in strikebreakers. Three days later the strikers forced out the newcomers, and in doing so clashed with officials of the company, one of whom was shot in the arm. The *Leader*, reporting the affair on page one under the head, "Mob Law—A Reign of Communism," painted a lurid picture of peaceful businessmen set upon by an armed mob "which would neither work nor allow others to do so." An editorial called for stern action to end "this kind of anarchy." [14]

James visited the scene, and while unfavorably impressed by the miners, felt that the reports had been exaggerated. On his return to Cleveland he tried to set the *Leader* straight in an interview. No one, he said, had been "dangerously hurt," and while the reports had

> in the main been true, still to a great extent they had been somewhat overdrawn. The miners have not had any desire to take life, nor in their sober moments to do injury, but merely to intimidate the operators, and prevent new men from working the mines, which he says they actually believe they have a right to do. . . .
>
> . . . Mr. Rhodes states . . . that the miners did not intend to shoot anyone, as the pistols were fired into the air on nearly every occasion. . . .[15]

The *Leader* made no comment on James' remarks, and he himself played no more public role in the strike, which collapsed shortly afterwards when Governor Rutherford B. Hayes sent in the National Guard.[16]

Here, surely, was the very stuff of history. Here, through Rhodes and Company, the young man with a bent for history could examine the hidden, interrelated functioning of business, labor and politics in a nation in rapid metamorphosis from agrarianism to industrialism. There is little indication that James realized his opportunity. He looked upon the firm, not as a laboratory in which to study American society, but as a means of making that "competence" which would enable him to indulge his literary ambitions. As Lucia McBride explains it, "He was not happy, he was not unhappy. It was simply a means of doing what he wanted to do." [17]

The heart of the matter is, of course, that James was not really interested in business, neither in its larger implications nor in its limited concern as a profit-making enterprise. He himself observed that the firm's success was due more to the talents of his partners than to his own contribution, and his brother, Robert, attributed it to Hanna's efforts and favorable economic conditions. Significantly, he made no mention of James.[18]

James' heart was in literature. Visitors to the office often found him secluded with a book.[19] He frequented the Cleveland Public Library, and avidly read *The Nation*, which, he said, was the "most important link between our practical world and the literary world." [20] He kept up his familiarity with French, and read novels and plays constantly, regarding this as a link with the literary world to which he had reluctantly said farewell.[21]

His significant associations, too, lay in what little of the literary world there was available in Cleveland. He was an ardent member of the Vampire Club, an organization of Clevelanders interested in cultural affairs. There he cultivated John Hay, diplomat and *littérateur*, whom Rhodes looked upon as "a superior person." Hay, enjoying the respectful attention of such provincials as James, held forth on the fascinations of cultural life in the East and of diplomatic life in the capitals of Europe—and quite inadvertently kept alive James' ambition to write.[22]

At Mark Hanna's home James hobnobbed with the celebrities of the stage who played at Hanna's Cleveland Opera House, including Edwin Booth, Henry Irving, Joseph Jefferson and Lawrence Barrett.[23] Years later he recalled with fondness the presentation of Booth in *Hamlet* and *Othello* and of Irving in *The Merchant of Venice*.[24]

Such interests, however, did not preclude a concern with the issues of the day. On these, his outlook was largely shaped by *The Nation*, the significance of which he himself described:

> The gospel which Godkin preached [revenue tariff, hard money, "home rule" in the South, morality in politics, supremacy of property rights in labor disputes, Anglo-American friendship] was needed much more in the West than in the East; and his disciples in the Western country had for him a high degree of reverence. . . . His influence was abiding. Presidents, statesmen, senators, congressmen rose and fell; . . . but Godkin preached to us every week a timely and cogent sermon.[25]

To that publication he attributed his favoring civil service reform; his feelings against Reconstruction were intensified by Godkin's frequent assaults upon it.[26] James' antagonism to "soft money," while no doubt partly due to the inconvenience caused Rhodes and Company by the Canadian discount of American currency, was based largely on *The Nation*'s defense of gold.[27] Under its inspiration, he deserted the Democratic party in 1875 because its candidate for the governorship espoused "soft money" heresies.[28] As in 1875, so he felt again in 1878, when Congress took up the Bland-Allison bill to expand the coinage of silver. James and his "gold men" were in a minority as they argued the matter with Cleveland businessmen, "but, fortified by *The Nation*, we thought that we held our own." [29]

During these eventful years James encountered problems of a more personal nature, for which even Godkin could furnish little guidance. In August, 1875, Daniel Rhodes died, and for the first time in his 27 years James could truly feel that he was his own man. Within a few months, he was put even more on his mettle, for Ann bore him a son, appropriately named Daniel Pomeroy Rhodes.[30]

The difficulties facing him as responsible head of a family were not to be taken lightly. As executor of Daniel's estate he had the unpleasant task of complying with an Illinois court order awarding $30,000 to the heirs of Stephen A. Douglas. James, governed as he was by high personal moral standards, was probably less disturbed by the loss of money than by the reflection cast on the character of his father, for in their suit the heirs had charged Daniel with conspiracy to defraud in his capacity as executor of the Douglas estate.[31]

Of more immediate personal consequence, James became a father while the country was in the grip of depression. The years following the Panic of 1873, he remembered from experience, were times in which "the depression and even despair of businessmen . . . can hardly be exaggerated." [32] It was a time, too, when the well-to-do thought the very foundations of society were crumbling as discontented farmers and workers sought relief from their burdens through organization, strikes and legislation such as the Granger laws. The disturbances attendant on these social upheavals, wrote James,

> came like a thunderbolt out of a clear sky, startling us unduly. For we had hugged the delusion that such social uprisings belonged to Europe and had no reason of being in a free republic where there was plenty of room and an equal chance for all. . . .[33]

Under these circumstances, and with Daniel no longer an obstacle, it is not surprising that James' thoughts should have turned to his first love. In "quiet moments" he wondered whether he could attain the literary ambitions of his early years.[34] While thus torn between the literary and the business worlds, he went to Boston in the summer of 1877, and while there learned of John T. Morse, Jr., the lawyer and legal writer of note who was preparing to abandon his profession for literature after having written a successful biography of Alexander Hamilton, which James admired.[35]

Here was the cue for which James had waited. As he confided to Morse later: "this was an incentive for me to shape my course in the endeavor to throw off eventually the shackles of business in order to devote myself to dearer and higher work." [36] If Morse furnished the inspiration, another writer, a historian, furnished the impetus. One evening, while reading Richard Hildreth's *History of the United States*, and perhaps recalling the youthful visions aroused by Buckle, James determined to write a history of his country. He would first make sufficient money on which to retire, and then devote himself to writing. In the meantime, he would read and amass notes with that end in view.[37]

The notes were accumulated methodically in an alphabetized volume of 230 pages about the size of a bookkeeper's journal, especially prepared for such a purpose by one Dr. John Todd and published under the title: *Index Rerum*.[38] The notes, which eventually filled four such volumes by the end of James' career, fall into four general categories: quotations he thought significant; references on relevant subjects; brief reports on his discussions with witnesses of or participants in historical happenings; and notes on literary style.

Unfortunately, few provide insight into James himself or into the trends of his thinking, but here and there an attitude may be gleaned from his choice of subject matter. The first entry, made in 1878, for example, is a quotation from Keats copied from *The Nation:* "I find I can have no enjoyment in the world but continual drinking of knowledge. I find there is no worthy pursuit but the idea of doing some good in the world." Sharing the place of honor is an observation from the Editor's Easy Chair of *Harper's Magazine*, although not added until much later: "In writing history the vital necessity is the historic sense, the ability to conceive the spirit of a time and to interpret it with candor." [39]

While these collections of notes furnish little light on James' thinking, they do bear witness to the scope and carefulness of his reading. The historians, of course, are well represented, with numerous lengthy citations from Gibbon, Macaulay, Mommsen, Bancroft, Thucydides and Lecky. The pages are also replete with quotations from such diverse sources as Aeschylus, Matthew Arnold, John Milton, Thomas De Quincey, Herbert Spencer, Goethe and Plato. Books which James considered of outstanding significance, such as *The Education of Henry Adams*, he outlined in full.[40]

The bulk of the material is heavily sober, but occasionally there is a lighter touch: William Dean Howells' observation, "How much easier it is to make one's peace with one's God than with one's wife"; a phrase from *Paradise Lost*—"secret, reluctant, amorous delay"; and Rhodes' own contribution, listed under "Reformers," that "radicals expected too much of America." [41]

James did not confine himself to reading and note-taking. In 1881, when he was placed in charge of the pig iron department of Rhodes and Company, he began writing circulars or monthly reviews of business which were sent to customers. To James, they meant rekindling of his ambition to write history, an opportunity to write and to prepare for a future literary career. With such an end in view, he tried to study businessmen from what he called "a philosophic point of view" as well as dealing with purely business matters.[42]

Unfortunately, little of that point of view is to be seen in the circulars that are available. They are rather optimistic appraisals, couched in pedestrian prose, of the recession which affected the iron industry from 1883 to 1885. Together with soothing, and unfulfilled, predictions of recovery, James coupled panaceas for hastening the process: limitation of production; expansion of the currency (from James, of all men!); maintenance of Protection; and cultivation of a spirit of optimism. In short, the kind of "philosophy" which explains why trade journals found the circulars "very valuable," "very comprehensive and intelligent." [43]

James' predictions are embarrassingly, if anachronistically, reminiscent of those of the soothsayers of a more recent depression. In June, 1883, while pig iron prices were sliding to a level of $7.50 a ton compared with $12.50 in 1880, James thought an improved crop situation would set the stage for a better iron market.[44] By September, he detected an improvement, a view he confirmed in October. The following month he conceded the vision had been a mirage, but solaced his readers with the reflection that since business was so bad "matters can be no worse." [45]

In fact, matters got much worse. Activity in the iron industry so declined that production of pig iron fell off nearly a million tons in 1884 and prices slumped to $3.50–$5.75 a ton.[46] James, however, maintained a determined optimism. Early in 1884 he foresaw an upturn, based on increased sales of public lands, consequent development of agriculture, the satisfactory condition of foreign trade and the "easy" state of the money market.[47] By October he was admitting that prosperity had failed to turn the corner, but, he argued, the gloomy state of things was more apparent than real, for America was blessed with abundant crops and when these were marketed the beneficial effects would be felt everywhere.[48]

With prosperity still elusive at the New Year, James speculated that recovery was bound to come in 1885, since there would be no "disturbing elements" such as a presidential election, "tariff tinkering" or financial panic.[49] In his last circular, February, 1885, he claimed that business had indeed improved, but not enough "to cause any degree of elation." [50] Actually, recovery did not get under way until much later that year.[51]

James, of course, like most of his fellow businessmen, firmly believed in economic "laws"; like them, too, he believed that certain measures might be adopted by which "the cure would be sooner effected than if left to the operation of natural causes." [52] Iron manufacturers, he urged, should curtail production to curb falling prices, citing the example of the nail manufacturers who had shown "that prices can be controlled" through such curtailment.[53]

Another remedial measure he recommended was mild inflation of the currency. The national banks, taking advantage of the premiums at which United States bonds were selling, had been disposing of their bonds at market prices. This led to a shrinkage in the amount of national bank notes in circulation, which, added to the fears of further currency contraction, contributed to the difficulties of business recovery.[54] To counteract this, James suggested that national banks be permitted to increase the issue of their notes up to 90 per cent of their market value, instead of the 90 per cent of face value required by law.[55] With the bonds selling at high premiums this would have resulted in some increase in the amount of circulating currency, and this, in turn, would have had some effect in stemming the price decline.

Such may seem strange doctrine coming from a man who broke with his party over "soft money," but it must be remembered that most Cleveland businessmen of this period were "soft money" men and that the iron and steel industry itself had endorsed inflationary policies during the Panic of 1873.[56] No doubt James was influenced by those factors—especially since his circulars were designed to attract business to Rhodes and Company from these very interests.

Above all, however, James wanted tariff protection for iron. The tariff of 1883 had cut the duty on pig iron from $7.00 to $6.72 a ton, a reduction which, as Professor Taussig pointed out, was insignificant.[57] To the iron industry, however, the tariff meant obstruction to its growth and destruction of the "nascent tin-plate industry." [58] James, voicing this view, called upon Congress to use the tariff to build the tin-plate industry and warned the Democrats and Liberal Republicans that "the political party which identifies itself with the anti-American idea [on the tariff] in the present critical condition of trade, cannot long retain power." [59] The case for Protection, he thought, was simple:

> The whole question of Protection lies in a nutshell. Our country is the granary of the world. Here must be raised the food to make up the deficit in Europe. The transportation of that grain implies a network of railroads. The construction of the railroads means an enormous consumption of iron. Shall that be furnished by well-fed American labor or by the pauper labor of Europe? If labor was equalized, the iron interest would not need protective duties. Which would tend to the highest welfare of the human race—the elevation of European labor to our standard, or the degradation of American labor to the European standard? We leave the revenue reformer to answer.[60]

To his proposals of output limitation, currency inflation and Protection, James added advice to businessmen themselves: they should cultivate positive thinking. He upbraided Wall Street for its current pessimism, and urged his fellows to change their attitudes:

> While conservatism is properly the order of the day, it is a question whether it is true conservatism to conduct one's business with the idea that a further decline in values is probable. Is it not more reasonable to base one's operations on the belief that if there is any marked change in prices, it will be in an upward direction? [61]

James himself, certainly, had need to develop an optimistic outlook. He had entered Rhodes and Company in the year following the Panic of 1873. In the ensuing months iron fell from $42 to $28 a ton; by the fall of 1874 nearly 43 per cent of the furnaces in the country were out of blast.[62] The downward trend continued until 1879. A four-year period of prosperity followed. In 1883 the old cycle of falling prices, shutdowns and unemployment resumed, as we have seen.

It was in this period, however, that James embarked on his venture to accumulate such a competence that he could retire to a life of literary leisure. Under the circumstances it is difficult to understand how he attained his objective: the available material sheds little light on how he acquired wealth in years of depression. He himself said later that he made money fast, although he also twice advanced the financial goal he had set for himself.[63] We may assume that the hard times delayed his retirement, and that the prolonged depression impressed upon him the need for a greater competence than he originally planned. It may also be assumed that under the direction of Mark Hanna the firm was quite capable of making money even in depression.[64] At any rate, in 1884, despite the gloomy aspect of business, James felt he could safely retire.[65] On April 1, 1885, Rhodes and Company was formally dissolved, to be succeeded by M. A. Hanna and Company.[66]

How much of a fortune did Rhodes accumulate? A family source believes he had about $250,000 when he went to Boston in 1891.[67] Charles K. Bolton, librarian of the Boston Athenaeum and a friend of Rhodes, noted that the newcomer possessed "half a million" when he arrived.[68] Whatever the amount, it proved sufficient—together with the increment derived from investments—for his purpose. Not as poor scholar, but as "gentleman historian," he lived out his life in Proper Boston and its breathtakingly beautiful resort, Seal Harbor, Maine, and in all the places to which Proper Boston progressed when it bestowed its presence on the Old World.

NOTES

[1] W. G. Rose, *Cleveland*, pp. 361–362, 376, 393–394.

[2] J. Wiggins & Company, *Directory of the City of Cleveland and Adjoining Towns for 1872–73* (Cleveland, 1872), p. 96.

[3] *History*, VII, 38.

[4] *Cleveland Leader Annual City Directory, 1868–69* (Cleveland, 1868), p. 128; W. S. Robison & Company, *Cleveland Directory, 1871–72* (Cleveland, 1871), pp. 66, 353. James said Daniel arranged a partnership for him with two older men, but available records list only Barrett. See M. A. D. Howe, *Rhodes*, p. 25.

[5] The marriage took place Jan. 4, 1872. Cleveland *Daily Leader*, Jan. 6, 1872; M. A. D. Howe, *Rhodes*, p. 29; Arthur M. Schlesinger, Sr., *The Rise of the City, 1878–1898* (New York, 1933), p. 126. Mrs. Bertha H. Rhodes and Mrs. Lucia McBride, interviews.

[6] *History*, VII, 104–105.

[7] Cleveland *Daily Leader*, Aug. 26, 1872; Cleveland *Daily Plain Dealer*, Aug. 23 and Aug. 24, 1872; J. F. Rhodes, *Historical Essays*, p. 281. Eric Goldman, *Rendezvous with Destiny* (New York, 1952), p. 21, puts James at the convention of the Liberal Republican party at Cincinnati in 1872. This appears to be a mistake in identification. The Cleveland delegate by the name of Rhodes was James H. Rhodes (no relative) who as an attorney and politician was active in the party. See *Proceedings of the Liberal Republican Convention in Cincinnati, May 1st, 2nd and 3rd, 1872* (New York, 1872), pp. 16–17, 40; Cleveland *Daily Leader*, May–November, 1872, *passim:* Cleveland *Daily Plain Dealer*, May 3, May 6, June 26, July 18, Aug. 24, 1872.

[8] Cleveland *Daily Plain Dealer*, March–April, 1873, *passim.*

[9] Rhodes, *Historical Essays*, p. 281; Cleveland *Daily Plain Dealer*, September–November, 1875, *passim.*

[10] H. Croly, *Hanna*, pp. 56–62.

[11] *Ibid.*, pp. 91–92; John R. Commons, *History of Labour in the United States* (New York, 1918), II, 180; Cleveland *Daily Plain Dealer*, April 15, 1875.

[12] Cleveland *Daily Leader*, Aug. 5, Aug. 6 and Aug. 18, 1875.

[13] Cleveland *Daily Leader*, April 18, 1876; Ohio Bureau of Labor Statistics, *First Annual Report, 1877*, p. 143, quoted in J. B. Whipple, "Cleveland in Conflict," p. 83.

[14] Cleveland *Daily Leader*, April 15 and April 18, 1876.

[15] Cleveland *Daily Leader*, April 18, 1876; Rhodes, *From Hayes to McKinley*, p. 63.

[16] Cleveland *Daily Leader*, May 3, May 5, May 12, June 26, 1876.

[17] Interview.

[18] H. Croly, *Hanna*, p. 54; M. A. D. Howe, *Rhodes*, p. 26.

[19] Harvey Cushing, M.D., "James Ford Rhodes," in Mark A. DeWolfe Howe (ed.), *Later Years of the Saturday Club, 1870–1920* (Boston, 1927), p. 350.

[20] Rhodes, *Historical Essays*, p. 293; M. A. D. Howe, *Rhodes*, p. 43.

[21] *Ibid.*, p. 26.

[22] *Ibid.* Rhodes to Henry Cabot Lodge, Jan. 15, 1909. Rhodes Papers.

[23] H. Croly, *Hanna*, p. 75; Edmund Pechin to Rhodes, July 19, 1918; Rhodes to Sir George Otto Trevelyan, June 12, 1920, Nov. 12, 1922. Rhodes Papers.

[24] Rhodes to Sir George Otto Trevelyan, June 12, 1920. Rhodes Papers.

[25] Rhodes, *Historical Essays*, pp. 279–280.

[26] *Ibid.*, pp. 280, 282.

[27] Thomas Beer, *Hanna*, p. 56.

[28] Rhodes, *Historical Essays*, pp. 280–281.

[29] *Ibid.*, pp. 281–282.

[30] Cleveland *Daily Plain Dealer*, Aug. 6, 1875; Cleveland *Daily Leader*, Aug. 6, 1875; M. A. D. Howe, *Rhodes*, p. 29. The son, born Jan. 20, 1876, was the only offspring of Rhodes' marriage.

[31] G. F. Milton, *Eve of Conflict*, pp. 145–146. Milton believes this experience "may have, unconsciously of course, colored the judgment" of Rhodes on Douglas. This view is also put forward by Frank H. Hodder, "Propaganda as a Source of American History," *Mississippi Valley Historical Review*, IX (1922), 10.

[32] *From Hayes to McKinley*, p. 99.

[33] *Ibid.*, p. 46.

[34] Rhodes to John T. Morse, Jr., May 6, 1893. Rhodes Papers.

[35] Morse wrote some volumes on the law of banking, arbitration and award. After his retirement from the law he edited the *American Statesmen* series of biographies. *National Cyclopedia of American Biography* (New York, 1940), XXVIII, 400.

[36] Rhodes to John T. Morse, Jr., May 6, 1893. Rhodes Papers.

[37] M. A. D. Howe, *Rhodes*, p. 26.

[38] John Todd, D.D., *Index Rerum: or Index of Subjects; Intended as a Manual to Aid the Student . . . With an Introduction Illustrating its Utility and Method of Use* (2nd ed., Northampton, Mass., 1861). This, together with three additional volumes, comprise Volumes IX, X, XI and XII of the Rhodes Papers.

[39] Rhodes Papers, IX, inside front cover, citing *The Nation*, LI, 444, and *Harper's Magazine*, July, 1890.

[40] Rhodes Papers, IX, X, *passim.*

[41] Rhodes Papers, IX, "Notes on Style"; XI, iR.

[42] M. A. D. Howe, *Rhodes*, p. 27. Thomas Beer, *Hanna*, p. 78 says the circulars were written at the "command" of Hanna but furnishes no source for the assertion.

[43] *The Trade Review* (Cleveland), June 16, 1883, p. 10. The circulars studied (sometimes available only as excerpts) were found in the files of this publication and its successors, *The Trade Review and Western Machinist* and *The Iron Trade Review and Western Machinist.* See also the last named, Oct. 4, 1884, p. 628.

[44] *The Trade Review*, June 16, 1883, p. 10; Victor S. Clark, *History of Manufactures in the United States* (New York, 1929), II, 194–195.

[45] *The Trade Review*, Sept. 8, 1883, p. 8; Oct. 6, 1883, p. 8; Nov. 10, 1883, p. 8.

[46] V. S. Clark, *History of Manufactures*, II, 161, 195.

[47] *Iron Trade Review*, Feb. 9, 1884, p. 88.

[48] *Ibid.*, Oct. 4, 1884, p. 633.

[49] *Ibid.*, Jan. 16, 1885, p. 41.

[50] *Ibid.*, Feb. 27, 1885, p. 137.

[51] V. S. Clark, *History of Manufactures*, II, 161, 225.

[52] *The Trade Review*, May 12, 1883, p. 10.

[53] *Ibid.*, April 7, 1883, p. 10; May 12, 1883, p. 10; June 16, 1883, p. 10; Dec. 15, 1883, p. 10; *Iron Trade Review*, April 5, 1884, p. 216.

[54] Davis R. Dewey, *Financial History of the United States* (8th ed., New York, 1922), pp. 411–413.

[55] *The Trade Review*, Dec. 15, 1883, p. 8.

[56] Rhodes, *Historical Essays*, pp. 281–282; V. S. Clark, *History of Manufactures*, II, 157.

[57] Felix W. Taussig, *The Tariff History of the United States* (5th ed., New York, 1910), p. 244.

[58] V. S. Clark, *History of Manufactures*, II, 304.

[59] *The Trade Review*, Dec. 15, 1883, p. 8; *Iron Trade Review*, Jan. 19, 1884, pp. 35, 38; March 8, 1884, p. 152; May 10, 1884, p. 296; Jan. 16, 1885, p. 41.

[60] *The Trade Review*, Feb. 17, 1883, p. 6.

[61] *Ibid.*, Dec. 15, 1883, p. 8.

[62] V. S. Clark, *History of Manufactures*, II, 157.

[63] M. A. D. Howe, *Rhodes*, pp. 47, 64.

[64] H. Croly, *Hanna*, p. 65.

[65] M. A. D. Howe, *Rhodes*, p. 27.

[66] *Iron Trade Review*, April 10, 1885, p. 233.

[67] Mrs. Bertha H. Rhodes, interview.

[68] *Notebook, 1886–1914*, p. 86 (June 5, 1898).

Chapter 4

THE NOVICE HISTORIAN

Now indeed was Rhodes his own man. A mature adult, free from his father's domination, he was now also released from the detested shackles of business. Now he was free to write that history of which he had dreamed. He had it planned—he would concentrate on the period from 1850 to 1885, treating it as a unit centered on the collapse and ultimate restoration to power of the Democratic party in national politics.[1]

Since the task involved knowledge of his own time, one might expect Rhodes to have steeped himself, at least for a time, in the life of his own day, and particularly in that of his own city, typical of the turbulent, bitter-sweet industrialism of the era. Slums were already a major problem. Capital and labor fought out their disputes on picket lines. Twice within three years (1882–1885) workers at the Cleveland Rolling Mills went on strike. Iron molders struck in 1884. In 1886 a street car dispute raged so fiercely that a local philanthropist called in Dr. Washington Gladden, the eminent Congregationalist exponent of the social gospel, to shed sweetness and light on the embittered parties.[2]

The labor problem was exacerbated by the presence of large numbers of unemployed, and the influx of Southern and Eastern European immigrants, who, while they tried to adapt to the new ways of life, had to cope with the hostility of both the old Yankee stock and the older immigrants from Germany, Britain and Bohemia.[3] Moreover, Cleveland was the center of operations of some of the great magnates of the time: John D. Rockefeller, Mark Hanna, the Mathers, the Chisholms. And it was a city of sharp class distinction. A Cleveland banker, recalling his impecunious youth, observed that when "the elect" wished to preempt Euclid Avenue, the town's main thoroughfare, for horse racing, the "common herd" had to obey.[4]

Rhodes was as deaf to the clamor of the city as he had been indifferent to the possibilities offered by Rhodes and Company. He immersed himself in ancient Greece and Rome with Grote, Mommsen and Gibbon and in the England of Macaulay.[5] He read voraciously in new books dealing with American history.[6] His personal relationships with fellow Clevelanders were centered largely around the Union Club, described by the *Daily Plain Dealer* as "the most elaborately 'gilt edged' and the most exclusive and expensive" of local clubs.[7]

Such restricted participation in the life of his day is reflected in Rhodes' first essays at historical writing, a series of articles and book reviews which appeared during 1885 and 1886 in the *Magazine of Western History*, a Cleveland publication designed for popular rather than scholarly consumption.[8] The first article, "The Coal and Iron Industry of Cleveland," traced with complacency the basic role of these industries in the development of the city and praised rather fulsomely those whom Rhodes considered to be the leaders in such progress. Among these were his father, to whose hard work and "early morning and all night labor" he attributed the substitution of coal for wood as fuel on lake steamers; Henry Chisholm, president of the Cleveland Rolling Mill Company, "the greatest of all the men who have had an honorable share in the development of these industries"; and Charles A. Otis of the Otis Iron and Steel Company, one of whose claims to fame was keeping his mills operating in face of strikes ordered by the Amalgamated Association of Iron Workers.[9]

Some Clevelanders were disturbed by the slums, strikes, and crudity of life in their city, but Rhodes was reminded of the cultural splendors of ancient Athens. Comparing the business leaders of Cleveland to Athenians, he noted that many rich men had given generously to education and other cultural endeavors, feeling that "there is something nobler in life than mere gain of money, and that something besides great wealth is needed to make the influence of a city enduring."[10]

Rhodes' next effort, a review of the second volume of John Bach McMaster's *History of the People of the United States*, is significant for its expression of Rhodes' concept of the role of the historian. After praising McMaster's literary style and use of newspapers as sources, Rhodes expatiated on that historian's frank statement of his opinions:

> This is the proper way to write history, for the expression of a decided opinion on men and events is what the annalist owes to his readers. . . . If he be honest, unprejudiced and has an impartial, enlightened judgment, his characterizations of men and his views of events are fully as important as the narration of facts and the coloring of his picture. . . . While it is desirable that Americans should have correct ideas of . . . Washington's

administration, it does not follow that they need go through the whole process of forming a right judgment. For all practical purposes a fair-minded and intelligent guide is ample.[11]

Having set forth his concept of the historian, Rhodes revealed that the "fair-minded and intelligent guide" would lead Americans down the road of Alexander Hamilton rather than that of Thomas Jefferson: "The Federalists were nearer right than their opponents and . . . it was fortunate that the ship of state on its first voyage was manned by Federalist officers." [12] Jefferson, thought Rhodes, "was a clog to the administration. . . . Under other circumstances he would have been a useful man, but his envy and jealousy of Hamilton were such as to make these feelings the crowning influence of almost every act." [13] The Virginia statesman, he continued, was not constructive, while Hamilton had "extraordinary ability, unbounded resources, and was fertile in expedients." [14] In Rhodes' estimate, Jefferson's work in connection with the Declaration of Independence, foundation of the Patent Office, religious liberty in Virginia, and personal liberties everywhere was of minor importance compared to "the good bargain he made for Louisiana." [15]

Even the most sagacious of guides may falter, however. In Rhodes' view, McMaster, whom he believed to be the fit successor to George Bancroft,[16] erred profoundly in his evaluation of George Washington. McMaster had written:

> We should respect and honor him [Washington] for being, not the greatest of generals, not the wisest of statesmen, not the most saintly of his race, but a man with many frailties and much common sense, who rose in the fullness of time to be the political deliverer of our country.[17]

Commented Rhodes: "This is certainly to damn with faint praise. Nor is it a true characterization. . . . [Washington] 'was the greatest of the good and the best of the greatest.' " [18] It is indicative of Rhodes' state of mind that he preferred the popular legend to the sober historical estimate of Washington. It is likewise indicative of Rhodes' weakness of perception that he failed to deal with the question implicit in his own formulation of the role of the historian: when guides fall out, whom is the layman to follow?

The attitude exemplified in Rhodes' espousal of the Washington myth is further illustrated in his review of Woodrow Wilson's *Congressional Government*.[19] This critical analysis of the American political system, with its suggestion that in some respects the

British parliamentary system might be preferable, called forth from Rhodes a patriotic affirmation of the superiority of his country's political institutions. Interestingly enough he based his case, not on the ground that the American system was more democratic than the British, but that it was less so! Under American practice, he pointed out, the Senate and Supreme Court act as brakes on popular feeling, while in Britain the trend toward a unicameral legislature had resulted in a tendency "towards destructive and even socialistic legislation and this suggests what is a serious defect in the British government [namely that] . . . the House of Commons is omnipotent." [20] This, together with the steadily broadening franchise in Britain, made it possible for the masses to pass laws against property "under the banner of equality." [21] Happily he saw such evil possibilities distinctly hampered by the American system.[22]

This satisfaction with things American he expressed even more forcefully in his essay, "Some Lessons of History." [23] A prime function of history, he wrote, was "the making of good citizens," [24] and, he continued:

> Most Americans, who are well read in history, are ready to affirm that, so far as having a good system of government is conducive to happiness, their lines have fallen in pleasant places. If one were to name the period of history during which men generally were most happy and prosperous, he could hardly fail to designate our country as the place, and the time as that from the adoption of our constitution to the present, making the exception of the twenty years from 1850–1870.[25]

There were Americans, of course, who, looking back at the Tweed Ring and Credit Mobilier scandals, at the tragic paradox of poverty amidst plenty, at the contrast between formal piety and actual materialism, thought the system something less than perfect: men like Henry George, Richard T. Ely, and Washington Gladden. With such critics Rhodes had little patience: "One might think that in no age before ours had the love of money been so strong . . . and that Mammon was the god of America and of our generation. But it was far worse in Rome during the last years of the republic." [26] Rather than listen to the critics, Americans should ponder the example of the wise democracy of Athens, where the people "identified inseparably the maintenance of property with their laws and institutions." [27] Americans, too, might well learn the lessons of the civil wars in Rome: "In such a state of society . . . the life and property of the burgess were no longer secure. The paramount end and aim of government were no longer realized."[28]

There were other lessons to be learned from history, as Rhodes interpreted it in the 1880's. The United States, he asserted, would not suffer the fate of Rome because she had rid herself of the incubus which destroyed the empire: slavery. Said he: "That slavery would have eventually destroyed our republic . . . can only be denied by those who will not heed the lessons of history."[29] Far from facing decline, the United States was destined to lead the onward march of civilization. After the collapse of Rome, civilization had been kept alive by the Christian Church, and in more recent times the mission had been carried out by the Anglo-Saxon peoples of England and America, who had well demonstrated how to combine liberty and order.[30] In his day, he believed, leadership had passed to the United States, which had shown marked superiority to Britain in meeting the social and political problems of the nineteenth century. He conceded, however, that America had possessed some significant advantages over Britain:

> We started, as it were, with a clean sheet. We had no relics of the feudal system. . . . We have such a boundless extent of land that there has never been any cause for agrarian disputes . . . ; the red men, whose land we took, are a race of barbarians that are being annihilated by contact with civilization, and thus we have avoided . . . never ending conflicts for the rightful ownership of the soil. . . . We started a democracy — . . . we were heir to all that was good in European civilization.[31]

No such spirit of satisfaction marked Rhodes' next excursion into historical criticism: a review of *Three Decades of Federal Legislation* by Samuel S. Cox, the noted Democratic congressman from Ohio.[32] Cox, wrote Rhodes, lacked literary style, ignored social history, and dealt inadequately with "our wonderful material growth." Rhodes chided the politician for neglecting the key roles of transportation and the iron and steel industries in post bellum America, although the work made no pretense of being an historical study of the period.[33] The book, said Rhodes, was dangerous for youth uninformed as to the real issues of the Civil War, although "those who are well grounded in the true faith . . . will find it instructive as well as entertaining."[34]

The reasons for this caveat soon appeared, for Rhodes espoused the conspiracy theory of the Civil War then dominant in the Republican North:

> No critical historian will write of Jefferson Davis in the kindly words that Mr. Cox has used. Davis and the senatorial clique had in the winter of 1860–61 the destiny of the South in their hands. . . . The South can charge them with their impoverishment, and ought never to forget that personal ambition . . . governed their leaders. . . . It was the old story of preferring rather "to reign in hell than to serve in Heaven." [35]

Davis, in Rhodes' opinion, was "a more infamous conspirator than Aaron Burr, . . . representing in a century of progress and light, the principles of darkness and oppression." [36]

Nor was Rhodes pleased with Cox's placing responsibility for the war at the door of the Republicans, inasmuch as they had rejected the Crittenden compromise proposals. Acceptance of the proposals, wrote Rhodes,

> would have given away everything for which they [the Republicans] had contended. If ever a political party fought a campaign for pure unadulterated principle, the Republicans did in 1860.
>
> * * *
>
> The Republicans were clearly in the right when they refused . . . to make any compromise on . . . slavery in the territories. Public sentiment in the North is pretty well settled on that point.[37]

"Public sentiment" may seem a strange basis on which to rest an historical judgment, even for a fledgling historian, but Rhodes followed with a generalization even more startling, coming, as it did, from one who had shown so much concern for the rights of property. The South, he explained, would not have accepted compensated emancipation because "the government of the Southern states was that of an oligarchy. Of all systems none are more selfish, and all history goes to show that rarely has an aristocracy given up the very base of their being, except through the shock of civil war." [38] There is ironic humor in the good bourgeois Rhodes expounding a philosophy of revolution more often associated with Karl Marx!

As to Reconstruction, Rhodes felt that Johnson's course was the "more merciful" but that the president was "entirely unfitted by nature, education or training to solve any such complex problem." [39] He conceded, on the other hand, that congressional Reconstruction "was by no means statesmanlike and wise." [40] In short, as Rhodes, in his circulars, had voiced the prevalent ideas of Cleveland businessmen, so in his initial historical writing he expressed the popular views of his class, region and time.

But Rhodes was not altogether satisfied with the cramped outlook of his fellows, however much he might make it articulate.[41] He felt the need for broader horizons, and these he sought, not in the American West, where history was being made by such diverse instrumentalities as Ignatius Donnelly, James J. Hill, Martin Irons and Jay Gould, but in Europe, where he and his family stayed for a year. He visited the House of Commons and heard Joseph Chamberlain inveigh against home rule for Ireland; [42] in France, he read, and probably saw, the popular play by Ernest Renan, *L'Abbesse de Jouarre;* in Rome he renewed his "vows to the Muse of History." In that city, he said, quoting Hawthorne, "the very dust is historical!" [43]

Shortly after his return to Cleveland he settled in a house at what was then 901 Euclid Avenue, in "Millionaire's Row," close to the residences of John D. Rockefeller; William Chisholm, the ironmaster; John H. Devereux, the railroad magnate; and Fayette Brown, a prominent banker.[44] Surrounded by such staid respectability, James undertook a work which indicated both that literature still attracted him and that his visit to Europe had vitally affected him. This was nothing less than a translation, in company with one Georges Delon, a teacher of French, of Renan's *L'Abbesse de Jouarre*, a play which is a frank avowal of the paramount role of sex in human life—an astonishing project for a respected citizen of a community where the clergy looked upon social dancing as an incitement to immorality.[45]

The collaborators were apparently undaunted by the broad views of Renan, who demanded open discussion of sex on the ground that, "Truth must not subordinate itself to the smallness of people who measure everything by their own mean thoughts." [46] The dramatist's viewpoint was quite explicit:

> if mankind should acquire the certainty that the world was about to end in two or three days, love would break out on all sides with a sort of frenzy; for that which restrains love, are the absolutely necessary conditions that the moral conservation of human society has imposed. If one should see oneself in the face of a sudden and certain death, nature alone would speak; . . . The world would drain to the dregs . . . a powerful aphrodisiac which would make it die of delight. . . .[47]

This is the theme of the play itself, most succinctly put by the Marquis D'Arcy in his successful attempt to seduce the Abbess while both await death during the Reign of Terror: "Nature intends us to enjoy. . . . She ordains that we should love, . . ." [48]

How can one explain such a work from the puritanical Rhodes? It is so far outside the orbit of his beliefs and behavior that one can only speculate that he was carried away by the play during his visit to France and that he thought to obtain entree to American literary circles by introducing a work daring enough to arouse defenders of conventional morality and significant enough as the work of a venerated author to win approval from the *literati*.[49] If this speculation is correct, the results were disappointing. None of the leading journals gave it even brief notice—which was perhaps just as well for Rhodes' later reputation! [50]

Rhodes had not lost sight of his main objective, however. Even while engaged on the translation he began study of the materials available for his projected history. Particularly concerned with the decade, 1850–1860, he was surprised to find a dearth of relevant sources. That deficiency he remedied by liberal use of newspapers. Following the examples of von Holst and McMaster he steeped his mind in journalistic material "to arrive at the spirit of the times." [51]

But Rhodes was far from relying on newspapers alone. He made good use of existing histories, especially that of von Holst.[52] He drew heavily upon the reports of travelers, such as Frederick Law Olmsted, Sir Charles Lyell, Frances Trollope and Alexis de Tocqueville. He read assiduously in memoirs and autobiographies, including those of Fanny Kemble, Thomas Hart Benton and Frederick Douglass.[53] All of these—newspapers, histories, travelers' reports, autobiographical material—he noted and digested.

Finally, in 1888, he began the actual writing, a task to which he devoted himself so wholeheartedly, even during "vacations," that occasional attention to personal financial affairs provided welcome change.[54] When the initial work, comprising two volumes, was finished, he commented that during the three and a half years of writing he had worked as he had never worked in business.[55]

The finished product, of course, was a tribute to his own efforts, but, as he himself generously admitted, he was fortunate in the quantity and quality of the assistance he received. His Negro barber, George A. Myers, not only brought him the books he required from local libraries, but also furnished him with insight into practical politics, for Myers was a power in the Negro Republican community.[56] William H. Brett, of the Cleveland Public Library, and Frederic Bancroft, librarian of the United States Department of State, procured him needed documents; the latter also assisted Rhodes for years through discussion and criticism.[57] Raymond St. James Perrin, a New Jersey varnish manufacturer with a flair for literature and philosophy, helped him with criticism, suggestions, and, more important, encouragement.[58] To help give his work literary finish, James employed Dr. Titus Munson Coan, professional magazine writer and literary advisor, who enjoyed the endorsement of George William Curtis, editor of *Harper's Weekly*.[59]

Of more basic significance was the aid rendered James by the brothers Henry E. and Edward G. Bourne, professional historians who taught at Western Reserve University in Cleveland. Rhodes hired Henry to do research for him on the period, 1854–1858, and his instructions show how well he understood the problem of the amateur collaborating with the professional:

> In general collect such material . . . as you would want yourself, were you writing a political history of the United States.
> I would like very much to have it full and complete, even if you do not cover the whole ground, as my experience is one cannot have too much material if someone gathers it for you.[60]

Rhodes' attitude toward the sources is also shown in his instructions: "The best hist. [sic] evidence is undoubtedly the private letters of men who have to do with the actions that become history." Next in importance were newspapers and the *Congressional Globe:* newspapers because, in the words of James Schouler, they mirrored "the passions and prejudices of the times," contained many significant letters, and published important correspondence from Washington; the *Congressional Globe* because it held hints on:

> the conduct of important events. Of course anything of that sort from the great men . . . does not escape the historians, but the admissions of the lesser lights are frequently more interesting for they let out that which the leaders keep secret.[61]

Rhodes found Henry's work eminently satisfactory. "First rate," he called it in one letter; and in another, he wrote, "with my own material and this [sent him by Henry] I can make a good account of 1855." [62]

Rhodes was even more impressed with the aid given him by Henry's brother, Edward, a historian deeply influenced by the Spencerian economics and sociology he had imbibed from his "guide and friend" at Yale, William Graham Sumner.[63] This assistance consisted both in research and in actual revision of the manuscript prepared by Rhodes, a revision which included both form and content. He thus described the spirit of their collaboration:

Bourne was a slow thinker and worker, but he was sure, and, when he knew a thing, his exposition was clear and pointed. . . . Two chapters especially attracted him, the one on Slavery in my first volume, and the one on general financial and social conditions at the beginning of the third; . . . not only every paragraph and sentence, but every important word in these two chapters was discussed and weighed. Bourne was a good critic, and, to set him entirely at ease, as he was twelve years younger, I told him to lay aside any respect on account of age, and to speak out frankly, no matter how hard it hit, adding that I had better hear disagreeable things from him than to have them said by critics after the volumes were printed.
. . . He was very strong on all economic and sociological questions, displaying in a marked degree the intellectual stimulus he had derived from his association with Professor Sumner. . . .[64]

To this collaboration is owed, no doubt, Rhodes' conversion to the doctrine of free trade. He needed no Sumner or Bourne to persuade him of the virtues of business civilization, but as one of these he had always reckoned the protective tariff. In that first chapter of Volume III of the *History*, however, he went over to free trade. Although Rhodes attributed his stand on the tariff to *The Nation* it is significant that he took no such open stand until after his discussions with Bourne.[65]

Rhodes completed his first two volumes, covering the years 1850 to 1860, in Cleveland, but he was increasingly restive with the cultural provincialism of his native city, where, as he put it, "a writer of books walking down Euclid Avenue would have been stared at as a somewhat remarkable personage." [66] The feeling was accentuated by the refusal of his friends to take his work seriously. The society in which he moved viewed him still as the dapper and fashionable Jim Rhodes and tolerantly indulged him in his harmless pastime of writing.[67] Besides, Cleveland lacked the libraries and other resources needed for his work. It is hardly surprising, then, that Rhodes should have turned his eyes to Boston, to him still the center of American culture. There, he thought, he would find intellectual companionship. There, the work of the mind was appreciated. There, were the libraries of Harvard and the Athenaeum, the latter possessing a wealth of sources on the Civil War. There, too, his family could be together while his son attended Harvard.[68] In September, 1891, the Rhodes family moved to Cambridge, Massachusetts.[69]

Before the year was out Rhodes submitted his manuscript to Harper and Brothers. They were sufficiently impressed to ask for an option on the remainder of the series. Rhodes agreed—and regretted it later, when the firm got into financial difficulties. "I would not have done that in pig iron," he wrote to Frederic Bancroft, "but I was too eager to get a good publisher and to get before the public." [70]

As a matter of fact, Rhodes was not quite so ingenuous. Harper and Brothers represented a shrewd choice. It was a publishing house of the first order, including among its authors Henry James, William Dean Howells, Arthur Conan Doyle and John Richard Green, the noted English historian.[71] In addition, the firm published two significant periodicals: *Harper's Magazine*, a monthly with "class" appeal; and *Harper's Weekly*, directed toward the "mass" market. Frank Luther Mott puts the circulation of the latter at 100,000, which made it one of the leading advertising media of the period.[72] How the *Weekly* maintained its dominance may be gathered from the fact that when the advertising of Rhodes' work first appeared, the magazine was serializing *The Adventures of Sherlock Holmes*—a coincidence obviously not at all harmful to the historian.

Indeed, Harper and Brothers launched him well on his new career. The *Weekly* ran a "puff" on Rhodes, written by Frederic Bancroft on the basis of a sketch submitted by the author himself, and followed it up with advertising. The *Magazine* published a laudatory review.[73] Rhodes himself took a hand in promoting sales. He suggested to the publishers that they send copies of his work to leading Englishmen and solicit their endorsements. He was reminded politely that what might appear sound sales technique to a Cleveland iron merchant was hardly proper for a publishing house dealing with distinguished foreigners:

> Early this year [wrote an official of the firm] you sent us a request to forward copies of your history to Mr. Gladstone, Mr. Lecky and two or three other gentlemen, with accompanying notes, for the purpose of eliciting letters from them which might help the sale. It was not thought advisable by us to follow your suggestion at that time, but now that the new edition is ready, it might be well to consider the matter again. I do not think, however, that it would be advisable to write to those gentlemen in any pointed or suggestive way. . . . A direct or pointed letter might excite an unfavorable feeling. . . .[74]

As we shall see, Rhodes' work needed little artifice to sell—at least in the United States. The two volumes set him apart as the historian for whom a substantial public had been waiting.

NOTES

[1] Rhodes, *History*, I, i.

[2] J. B. Whipple, "Cleveland in Conflict," pp. 94–111, 237, 240–243; E. J. Benton, *Cultural Story*, III, 91; Washington Gladden, *Recollections* (Boston, 1909), pp. 300–301; Cleveland *Leader*, Feb. 6, 1884.

[3] Cleveland *Leader*, Jan. 25, 1884; Mary Land, "The Malcontents and the Melting Pot: The Cleveland Story; A Study in American Civilization" (Unpublished M.A. thesis, Western Reserve University, Cleveland, 1946), *passim*.

[4] Charles A. Post, *Those Were the Days* (Cleveland, 1935), p. 25.

[5] M. A. D. Howe, *Rhodes*, p. 28.

[6] *Ibid.*

[7] Cleveland *Daily Plain Dealer*, Oct. 19, 1872. Rhodes maintained active membership in the Union Club from 1874 until his leaving the city in 1891. *Charter, By-Laws, Rules; Officers and Members of the Union Club of Cleveland* (Cleveland, 1891), p. 6. See also Rhodes, *Historical Essays*, pp. 281–282.

[8] J. B. Whipple, "Cleveland in Conflict," p. 449.

[9] *Magazine of Western History*, II (1885), 338, 343.

[10] *Ibid.*, p. 345.

[11] *Ibid.*, pp. 464–465.

[12] *Ibid.*, p. 467.

[13] *Ibid.*

[14] *Ibid.*, p. 468.

[15] *Ibid.*, p. 467.

[16] *Ibid.*, p. 477.

[17] Quoted in *ibid.*, pp. 472–473.

[18] *Ibid.*, p. 473.

[19] *Ibid.*, III (1885–1886), 15–25.

[20] *Ibid.*, pp. 20–22.

[21] *Ibid.*, p. 21.

[22] *Ibid.*

[23] *Ibid.*, pp. 148–157.

[24] *Ibid.*, p. 149.

[25] *Ibid.*

[26] *Ibid.*, p. 152.

[27] *Ibid.*, p. 150.

[28] *Ibid.*, pp. 152–153.

[29] *Ibid.*, pp. 153–154.

[30] *Ibid.*, pp. 154–156.

[31] *Ibid.*, pp. 156–157.

[32] *Ibid.*, pp. 356–366.

[33] *Ibid.*, pp. 356–357. For Cox, see the biography by David Lindsey, "*Sunset*" *Cox, Irrepressible Democrat* (Detroit, 1959).

[34] *Magazine of Western History*, III, 358.

[35] *Ibid.*, p. 359.

[36] *Ibid.*, p. 361.

[37] *Ibid.*, pp. 360–361.

[38] *Ibid.*, p. 362.

[39] *Ibid.*, p. 365.

[40] *Ibid.*

[41] Rhodes, *Historical Essays*, p. 293.

[42] The family was in Europe during 1886–1887. Rhodes to Sir George Otto Trevelyan, Nov. 20, 1921. Rhodes Papers.

[43] M. A. D. Howe, *Rhodes*, p. 28.

[44] Ella G. Wilson, *Famous Old Euclid Avenue of Cleveland* (Cleveland, 1937), II, 87, 90, 107; J. B. Whipple, "Cleveland in Conflict," p. 233; *Cleveland Directory for the Year Ending July, 1890* (Cleveland, 1889), pp. 317, 329, 627, 730, 798.

[45] Ernest Renan, *The Abbess of Jouarre*, authorized translation by James Ford Rhodes and Georges Delon (New York, 1888); J. B. Whipple, "Cleveland in Conflict," pp. 457–487; M. A. D. Howe, *Rhodes*, p. 59.

[46] *Abbess of Jouarre*, p. 6.

[47] *Ibid.*, pp. 10–11.

[48] *Ibid.*, p. 47.

[49] Some indication of the high regard held by American intellectuals for Renan may be found in L. J. Huff, "Renan's Dramas," *Atlantic Monthly*, LXIII (1889), 558–562; and R. G. Ingersoll, "Ernest Renan," *North American Review*, CLV (1892), 608–622.

[50] No mention of the work was found in *Harper's Magazine*, *Atlantic Monthly*, *North American Review*, *The Nation*, *Book Buyer* or *The Literary World* (Boston). Significantly, Rhodes made no reference to it in the autobiographical sketch he prepared for *Harper's Weekly* in 1892. Text of the sketch may be found in M. A. D. Howe, *Rhodes*, pp. 17–29.

[51] Rhodes, *History*, I, 1; *Historical Essays*, p. 84.

[52] Rhodes to Frederic Bancroft, Oct. 5, 1893, quoted in M. A. D. Howe, *Rhodes*, p. 80; Rhodes, *History*, I, *passim.*

[53] *Ibid.*, I, II, *passim.*

[54] M. A. D. Howe, *Rhodes*, p. 28.

[55] Rhodes to Frederic Bancroft, March 26, 1892, in *ibid.*, p. 64.

[56] M. A. D. Howe, *Rhodes*, pp. 62–63. Myers had been established in a barber shop at the Hollenden Hotel (Cleveland) by a group of local businessmen, including Rhodes. George A. Myers to Rhodes, March 15, 1921. Rhodes Papers.

[57] Rhodes, *History*, I, 208 n; Rhodes-Bancroft correspondence, Rhodes Papers.

[58] Rhodes, quoted in M. A. D. Howe, *Rhodes*, p. 29; Rhodes, *History*, I, 383 n; *Who's Who in America, 1906–1907*, p. 1396.

[59] Rhodes, *History*, III, 637 n; *Rhodes Papers*, X, aA, wA; *The Book Buyer*, V, 553. Lucy C. Ball to Rhodes, July 29, 1892. Rhodes Papers. Miss Ball was an employee of Coan.

[60] Rhodes to Henry E. Bourne, July 22, 1890, and undated memo. Rhodes Papers.

[61] Rhodes to Henry E. Bourne, Aug. 2, 1890, and undated memo. Rhodes Papers.

[62] Rhodes to Henry E. Bourne, Aug. 10, Aug. 13, 1890. Rhodes Papers.

[63] Rhodes, *Historical Essays*, p. 192.

[64] *Ibid.*, pp. 197–198.

[65] *Ibid.*, p. 280.

[66] *Ibid.*, p. 293.

[67] Harvey Cushing, "James Ford Rhodes," in M. A. D. Howe, *Later Years of the Saturday Club*, pp. 350–352; Charles K. Bolton, *Notebook, 1886–1914*, p. 86 (June 5, 1898).

[68] Mrs. Lucia McBride, interview.

[69] M. A. D. Howe, *Rhodes*, p. 65.

[70] Quoted in *ibid.*, p. 67.

[71] *Harper's Weekly*, Jan. 14, 1893, p. 27.

[72] Frank Luther Mott, *A History of American Magazines, 1865–1885* (Cambridge, Mass., 1938), III, 6, 10.

[73] *Harper's Weekly*, Dec. 7, 1892, pp. 1218–1219; *Harper's Magazine*, LXXXVI (1893), Supplement 2, p. 324.

[74] J. F. Phayre to Rhodes, March 23, 1893. Rhodes Papers.

Chapter 5

THE SUCCESSFUL HISTORIAN

FOR Rhodes' work the audience was at hand, drawn from that middle class which had grown and prospered from the post–Civil War economic expansion. It was an audience which, taking matters of culture seriously, provided a foundation for that impressive group of magazines typified by the *Atlantic Monthly* and the *Century* and a public eager for the writings of Zola, Tolstoy and Flaubert. It was, as Richard Watson Gilder, editor of *The Century*, observed, "anxious to be historically educated," particularly about the Civil War, which, to this audience had ceased to be a source of bitterness and was now viewed in the mellow light of the sectional reconciliation which marked the '90's.[1]

Proud of their country's recent material achievements, the new public was no less satisfied with the attainments of American scholarship, symbolized by the work of Edward Morley, Albert Michelson, and Willard Gibbs, and of American culture, which, in their own time, had produced Mark Twain, Louis Sullivan and Winslow Homer. They shared the view of that ardent spokesman of the New South, Henry W. Grady, that American society from its inception had been "a constant and expanding miracle," a miracle which, as they saw it, demonstrated in most satisfactory fashion the truth of Herbert Spencer's "law" of social progress through survival of the fittest. It was not at all difficult to believe with Josiah Strong that God Himself was preparing mankind the world over to receive the impress of Anglo-Saxon America. To the middle-class American, James Bryce had stated the obvious when he described life in America as floating "in a sense of happiness like that of a radiant summer morning."[2]

But there is no Eden without its serpent; in this case, discontent—massive, articulate discontent which, pervading every aspect of life, gave ample cause for disquiet to the otherwise complacent citizen. Populism, rooted in the grievances of the farmers, openly advocated an income tax, government ownership of railroads and abandonment of the gold standard. Workers, refusing to accept meekly the outcome of the survival of the fittest, battled troops and strikebreakers in the struggle to establish unions, while the infant American Federation of Labor actually avowed the existence of a class struggle in the United States. Some men who should have known better, wealthy men like Henry Demarest Lloyd, publicly branded the great business leaders as "public enemies." [3]

In the churches, the ancient peace was disturbed aplenty by the turmoil accompanying the spread of evolutionary theory and the higher criticism, but perhaps more menacing to the good middle-class Christian was the growing popularity of the social gospel preached by firebrands like Walter Rauschenbusch and John A. Ryan. The comfortable doctrines of William Graham Sumner were now disputed in the universities by young men of the stripe of Thorstein Veblen, Lester Ward and Richard T. Ely who extolled collectivism and decried *laissez faire* as "unsafe in politics and unsound in morals." The peace of the domestic hearth itself seemed in danger as young women demanded the right to vote, the single standard of morals, and a voice in shaping their careers while they ridiculed the aged Francis Parkman's pronunciamento that the major function of good middle-class women was the production of numerous offspring lest "the masses of the coarse and unintelligent . . . overwhelm us and our institutions." As a writer in the *Ladies' Home Journal* observed sadly, the typical young woman was "absolutely restless and dissatisfied." [4] As he looked about him, the proud but disturbed middle-class American could well share Henry Adams' feeling that American society no less than that of Europe was "shaking." [5]

Within a few months after the appearance of Rhodes' volumes it seemed as if the worst apprehensions of middle-class America were to be realized. The Panic of 1893 swiftly developed into one of the worst in the nation's history; before the year was out 491 banks and more than 15,000 business firms had closed their doors. As Henry Adams recalled, "Men died like flies under the strain, and Boston grew suddenly old, haggard, and thin." [6]

Worse was to come. Governor Altgeld of Illinois pardoned the surviving Chicago anarchists, thus suggesting to some that socialism and anarchism had infiltrated high places in the republic.[7] In 1894 Chicago fell into the hands of bloodthirsty foreigners and revolutionists—or so thought those who believed the newspaper accounts of the Pullman strike.[8] In that same year, "General" Jacob Coxey marched on Washington with his "army" of unemployed, a demonstration which appeared to at least one middle-class spokesman as a crusade of thieves, rapists, and murderers, led by a "would-be Robespierre." [9]

Faced thus suddenly with the problems arising from triumphant industrial capitalism, from the subordination of the farm to the factory, from the general practice of the principles of Spencer, the distracted citizen, unaware of the sources of his distress, found some stability in clinging to the symbols and values of the past. There were many to help him intone the old litanies, but few so persuasive as James Ford Rhodes. For Rhodes spoke as with authority; with the voice and manner of a Daniel come to judgment he brought assurance that the values of the middle-class were indeed rooted in the eternal verities. It is not surprising then, that, as John T. Morse, Jr., put it with some exaggeration:

> Appreciation came with surprising speed. Precisely such a book had been keenly desired, but by whom it should be written no one had been able to suggest. Now this secret was made known. . . . There was one universal acclaim of praise. . . .[10]

This is not to say that Rhodes' work represented a conscious attempt to supply a *rationale* for a class shaken by the wreck of '93. Rhodes was not the subtle thinker required for such an effort. He was simply the uncritical child of his time, region and class. He knew his public, not by analysis, but by that process of identification which goes deeper than and beyond mere intellectual acumen. Its interests, its ideals, its morality, its unconscious motivations and its felt needs were his own. In sounding his reassuring note he was doing so, not so much because he felt society to be in need of it as because he was expressing what were to him the basic truths of American experience. It was his good fortune that such expression came at a moment when the American reading public hungered for just such positive expression.

In the midst of the agitations of socialists and anarchists it was good to be reminded that except for its provisions on slavery the Constitution of the United States was a "perfect work." [11] Populists might call upon voters to follow the primrose path of political dalliance; Rhodes emphasized that all the great Americans—Washington, Hamilton, Webster and Lincoln—were conservatives.[12] Free silverites might clamor against the gold standard; Rhodes recalled to his readers "the sacredness of money obligations" and pointed out that without thrift even the "morally sound" may be "continually in trouble." [13] Corruption in local governments was offensive to the middle-class citizen; Rhodes assured him it arose from the "ignorant foreign vote." [14]

Indeed, in matters of nationality and race Rhodes well represented the dominant feelings of the time. The relations between Spain and the United States, he indicated, were those "of a weak, degenerate nation to a strong, energetic people." [15] It was "scientific truth" that "the negro race was inferior to the Caucasian." Negro women were "naturally" unchaste, and at least under slavery, "felt only pride at bearing offspring that had an admixture of the blood of the ruling class." [16] To a reading public disturbed by an upsurge of lynchings in the South, Rhodes proffered reflections from Thomas Jefferson, William Seward and Herbert Spencer that since Negroes were "insensible" their griefs were "transient." [17] For the racial problem which vexed the nation then as now he pontifically offered the currently popular solution: "wisdom of action on the part of the South, . . . wisdom of forbearance on the part of the North." [18]

If middle-class Americans generally responded warmly to such sentiments, certain significant segments of the public found that Rhodes had a message of special import to them.

The "restless" women, thousands of whom were organized in clubs to develop "culture," could well agree with Rhodes that women "were well fitted to grasp" the moral issues in politics and that popular government "has shown few more inspiring spectacles" than that of the indirect intervention of women against the slave power in the elections of 1856.[19]

Protestant clergymen perennially engaged in campaigns to "clean up" municipal politics, could assent to Rhodes' stricture that ministers should stay out of politics—for he hastened to add, "when the paramount political issue becomes intertwined with a sacred moral principle, it is the duty of the preacher to declare that principle." [20] What more could reformers like Washington Gladden and Charles H. Parkhurst ask?

Newspapermen, sensitive to the implications of "yellow journalism," could reflect that on great occasions the press rose to its responsibility. In arousing the country to the evils of the slave power, wrote Rhodes,

> The power of the newspapers was exercised in a manner to justify all the praise that has ever been bestowed upon an unrestrained press. . . . [It is] a record of pure and unselfish labors in a holy war. . . . Apparently the editors determined their course without ulterior thoughts as to what the effect might be on their pecuniary interest, or whether it would suit their party or faction.[21]

Scholars, usually neglected by the historians of the period, could not fail to respond to the lofty ideals held up for them by Rhodes, as he quoted at length from a speech by George William Curtis:

> The scholar is the representative of thought among men, and his duty to society is the effort to introduce thought and the sense of justice into human affairs. He was not made a scholar to satisfy the newspapers or the parish beadles, but to serve God and man. While other men pursue what is expedient, and watch with alarm the flickering of the funds, he is to pursue the truth and watch the eternal law of justice. . . .[22]

Rhodes had even more substantial fare to offer his readers, however. The sole cause of the Civil War, he averred, was slavery,[23] and in going to war over that issue the North had fought on the side of morality and civilization: "it was an unrighteous cause which the South defended by arms; and at the tribunal of modern civilization [John C.] Calhoun and [Jefferson] Davis must be held accountable for the misery which resulted." [24] All that was shameful in our history between 1846 and 1860—the Mexican war, the Ostend Manifesto, the Kansas-Nebraska bill—was due to the pro-slavery policies of the Democratic party.[25] All that was good flowed from the work of the anti-slavery elements,[26] especially the Republican party:

> the historian has no difficulty in affirming that . . . the Republican party of 1856 had more disinterested and sincere men in its ranks than any party in this country before or since, . . . its members were honestly devoted to a noble principle, . . .[27]
>
> * * *
>
> Never in our history, and probably never in the history of the world, had a more pure, more disinterested, and more intelligent body of men banded together for a noble political object than those who now enrolled themselves under the Republican banner [in 1856]. . . .[28]

To be sure, the pristine purity was somewhat sullied by 1860, but to Rhodes the maneuvering of the politicians and the clamor of those eager for pelf and place were of no real significance; the real significance of the Republican party was that "in truth they represented the noblest conservatism. They simply advocated a return to the policy of Washington, Jefferson and Madison." [29] And as if to set at rest any doubts as to his authority, Rhodes, with the supererogation of a John Marshall, laid down the dictum: "The historian whose sympathies are with the anti-slavery cause . . . can most truly write the story." [30]

Readers of Democratic persuasion, then, could be grateful for such an historian's observation that the election of Grover Cleveland in 1884 "showed the belief by the people that the Democratic party could be safely trusted to cope with the . . . problems that were likely henceforward to engage the attention of the country." [31] Likewise, Southerners could find solace in such an historian's reference to them as "a proud, high-spirited people," whose way of life typified "good breeding, refined manners, and dignified deportment. . . . physical courage, a habit of command, a keen sense of honor, and a generous disposition." [32] They could ponder, too, what might have been Rhodes' conclusions had he developed his speculation that it was not impossible "that if the Puritan had settled Virginia and the Cavalier had settled Massachusetts, . . . , the Puritan might have fought for slavery and the Cavalier for liberty." [33]

In these diverse ways did Rhodes provide historical sanction for the then dominant feelings, prejudices and opinions of the American middle class. Yet this, in itself, does not explain Rhodes' popularity; numerous apologetics for the *status quo* end up as publishers' remainders. What other factors help to account for his success?

One such was the simple fact that no one else had worked in the field now occupied by Rhodes. As Edward L. Pierce, the scholarly biographer of Charles Sumner, wrote to him:

> You are most happy in choice of theme. You are not likely to have rivals. . . . [Carl] Schurz and [Goldwin] Smith and such writers may evolve good things from memory and consciousness but they have not the strength and devotion for heavy research. It was well for you also that [James] Schouler and [Hermann] Von Holst stop where they do so as to leave you the exclusive field. . . .[34]

Another factor was that Rhodes dealt with a period with which many of his readers were personally familiar. For them he recreated the days of childhood and youth, awakened nostalgic memories of the past; rapport with such an audience was established easily and effectively. Numerous letters to Rhodes from obscure readers testify to the strength of this appeal. Perhaps most important, Rhodes' work was *interesting*. In common with his readers he believed that history was basically literature, and since he held the greatest historians to be Homer and Shakespeare, it is not surprising that his work should bear the hallmarks of drama—or rather, since Rhodes was indeed a product of the gaslight era, of melodrama.[35]

Viewed in this light, the decade before the Civil War was a period during which the villains, John C. Calhoun and Jefferson Davis, sought to seduce the maiden, the United States, through the medium of slavery, "an idea utterly condemned at the tribunal of modern civilization." [36] Frustrated in their designs, they, and others, conspired to tear down the Union.[37] To the rescue came many heroes, among whom towered Daniel Webster, "our great conservative," and Abraham Lincoln, a backwoods Socrates with "the instincts of a gentleman." [38]

The clash between good and evil was enlivened by the actions of the repentant sinner, Stephen A. Douglas. By forcing through the Kansas-Nebraska bill he sacrificed "the peace of his country, . . . , to his own personal ambition" for the presidency; he "hastened the struggle; he precipitated the civil war." [39] But apart from politics, Douglas "was a man of honor"; when it appeared in 1857 that the Buchanan administration was about to sacrifice Kansas to slavery, in violation of the wishes of the settlers, he broke with the administration and sacrificed his nomination by a united Democratic party. "No Democrat but one of rare courage and indomitable energy" would have followed this course, wrote Rhodes, adding, "Four years before he had committed a grievous fault; he was now beginning the atonement." [40] Thereafter Douglas' fight against the Southern wing of his party "was actuated by a bold and sincere patriotism." [41]

Quite apart from the interest of its central theme the *History* was replete with what today would be called "human interest." Funerals of celebrities, like President Zachary Taylor, Henry Clay and Daniel Webster were described in the terms dear to Victorians, with guns booming, bells tolling, buildings draped in black.[42] Scenes of violence, such as the Foote-Benton fracas in the Senate, the Oberlin-Wellington slave rescue, and the Anthony Burns incident in Boston were portrayed in rich, dramatic colors.[43] Episodes of horror, such as the yellow fever epidemic in New Orleans in 1853, were presented with a wealth of circumstantial detail.[44] The famous chapter on slavery was not least interesting because of its frank discussion of Negro-white sexual relations in the *ante bellum* South.[45]

The treatment of John Brown's raid was that of a drama within a drama, with its descriptions of sober New Englanders financing the conspiracy, of Brown and Frederick Douglass meeting secretly at night in an abandoned stone quarry, of Brown's conduct at his trial, which "showed him a hero, and won him that admiration of choice spirits that is granted only to those who dare much and sacrifice much in the cause of humanity." [46]

Many of his women readers must have responded sympathetically to his sketch of Harriet Beecher Stowe as she composed *Uncle Tom's Cabin:*

> Worn out with the care of many young children; overstrained by the domestic trials of a large household; worried because her husband's small income did not meet their frugal needs; eking out the poor professor's salary by her literary work in a house too small to afford a study for the author— . . .[47]

Indeed, the sketch of Mrs. Stowe provides yet another clue to the popularity of Rhodes' work. History to him was not so much the development and clash of impersonal forces as it was the struggle of men and women, good and evil—and such history, to the layman, is both understandable and interesting. Rhodes' *History*, interlarded with numerous character sketches, gave his work more popular appeal than that of scholars like von Holst and Schouler. Finally, to a public which looked for such qualifications in a historian, Rhodes amply filled the roles of guide and judge. The Fugitive Slave Law was an "infamous act." [48] The Ostend Manifesto "contained notions abhorrent to justice and at war with the opinion of the civilized world." [49] The Pierce Administration in domestic affairs "was characterized by an utter disregard of plighted faith; the avowed foreign policy was marked by the lack of justice as understood by all civilized nations." [50] The Personal Liberty laws passed by Northern states in retaliation for the Fugitive Slave Law were indeed "dangerously near . . . nullification . . . Nullification cannot be defended; but in a balancing of the wrongs of the South and the North, it must be averred that in this case the provocation was vastly greater than the retaliation." [51] In Kansas, "in a balancing of acts and character, the free-state adherents . . . stand immeasurably superior to the proslavery partisans in everything that goes to make up industrious, law-abiding, and intelligent citizens." [52] In the Dred Scott decision, "Taney committed a grievous fault . . . he allowed himself to make a political argument, when only a judicial decision was called for. . . . Posterity must condemn Taney as unqualifiedly as Douglas." [53]

In short, Rhodes, writing history as he and his public thought it should be written, had something to offer practically every section of the reading public. The middle class generally was assured that the American way of life was rooted in the values of economic and political conservatism, represented by the Republican party, and in the maintenance of Anglo-Saxon supremacy. Northerners received the accolade of a superior morality; Southerners that of a gentlemanly society, together with positive support for their position that the South be left to handle the racial problem in its own way. Those who sought diversion of an elevating kind found it in history told as a tale. Those who sought in history a moral significance found in Rhodes the patriarchal guide and judge.

That this was the kind of history American readers wanted is indicated by the reception of the work by both public and reviewers. The first edition sold so well that by October, 1895, another edition was issued—no small tribute to a work which cost five dollars (per set of two volumes) at a time when a suit of men's clothing could be purchased for ten dollars and when the country was in the slough of an economic depression.[54] Newspaper reviewers reflected the public enthusiasm. To the Chicago *Inter-Ocean* the work was "excellent history"; to the Philadelphia *Ledger*, "The best all-around history of the period that has yet appeared"; to the New York *Tribune*, "a work of great dignity and purpose, . . . rich in sources of learning and political and moral philosophy"; to the New York *Sun*, "the only book which presents a tolerable approach to an adequate and trustworthy record of the period." [55] The Cleveland *Leader* declared:

> Few better histories have been written that enable the student to see and weigh these causes [of the Civil War] more justly than Mr. Rhodes', while for the purpose of recalling the political events which led to the downfall of the Democratic party . . . , it has no competitor . . .[56]

There was also praise from more discriminating sources. Edward L. Pierce wrote to Rhodes, attributing his success to "thorough and exhaustive research." [57] John T. Morse, Jr., thought the *History* a great work despite his disagreement with some of Rhodes' judgments.[58] Carl Schurz wrote, "Your work has constantly grown upon me as I went on." [59] From across the Atlantic came warm words. W. E. H. Lecky, the famous English historian, declared, "Very few books indeed have helped me so much to understand American politics, and the desire you show to do justice to all sides and to tell the exact truth . . . is very manifest on every page. It is a rare quality."[60] Albert V. Dicey, the learned authority on English law, wrote, "I am greatly impressed with the fairness of your book. It is quite the most just and the most comprehensive account I have read of the course of events which led up to the Civil War."[61]

There must have been a special piquancy for Rhodes in the message he received from Tom L. Johnson, the arch-foe of Mark Hanna and no idolator of that conservatism so esteemed by Rhodes, retracting a charge of inaccuracy Johnson had leveled against Rhodes' account of a filibuster in Cuba in 1851.

> Your history [Johnson continued] I regard as accurate, well-written and above all, told in a spirit of perfect fairness to the southern people; I feel competent to speak for them, as I was born and reared there. Your history is one of the few which hold one's attention like a work of fiction, . . .[62]

But there were those who suggested, in no friendly manner, that Rhodes' work was fiction rather than history. One such, an anonymous reviewer in the *Atlantic Monthly*, asserted that Rhodes did not possess the broad viewpoint, wide sympathy and literary skill required of a historian. The *History*, in his opinion, was "a superior sort of antislavery pamphlet" that not only presented a biased picture of slavery but also distorted the history of the nation. Rhodes, wrote the critic, had "no insight . . . into complex characters, taking men either individually or in the mass." Finally, Rhodes' judicial manner was assumed because Rhodes was "aware that it is 'bad form' to be dogmatic; [the *History*] is strongly dogmatic in spirit."[63]

Rhodes, stung by such criticism, and under the impression that the review had been written by Professor Nathaniel Southgate Shaler of Harvard, who was regarded in academic circles as a Southern sympathizer, objected to Horace E. Scudder, editor of the *Atlantic Monthly*.[64] Scudder replied:

> I am not a mere editorial machine, and it was not an agreeable experience to print the notice of your book . . . Of course, if I had thought my reviewer seriously in the wrong I should have set the paper aside; but I am disposed when once I have taken the risk of assigning a book to a man in whose qualifications of knowledge and honesty I have confidence, to let him have his say.[65]

He did not reveal to Rhodes that the critic had been, not Shaler, but a professor at Princeton named Woodrow Wilson.[66]

Wilson was not alone in his judgment. Professor John W.

Burgess, who was expounding Nordic supremacy at Columbia, complained that Rhodes was neither impartial nor unprejudiced. Much of Volume I, he charged, was made up of "abolitionist prejudices"; the chapter on slavery was not history but propaganda. Slavery, said Burgess, was not as bad as it was painted by Rhodes, and, he added:

> The time has arrived for the cooler impartial study of the nature of this temporary relation between the highly civilized white race and the deeply barbarous negro race—for the discernment of the great problem of history which was solved through this relation. Such study Mr. Rhodes has not pursued, and of such discernment, he has not given the slightest evidence.

Despite such weaknesses, however, Burgess concluded: "Viewed as a whole, it is in my opinion the best work which has as yet appeared on the period which it covers." [67]

Professor David E. Spencer of the University of Michigan praised Rhodes' use of newspapers as sources, his character sketches, and his fairness but noted as a basic weakness that Rhodes had written "as if but for the slavery question we should have had no history worth the writing." [68]

An anonymous reviewer in *The Nation* criticized the *History* from other viewpoints. Rhodes was commended for his research; his chapter on slavery was said to be a model of "judicial summing up"; and his estimate of Stephen A. Douglas, while unusually kind, was basically "reasonable and just." But, the reviewer went on, von Holst was a much better historian for the period; Rhodes used newspapers too uncritically; failed to analyze the relationship between slavery and western settlement; and lavished space on inconsequential details like the yellow fever epidemic in New Orleans while dismissing in a footnote such significant developments as Commodore Perry's expedition to Japan. The reviewer concluded that if Rhodes carried through his projected series, "we shall have a noteworthy and valuable addition to our solid literature." [69]

With such growls and grumbling did the guardians of the academic groves greet the trespasser—but even there James found compensation. Undaunted by academic criticism, impressed by the public acclaim of Rhodes' work, Western Reserve University in June, 1893, conferred on him the honorary degree of Doctor of Laws.[70] His triumph was almost complete. There remained only the question of how Boston society would treat this intruder in its midst.

NOTES

[1] Henry S. Commager, *The American Mind: An Interpretation of American Thought and Character Since the 1880's* (New York, 1950), pp. 43, 74; Frank L. Mott, *Golden Multitudes: The Story of the Best Sellers in the United States* (New York, 1947), pp. 173–174, 310–311; Thomas Beer, *The Mauve Decade* (New York, 1926), p. 217; A. M. Schlesinger, Sr., *The Rise of the City*, pp. 256–257, 413; *The Century*, XLVI (1893), 952.

[2] James Bryce, *The American Commonwealth* (2nd ed., revised, New York, 1891), II, 692; Josiah Strong, *Our Country: Its Possible Future and Present Crisis* (Revised ed., New York, 1891), pp. 220–222; Thomas C. Cochran and William Miller, *The Age of Enterprise: A Social History of Industrial America* (New York, 1942), p. 136; Harvey Wish, *Society and Thought in Modern America: A Social and Intellectual History of the American People* (New York, 1952), pp. 306–307, 313; Grady quoted in Willard Thorp (ed.), *American Issues: Volume I—The Social Record* (Chicago, 1955), p. 615.

[3] *Wealth Against Commonwealth* (Washington, D. C., 1936), p. 347.

[4] Francis Parkman, "The Woman Question Again," *North American Review*, CXXX (1880), 21; A. M. Schlesinger, Sr., *The Rise of the City*, p. 144.

[5] Quoted in Henry S. Commager, *The American Mind*, p. 52.

[6] Henry Adams, *The Education of Henry Adams* (New York, 1928), p. 338; Richard B. Morris (ed.), *Encyclopedia of American History* (New York, 1953), p. 510.

[7] *The Century*, XLVI (1893), 792; Cleveland *Leader*, June 30, 1893, p. 4.

[8] Almont Lindsey, *The Pullman Strike* (Chicago, 1942), ch. XIII; Robert Cruden, "Representative Cleveland Newspapers and the Pullman Strike, 1894–1895" (Unpublished M.A. thesis, Western Reserve University, 1952), *passim.*

[9] Harry Thurston Peck, *Twenty Years of the Republic, 1885–1905* (New York, 1906), pp. 373–375.

[10] "James Ford Rhodes," *Proceedings, Massachusetts Historical Society*, LX (1927), 179.

[11] Rhodes, *History*, I, 19.

[12] *Ibid.*, I, 156, 160–161; II, 502.

[13] *Ibid.*, I, 143, 215.

[14] *Ibid.*, II, 51.

[15] *Ibid.*, II, 21.

[16] *Ibid.*, I, 318, 335, 370.

[17] *Ibid.*, I, 321–322. See Frederick Douglass, "Lynch Law in the South," *North American Review*, CLV (1892), 17–24.

[18] *History*, I, 383. For prior presentation of this viewpoint see James Bryce, "Thoughts on the American Negro Problem," *North American Review*, CLIII (1891), 641–660; and Thomas Nelson Page, "A Southerner on the Negro Question," *ibid.*, CLIV (1892), 401–413.

[19] *History*, II, 220–221.

[20] *Ibid.*, I, 479–480.

[21] *Ibid.*, I, 463.

[22] *Ibid.*, II, 213.

[23] *Ibid.*, I, 27, 53.

[24] *Ibid.*, I, 380.

[25] *Ibid.*, I, 79; II, 44, 266.
[26] *Ibid.*, I, 55, 63, 75; II, 217.
[27] *Ibid.*, II, 175.
[28] *Ibid.*, II, 210.
[29] *Ibid.*, II, 502.
[30] *Ibid.*, I, 152.
[31] *Ibid.*, I, 3.
[32] *Ibid.*, I, 94, 359.
[33] *Ibid.*, I, 381.
[34] Edward L. Pierce to Rhodes, June 21, 1893. Rhodes Papers.
[35] *Infra*, 231.
[36] *History*, I, 95.
[37] *Ibid.*, I, 94–95, 380, 390, 421, 438, 482; II, 24, 359, 373.
[38] *Ibid.*, I, 161; II, 309, 312.
[39] *Ibid.*, I, 435, 494.
[40] *Ibid.*, II, 285, 286–287.
[41] *Ibid.*, II, 373.
[42] *Ibid.*, I, 174–177, 261, 287.
[43] *Ibid.*, I, 171, 500–506; II, 361–367.
[44] *Ibid.*, I, 402–413.
[45] *Ibid.*, I, ch. IV.
[46] *Ibid.*, II, 406.
[47] *Ibid.*, I, 279.
[48] *Ibid.*, I, 188.
[49] *Ibid.*, II, 40.
[50] *Ibid.*, II, 44.
[51] *Ibid.*, II, 74.
[52] *Ibid.*, II, 217.
[53] *Ibid.*, II, 261.
[54] Harper & Bros., to Rhodes, Feb. 25, 1896. Rhodes Papers. Advertisements of E. R. Hull & Dutton and of Steinfeld's, Cleveland *Plain Dealer*, Jan. 20, 1893, pp. 3, 5.
[55] Quoted in *Harper's Weekly*, Dec. 24, 1892, p. 1247; Dec. 31, 1892, p. 1269; Jan. 14, 1893, p. 48.
[56] Cleveland *Leader*, Dec. 4, 1892, p. 24.
[57] Edward L. Pierce to Rhodes, June 21, 1893. Rhodes Papers.
[58] John T. Morse, Jr., to Rhodes, May 4, 1893. Rhodes Papers.
[59] Carl Schurz to Rhodes, Feb. 4, 1893. Rhodes Papers.
[60] W. E. H. Lecky to Rhodes, Sept. 5, 1893. Rhodes Papers.
[61] A. V. Dicey to Rhodes, Dec. 3, 1894. Rhodes Papers.
[62] Tom L. Johnson to Rhodes, Oct. 14, 1895. Rhodes Papers.
[63] "Anti-Slavery History and Biography," *Atlantic Monthly*, LXXII (1893), 272–274.
[64] Rhodes to Edward L. Pierce, Oct. 7, 1893; Pierce to Rhodes, Oct. 22, 1893. Rhodes Papers.
[65] Horace E. Scudder to Rhodes, Aug. 7, 1893. Rhodes Papers.
[66] *The Atlantic Index Supplement: A List of Articles with the Names of Authors Appended, Published in "The Atlantic Monthly," 1889–1901* (Boston, 1903), p. 70.
[67] *Political Science Quarterly*, VIII (1893), 342–346.
[68] *The Dial*, XIV (1893), 280–281.
[69] *The Nation*, LV (1893), 499–500.
[70] Minutes, meeting of Board of Trustees, Adelbert College, Western Reserve University, June 20, 1893. Copy furnished by Dean Carl F. Wittke, Graduate School, Western Reserve University.

Chapter 6

THE PROPER BOSTONIAN

THE BOSTON to which Rhodes migrated in 1891 [1] exhibited the typically distressing symptoms of rapid urbanization which he had witnessed in Cleveland, but in addition it suffered from strains peculiar to itself. Like Cleveland, it was growing fast, due largely to foreign immigration, but the tensions inherent in the conflict of values between older residents and newcomers were heightened by the protracted and bitter struggle between the native Protestant stock and the Irish Catholics. While the Irish, by virtue of numbers, had captured the political strongholds of the city, the native element had firmly entrenched itself in the heights of industry and finance, and thus added to an ethnic and religious quarrel the bitterness of a class struggle, a conflict further accentuated by frequent strikes and by a poverty so widespread that even in the relatively prosperous year, 1900, it was estimated that 20 per cent of the population had to apply to public agencies for some sort of relief.

It was exactly in such waters, however, that shrewd promoters of the day made their hauls—and Boston proved no less an attraction than did Chicago and other cities of the interior. Corruption in business and politics was rife as disciples of Spencer fought over street railway and gas line franchises, and as public utilities and the liquor industry battled regulation. To young idealists like Louis Brandeis and to older Proper Bostonians like Henry Lee Higginson the situation proved a challenge; they organized Public Franchise Leagues and Good Government Associations to bring some measure of integrity into public and private business.[2] Rhodes was as indifferent to such concerns as he had been in his native city.

Neither was Rhodes distressed by the uneasy consciousness of older Bostonians that their city's day of cultural leadership had passed. They sensed only too keenly that their fellows of the '90's no longer "shared heroic passions," and too well they knew what was involved in the supplanting of poetry by learning, of the cult of Emerson by that of Lucretius, of the creation of art by the conspicuous display of art collections.[3]

Of all this Rhodes was actually unaware. To him, Boston was

Boston, still the center of the nation's culture; to him culture meant learning, the book-filled study, quiet and comfortable, with a coal fire burning cozily in the grate. Bostonians might sense the loss of power in the decline from poetry to learning, but to Rhodes this learning was all-sufficient, and for it he was eternally grateful to Boston. That is, he was grateful to a special kind of Boston, the kind of Boston which Josiah P. Quincy prematurely thought had passed away:

> A Boston within Boston, cultured, moral, conservative, and—*proper*. . . . there was in it a certain narrowness of perception, . . . It was apt to take its own notions of what was proper as a criterion for the rest of mankind; . . .[4]

To this Boston Rhodes owed allegiance; he shared its aversion to those *parvenus* of business who sought to breach the walls of its society, which was based on Family no less than on Wealth. He sympathized with the central character of Robert Grant's sociological novel, *The Chippendales*, who was appalled no less by "strangers forcing their way into prominence" than by their new business methods which to him seemed gambling.[5] To Rhodes, as to another of Grant's characters, such Brahmins may have been "merely left-overs" but in Rhodes' opinion they represented the best in society; they formed a narrow caste, perhaps, but one to which he "really . . . should have liked to belong."[6] He admired "Boston people, whose good manners and cultivation give them a distinction rarely seen elsewhere."[7] Significantly one of Rhodes' earliest and most enduring friendships in Boston was with Barrett Wendell, the literary historian who was called "the Brahmin of Brahmins" and who styled himself the "last of the tories."[8]

Boston, wrote Charles Francis Adams, recalled to him "little that was pleasant," but he conceded that, "For strangers, well introduced, it is a delightful city." More recently, Cleveland Amory has noted that the Brahmins welcomed the vistor who showed the "same sort of awesome respect for what he sees that his hosts have always had."[9] Rhodes qualified on both counts. He was "well introduced," not so much by his money, as by his *History*, and he so modestly refrained from presuming even on this introduction that Justin Winsor, the historian who served as librarian at Harvard, was not only unaware of the identity of the author but also of the fact that Rhodes lived within a stone's throw of the Harvard Yard.[10]

This, of course, was precisely the type of behavior that appealed to Proper Boston. As to Rhodes' respect for things Bostonian, no one could doubt. He never wearied of praising his adopted city, and while words might have proved vain with skeptical Yankees they could not well overlook the subtle flattery involved in Rhodes' moving from Cleveland to Boston to take up the life of the mind.

Even so, Proper Boston might well have proved chilly had Rhodes fitted the stereotype of the boorish, pushing Westerner.[11] But Rhodes, sometimes with a delicacy that seems now somewhat strained, never ventured beyond the metes and bounds set by Boston society. Conscious that he was no scion of Beacon Hill, he continuously reminded Bostonians of the fact. In praising a play of Barrett Wendell's he wrote apologetically to the author: "I shall have to use an Americanism I had vowed never again to employ, . . . but I had a very good time." [12] To John T. Morse, Jr., he expressed gratitude in the third person: "it is lucky that a Westerner fell in with him [Morse] and learned how to conduct himself in the cultivated Back Bay." [13] When friends urged him to become a vice-president of the Massachusetts Historical Society in 1904 he objected in part because of his Ohio nativity; [14] and while he finally accepted the post he never could be persuaded to accept the presidency. That exalted position, he felt, should be reserved for those Boston-born and bred.[15]

Such an attitude Bostonians could appreciate. That Rhodes, with ever-growing fame, should fail to presume upon it to push his way into their tight little society, marked him as one of their own. So far as was possible, they did make him one of themselves; in the words of Mark A. DeWolfe Howe, Rhodes became "as nearly an Inner as any Outer Bostonian could become." [16]

The first sign of his acceptance was election to membership in the Massachusetts Historical Society in December, 1893, the news of which was conveyed to him by the society's secretary, Mellen Chamberlain, in typically discreet Boston fashion: "[Justin] Winsor was your sponsor, and stated your claims none too strongly, but in a way that . . . would not have allowed of your presence." [17] This society was not only the oldest and wealthiest historical organization then in existence; it was also the center which brought together in serious pursuits those three basic elements of Brahminism: family, wealth and culture.

Among its 97 members when Rhodes was elected were the scholars Albert Bushnell Hart, John Fiske, Edward Channing, A. Lawrence Lowell, Charles W. Eliot, president of Harvard, and Francis A. Walker, president of the Massachusetts Institute of Technology, an outstanding economist of the day who believed that the single tax theory of Henry George was "a project steeped in infamy."[18] Probably the most distinguished lay member was Charles Francis Adams, of *the* Adams family, whose experiences as director and president of the Union Pacific Railroad and as associate in other enterprises, led him to excoriate "successful" businessmen:

> a less interesting crowd I do not care to encounter. Not one that I have ever known would I care to meet again, either in this world or the next; nor is one of them associated in my mind with the idea of humor, thought or refinement. . . .[19]

Included in the membership were men successful in business and politics in the traditional First Family manner: William C. Endicott, William S. Appleton, Roger Wolcott, Leverett Saltonstall, Samuel Eliot, and Robert C. Winthrop. Better known to the public, perhaps, were members Gamaliel Bradford, the author; George F. Hoar, United States Senator from Massachusetts; Horace E. Scudder, editor of the *Atlantic Monthly;* and Thomas Wentworth Higginson, still the embattled friend of the Negro.[20] Rhodes valued his membership highly. He used it as his sole identification on the title pages of Volumes V, VI and VII of his *History*. And, of course, election to this select group must have tasted more sweet by its coming hard on the heels of the hostile remarks of academic critics.

Within the next few years the gates of Proper Boston swung open to receive this pilgrim from the West. Not only did he become friends with such individuals as Henry Lee Higginson, Charles Eliot Norton, Charles W. Eliot, Barrett Wendell and John T. Morse, Jr.; he was also admitted to those gatherings of the élite which were exclusive even within exclusive Proper Boston: the dinner clubs, devoted to good food, good drink and good talk among approved males. The St. Botolph's, Wednesday Evening, Tavern, Winter's Night, and Saturday Clubs—and that ultra-select group which called itself simply "The Club"—were proud to list Rhodes on their rosters.[21] Through these clubs he made intimate acquaintance with the leading figures in the life of Boston, including William James, William Dean Howells, Dr. Harvey Cushing, Judge Oliver Wendell Holmes, Jr., William Cardinal O'Connell, Thomas Sargent Perry and Moorfield Storey.[22]

In turn, Rhodes himself became something of a social institution. When he moved to Boston from Cambridge in 1895 he went, significantly, not to the new and fashionable suburb of Brookline, but to the very heart of Proper Boston: first to Newbury Street, and then (in 1899) to the "water side" of Beacon Street.[23] His dinners, famous for their food, wine and talk, were acclaimed by Bostonians and welcomed by the staff of the history department at Harvard.[24] As Dr. Sidney B. Fay recalls:

> These dinners were most enjoyable with their many dishes and many kinds of wine—so munificent in fact that they were almost too much for some of the staid members of the department. But his genial presiding figure and hearty cordiality made them, . . . , most enjoyable and long to be remembered.[25]

Indeed, Rhodes became the recognized host for visiting dignitaries; his guests included James Bryce, the eminent historian who became British ambassador to the United States; John Morley, the distinguished British biographer; George Macaulay Trevelyan, of the Macaulay-Trevelyan clan of great historians and Theodore Roosevelt, with whom Rhodes developed such warm relations as to become a welcome guest at the White House. Rhodes may not have "dined himself into popularity" as Edward Channing once remarked with asperity,[26] but he did become so well established in the society of his adopted city that he could afford to decline one of its signal honors: an appointment to the Harvard faculty.[27] He contented himself with accepting appointment as member of the visiting committee of the history department—and with the unofficial role as permanent and enthusiastic member of the Harvard cheering section at football games.[28]

Rhodes' wealth, his *History*, his respect for the *lares et penates* of Proper Boston, his scrupulous regard for the social niceties, his famous dinners—these, while they might explain a measure of the welcome given him by Boston, fail to do justice to the extraordinary and enduring warmth felt for this Westerner by usually staid Bostonians. Basically, the explanation seems to lie in the personality of Rhodes himself: he was "the kind of man whom people naturally liked," a "big, brotherly man," in the words of Lord Charnwood.[29]

Men and women of Boston provided ample confirmation of Charnwood's judgment. Judge Robert Grant, who knew Rhodes intimately for nearly thirty years, wrote:

> He was a very unaffected human person, with clearcut views on matters on which he was informed. His opinions on these, enunciated lucidly in a rather harsh but penetrating voice, carried conviction in any company. In spite of a matter-of-fact, breezy Western manner, he speedily won liking and respect in an orbit

> bounded, except for an occasional visit to his brokers on State Street, by the Boston Athenaeum Library, the Tavern and Somerset Clubs, and the Massachusetts Historical Society. He had very hospitable instincts, and at the large dinners given at his house on Beacon Street, . . . the intellectual and the fashionable were agreeably mixed. Because of being strangers, the acquaintance of the Rhodes continued somewhat narrow, but was always well chosen, and as his books won fame abroad, the occasion for entertaining was likely to be the presence of some celebrity such as one of the Trevelyans or John Morley. There was rarely a foreigner of note in Boston whom the Rhodes did not entertain.
>
> At the dinner clubs which he joined the members took to him at once because of his heartiness and mental integrity. . . .[30]

John T. Morse, Jr., who was on such terms with Rhodes that he could write, "you are always so sweet-tempered that I'm really not much afraid of you," recalled that "where other men made acquaintances, Rhodes made friends." [31] Morse drew an engaging picture of the historian at home:

> He heartily enjoyed [a chat], settling himself comfortably in his capacious easy chair, with the expanse of the Charles River visible through the broad windows behind him, his bookshelves ascending to the ceiling, a cheerful fire in the open grate—(he was the last man in Boston to secure that old cannel coal).[32]

Perhaps most impressive is the simple tribute of Annie B. Perry, wife of the famous student of New England culture, on the occasion of Rhodes' 70th birthday:

> if Bliss and I were to count up our blessings since coming to live in this part of the country . . . your friendship and the inspiration that have come from knowing you would be among the very first.[33]

So much for the testimony. What was there in the man that made him so well liked?

Physically, he was an imposing man: tall, "towering above every one" at gatherings, despite his slight, scholarly stoop and his heavy figure.[34] His hair was dark, his beard neatly trimmed. His features in repose wore a serious, shrewd, but kindly mien. His voice was loud and penetrating, and when he told a story his face lit up pleasantly; when he heard a good story, as Dr. Harvey Cushing recalled, he greeted it with a "deep voiced chuckle. . . . That generous, whole-hearted, and sympathetic laugh, the laugh of a good listener." Easterners were impressed by what Prof. Sidney B. Fay calls his "somewhat uncultured manner of speech. For instance, he never bothered to pronounce the final 'g' in words ending in 'ing.' " Charles K. Bolton also noted that Rhodes habitually mispronounced such words as *diplomatically* (to which Rhodes gave a long *i*) and *prestige* (in which Rhodes accented the first syllable). Prof. Fay also observed, however, that Rhodes' conversation was marked by "vigor, force, clarity and simplicity." [35]

Rhodes, indeed, enjoyed a reputation as a good conversationalist, but in that, as in other aspects of his character, he demonstrated the modesty on which his friends made such frequent comment. He rarely talked about himself, and while he did not hesitate to voice his opinions on subjects on which he felt competent to speak, he was deferential to the opinions of others, and particularly so toward those of individuals informed on matters of which Rhodes felt himself ignorant.[36] Grant remembered that

> Definite as he was in his convictions as an historian, Rhodes habitually disclaimed any capacity to forecast the future, and even regarding the import of current events was self-distrustful. Time and again I have heard him seek information concerning politics from men . . . whom he considered best informed. . . .[37]

President Arthur T. Hadley of Yale University, although not a close friend, emphasized another significant element in Rhodes' personal talk:

> He had a singular talent for constructive conversation—for talk that left you with your ideas cleared up and enlarged. This, I think, was due to a combination of two qualities: vast knowledge of the important facts of political history, and a cheerful optimism which underlay all his views and conclusions. It sometimes happens that wide knowledge makes people cynical or even pessimistic. Of such cynicism there was not a trace in James Ford Rhodes. He had observed large fields of human activity and had found them good. . . . his eye was always open for the good.[38]

Even more impressive, in a man of so great a reputation, was his respect for the opinions of adolescents. His niece, Mrs. Lucia McBride, remembers that on her frequent visits to the Rhodes home in the '90's he listened carefully to her discussions of current questions, interjecting now and then, "Are you sure these are the facts?," or "Where did you get that information?" Usually he concluded such observations as he had to make with the advice, "Be sure you've got your facts straight." [39] Not once did he show condescension to nor impatience with what she now feels must have sounded to him like sketchy arguments indeed.

Rhodes' modesty manifested itself in yet other ways. Conscious of his deficiencies in formal education, he freely admitted his own weaknesses.[40] He conceded to Morse "that your judgment of [Charles] Sumner is better than mine." To Barrett Wendell he confessed, "I am amazed at the gaps in my knowledge. The Renascence in Italy and the literature of the subject is (sic) one of my bits of colossal ignorance." To an English correspondent he candidly admitted he knew little about German historians.[41] When he accepted an invitation in 1915 to address the Harvard chapter of Phi Beta Kappa he wrote to a friend: "I ought not to have accepted . . . , as I read badly and should never attempt what is called an 'oration,' but, . . . I have such an idea of the high honor of being a Phi Beta Kappa orator that I could not resist the temptation." [42] Willing to confess his failings, he was shy about his work and honors. In a letter describing the commencement at the University of California in 1916 he did not even hint that he had received an honorary degree.[43] His refusal to talk about his work for publication caused James B. Morrow, a noted newspaper correspondent of the time, to "mourn because you would not talk to me for publication . . . And I shall continue to mourn." [44] As a matter of fact, Rhodes had an aversion to newspaper publicity of any kind; he advised Morse to ignore newspaper criticism of Morse's work.[45]

As he shrank from publicity, so did he shrink from money-raising, even for what he felt were good causes, but in giving he was generous—and anonymous.[46] In Cleveland he had comfortably assumed that no one need go hungry in America but he discovered in Boston that very worthy people indeed, such as aged university professors, were in danger of doing just that.[47] He responded liberally to appeals for aid made by mutual friends.[48] On one occasion Rhodes himself took responsibility for fighting for a Carnegie pension for the widow and family of a professor whom he had known. Pres. Henry S. Pritchett of the Carnegie Foundation for the Advancement of Teaching, reported the result: "my executive committee voted [the] pension . . . When I read the letter which you wrote . . . it melted them at once." [49]

Rhodes, in fact, fought for others as he rarely fought for himself. When a friend, Major William R. Livermore, was removed from the Nicaraguan Commission of the United States government, Rhodes interceded, albeit unsuccessfully, with both Secretary of War Russell A. Alger and President William McKinley.[50] After the outbreak of the Spanish-American War he appealed to Mark Hanna to see that Livermore got "favorable consideration"—a request which Hanna promptly approved and sent to the White House.[51] When Hanna himself was attacked for his political practices by a writer on the *Boston Herald* Rhodes protested with such effect that the author, a personal friend of the historian, promised, "I will pursue him as little as possible hereafter, . . . , for your sake." [52]

During World War I he pestered the Assistant Secretary of the Navy, Franklin D. Roosevelt, with requests for special consideration for a nephew.[53] He helped obtain Lowell lectureships for Frederic Bancroft, Charles Harding Firth, and Sidney Lee.[54] Rhodes' generosity went even further. With friends he shared private information on investments he obtained from such associates as Henry Lee Higginson.[55] And during prohibition he sacrificed to friends some of the choicest samples of his liquor closet.[56] What more could mortal ask?

Rhodes' generosity, however, was not prodigal; it was, rather, the careful—but not mean—giving of a thrifty man: indeed, Rhodes, like his Boston associates, embodied that basic Yankee virtue. He saved his ties and sent them to George Myers for use when he had no more use for them.[57] He labeled and used his underwear in chronological sequence of purchase so as to get maximum wear.[58] On the occasion of a birthday dinner in his honor he cautioned his hosts about wasting champagne: "have it as cheap as will possibly pass muster. Much will be left in glasses and the quantity of champagne on the market is growing less from month to month. Therefore it is an article not to be wasted." [59]

Thriftily, he never allowed his preoccupation with the *History* to cause neglect of his business interests. His relations with Henry Lee Higginson were business as well as personal; through his associations with State Street brokers he was enabled to increase substantially his original assets.[60] He discussed with Mark Hanna his holdings in Cleveland street railway stock.[61] He kept so close watch on a Cleveland bank in which he was interested as to express objection when it appointed an official in whose integrity Rhodes had little faith.[62]

If he did not slight his business interests, neither did he attempt to deceive himself or others as to their significance in his life. Quite frankly he told college students that they should not make the study of history a career unless they enjoyed inherited wealth or planned to accumulate a fortune as the necessary prerequisite.[63]

Unlike many Proper Bostonians, however, Rhodes did not indulge his thrift at the expense of others. Toward the staff of servants who cared for his family's needs in Boston and Seal Harbor he was generous in compensation and thoughtful in attitude. As he respected the opinions of people of his own class, so did he respect the feelings of those who worked for him. His "orders" were polite requests; he made sure that none felt slighted or overworked. At home and abroad he demonstrated the same attitude toward those who rendered temporary service: waiters, chauffeurs, chambermaids, and the like. Liberal in reward and gracious in word and deed he encountered no difficulty in getting help or food or lodging—or in making friends.[64]

Together with thrift, Rhodes exemplified the Yankee passion for neatness and order. Even in boyhood this trait was well developed. Each night he undressed methodically, carefully placing each article of clothing on top of the other in such sequence that he could dress again with a minimum of time and bother. The habit was so ingrained in James that his brother, Robert, counted upon it in emergencies. When firebells rang in the night, for instance, Robert would bound out of bed, slip rapidly into James' clothes, and be out of the house in full pursuit of the fire engines while James sleepily fumbled among Robert's garments, strewn carelessly over the floor.[65] As an adult, he even kept detailed notes on his eye examinations, giving the exact dates of each and the recommendations of the oculists.[66] Study of his books shows the same methodical approach. Material he considered important he underlined; that which he considered outstanding he noted on the back covers, citing their substance and page number.[67]

Desirable as such a habit may have been in a scholar, it must have made Rhodes somewhat hard to live with as a human being. His days were planned almost to the minute, and to these plans he rigidly adhered. His mornings were devoted to his work, his afternoons to callers and calling, his evenings to his family, his clubs, or his study. In his family he was "nearly a martinet of punctuality and punctilio," but he held himself to the same standard.[68] Mrs. Bertha H. Rhodes recalls that James' wife once remonstrated about his leaving the house early for an appointment, protesting, "If you start so early, James, you'll only have to wait at the other end." To which he replied, "You're right. 'Time was made for slaves,'" and, with a glance at his watch, departed "at the precise minute he had previously planned." [69] Even James' letters to his mother were written on schedule.[70]

As might be expected, Rhodes was a stickler for propriety. With a high regard for dignity, he disliked controversy, believing with Thomas Huxley, "Controversy always tends to degenerate into quarreling." For displays of emotion or ill-temper he had a positive distaste.[71] When people around him became excited over some reported development he would try to quiet them with a smile and the remark, "Maybe t'aint so." [72] How deeply Rhodes felt about the troubles common to families with normal boys in the process of growing up is indicated in one of the few letters in which he gave vent to personal feelings:

> a daughter is the thing to have. When she is growing up and when she is grown, you can always lay your hands on her and she is the joy of the house but you never know where a boy is and when he is around he is apt to be noisy, restless and headstrong.[73]

Rhodes' respect for the conventions went beyond the limits of his family. After his daughter-in-law heard James Bryce bitterly criticize an English politician at a function in the British Embassy in Washington Rhodes cautioned her: "Remember, whatever you hear in an embassy, you must not repeat it." [74] He disliked Edward VII largely because Edward amused himself with "high-born ladies and pretty married women." [75]

Rhodes' notions of propriety even colored his approach to history. President Hadley recalled how Rhodes had omitted from his *History* material reflecting on the character of a leading Republican at the convention of 1864:

> He [Rhodes] said frankly that the incident . . . had probably occurred—almost certainly—but that it appeared unwise to him to damage good men's reputations unnecessarily on anything short of a certainty. . . .[76]

When George A. Myers, the confidant of Mark Hanna, complained that Herbert Croly's biography did not tell the whole story, Rhodes advised him to "garner up your facts and impressions" for a future historian, "if you deem that propriety will approve your telling." [77] If we are to accept the report of Charles K. Bolton, Rhodes went to the extent of destroying historical documents in the interests of propriety. Discussing a meeting of the Massachusetts Historical Society, Bolton noted:

> [Worthington C.] Ford got up and read a letter of Charles Sumner . . . in which Sumner blackguarded his own divorced wife and the Hooper family in general. . . .
>
> After the meeting [Henry Cabot] Lodge and Rhodes forced Ford to destroy the Sumner letter then and there.[78]

On matters of art and literature Rhodes was equally positive. He thought that a painting by Frank Cadogan Cowper, showing, "How the devil, disguised as a vagrant troubadour, having been entertained by some charitable nuns, sang to them a song of love," displayed a "style of painting [that] does not suit the highest taste." [79] On the other hand, he thought John Singer Sargent "a wonderful genius. I have found him socially attractive. He has a keen sense of the artistic." [80] Balzac's *Cousin Bette* he found objectionable because of its "lubricity" and Hardy's *Jude the Obscure* he found so disgusting that he threw it into the sea! [81] But *The Chippendales*, he wrote, was better than "the novels of Maupassant. It is indeed a triumph to write an intensely interesting tale which any mother can put into the hands of her young daughter." [82]

Rhodes' taste in literature, apart from historical works, covered a wide field: Milton, Eckermann, Goethe, Henry Adams (whose *Education* he read three times), Shakespeare ("who has written for all time so far as we know it"), and the Odyssey ("which I read every summer. I think it is the greatest narrative ever written").[83] He had little taste for the familiar essay: he disliked Lamb and at the age of 74 he could not remember whether he had read Robert Louis Stevenson's essays.[84] His taste in poetry was equally set. Asked if he had read any of Amy Lowell's, he replied: "No, and I don't intend to." [85]

If propriety required that young daughters and descendants of illustrious families be shielded behind its taboos it also permitted gentlemen to discuss between themselves what Rhodes euphemistically termed "the infraction of the Seventh Commandment." Thus, the historian recalled to Judge Grant a talk with Barrett Wendell about the comment made by a Canadian woman after reading some French novels: "Les Français le disent, et les Americains le font." [86] And he asked Worthington C. Ford, director of the Massachusetts Historical Society, to confirm a story of Charles Francis Adams

> that Lord Palmerston was a great sinner . . . ; that when he visited at country houses it was an understood thing that his bedroom was next to that of Lady ——, making night visits convenient. . . .[87]

Rhodes' propriety, however, was far from being a gloss for pruriency; it was deeply imbedded in his character, reflected in his shrinking from personal revelation and from inquiring into the feelings of others, even of those of the characters portrayed in his *History*. As Mrs. Bertha H. Rhodes puts it, "He was not an intimate man, he did not want to delve into personal feelings." [88] His correspondence offers little of that inner glow which lights up a writer's personality; it is pitched almost invariably at the intellectual level, and then only as the result of deliberation, as is indicated by the frequent penciled drafts of letters which he prepared before the final writing in ink.

His attitude is perhaps best expressed in his comments on the *Autobiography* of Charles Francis Adams:

> It is a notable story written with sincerity, but it need not have been such a bare disclosure of his soul. Rousseau said of his Confessions that no man was truthful enough to narrate his whole life and he was going to do it. . . . Parisian critics of our day have found fault with his indecent frankness. So with Mr. Adams. It was not necessary to tell that he had been drunk, and the reiteration of how he had missed many chances becomes tiresome. . . . my Mr. Adams is a more worthy man than the Adams of the biography. . . .[89]

Rhodes' strait-laced morality may be attributed to the Puritan atmosphere of his childhood and youth, for it seems to have had little relation to such religious views he held as an adult. Indeed, to the mature Rhodes religion was unworthy the serious attention of a thoughtful man. "From Episcopalian to Unitarian to agnostic," was his own summary of his religious progress.[90] G. Winchester Donald, rector of fashionable Trinity Church, labored unsuccessfully to return Rhodes to the fold, finally telling the historian, "The difficulty is wholly in you." [91]

In Rhodes' view the Christian churches, with the exception of the Roman Catholic, had lost their power, and one reason for their loss of power was that Christians basically had no faith in their own creeds. As a case in point he cited to William James the example of his own mother:

> I have a concrete example which properly raises a doubt whether there is much of anything in the Christian religion. My mother is eighty-six years old and has always been a religious woman, . . . She has been kind, amiable and good, and during the whole course of her life I do not believe she has ever done anything herself which has caused her bitter regret. . . . Now

> she is failing fast physically and while up and about, is physically uncomfortable a good deal of the time. She cannot possibly live much longer and that fact must be apparent to her. Now here is a case when the person should welcome death, when she should be so sure of the eternal bliss awaiting her that she should be ready and anxious to go. On the contrary her clinging to life and her desire to live is positively painful and could not be greater in an infidel or agnostic.[92]

He found humorous the attempts of Protestants to attribute divine inspiration to the Bible, recalling the days "when young and pious, I tried to reconcile the four gospels." [93] He found objectionable what seemed to him the superstition and commercialization fostered by the Roman Catholic Church at Lourdes. Discussing a visit to that famous shrine, he wrote:

> many pilgrims were there humbugging themselves and being humbugged. The evidences of sincere piety and the desire of relief, if it be God's will, we saw at the Grotto were in striking contrast with the mercenary demeanour of the shopkeepers, who pressed upon you their pious wares. . . . we reflected on the immense investment at Lourdes, in churches, shops and merchandise, and hotels, all based on the silly story. . . .[94]

Rhodes never elaborated his own beliefs, and indeed there is little evidence that he gave much thought to such matters. The closest he came to stating his own philosophy was an enthusiastic endorsement of William James' *Pragmatism*, in which he found the basic elements of the philosophy of John Stuart Mill. He praised both for their "sanity" and for making philosophic ideas comprehensible to laymen.[95] Actually, his attitude toward philosophy was much like that toward religion, summed up in his comment on William James: "Unfortunately he was a philosopher and philosophers never seem to agree." [96]

Despite his adherence to a rather strict code, Rhodes does not fit our stereotype of the Puritan. There was little of the austere or grim about him. He liked the society of Boston men, and while he found little to amuse him in the Symphony he indulged his love for the theatre.[97] He had a positive enjoyment in good fellowship mellowed by good food and good drink. In recalling one dinner, he wrote "how nice and wholesomely dissipated it was when we sat around the driftwood fire with the jug of whiskey on the table." [98] On another occasion he recalled "How good meat and drink do clarify one's ideas and help expression!" [99] Some times, indeed, he had to be careful lest his appetites run away with him. "When I go to one of these feasts," he wrote to William R. Thayer, "I think of what Petronius said, 'Good wine should be drunk slowly'—a necessary thought for me." [100]

Rhodes, for all that he was a serious man, a man with no *joie de vivre*, to use the phrase of Mrs. Lucia McBride,[101] was a man of gentle, somewhat ironic, humor. During a discussion of keeping the Boston Athenaeum open on Saturdays during summer, Rhodes observed, "A library is like a bar-room; when you want it open you want it badly." [102] At a meeting where a gift of five million dollars to Harvard by a millionaire was the subject of discussion, Rhodes was pressed for an opinion on the donor's business ethics. Finally he answered, with a twinkle in his eye, "Could a man who would give five millions be dishonest?" [103] On a trip to Europe he wrote ironically to Barrett Wendell:

> I would write you much more about what we saw . . . but unfortunately I lost my Baedeker's N. Italy (sic) in Venice, with its marks of emphasis and praise and so am at a bit of a loss how much I loved the Giotto's (sic) frescoes at Padua and what was the difference between my admiration of the equestrian statue at Padua and the Cellini at Venice. . . .[104]

And serious though Rhodes himself might be, he distrusted those who took life too seriously. As he put it to a friend:

> We have a few friends . . . who are Catholics but I always aver that they are the harmless kind just as I do not like our socialistic friends to carry bombs in their pockets. Zeal in either case might be disturbing to social doings.[105]

Perhaps the most charming aspect of Rhodes' private life was his relationship with his grandchildren and his wife. Mrs. Bertha H. Rhodes, who lived for many years with the elder Rhodeses, recalls that when James had to take meals with her children he always made a success of them. He talked seriously or humorously with the youngsters as the occasion demanded, showing the same respect for their feelings that he showed toward those of adults. Somewhat diffident in the presence of children he proved a boon companion once his reserve was overcome. They never tired of hearing him render "Johnny Smoker," an animated song about the instruments of a symphony orchestra.[106]

In his wife Rhodes had an ideal companion. While she believed wholeheartedly in his work, and had cooperated loyally in the move to the East, she maintained a sense of humor and perspective which helped her husband to take himself a little less seriously

—a genuine help to a man who, in the words of his old barber, was "always of a settled nature—[who] played but little."[107] His fits of moodiness, his obsession with punctuality and order, she took with the same good humor with which she chaffed him about them.[108] The picture of the couple at their summer home at Seal Harbor, Maine, sketched by Mrs. Bertha H. Rhodes, seems symbolic of their relationship:

> On clear, warm evenings it interested J. F. R. (sic) to go out on the large verandah [facing the Atlantic] . . . and peer forth to see . . . the light on Mt. Desert Rock and come back and report to Mrs. R.
>
> On moonlit nights, the full moon was often extraordinarily clear and the sheen upon the waters far extended. On such nights Mrs. R. would come outside and the pair of them would sit in calm and friendly silence, wrapped up warmly, perhaps with steamer rugs over their knees, in two chairs close together.[109]

Rhodes put it more prosaically. He loved study better than anything, he wrote—"Next to my family."[110]

Rhodes, then, exemplified many of the personal qualities which Proper Boston valued. He was a good conversationalist without being egotistical; a lover of the good things of life who, despite his agnosticism, rigidly observed the proprieties; a scholar who respected the beliefs and feelings of others; a man of business who was thrifty without meanness; a friend generous in money and effort to those in need but never prodigal; a paragon of punctuality, neatness and order humanized by a gentle, ironic humor, an entire lack of fanaticism, and a genuine affection for his family. In short, Rhodes embodied, despite his Western accents, that "spirit of a gentleman" which Cleveland Amory declares still "remains of great importance to the Proper Bostonian."[111]

NOTES

1 Rhodes actually moved to Cambridge, Mass., and later to Boston.

2 Summary based upon the following: Oscar Handlin, *Boston's Immigrants, 1790–1865: A Study in Acculturation* (Cambridge, Mass., 1941), pp. 146, 221; Albert B. Hart (ed.), *Commonwealth History of Massachusetts* (New York, 1930), V, chs. III, VI; Alpheus T. Mason, *Brandeis: A Free Man's Life* (New York, 1946), pp. 89–90, 106–107, 109, 115; Thomas C. Cochran and William Miller, *Age of Enterprise*, p. 280; A. M. Schlesinger, Sr., *Rise of the City*, p. 151; "Boston," *Encyclopaedia Britannica* (11th edition), IV, 295.

3 Van Wyck Brooks, *New England: Indian Summer, 1865–1915* (New York, 1940), pp. 422, 435–438, 476 n.

[4] Josiah P. Quincy, "The Character and Services of Alexander Vattimare," *Proceedings, Massachusetts Historical Society* (2nd series), I (1884–1885), 263.

[5] Robert Grant, *The Chippendales* (New York, 1909), pp. 132–134.

[6] *Ibid.*, p. 209; Rhodes to Robert Grant, quoted in M. A. D. Howe, *Rhodes*, pp. 198–199.

[7] Rhodes to Robert Grant, March 3, 1912. Robert Grant Papers, No. 530. Houghton Library, Harvard University.

[8] Cleveland Amory, *The Proper Bostonians* (New York, 1947), p. 24; Van Wyck Brooks, *New England: Indian Summer*, p. 426.

[9] Charles Francis Adams, *An Autobiography; 1835–1915* (Boston, 1916), p. 39; Cleveland Amory, *The Proper Bostonians*, p. 25.

[10] M. A. D. Howe, *Rhodes*, p. 66. Rhodes lived on Reservoir Street, Cambridge, in a house owned by Prof. Adams Sherman Hill of Harvard. *Ibid.*, p. 65.

[11] Rhodes wrote to Grant he was glad that the rich man of the book [*The Chippendales*] was from Maine, not from Ohio. M. A. D. Howe, *Rhodes*, pp. 198–199.

[12] Rhodes to Barrett Wendell, Feb. 23 [1897?]. Rhodes Papers.

[13] Rhodes to John T. Morse, Jr., Nov. 13, 1920. John T. Morse, Jr., Papers, Massachusetts Historical Society.

[14] A. McF. Davis to Rhodes, March 16 and March 21, 1904. Rhodes Papers.

[15] Mrs. Bertha H. Rhodes, interview.

[16] Mark A. DeWolfe Howe, "Inner and Outer Bostonians," *Saturday Review*, XXXVII (1954), 9.

[17] Mellen Chamberlain to Rhodes, Dec. 15, 1893. Rhodes Papers.

[18] Quoted in H. S. Commager, *The American Mind*, p. 233; *Proceedings, Massachusetts Historical Society* (2nd series), VIII (1892–1894), xvi–xvii.

[19] Charles Francis Adams, *Autobiography*, p. 190.

[20] *Proceedings, Massachusetts Historical Society* (2nd series), VIII (1892–1894), xvi–xvii.

[21] Letters to Rhodes from: Henry Lee Higginson, Dec. 27, 1906, quoted in Bliss Perry, *Life and Letters of Henry Lee Higginson* (Boston, 1921), p. 402; Francis A. Walker, Nov. 11, 1895; Holden Abbott, May 18 [1903?]; Charles E. Gruinel, Sept. 31 (sic), 1898. Rhodes Papers. Rhodes to Sir George Otto Trevelyan, Jan. 20 and May 23, 1921; to Robert Grant, Jan. 29, 1925. Rhodes Papers.

[22] Charles E. Gruinel to Rhodes, Sept. 31 (sic), 1898; William Cardinal O'Connell to Rhodes, Feb. 5, 1912. Rhodes to Sir George Otto Trevelyan, May 23, 1921. Rhodes Papers. Bliss Perry, *Henry Lee Higginson*, p. 403. Robert Grant, *Fourscore: An Autobiography* (Boston, 1934), p. 258.

[23] H. S. Commager, *The American Mind*, p. 46; Cleveland Amory, *The Proper Bostonians*, pp. 30–31.

[24] Mrs. Bertha H. Rhodes, interview. Barrett Wendell said he had dined with Rhodes on three continents "and never a poor dinner." Mark A. DeWolfe Howe, *Barrett Wendell and His Letters* (Boston, 1924), p. 114.

[25] Dr. Sidney B. Fay to Robert Cruden, July 1, 1954.

[26] Mark A. DeWolfe Howe, interview. Howe noted that Channing's remarks often sounded more caustic than he intended them.

[27] Charles W. Eliot to Rhodes, Jan. 18, 1902. Rhodes Papers.

[28] Mrs. Lucia McBride, interview. Rhodes to Mrs. McBride, Oct. 31, 1911. Letter in possession of Mrs. McBride.

[29] Mrs. Bertha H. Rhodes, interview; Charnwood quoted in M. A. D. Howe, *Rhodes*, p. 295.

[30] Robert Grant, *Fourscore*, p. 278.

[31] John T. Morse, Jr., to Rhodes, April 14, 1912. Rhodes Papers. John T. Morse, Jr., "James Ford Rhodes," *Proceedings, Massachusetts Historical Society*, LX (1927), 185.

[32] *Ibid.*

[33] Annie B. Perry to Rhodes, April 30, 1918. Rhodes Papers.

[34] Charles K. Bolton, *Notebook*, 1886–1914, p. 86 (June 5, 1898).

[35] Sidney B. Fay to Robert Cruden, July 1, 1954; Charles K. Bolton, *Notebook, 1886–1914*, p. 86 (June 5, 1898); p. 100 (Dec. 6, 1900); Harvey Cushing, "James Ford Rhodes," in M. A. D. Howe, *Later Years of the Saturday Club*, pp. 346–347, 353–354.

[36] *Ibid.*, p. 347; John T. Morse, Jr., "James Ford Rhodes," *Proceedings, Massachusetts Historical Society*, LX (1927), 183.

[37] Robert Grant, *Fourscore*, p. 279.

[38] Quoted in M. A. D. Howe, *Rhodes*, p. 189.

[39] Mrs. Lucia McBride, interview.

[40] Harvey Cushing, "James Ford Rhodes," in M. A. D. Howe, *Later Years of the Saturday Club*, p. 352.

[41] Rhodes to John T. Morse, Jr., May 16, 1893; Barrett Wendell, Feb. 2, 1907; G. W. Prothero, Sept. 4, 1910. Rhodes Papers.

[42] Rhodes to William R. Thayer, Feb. 16, 1915. Rhodes Papers.

[43] Rhodes to Sir George Otto Trevelyan, June 9, 1916. Rhodes Papers.

[44] James B. Morrow to Rhodes, March 1, 1910. Rhodes Papers. Morrow had been previously editor of the Cleveland *Leader*.

[45] Rhodes to Robert Grant, May 7, 1922. Rhodes Papers. Rhodes to John T. Morse, Jr., May 30, 1893. Morse Papers.

[46] "I never could ask a man for a contribution," Rhodes wrote to William R. Thayer, Dec. 3, 1919. Rhodes Papers.

[47] Mrs. Bertha H. Rhodes, interview.

[48] Charles Eliot Norton to Rhodes, May 3, 1905; Charles W. Eliot to Rhodes, Nov. 4, 1914; Oct. 16, 1915. Rhodes Papers.

[49] Henry S. Pritchett to Rhodes, March 28 [1908?]. Rhodes Papers.

[50] William R. Livermore to Rhodes, Oct. 13, 1897; Russell A. Alger to Rhodes, Oct. 19, 1897. Rhodes Papers.

[51] Mark Hanna to Rhodes, Dec. 2, 1898. Rhodes Papers.

[52] George H. Monroe to Rhodes, April 9, 1898. Rhodes Papers.

[53] Franklin D. Roosevelt to Rhodes, April 19, 1918; Henry Cabot Lodge to Rhodes, Nov. 17, 1917; April 18, 1918. Rhodes Papers.

[54] Letters to Rhodes from: Frederic Bancroft, Nov. 14, 1901; Charles H. Firth, Nov. 7, 1902; Sidney Lee, Nov. 18, 1902. Rhodes Papers.

[55] Rhodes to Sir George Otto Trevelyan, Dec. 9, 1912; July 10, 1913. Trevelyan to Rhodes, Oct. 17, 1911; Dec. 21, 1912; June 4, 1913; Aug. 1, 1913. Rhodes Papers.

[56] Rhodes to William R. Thayer, Nov. 21, 1921. Rhodes Papers.

[57] George A. Myers to Rhodes, Sept. 20, 1913. Rhodes Papers.

[58] Mrs. Lucia McBride, interview.

[59] Rhodes to William R. Thayer, April 23, 1918. Rhodes Papers.

[60] Mrs. Bertha H. Rhodes, interview.

[61] Mark Hanna to Rhodes, Feb. 12, 1899; April 29, 1899. Rhodes Papers.

[62] H. R. Newcomb, President, Citizens Savings and Trust Company, Cleveland, Ohio, to Rhodes, July 19, 1906. Rhodes Papers.

[63] *Historical Essays*, pp. 78–79.

[64] Mrs. Bertha H. Rhodes and Mrs. Lucia McBride, interviews.

[65] Mrs. Lucia McBride, interview.

[66] Rhodes Papers, XI, inside front cover, unlettered.

[67] See Rhodes' copies of Tacitus, Macaulay, Aeschylus and Homer in

library of Rhodes' summer home at Seal Harbor, Maine, and his personal books in possession of the Massachusetts Historical Society.

[68] M. A. D. Howe, *Rhodes*, p. 340.

[69] Mrs. Bertha H. Rhodes to Robert Cruden, Aug. 29, 1954.

[70] Mrs. Lucia McBride, interview.

[71] Rhodes to George A. Myers, Jan. 16, 1918, in John A. Garraty (ed.), "Correspondence of George A. Myers and James Ford Rhodes, 1910–1923," *Ohio Historical Quarterly*, LXIV (1955), 256; Mrs. Bertha H. Rhodes, interview.

[72] Mrs. Bertha H. Rhodes, interview.

[73] Rhodes to Mrs. Lucia McBride, Oct. 27, 1907. Letter in possession of Mrs. McBride.

[74] Mrs. Bertha H. Rhodes, interview.

[75] Rhodes to Robert Grant, Oct. 21, 1914. Rhodes Papers.

[76] Quoted in M. A. D. Howe, *Rhodes*, p. 190.

[77] Rhodes to George A. Myers, Jan. 7, 1913, in John A. Garraty (ed.), "Correspondence," *Ohio Historical Quarterly*, LXIV (1955), 127.

[78] *Notebook, 1920–1922*, p. 54 (Oct. 21, 1920).

[79] Rhodes to Barrett Wendell, May 7, 1907. Rhodes Papers. Cowper was a noted English painter of the day. *Who's Who, 1908*, p. 411.

[80] Rhodes to A. Lawrence Lowell, May 10, 1920. Rhodes Papers. Rhodes to John T. Morse, Jr., Jan. 28, 1918. Morse Papers.

[81] Rhodes to Mrs. C. H. Toy, Aug. 7, 1906, quoted in M. A. D. Howe, *Rhodes*, pp. 133–134. Rhodes to Barrett Wendell, Aug. 6, 1906; Nov. 4, 1906. Rhodes Papers.

[82] Rhodes to Robert Grant, April 11, 1909. Rhodes Papers.

[83] Rhodes to Charles H. Firth, Jan. 24, 1909; Barrett Wendell, Aug. 25, 1911; Sir George Otto Trevelyan, Aug. 18, 1920; Sept. 19, 1920. Rhodes Papers. Rhodes to Worthington C. Ford, Sept. 22, 1922, quoted in M. A. D. Howe, *Rhodes*, p. 330.

[84] Rhodes to Sir George Otto Trevelyan, Feb. 18, 1916; Oct. 29, 1922. Rhodes Papers.

[85] Charles K. Bolton, *Notebook, 1917–1920*, p. 164 (Oct. 23, 1918).

[86] Rhodes to Robert Grant, Sept. 24, 1922. Rhodes Papers.

[87] Rhodes to Worthington C. Ford, Aug. 1, 1917. Photostat fragment, Rhodes Papers.

[88] Mrs. Bertha H. Rhodes, interview.

[89] Rhodes to John T. Morse, Jr., April 16, 1916, quoted in M. A. D. Howe, *Rhodes*, pp. 261–262. Rhodes' letter to Sir George Otto Trevelyan, April 20, 1916, is in the same vein. Rhodes Papers.

[90] Mrs. Bertha H. Rhodes, interview.

[91] G. Winchester Donald to Rhodes, March 30, 1903; Nov. 11, 1903. Rhodes Papers.

[92] Rhodes to John T. Morse, Jr., Nov. 25, 1921, in M. A. D. Howe, *Rhodes*, p. 321; Rhodes to William James, Aug. [ ], 1907, in *ibid.*, p. 161.

[93] Rhodes to Frederick Shattuck, M.D., Jan. 18, 1907. Rhodes Papers.

[94] Rhodes to Barrett Wendell, Nov. 4, 1906. Rhodes Papers.

[95] Rhodes to William James, Aug. [ ], 1907, in M. A. D. Howe, *Rhodes*, p. 160.

[96] Rhodes to Sir George Otto Trevelyan, Jan. 20, 1921. Rhodes Papers.

[97] Mrs. Lucia McBride, interview.

[98] Rhodes to John T. Morse, Jr., Jan. 6, 1912. Rhodes Papers.

[99] Rhodes to Barrett Wendell, Jan. 18, 1918. Rhodes Papers.

[100] Rhodes to William R. Thayer, May 3, [1915?]. Rhodes Papers.

[101] Mrs. Lucia McBride, interview.

[102] Charles K. Bolton, *Notebook, 1886–1914*, p. 99 (April 26, 1900).
[103] *Ibid., 1922–1925*, p. 238 (Oct. 20, 1924).
[104] Rhodes to Barrett Wendell, June 5, 1911. Rhodes Papers.
[105] Rhodes to Sir George Otto Trevelyan, March 6, 1920. Rhodes Papers.
[106] Mrs. Bertha H. Rhodes, interview. Mrs. Rhodes to Robert Cruden, Aug. 29, 1954.
[107] George A. Myers to Rhodes, April 15, 1921. Rhodes Papers. Mrs. Bertha H. Rhodes and Mrs. Lucia McBride, interviews.
[108] Mrs. Bertha H. Rhodes and Mrs. Lucia McBride, interviews.
[109] Mrs. Bertha H. Rhodes to Robert Cruden, Aug. 29, 1954.
[110] Rhodes to his wife, Aug. 3 [1892?]. Rhodes Papers.
[111] *The Proper Bostonians*, p. 58.

Chapter 7

COMPLETING THE HISTORY

RHODES had attained two objectives: his initial two volumes had proved successful and he and his family were firmly established in Proper Boston. Now he set himself to completion of the *History*. He permitted nothing to interfere. Devoted to his task, he turned down suggestions from distinguished publishers and institutions that he write or lecture for them on historical subjects —including a request from Lord Acton that he write a history of the United States for the Cambridge Modern History series, no mean tribute to a newcomer in the field! [1]

So assiduously did he apply himself that fears expressed about his health were realized. Upon the completion of the third volume in 1894 he suffered a collapse from which he never quite recovered; the delay in finishing his work was due in large part to the frequent rests he was compelled to take.[2] His trips to Europe, for instance, were dictated to a considerable degree by reasons of health.

Despite such interruptions, Rhodes stuck to his last. Volume III appeared in 1895; Volume IV in 1899; Volume V five years later; the two concluding volumes in 1906. In the course of writing he made a significant change: instead of ending his work with the year 1885 he chose to end it with 1877.[3] He believed that the withdrawal of the federal troops from the South marked the ending of one era and the inauguration of a new one, based on reconciliation between the sections and recognition by the North that the South should solve the Negro problem in its own way. Old issues had passed away, he thought, and for discussion of the social questions involved in the new issues which had arisen since 1877 he felt "a lack of basic knowledge." [4]

There may well have been another factor in Rhodes' decision to abbreviate his *History:* fatigue. The last two volumes show many signs of weariness: rough literary style, much undigested material, lack of exploring the relationships of factors discussed. Rhodes' own comment on the conclusion of his work is that of a tired man:

> Jan. 24, 1906. I have this day completed my draft . . . to the Inauguration of Hayes and the Restoration of Home Rule at

> the South. I will . . . complete my history, but I am not singing nunc dimittus. Almost steady work for two years on this volume.[5]

In this work, as in his first two volumes, Rhodes enjoyed talented assistance. In addition to help given by old professionals like Edward G. Bourne and Titus M. Coan [6] he benefitted from the advice and criticism of a host of gifted amateurs and experts in various fields. Jacob D. Cox, a former major-general in the Union Army and an authority on the military history of the Civil War, not only read manuscript but also furnished reminiscences of the war, leads to materials, and critical analysis of sources.[7] Edward L. Pierce permitted Rhodes to use the materials he had used in his biography of Charles Sumner, cautioned him against uncritical use of such sources as *The Diary of a Public Man*, and discussed with him the evaluation of some of Lincoln's cabinet members. On one occasion he lectured Rhodes on historical method, chiding him for writing in a letter "that the suspicion existed that [Secretary of War Simon] Cameron himself was not above taking a share in graft." Said Pierce:

> I think an historian should in general limit himself to certainties and that he should avoid *on dits*, "it is said," "it was suspected," "there is grave reason to suppose," and all that class of expression. . . . What cannot be fairly proved may well be allowed to die. . . .[8]

Charles Francis Adams gave Rhodes access to his father's diaries. Carl Schurz furnished documents covering his relations with William H. Seward, Secretary of State. James Longstreet, former general in the Confederate army, supplied details about the war and Reconstruction in Louisiana. Prof. W. T. Sedgwick of the Massachusetts Institute of Technology prepared for Rhodes a brief history of the canning industry, designed to show that few canned goods were available to the armies during the Civil War.[9] Brig. Gen. F. C. Ainsworth, Chief, Records and Pension Office, United States War Department, liberally supplied the historian with both official and unofficial source material. Perhaps most interesting among the latter was a comment on Sherman's March to the Sea. Wrote Ainsworth:

> Confidentially, it is my opinion that Gen. Sherman never took any active measures to enforce his own orders prohibiting the pillage and destruction of property . . . Officers who were with Sherman during this period laugh at the idea of his making any

special effort to enforce these orders. It is pretty generally understood that he was quite willing that the inhabitants of the country . . . should fully realize the horrors of war, and that he contemplated with a good deal of equanimity the destruction wrought by his troops. . . .[10]

In addition to such help, Rhodes enjoyed a boon denied to most historians: personal discussions with some of the principal actors in the period of which he wrote and with other men who had personal acquaintance with leading characters. The results of such personal discussions Rhodes carefully noted in his *Index Rerum*, as indicated by the following examples:

> Carl Schurz, Jan. 18, 1894, thinks of [William H.] Seward's diplomatic achievements very much as I have written up to this time—a poor diplomatist—a poor Secy. (sic) of State.
>
> When [Senator] Potter of Wis. (sic) went to Seward to prop (sic) Schurz's appointment he said there wd (sic) be great disappointment if it was not made. Disappointment, said Seward, who has been more disappointed than me. I ought to be Pres. (sic) and am now only chief clerk for an Illinois attorney. One night when going to give a dinner at his house, several ladies and Schurz were in the library laying off their wraps—an open fire was there. Seward came in from outside, took off his shoes and socks and warmed his naked feet at the fire.[11]
>
> . . . J. C. Ropes told me March 6, 1894, of a conversation he had with [Senator Charles G.] Sumner. Sumner said it [Negro suffrage] was foreign to his convictions and his whole habit of thought but the fact of it was that it was necessary to protect the negro.[12]
>
> . . . Charles Eliot Norton, Nov. 3, 1902. Read me a letter from George W. Curtis in Feb. 1876 saying the whole Supreme Court the Chief Justice at their head had been to dine with Sam Ward the lobbyist . . .[13]
>
> . . . Henderson, Senator, at time of impeachment [of Andrew Johnson] engaged to Miss Foote, daughter of ex-senator Foote of Mississippi. Wavered about his vote. . . . Miss Foote wrote him if he voted for conviction he need never come to see her again. Mrs. [Justice] Miller saw the note and told [Henry F.] Pritchett. Pritchett to me, April 16, 1904.[14]

Fortunate in getting assistance from friends, Rhodes enjoyed also an almost complete freedom from the drudgery of scholarship. His devoted secretary, Almira T. Wyman, copied documents and manuscripts and transcribed many of his notes. Mrs. Mary

Stevens Beall did much of the necessary research in Washington, often under drastic handicaps imposed by officialdom. His son, Daniel, revised the manuscript and gave it literary finish.[15] In Volume III, he relied heavily, of course, upon Edward G. Bourne, but thereafter his principal assistant was David M. Matteson, one of those scholars with a passion for anonymity whose burrowings in the archives throw up the material which a Rhodes transforms into history.

A native of California, Matteson became deaf as the result of an accident while he was a student at Harvard, and thus frustrated in his ambition to become a teacher, devoted himself to a lifetime of research in the libraries of Cambridge and Boston. Rhodes was so impressed with the quality of Matteson's work that eventually he assigned Matteson not only to collect material but also to analyze and organize the data.[16] Thus freed from many chores of scholarship, helped by the counsel of friends and the first-hand accounts of participants, Rhodes devoted himself to re-creating the years of Civil War and Reconstruction.

The public to which he addressed his work was quite different in mood and temper from that which had welcomed his first two volumes. The fading of the Panic of '93 persuaded middle-class Americans that their economic system was fundamentally sound, while the defeat in 1896 of "Bryan and his gang" in what even a sober scholar like Edward L. Pierce regarded as "a great struggle for civilization" reassured them as to the future of their country.[17] The feeling of this public was echoed in a magazine editorial:

> leaving unknown Russia out, no country in the world has the economic advantages we have, nor the independent position for the coming centuries as far as economics dare look.
>
> * * *
>
> the American workman, the American machine, the American organizer, have the lead. . . .[18]

With civilization saved at home it was but a step to impose it abroad. Filipinos and Puerto Ricans were brought under the rule of the Stars and Stripes, if not of the Constitution, and American business embarked on a golden crusade for international commercial predominance.[19]

It was symbolic of the times that the American hero of the best-seller, *Graustark*, should carry off his bride for a honeymoon in Washington, D. C., capital of

> the greatest nation in the world . . . [where] you will find the poor man climbing to the highest pinnacle, side by side with

> the rich man. . . . [Where] We recognize little as impossible. . . .[20]

The feelings of complacency and optimism were strengthened by developments in science and technology, ranging from the invention of the safety razor to the discovery of X-rays, which not only brought immediate benefits but also promised longer and better living in the future. To Americans generally, life appeared as bright as it did to Walter Hines Page, the transplanted Southerner who edited the foremost journal dedicated to American business enterprise, *World's Work:* "The outward din of progress is only an indication of the silent, steady advance beneath." [21]

This atmosphere pervades the last five volumes of the *History.* Symbolically, Volume III opens with a chapter, 113 pages long, which is in effect a panegyric of American business and character; Volume VII closes with the assurance that whatever abuses may have developed in American life, "the American people remained sound at the core." [22] Volume III, it will be recalled, appeared in 1895, when the country was still trying to find its way out of the wreckage of '93. Rhodes was certain not only that prosperity would return but also that it would reach new heights:

> The great material prosperity of the country amazed De Tocqueville in 1832 and Bryce in 1881. Since the adoption of the Constitution the progress has been certain from decade to decade. War has checked it, political troubles have weighed upon it, financial panics have interrupted it, but each wave of prosperity has been higher than the preceding. . . .[23]

The secret of this prosperity was to be found in the energetic and independent character of the people rather than in the material resources of the continent.[24]

The superiority of native American character Rhodes found manifested in other ways. His fellow-countrymen were good-natured, he wrote; in many ways Abraham Lincoln was the typical American. American taste and manners, as well as physique, had unquestionably improved since 1850. As to sexual morality, the American standard was high, thanks to the influence of women and to the fact that Americans worked too hard to be immoral.[25] Business morality, aspersed by foreigners, was such that he did not hesitate to compare it with that of any European country. As to the pursuit of wealth in his own country, he conceded

> that there is a higher end of effort than the gain of money; but an honest striving for wealth is better than idleness; and habits of

> industry, acquired in the pursuit of riches through many generations, may be directed by some of their inheritors to the most noble aims.

In America, too, the accumulation of wealth had not been accomplished at the expense of the poor. American businessmen, besides, were far from being mere money-grubbers: "the energetic spirits of the country were willing to embark in hazardous enterprises, . . . [for] honor as well as profit." [26]

This note of satisfaction with his compatriots, sounded throughout Volume III, is echoed in the remainder of his work. No other country was so sensitive to the influence of good women.[27] Southern white people, he wrote, quoting Senator Hoar of Massachusetts, were "a noble race." [28] Residents of the Western Reserve in Ohio were "intelligent and high-minded people." [29] Northerners and Southerners alike shared "the political aptitude which is the peculiar attribute of Americans." Congress, with few exceptions, was immune to corruption. The American cabinet system was preferable to that of England. After the unfortunate example of Andrew Johnson the character of vice-presidents had been such that they would have made fairly good presidents. The grave and dignified conduct of the impeachment of Andrew Johnson shed lustre on both American character and institutions.[30]

Indeed, Americans, on occasion, could rise to "sublime" heights, as when they refused to punish Jefferson Davis, when they peacefully accepted the election of Hayes in 1876, and when, despite the blunders and crimes of Reconstruction, they refrained from savage reprisals after the Civil War:

> the common sense of the American people saved them from crowning blunders. They confiscated (practically) none of the land of their prostrate foe; they hanged nobody for a political crime. These are grand results furnishing a new chapter in the world's history. . . .[31]

In the expression of these views Rhodes mirrored the beliefs of the overwhelming majority of his countrymen, whatever their economic and social status may have been. In his economic and social observations, however, he voiced considerations of class rather than of the mass. Government, he wrote, properly belonged to "intelligence and property." Many of the evils of Reconstruction arose from the fact that political power rested in "an ignorant and propertyless constituency." [32] Municipal corruption, too, originated in the poor and ignorant having the right to vote.

> The remedy [wrote Rhodes] was a restriction of right of suffrage to those qualified for it by education and by property. . . .
>
> The management of our cities is purely a business matter, and so, for the most part, is that of our States. . . . For the greatest good of the greatest number the rule of an intelligent minority is, in city and State affairs at least, preferable to the rule of an unintelligent democracy.[33]

It is not surprising, then, to discover that Rhodes thought it fitting for the leading bankers of the country to intervene in governmental affairs to procure the appointment of an acceptable secretary of the treasury in 1861; [34] that the human aspect of business depressions which he deemed worthy of note was the distress of many employers in contemplating the suffering of their workingmen; [35] and that in discussing the contributions of Northern people to the Civil War effort he ignored those of farmers and laborers and concentrated on those of businessmen:

> energetic and patriotic men who gave their time and their money to their country; . . . These citizens helped to raise troops and carry elections and were relied upon by their governors and mayors for counsel and support. They were men of high moral and business standing whose advice was always disinterested and often of great value. . . .[36]

Railroads were praised for their "patriotic and generous" behavior during the war; Thomas A. Scott, president of the Pennsylvania railroad, was singled out for special attention because he "was always ready to help efficiently the government in a time of trouble." [37] In contrast to such voluntary assistance to government Rhodes pointed to the horrid example of the Confederacy, "a grand socialized state in which the government did everything." [38]

In his economic views, too, Rhodes reflected the concerns of the Eastern business and financial community of his day, faced with demands from Western farmers and small businessmen for an expanded currency and with the necessity for downward tariff revision dictated by the entrance of American business into world markets. There were basic economic truths, said Rhodes, and of these none was so certain as that only "hard money" was "honest money." [39] The issue of greenbacks during the Civil War was a "scheme . . . at war with economic truths." [40] President Grant's veto of a measure to expand the issue of greenbacks was "a brave and noble act." [41] Resumption of specie payments was a statesmanlike act, while the decision of the Supreme Court in *Juilliard vs.*

Greenman (March 3, 1884), upholding the right of Congress to authorize issuance of paper currency, opened the door to financial disaster.[42]

Equally positive were Rhodes' views on the tariff. Influenced by *The Nation* and by Edward G. Bourne, he had abandoned the protectionist views expressed in his circulars of the '80's:

> The economists maintain [wrote Rhodes] that a protective tariff does not in our country provide the greatest good of the greatest number; . . . History, . . . , confirms the teachings of the economists. . . .[43]

The revenue tariffs of 1846 and 1857, in his opinion, "demonstrated a fact of great value—that a high protective tariff is not necessary for the growth of our manufacturing industries." [44]

In still another area did Rhodes share the views of the business community of his day: antagonism to the Spanish-American war and to an overgrown military establishment. He deplored the intense emotion of wartime which weakens objective judgment; and concluded that, "No matter how mercifully war may be carried on, it is at the best a rude game." [45]

These attitudes, expressed in the volume which appeared shortly after the war ended, were emphasized in the ensuing volumes. War, he wrote, "is not a business for us. The genius of the American Commonwealth lies in peace." [46] Hamilton Fish, secretary of state in the Grant administration, drew high praise for standing out against war with Spain, "when so many strong men were swayed by the war sentiment of the country." [47] Rhodes felt a thrill of satisfaction in the settlement of the *Alabama* claims by arbitration, because, he believed, it established a precedent for the settlement of irritating international issues by law.[48]

As to the place of the military in a constitutional government, Rhodes had no doubts. Military officers must always be subordinate to the civil power: one of McClellan's great weaknesses was that he did not conduct himself "as a general subject to the civil power ought to have done." [49] The historian's distaste for military rule found expression in repeated condemnation of the suspension of *habeas corpus* and of the policy of arbitrary arrests in the North during the Civil War.[50] Nor did Rhodes content himself with merely negative criticism. He affirmed "the necessity in a constitutional government of an opposition party even when the life of the nation is at stake," and emphasized the duty of the historian to uphold freedom of dissent even in time of war.[51]

It was in matters of race and nationality, however, that Rhodes most clearly identified himself with his public. He matured and wrote in a period dominated by the ideas of Count Joseph de Gobineau, the Frenchman whose teachings of "Aryan" racial superiority later proved so useful to the Nazis. His ideas were given an American gloss by such leading publicists as Lyman Abbott, John Fiske and Josiah Strong, who saw in the American Anglo-Saxon the highest product of biological and social evolution. Apart from flattering the Anglo-Saxon ego, such doctrines proved popular since they afforded moral and "scientific" sanctions for relegating the Negro to second-class citizenship under the watchful eye of Anglo-Saxon Southerners.[52]

All this Rhodes accepted without question. Science, said he, demonstrated the inferiority of the Negro race throughout history.[53] He himself held the race to be "one of the most inferior races of mankind."[54] The basic blunder of Reconstruction was the overrating of the mental and moral capacities of Negroes. The Radical Republicans "did not appreciate the great fact of race, that between none of the important races of mankind was there a difference so wide as between the Caucasian and the negro."[55] Negro suffrage, given a fair trial in the South, had proved the black American to be a political failure, as indeed he had proved to be also in the North.[56] Only twice in his work did Rhodes have a kind word for his colored countrymen. He praised some for showing fidelity to their owners during the war and others for displaying bravery as soldiers in the Union army.[57]

At the other end of the scale was the Anglo-Saxon. In the South, the Anglo-Saxon spirit of resistance to oppression helped explain the length of the war; on the other hand, Abraham Lincoln typified the Anglo-Saxon respect for law, Northern Democrats the Anglo-Saxon sense of political responsibility, and the Union troops at Gettysburg Anglo-Saxon zeal in defense of their own land.[58] Lincoln's plan for Reconstruction displayed Anglo-Saxon practicality.[59] Maintenance of peace between the United States and England was not only of importance to the world at large but also to the Anglo-Saxon race itself.[60]

Apart from the Scotch-Irish of the South, whose Calvinist faith and physical courage he found praiseworthy,[61] Rhodes had little good to say about other peoples in the American cultural stream. If poverty became more abject, said he, it was due to the low character of European immigrants rather than to conditions of American society.[62] Defects in American business morality he attributed largely to the knavery of immigrants and their offspring.[63] Of Americans of foreign background, Rhodes entertained a particular antipathy to those of Jewish origin, whom he lumped together, regardless of place of birth or length of residence in the United States, with "other foreigners." [64] His discussion of Irish participation in the New York draft riots, for example, was fairly dispassionate,[65] but he rarely mentioned Jews without invidious comment. Judah Benjamin, the Confederate Secretary of State,

> was of Hebrew parents, wealthy, the ablest lawyer of the South in public life, and a fit representative of Louisiana, one of the more conservative of the cotton States. . . . sincerity does not inhere in his utterances as it does in so marked a degree in those of the South Carolina leaders, of Toombs, Stephens, and Jefferson Davis. . . .[66]

Not only did Benjamin live well in the midst of general distress; in Rhodes' opinion he also connived at carrying the war to Northern civilians—something impossible to believe of a Jefferson Davis.[67] The historian's anti-Semitism was not confined to discussions of Benjamin; in his treatment of those whom he considered scoundrels, Jay Gould and Governor F. J. Moses, for example, he emphasized the matter of origins mainly in the case of Jews.[68] In his discussion of the illicit trade between North and South during the war, only Jewish smugglers and merchants were given special mention and the anti-Jewish tirades of Grant and Sherman were taken at their face value without analysis.[69] Of this overt anti-Semitism no trace is to be found in the first two volumes, written in Cleveland. One may well wonder how much of it in the later volumes stemmed from Rhodes' close contacts with the Boston Brahmins, among whom anti-Semitism has long been endemic.[70]

As in his first two volumes, Rhodes appealed to his public not only with affirmation of their own beliefs, prejudices and attitudes but also with material that was of genuine interest in itself. There were numerous character sketches, giving an intimate, personal turn to the impersonal stuff of history. A few examples will show how skillfully the historian used this device: Robert E. Lee was

> physically and morally a splendid example of manhood. . . . , the best blood of Virginia ran in his veins. . . . Drawing from a knightly race all their virtues, he had inherited none of their vices. Honest, sincere, simple, magnanimous, forbearing, refined, courteous, yet dignified and proud, never lacking self-command, he was in all respects a true man. . . . Sincerely

> religious, Providence was to him a verity, and it may be truly said he walked with God.[71]

No one was more devout than "Stonewall" Jackson:

> his religion became a part of his being, influencing every act. . . . His communion with his Maker seemed complete. He prayed without ceasing . . . These traits were a rightful inheritance from Jackson's Scotch-Irish ancestry.
>
> He loved liquor, but would not drink it. . . . Morally he was conscientious to a nicety that appears extreme, but his exact truthfulness and ready self-denial were traits of a noble soul. . . .[72]

Rhodes sketched at some length the early history of U. S. Grant, describing his hard childhood and youth, his undistinguished record in the Army after his graduation from West Point, his falling "into habits of intemperance," his repeated failure to make a success of life as a civilian. But, wrote Rhodes,

> Breaking through this wretchedness, however, there were gleams of true manhood. He was honest and truthful, and he had the instincts of a gentleman, which prevented him from becoming a loafer. He never used profane language; he did not tell obscene stories; and this was not from refinement of taste, for that he lacked, but from his purity of soul.[73]

Lucius Q. C. Lamar, in the days of Reconstruction in Mississippi,

> might be seen of a pleasant evening leaning over the white picket fence in front of his humble cottage. Bare-headed, clad in a frayed, ink-stained study-gown, he seems drooping like a wounded soldier. His sombre, thoughtful face . . . tells of the sorrowful heart within that broods upon his dear suffering State. . . . the effect of these days of melancholy and anxious reflection, when he generously took to himself the sorrows of his community, was to prepare him for one of his greatest efforts.[74]

For Andrew Johnson, Rhodes had quite a different approach:

> Of all men in public life it is difficult to conceive of one so ill-fitted for this delicate work [of Reconstruction] . . . Born in the midst of degrading influences . . . , brought up in the misery of the poor white class, he had no chance for breeding, none for book education, none for that half-conscious betterment which comes from association with cultivated and morally excellent people. It is said that he never went to school for a day. Apprenticed to a tailor at the age of ten, he had only manual labor to perform, . . . a born politician and speechmaker . . .

> a reader of books . . . but his reading was a veneer and he never mastered a book as Lincoln did . . . He went directly from the tailor's bench to the mayor's chair and the legislative hall, and indeed worked intermittingly at his trade until elected to Congress. This was much to Johnson's credit but it was not a suitable training for a President of the United States.[75]

Interlarded with character sketches were many accounts of happenings which lent themselves easily to dramatic treatment: the reduction of Fort Sumter; the cabinet meeting at which Lincoln read the Emancipation Proclamation; the New York draft riots; the rejoicing in the North when Lee surrendered; the anguish and anger in the North at Lincoln's assassination: "Magnanimity to the beaten foe was the sentiment of Monday; . . . justice and vengeance . . . on Saturday." [76]

There were also fascinating chapters describing life behind the lines in both North and South, telling of luxury, immorality, blockade-running, bread riots and slave auctions in the midst of war.[77] There was even a chapter on the still-controversial topic of treatment of prisoners of war, in which Rhodes asserted

> In no part of the history of the Civil War is a wholesome scepticism more desirable and nowhere is more applicable a fundamental tenet of historical criticism that all the right is never on one side and all the wrong on the other.[78]

It was certain, he concluded,

> that no deliberate intention existed either in Richmond or Washington to inflict suffering on captives more than inevitably accompanied their confinement. Rather than to charge either section with inhumanity it were truer to lay the burden on war, . . .[79]

These however, were but parts of the great tragic dramas of Civil War and Reconstruction which dominate these five volumes. That slavery was the sole cause of the war Rhodes still did not doubt, but he had abandoned his old belief—shared by most Northerners—that secession was the result of an unholy conspiracy.[80] He now thought, as Southern whites had long contended, that secession had been the product of a popular demand so strong that had not men like Jefferson Davis led the movement the people would have found other leaders.[81] Nevertheless, Rhodes was far from absolving such leaders of guilt. Their folly and rashness led to war; their outcries against the tariff were insincere; and even to save slavery their policy was suicidal.[82]

Despite their folly, the Southern people won Rhodes' admiration,[83] and he deplored the sacrifice made of them by Jefferson Davis, an ambitious and selfish leader who blocked a negotiated peace:

> Congress [of the Confederacy] would undoubtedly have authorized negotiations had it believed that such authorization would be acceptable to Davis. . . . It was Jefferson Davis who in this matter imposed his will . . . and it was he more than anybody else who stood in the way of an attempt to secure favourable terms for the South in the reconstruction of the Union. . . . In this dogged resolution, this repugnance to own up that he was beaten, there was more of selfishness than of regard for the best interests of his people. . . .[84]

The North, in Rhodes' view, fought on the side of the angels. Anxious to avoid war, Northerners had offered to modify their Personal Liberty Laws and to guarantee the continuation of slavery in states where it existed, but once forced into the field, their concern was for human freedom. The Emancipation Proclamation simply made clear the basic issue of the war.[85] Considerations of tariff and economic policy Rhodes thought of so little significance that he dismissed them with bare mention.[86] Rather, his attention on the war, apart from political considerations, was focused largely on military affairs.[87] Only belatedly he acknowledged the historian's obligation to deal with other matters and expressed doubts as to the value of a civilian's criticism of strategy and tactics, but this did not prevent him from passing judgment on the various campaigns, including those of Lee, Jackson, and Grant.[88]

As seen through Rhodes' eyes it was rather a curious war in some respects. One gathers that it was indeed a bloody affair, waged bitterly against civilians as well as soldiers by the governments of both North and South—but somehow a war fought by gentlemen who cheered their opponents, refrained from pillage, and "frowned forbiddingly on the crime of rape." [89] As to the conduct of Sherman's troops, much criticized in the South, Rhodes concluded: "The men who followed Sherman were probably more humane generally than those in any European army that marched and fought before our Civil War." [90] Such an opinion, appearing in 1904, may well have proved reassuring to a public still uneasy over reports of atrocities committed in the Philippines by American troops.

If much of the appeal of Volumes III–V lay in their portrayal of the war, the impact of Volumes VI–VII lay in their sweeping indictment of Reconstruction and in their reinforcement of the popular belief in the unfitness of the Negro for full citizenship.

In his last two volumes, Rhodes articulated this popular feeling, provided it with scholarly backing deriving from the work of Professor William A. Dunning and his associates, and gave it such wide currency among the educated that for decades it was the standard view of Reconstruction, accepted alike by laymen and scholars. In this view, Reconstruction was a period of unmitigated evil, brought about by the subjection of intelligent, property-holding Anglo-Saxons to ignorant, barbaric, propertyless Negroes, who were sustained in power through the manipulations of unprincipled "carpet-baggers" and "scalawags"; a condition so revolting to decent white men that in desperation they were forced to resort to intimidation and violence to secure the restoration of honest and efficient government.[91] As Rhodes saw it:

> No large policy in our country has ever been so conspicuous a failure as that of forcing universal negro suffrage upon the South. The negroes who simply acted out their nature were not to blame. . . . The scheme of Reconstruction pandered to the ignorant negroes, the knavish white natives and the vulturous adventurers who flocked from the North; . . . intelligence and property stood bound and helpless under negro-carpet-bag rule. . . .[92]

Indeed, thought Rhodes, Reconstruction was worse than a failure: it was "an attack on civilization" which cost the North much of its standing in European opinion.[93] Overthrow of the Reconstruction governments was "a victory for righteousness," at which "all lovers of good government must rejoice." [94]

NOTES

[1] S. Weir Mitchell, for the Century Company, to Rhodes, Nov. 27, 1902; Horace E. Scudder, for Houghton Mifflin Company, to Rhodes, Oct. 26, 1901; Captain C. H. Stockton, U. S. Naval War College, to Rhodes, May 4, 1900; Lord Acton to Rhodes, Dec. 19, 1896. Rhodes Papers.

[2] Albert B. Hart to Rhodes, July 11, 1894. Rhodes Papers.

[3] The change had been suggested by Charles Francis Adams. Rhodes to Adams, May 10, 1907, in M. A. D. Howe, *Rhodes*, p. 155.

[4] *History*, VI, v–vi.

[5] Rhodes Papers, XI, unlettered page. Rhodes noted that two volumes were actually made out of his manuscript.

[6] Rhodes, *History*, III, 637; IV, 539; Rhodes Papers, XI, Fa–eF.

[7] Jacob D. Cox to Rhodes, correspondence in Rhodes Papers, 1893, 1894, 1896, 1898, 1900, *passim*.

[8] Edward L. Pierce to Rhodes, June 15, 1893; May 4, 1894; June 3, 1894. Rhodes to Pierce, April 28, 1894. Rhodes Papers.

[9] Rhodes, *History*, IV, 83 n. Carl Schurz to Rhodes, Feb. 26, 1894; James Longstreet to Rhodes, Nov. 18, 1896; Jan. 30, 1897; W. T. Sedgwick to Rhodes, Jan. 21, 1902. Rhodes Papers.

[10] F. C. Ainsworth to Rhodes, Feb. 1, 1901. Rhodes Papers. See also Ainsworth to Rhodes, March 18, 1902; Nov. 24, 1902; and May 8, 1903. Rhodes Papers.

[11] Rhodes Papers, X, uQ.

[12] *Ibid.*, p. iN. Ropes was a noted military historian of the time.

[13] Rhodes Papers, XI, unlettered page.

[14] *Ibid.*, p. He.

[15] Rhodes, *History*, IV, 539; V, 626. Mrs. Bertha H. Rhodes, interview. F. C. Ainsworth to Rhodes, Nov. 13, 1900; William R. Day, U. S. State Department, to Mrs. Mary Stevens Beall, July 28, 1898. Rhodes Papers.

[16] Rhodes to Charles H. Firth, Dec. 16, 1902. Rhodes Papers. Dr. Frederick Merk, emeritus professor of history, Harvard University, interview.

[17] Edward L. Pierce to Rhodes, Aug. 4, 1896. Rhodes Papers.

[18] *World's Work*, III (1901), 1359.

[19] Sydney Brooks, "Problems of the British Empire," *ibid.*, p. 1393. The early volumes of this magazine are replete with articles designed to promote international expansion of American business.

[20] George Barr McCutcheon, *Graustark*, quoted in Frank L. Mott, *Golden Multitudes*, p. 209.

[21] *World's Work*, III (1901), 1453.

[22] *History*, VII, 291.

[23] *History*, III, 4.

[24] *Ibid.*, p. 15.

[25] *Ibid.*, p. 72, 82, 97–99, 109, 110.

[26] *Ibid.*, pp. 14, 65 n., 100, 111.

[27] *History*, V, 260.

[28] *History*, VII, 173.

[29] *Ibid.*, p. 17.

[30] *History*, III, 296; V, 269–271; VI, 154, 155.

[31] *History*, VI, 49; VII, 174, 255, 284–285.

[32] *History*, VII, 78, 112, 128, 147, 174, 195, 290.

[33] *History*, VI, 410–411.

[34] *History*, III, 251.

[35] *Ibid.*, p. 48.

[36] *History*, V, 243.

[37] *History*, IV, 508; V, 225, 242.

[38] *History*, V, 475.

[39] *History*, III, 567; IV, 509; VII, 56, 176, 242.

[40] *History*, III, 567.

[41] *History*, VII, 64.

[42] *History*, VI, 228, 270; VII, 56.

[43] *History*, III, 31–32.

[44] *Ibid.*, p. 58.

[45] *History*, IV, 140, 181, 275.

[46] *History*, V, 238.

[47] *History*, VII, 36.

[48] *History*, VI, 375–376.

[49] *History*, IV, 191, 253–254; V, 167.

[50] *History*, IV, 165, 169, 171, 230–234, 248, 249–250, 253.

[51] *Ibid.*, pp. 168, 227, 532.

[52] Rayford W. Logan, *The Negro in American Life and Thought: The Nadir, 1877–1901* (New York, 1954), ch. 9.

[53] *History*, VI, 36–37.

[54] *History*, V, 556.

[55] *History*, VII, 95.

[56] *Ibid.*, pp. 141, 143, 149, 170.

[57] *History*, IV, 333, 334 n.; V, 460–461.

[58] *History*, III, 117, 402; IV, 213, 228, 286.

[59] *History*, V, 55–56. In contrast, wrote Rhodes, Sumner's plan calling for Negro suffrage "smacked of the logic of the French." *Ibid.*

[60] *History*, VI, 376.

[61] *History*, IV, 265.

[62] *History*, III, 64.

[63] *Ibid.*, p. 111.

[64] *History*, V, 420.

[65] *History*, IV, 321–330.

[66] *History*, III, 241.

[67] *History*, V, 63, 341, 481.

[68] *History*, VI, 247; VII, 146.

[69] *History*, III, 549; V, 216, 285–290, 420.

[70] Alpheus T. Mason, *Brandeis*, pp. 203–204.

[71] *History*, III, 411–412.

[72] *Ibid.*, pp. 460–461.

[73] *Ibid.*, pp. 594–596.

[74] *History*, VII, 97–98.

[75] *History*, V, 517–519.

[76] *History*, III, 221–249; IV, 160–161, 322–327; V, 131, 147–148.

[77] *History*, VII, chs. XXVII, XXVIII.

[78] *History*, V, 485.

[79] *Ibid.*, p. 508.

[80] *History*, III, 119, 122, 280; IV, 1, 215.

[81] *History*, III, 278. Rhodes added that he was encouraged to adopt this view because von Holst and James Schouler had already done so. *Ibid.*, p. 279 n.

[82] *Ibid.*, pp. 177, 204, 297–298, 324.

[83] *History*, IV, 320.

[84] *History*, V, 79–80.

[85] *History*, III, 144–145, 147, 169–170, 177; IV, 215.

[86] *History*, III, 204, 315, 397–398; IV, 239, 428.

[87] *History*, IV, ch. XVII, 127, 146, 179, 280–298, 304–319; V, 7–31.

[88] *History*, III, 451 n.; IV, 13, 239, 282, 291, 295, 445.

[89] *History*, IV, 318; V, 25, 88, 100–101.

[90] *History*, V, 104.

[91] *History*, V, ch. XXX; VI and VII, *passim*.

[92] *History*, VII, 168–169.

[93] *History*, VI, 35; VII, 171.

[94] *History*, VI, 309; VII, 140.

Chapter 8

THE POPULAR HISTORIAN

RHODES, then, in his last five volumes, appealed to numerous publics within the larger reading public. He not only presented readable accounts of the Civil War and Reconstruction; he also made articulate basic feelings and attitudes of these publics and in sustaining such attitudes in relation to current problems lent them the weight of history, an influence all the more telling in that Rhodes spoke with the voice of learning and moderation, rendering his historical verdicts with what seemed to his contemporaries almost godlike impartiality. To such history, readers—laymen and professional historians alike—responded with appreciation.

Obviously, Rhodes was far from being in a class with such "best sellers" as Rudyard Kipling and Richard Harding Davis, but for a solid, responsible historian who avoided the directly popular appeal of a John Bach McMaster, his sales were far from negligible. In the last eight months of 1895, a year of economic depression, 2580 copies of Rhodes' work were sold; most of these, it may be assumed, were copies of the newly published Volume III.[1] In the ensuing three years, despite a slump in the book trade resulting from the Spanish-American war, 2387 copies were sold, and the demand for Volume IV was so strong that the publishers pressed Rhodes for its early completion.[2] Of this volume, 1696 copies were sold in 1899, the year of its appearance; at least 1423 were sold in the next four years. During that period, 1899–1903, the earlier volumes continued to be in moderate demand: sales of Volume I amounted to more than 1381; of Volume II to more than 1391; of Volume III to more than 1423.[3]

Such figures may seem unimpressive to a generation accustomed to think in terms of millions, but to publishers of that day they were impressive enough. When Harper and Brothers underwent an internal reorganization in 1899 which caused them to relinquish many of their outstanding authors, Rhodes, who owned his own plates and copyrights, did not lack for other houses eager to produce his work. Houghton Mifflin and Company; Doubleday, Page and Company; the Macmillan Company—they all solicited his association, as did that redoubtable muckraker, S. S. McClure.[4]

Rhodes chose Macmillan: it already published his work in England; it enjoyed international prestige; and it pursued an aggressive sales policy—a point on which Rhodes was always sensitive.[5] On this score, he could find little fault with his new publisher. Even before Volumes VI and VII appeared, Macmillan had orders for at least 250 *sets* of the entire seven volumes. George P. Brett, vice-president of the company, informed the sales force he expected them to sell at least 1000 sets of the completed work within a year of publication.[6] Individual copies of the last two volumes sold 3100 each in that period.[7]

The influence of Rhodes' work is not to be measured entirely in terms of sales. Many of the purchasers were opinion-makers of the day: editors, teachers, clergymen, political leaders. Through them the contents of the *History* reached a much wider public. Indeed, Brett saw in this one of the values of Rhodes' work: "to set the public right on many matters on which they are not capable of taking time to form for themselves a correct judgment." [8]

The public was apparently delighted to be set right. Theodore Roosevelt favorably compared Rhodes to his idol, Macaulay. He singled out for praise Rhodes' treatment of Reconstruction, which he thought marked by ability and fairness.[9] *The International Socialist Review*, the intellectual organ of Roosevelt's arch enemies, the Socialists, while criticizing Rhodes' lack of class analysis, shared Roosevelt's view on the discussion of Reconstruction. It observed that Rhodes' history of the Civil War was by far the best yet written. The magazine had special praise for the description in Volume V of life behind the lines: "There is nothing in the whole field of historical literature in any way comparable to these two chapters." [10]

A prominent Negro churchman, Benjamin W. Arnett, acclaimed the first three volumes as "a beacon light to the heroes of freedom." [11] A leading white Southerner, Dunbar Rowland, wished that copies of the *History* "could be placed in every Southern home for it would impress the truth that justice finally prevails." [12] Another Southerner, the historian William E. Dodd, used Rhodes' *History* "in preference to any others." In Dodd's view this "masterly History has done more than any other historical agency—perhaps any other agency of any sort—to bring about" reconciliation between North and South.[13]

New Englanders were no less enthusiastic. Barrett Wendell compared Rhodes with Thucydides and Tacitus. "In all seriousness," he wrote to his friend, "your grasp and your poise as a narrator do not shrink beside a comparison like that."[14] William James, who thought the *History* "admirable," used it for lecture material.[15] John T. Morse, Jr., praised Rhodes for "the 'equal mind' which you preserve concerning men and events. Your justice, freedom from passion and prejudice, from love and hates, are remarkable."[16]

Such messages, a slight sampling of the encomia which flowed in on Rhodes privately, mirrored public expressions in leading magazines.[17] *The Nation*, devoting an entire page to reviewing the seven-volume set, commented:

> Of Mr. Rhodes' success in his published volumes there can be only one opinion. He has written a history of an eventful, even critical, period, that will long remain a standard; and he has to a remarkable degree met the principal requirements of modern historical methods. Great industry in compiling his authorities, marked capacity for weighing them, clear arrangement, and a balanced judgment of men and events—such qualities have resulted in a series of notable volumes, in a dispassionate tone. . . . That there are defects and omissions is not to be denied; specialists may find faults in every chapter. But, as a whole, the work has been well done. It describes a period of sectional difference and strife, in a manner that will appeal to the whole country.
>
> It does not follow that Mr. Rhodes is without definite opinions or is backward in expressing them. On the contrary, his pages bristle with praise and blame. Their value lies in the fact that they have been judicially bestowed. . . . If in these matters Mr. Rhodes has not uttered the final word, he has offered one that will stand the tests of present knowledge.[18]

The Outlook, under the heading, "A Great American History," gave more than two pages to a review of the set, concluding that the *History* would prove to be the standard work for the period because of its "noteworthy fairness, sound scholarship, and . . . high degree of narrative skill."[19] The *World's Work*, deviating for a moment from crying up the manifold virtues of business and its votaries, hailed the *History* editorially as "a monument of industry and (rarer yet) of fair judgment." Even in this it found a moral, however:

> it was a distinct advantage that Mr. Rhodes had his early training in an orderly business pursuit rather than in a university. He learned in business to make good judgments of living men, and he has, therefore, the better made just judgments of men in a turbulent era of the past.[20]

The *Atlantic Monthly*, which had presented Woodrow Wilson's trenchant criticism of the first two volumes, now made handsome amends in an extended article by Bernadotte Perrin, professor of Greek literature and history at Yale University, which extolled the *History* as "in truth a national treasure." Perrin commended Rhodes for his broad sympathies, high standards of research, literary craftsmanship and rigorous impartiality of judgment. He was grateful to Rhodes for showing that through its resistance to Congressional Reconstruction the South had saved the nation in the '70's, just as the North had saved it during the war in the '60's.[21]

There also came to Rhodes that "Appreciation by brothers in the craft" which he thought "of all things the most desirable." [22] Andrew C. McLaughlin, managing editor of the *American Historical Review*, congratulated Rhodes on "the reserve, the fairness, the modesty, the frankness and the lack of affectation with which you tell your story." [23] Edward Channing wrote that the first five volumes "placed [the] author at the head of living historical students." [24] Albert Bushnell Hart thought Volumes III and IV the best work done on the periods covered.[25] William A. Dunning, then engaged in writing his significant work on Reconstruction for *The American Nation* series, sadly confessed that his book

> in its later parts will create the impression of a faithful but inferior summary of yours [Volumes VI and VII]. I am not mourning over the situation, however, for nobody will be the loser. It certainly is remarkable how many instances struck me in which, not only your method, but also your expression, anticipated mine. . . .[26]

James Schouler, whose work covered the same period as that of Rhodes, was ungrudging—and somewhat wistful—in his commendation:

> Those reconstruction years are very difficult to describe dispassionately, but I think you have told the story very well. Your style is clear, your materials are ample, and your known sense of fairness predominates. While my own path was always thorny as historian, you seem to have found constant encouragement and appreciation, and I congratulate you upon your well-deserved fame and honors.[27]

H. Morse Stephens, discussing the first four volumes, ranked Rhodes among the

> five contemporary American writers of history, who meet all the canons of the severest historical criticism, and who have at the

same time written histories which are eminently readable and mark solid advances in the world's knowledge of its past. . . .

Stephens went on to say, "Among living and working writers of American history the palm undoubtedly belongs to Mr. James Ford Rhodes," emphasizing that while the passions and controversies arising from the Civil War had not yet died down, Rhodes had shown that

> the history of a comparatively recent epoch, instinct with political and personal controversies, can be handled with the same impartial spirit that underlies the work of modern historians of the scientific school in dealing with more remote periods, . . .[28]

Southern historians, while finding some flaws in Rhodes' work, were no less enthusiastic. Walter L. Fleming noted that Rhodes was too apt to accept laws and official statements at face value without inquiring into their actual administration and implementation; he thought Rhodes did not present, in many cases, sufficient evidence to support his conclusions: "In other words, the author's conclusions are more unbiased than is warranted by the evidence presented." In general, he concluded that so far as the first five volumes were concerned, the *History*

> while as fair and judicial as any American can now make it, is distinctly from the northern standpoint; . . . there is the intent, usually successful, to treat the other side with fairness, though a sympathetic treatment of both sides is naturally impossible at present; . . . the book is far superior in liberality to anything that has yet been written . . . It is to be hoped that the fine spirit and admirable temper shown in this work will have definite results in correcting the bias of the average school histories, the most potent agencies for perpetuating sectional misunderstandings.[29]

William Garrott Brown thought that in his treatment of the Civil War

> Mr. Rhodes tells the truth. It would probably be hard to improve on that plain statement of the solid excellence of his work. . . . I cannot think of another historian who so constantly produces the effect of complete candor, who is so indefatigably minded to tell all that can be reckoned of consequence, and to display unreservedly the sources of his knowledge and the grounds of his opinions. . . .[30]

Volumes VI and VII Brown termed "the best history yet written of Reconstruction . . . until these two volumes appeared there was no work covering the period . . . which could be commended." [31] J. G. de Roulhac Hamilton wrote that the *History* "as a whole will not soon be surpassed, if indeed it is not as nearly correct as a history of that period can ever be." [32]

The plaudits of the profession were not confined to this side of the Atlantic. W. E. H. Lecky described Volume IV as

> a truly impartial account of a period within the memory of living men and hitherto obscured by the most violent party and national passions. You are doing a good service not only to your own country but also to the interests of historical truth . . .[33]

Charles Harding Firth thought Rhodes' volumes on Reconstruction "sound solid work, as any brother in the trade can see." [34] Commendation in similar strain came from H. Spencer Walpole, A. V. Dicey, Samuel R. Gardiner and J. A. Doyle, a specialist in American colonial history who reviewed Rhodes' work for the *English Historical Review*.[35]

There were dissenters, of course. Moorfield Storey, a personal friend of Rhodes who was also a practical friend to the Negro, thought Rhodes was wrong in attributing the Reconstruction measures to Northern vindictiveness against the South.[36] Leslie Hopkinson of Cambridge, Mass., in discussing that same subject, raised a point which historians other than Rhodes have failed to consider:

> It is easy now to see how blind . . . they [Radicals] were, but then how intense must have been the determination, sharpened in so many cases by personal grief and loss, that our dead should not have died in vain, . . . I at least can see that reconstruction was a terrible bungle; my aunt Mrs. Eliot, when I referred to it one day in that sense, answered with absolute conviction, "It had to be done. If you have (sic) lived then you would have known it was the only way.". . . So I think there was another feeling, not revengefulness and not exactly philanthropy; nor interest primarily in the negro as such, but desire for justice —such abstract, ideal justice, no doubt, as our rough human means never can effect in this world— . . .[37]

Thomas G. Shearman of New York City, a lawyer and writer of legal textbooks, criticized Rhodes' failure to grasp the relation between economics and politics. Shearman, who had been chief counsel for Henry Ward Beecher in that clergyman's famous trial, also felt that Rhodes had not given "suitable recognition of the great influence which Mr. Beecher had in shaping the course of events before and during the war." [38] Simeon E. Baldwin, Chief Justice of the Supreme Court of Connecticut, wrote that Rhodes had not done Salmon P. Chase full justice for his part in quashing the indictment against Jefferson Davis after the war.[39]

George H. Monroe, of the Boston *Herald*, disagreed with Rhodes' estimate of Stephen A. Douglas as a noble patriot during his last years. Wrote Monroe, "There was as little nobility in him as in any statesman I remember. He seemed to me low in aspiration and vulgar in method." [40] Andrew C. McLaughlin, for all his warm welcome to the first three volumes, thought they also showed serious weaknesses. The author, he wrote, lacked a sense of geography, insight into the temper of the public in the years immediately preceding the war, knowledge of the importance of the West, and thoroughness in exploring the legal problems involved in rebellion.[41]

More trenchant criticisms, came from other and widely different sources: Frederick Jackson Turner, the historian; Paul Leland Haworth, a student of the Reconstruction period; Thomas Wentworth Higginson, the Boston Brahmin who never lost the fervor of his abolitionist convictions; Louis Marshall, the noted constitutional lawyer who was the outstanding leader of the conservative group in the Jewish community; and paradoxically, in view of his warm personal comments to Rhodes, William A. Dunning.

Turner, in a review for the *Atlantic Monthly*, took Rhodes to task for his preoccupation with slavery in the background of the Civil War. The decade, 1850–1860, he pointed out,

> was a decade of American expansion . . . of transformation of the social organism by immigration and industrial change, of the reorganization of sectional relations by railroad building, by the revolution of commercial connections, and by interstate migration. These and similar topics demand as serious study as does the slavery struggle. . . . only the historian who has the insight and the power rightly to analyze and interpret the economic and social evolution of American society in this era will correctly write its history. . . .[42]

As before, Horace Scudder, the editor, had to defend his reviewer against Rhodes' objections:

> It is possible you are right [he wrote] in assuming the overwhelming importance of the abolition of chattel slavery; but is it not part of the historian's business to take account of the less obvious forces which were very present in the actual society of the time? Our social life is pretty complex and a writer may get lost in the complexity, but as an analyst of historic movements I think he must keep his eye on a good many parts of the field beside that where the contest is hottest. . . .[43]

Haworth, writing in 1907, foreshadowed criticisms of Rhodes' interpretation of Reconstruction made by historians of our own day. Praising Rhodes for his work in the sources and for his attempts to be fair, Haworth indicated that

> in his efforts to be impartial and please both sides he sometimes goes so far as to leave out coloring that ought to be put in. This is not the best method for arriving at historical truth, but it goes far toward closing "bloody chasms" and "keeping peace in the now reunited family. . . ." [44]

The volumes on Reconstruction, he continued, were not up to the standard of the earlier volumes; Rhodes was fitted neither by training nor by temperament for dealing with such complicated problems. Rhodes made a basic error in approaching Reconstruction as if it were a peacetime choice of alternatives, when in actuality it was a war policy, designed to safeguard the gains of the war itself. Further, Rhodes ignored the constructive achievements of the Reconstruction governments, particularly the establishment of public school systems for the first time in the South; and he distorted the waste and fraud by omitting the elements of physical rebuilding required after the destruction caused by the war, of social obligations undertaken by the new governments, of the financial burdens imposed by Northern financiers, and of the corruption in the entire nation at that time. Rhodes also neglected to discuss how Reconstruction had enabled the South to make a swift economic recovery after a devastating war.[45]

Higginson, at a meeting of the Massachusetts Historical Society where Rhodes spoke on Reconstruction, attacked Rhodes' view of the process. The historian, he charged, had been neither fair nor exhaustive in his treatment; Rhodes "had drawn his story from Southern papers owned by Southern whites, . . . had not consulted those who fought for the freedom of the slaves." [46]

Marshall raised the issue of anti-Semitic bias in the *History*. Apparently unfamiliar with Rhodes' numerous anti-Jewish references he confined himself to Rhodes' identification of a corrupt Reconstruction governor, F. J. Moses of South Carolina, as a Jew. Asked Marshall:

> Why, pray, was it necessary to refer to one of those thieves as a Jew? If historic verity required reference to his religious faith, why did not your research include . . . the special form of Christianity professed by the other and more experienced thief? [R. K. Scott, who preceded Moses as governor.]

> If you use the word, Jew, in an ethnological sense, would it not have been equally interesting for your readers to learn of the stock whence Scott was derived? Throughout the seven instructive volumes, in which you have laid bare the rascality of a quarter of a century, you did not find it necessary, save in this solitary instance, to indulge in such characterization. What is to be inferred from this extraordinary lapse? I sincerely hope that it is not, that you have been infected with that blind and unreasoning prejudice which has constituted the saddest blot on modern civilization.

Marshall declared that Moses' mother had been a Christian and that he had not been brought up as a Jew: "Why, then, charge the crimes of this degenerate son to the Jewish rather than to the Christian strain of blood that mingled in his veins?" [47]

Dunning, in a lengthy review, lauded Rhodes for writing the kind of history that contributes "most to men's accurate understanding of their kind" but even so Rhodes had fallen far short of writing an adequate history of the period, 1850–1877. To the decade prior to the Civil War Rhodes gave approximately 1350 pages of text; to the four war years, about the same; and to the twelve significant years of Reconstruction, only about 850 pages. In dealing with these years, Rhodes showed a lack of interest, gave "a certain impression of ennui," although Dunning agreed that the volumes on Reconstruction provided "the only comprehensive account yet written." Dunning was also disturbed by Rhodes' ignoring of the elements and significance of Western expansion. Dunning speculated that Rhodes' myopia derived from his migration to New England and his uncritical adoption of the traditional New England view of American history. He wondered whether, if Rhodes had gone to Chicago or St. Louis instead of Boston "the contents of his last volumes would have been any different." [48]

Such criticisms had little influence on a public that came to look upon Rhodes as guide and teacher. The historian's correspondence is interspersed frequently with letters from readers expressing fervent admiration. One such writer expressed gratitude because the *History* helped him "to be a better American." [49] A teacher valued the work so highly that he wanted a portrait of Rhodes to hang in his classroom.[50] An editor in Texas used the *History* to help promote a local road building program.[51] A veteran of the Army of the Cumberland was pleased that Rhodes had rehabilitated the reputation of General George H. Thomas.[52]

Nor was recognition lacking in a more formal sense. In 1898

Rhodes was elected to the highest office within the gift of the professional historian: the presidency of the American Historical Association.[53] Four years later he was elected a fellow of the American Association for the Advancement of Science. Universities continued to shower him with honorary degrees. He received the Doctor of Laws degree from Harvard (1901), Yale (1901), and Wisconsin (1904), and a Doctor of Letters degree from Kenyon College (1903). Such honors were not confined to his own country. Oxford University conferred on him an honorary Doctor of Laws degree in 1909, and the Royal Academy of Science in Berlin awarded him the Loubat Prize—the proceeds of which Rhodes used to purchase a bust of Goethe for his library.[54]

Historical scholars, too, delighted to honor him. Albert Bushnell Hart dedicated a volume to him. Edward Channing candidly based a portion of one of his works on "Mr. Rhodes' excellent work." Frederic L. Paxson, in a popular book on the Civil War, noted that his greatest debt was "to the profound, judicial, and enlightened pages of James Ford Rhodes." Rhodes' erstwhile critic, Woodrow Wilson, now cited the *History* as "Perhaps the finest piece of historical work yet done by an American." [55]

"Jim" Rhodes, the genial iron dealer of Cleveland with a taste for literature, had arrived indeed! He was established, not only as an historian but also as *the* historian for that important period which his work covered. There was criticism of that work, to be sure, but it was minor compared to the acclaim which greeted it among scholars and laymen alike. For many scholars he had written what Charles Eliot Norton called "the permanent history of the time." [56] For many citizens he was the teacher and guide whose *History* was, in the words of Albert Shaw, editor of the *Review of Reviews*, "like finality itself." [57]

NOTES

[1] Harper and Brothers to Rhodes, Nov. 1 and Dec. 31, 1895. Rhodes Papers.

[2] Harper and Brothers to Rhodes, Dec. 31, 1896; Aug. 25, 1897; Dec. 31, 1897; May 27, 1898; June 30, 1898; June 30, 1899. Rhodes Papers.

[3] No complete record of sales for 1901 is available. For other years see Harper and Brothers to Rhodes, Dec. 31, 1899 and Nov. 1, 1900; Macmillan Company to Rhodes, July 31, 1902 and April 30, 1903. Rhodes Papers.

[4] Harper and Brothers to Rhodes, June 20, 1894; May 1, 1895; Nov. 1, 1895; June 30, 1899. Houghton Mifflin Company to Rhodes, Dec. 13,

1899. Walter Hines Page to Rhodes, Feb. 3, 1900. S. S. McClure to Rhodes, Feb. 15, 1900. Rhodes Papers.

[5] Rhodes to Charles Francis Adams, Dec. 9, 1906, in M. A. D. Howe, *Rhodes*, p. 141.

[6] George P. Brett to Rhodes, Aug. 22, 1906. Rhodes Papers.

[7] Macmillan Company to Rhodes, April 30, 1907. Rhodes Papers.

[8] George P. Brett to Rhodes, Aug. 22, 1906. Rhodes Papers.

[9] Theodore Roosevelt to Rhodes, Nov. 29, 1904, in Elting E. Morison (ed.), *The Letters of Theodore Roosevelt* (Cambridge, Mass., 1951–1954), IV, 1049.

[10] *International Socialist Review*, V (1905), 572; VII (1907), 635–636.

[11] Benjamin W. Arnett, secretary, Bishops' Council, African Methodist Episcopal Church, to Rhodes, Nov. 11, 1896. Rhodes Papers.

[12] Dunbar Rowland, director, Department of Archives and History, State of Mississippi, to Rhodes, Nov. 28, 1906. Rhodes Papers.

[13] William E. Dodd to Rhodes, Feb. 22, 1907. Rhodes Papers.

[14] Barrett Wendell to Rhodes, Nov. 18, 1906. Rhodes Papers.

[15] William James to Rhodes, June 5, 1897. Rhodes Papers.

[16] John T. Morse, Jr., to Rhodes, Nov. 18, 1899. Rhodes Papers.

[17] For example, see letters to Rhodes from Senator George F. Hoar, Aug. 21, 1901; Owen Wister, Nov. 19, 1906; Carl Schurz, Aug. 19, 1905; Senator Henry Cabot Lodge, Dec. 20, 1904; President William McKinley, Oct. 24, 1899. Rhodes Papers.

[18] *The Nation*, LXXXIV (1907), 14–15.

[19] *The Outlook*, LXXXVI (1907), 114–115.

[20] *World's Work*, XIII (1906–1907), 8378–8379.

[21] Bernadotte Perrin, "Mr. Rhodes' History of the United States," *Atlantic Monthly*, XCIV (1907), 859–867.

[22] Rhodes to Charles H. Firth, March 1, 1907. Rhodes Papers.

[23] Andrew C. McLaughlin to Rhodes, Sept. 8, 1902. Rhodes Papers. McLaughlin had previously written a highly laudatory review of Rhodes' first three volumes. *American Historical Review*, I (1895), 367.

[24] Edward Channing to Rhodes, Nov. 19, 1904. Rhodes Papers.

[25] Albert B. Hart to Rhodes, Aug. 28, 1895; Oct. 16, 1899. Rhodes Papers.

[26] William A. Dunning to Rhodes, Nov. 19, 1906. On Oct. 19, 1899, he had written that he was "carried way" by Volume IV. Rhodes Papers.

[27] James Schouler to Rhodes, Nov. 28, 1909. Rhodes Papers.

[28] H. Morse Stephens, "Some Living American Historians," *World's Work*, IV (1902), 2321, 2324. For other laudatory reviews see George W. Julian, "The Third Volume of Mr. Rhodes' History of the United States," *The Dial*, XIX (1895), 68–70; Francis W. Shepardson, "The Heart of the Civil War," *ibid.*, XXVII (1899), 312–314; William A. Dunning, *American Historical Review*, V (1899–1900), 371–374; John S. Bassett, *Political Science Quarterly*, XV (1900), 131–134.

[29] *Political Science Quarterly*, XX (1905), 535–539.

[30] *American Historical Review*, XI (1905–1906), 183–184.

[31] *Ibid.*, XII (1906–1907), 681–682.

[32] "A Notable Achievement in Historical Writing," *South Atlantic Quarterly*, VI (1907), 87–91.

[33] W. E. H. Lecky to Rhodes, Nov. 11, 1899. For similar praise of Volume III see Lecky to Rhodes, Aug. 25, 1895. Rhodes Papers.

[34] Charles H. Firth to Rhodes, Jan. 31, 1907. For like comments about

Rhodes' earlier work, see Firth to Rhodes, Jan. 28, 1900, and Dec. 29, 1904. Rhodes Papers.

[35] H. Spencer Walpole in *Edinburgh Review*, CXCIII (1901), 2–3. *English Historical Review*, XI (1896), 604–605; XV (1900), 822–823; XXI (1906), 183–184. Samuel R. Gardiner to Rhodes, Oct. 13, 1895; A. V. Dicey to Rhodes, Jan. 3, Jan. 11, 1907 (one letter with both dates). Rhodes Papers.

[36] Moorfield Storey to Rhodes, Dec. 12, 1906. Rhodes Papers.

[37] Leslie Hopkinson to Rhodes, Jan. 9, Jan. 26, 1907, (one letter with both dates). Rhodes Papers.

[38] Thomas G. Shearman to Rhodes, Jan. 3, 1900; Jan. 11, 1900. In a letter of Jan. 17, 1900, Shearman said that if Rhodes revised his work to discuss Beecher he should not mention Theodore Tilton "as it is undesirable that so evil-smelling a creature should be dignified by mention in your history." Rhodes Papers.

[39] Simeon E. Baldwin to Rhodes, March 13, 1908. Rhodes Papers.

[40] George H. Monroe to Rhodes, July 19, 1895. Rhodes Papers.

[41] *American Historical Review*, I (1895), 369–370.

[42] *Atlantic Monthly*, LXXVI (1896), 841. Turner made similar criticisms in his review of Volume III in *Political Science Quarterly*, II (1896), 167–170.

[43] Horace E. Scudder to Rhodes, May 6, 1896. Rhodes Papers.

[44] *Political Science Quarterly*, XXII (1907), 517.

[45] *Ibid.*, pp. 513–516.

[46] Charles K. Bolton, *Notebook, 1886–1914*, p. 121 (May 11, 1906). Bolton noted that Moorfield Storey spoke in the same vein. See also *Proceedings, Massachusetts Historical Society*, Second series, XX (1906–1907), 256–257.

[47] Louis Marshall to Rhodes, Dec. 10, 1906. Rhodes Papers.

[48] William A. Dunning, "Rhodes' History of the United States," *Education Review*, XXXIV (1907), in his *Truth in History* (New York, 1937), 184–191.

[49] Archibald M. Howe to Rhodes, Nov. 22, 1904. Rhodes Papers.

[50] Lewis R. Harley, Central High School, Philadelphia, Pa., to Rhodes, Oct. 7, 1899. Rhodes Papers.

[51] Thomas J. Middleton, editor, *Ellis County Mirror*, Waxahachie, Texas, to Rhodes, Aug. 16, 1907. Rhodes Papers.

[52] E. A. Otis to Rhodes, Jan. 31, 1900. Rhodes Papers.

[53] *American Historical Review*, IV (1898–1899), 421.

[54] Letters to Rhodes from Charles W. Eliot, May 25, 1901; Frederick Jackson Turner, Jan. 28, 1904; Königliche Akademie der Wissenschaften, Berlin, July 4, 1901. Certificate of election, American Association for the Advancement of Science, Dec. 31, 1903. Rhodes Papers. "James Ford Rhodes," *Who's Who in America, 1912–1913*, p. 1745.

[55] Albert Bushnell Hart, *Slavery and Abolition, 1831–1841* (New York, 1906); Edward Channing, *The United States of America, 1765–1865* (New York, 1896), pp. vii–viii; Frederic L. Paxson, *The Civil War* (New York, 1911), p. x; Woodrow Wilson, *Division and Reunion, 1829–1909* (New York, 1909), p. xi.

[56] Rhodes Papers, XI, oN (Dec. 13, 1904).

[57] Albert Shaw to Rhodes, Feb. 14, 1907. Rhodes Papers.

Chapter 9

TRAVEL AND POLITICS

WITH the passing of the years, the success of the *History*, and freedom from the demands of scholarship, Rhodes emerged increasingly from that seclusion to which he had committed himself. He kept his mornings sacred to his writing, of course, and he dedicated his afternoons and evenings to study and companionship, but he made time for other interests.

For a friend, Charles Dudley Warner, editor of a popular book series, *The Library of the World's Best Literature*, he wrote an essay on another friend, Carl Schurz, in which he extolled that immigrant for impressing upon laboring men "the elementary truths of sound finance" and defended the right of Americans, even foreign-born Americans, to be "cosmopolitan." [1] August Lowell finally prevailed upon him to deliver the Lowell Institute Lectures in 1902–1903, on a subject closely related to the *History:* "Commercial Intercourse Between the North and South during the Civil War." While his audiences were small (Rhodes was not a good lecturer. As he himself explained, "I read with neither expression nor effect,") what he had to say was considered of sufficient importance to warrant renewed appearances. It is symptomatic of the state of opinion in New England in the early years of this century that in these lectures he inveighed against Radical Reconstruction and Negro suffrage.[2]

Rhodes also played an active part in the Massachusetts Historical Society, contributed to leading magazines, lectured to students at Harvard, Yale and Western Reserve Universities, and played host to distinguished foreign visitors, including John Morley, James Bryce and Mrs. John R. Green, widow of the noted English historian.[3]

Also indicative of Rhodes' easing of the schedule to which he had set himself were his frequent trips abroad. These were forced on him, in part, by failing health; after 1894 rarely free from chronic ailments, he found some relief in the "moist climate of Europe." [4] Besides, he had a restless streak in his temperament, particularly when work was finished: he felt a real need to move physically away from Boston or Seal Harbor.[5] He also wanted to talk personally to leading historians, especially Samuel R. Gardiner, W. E. H. Lecky and James Bryce.[6] In 1902 there was a family reason for going to England: his son, Daniel, married in London Miss Bertha Johnson, a young Englishwoman whom he had met in Switzerland.[7] In 1906 he had yet other grounds for going abroad. As he explained to Theodore Roosevelt, the writing of American history beyond 1877 required knowledge of social problems and he hoped to acquire some understanding of them by study in Europe. Such study would be:

> a fitting preparation for the continuation at some future day of the history of the United States from 1877 on.
>
> My study during the next three years will comprise those social questions [which concerned Theodore Roosevelt]. I have little doubt that I shall arrive at your conclusions but I am going to attack the questions with an effacement, so far as possible, of any preconceived notion.[8]

Certainly, for a historian seeking insight into the experiences of highly industrialized states for such clues as they might afford for understanding an industrialized America, these were stirring years to be abroad. Rival empires clashed in Morocco, China, Bosnia-Herzegovina, and the Dardanelles. While Germany planned a railroad to link Berlin with the oil fields of the Middle East and a navy strong enough to challenge that of Britain, Britain itself was undergoing a transformation. With the passing of Victoria classical Liberalism gave way to the Radical Liberalism of a Lloyd George, Fabian socialism made converts among intellectuals and a new Labor Party gave voice to workingmen in the halls of Parliament.

In Germany, too, despite its elaborate system of social insurance, the urban masses were on the move; by 1903 the Social Democrats occupied 81 seats in the Reichstag, and Eduard Bernstein was showing how Marxism could be adapted to the uses of a parliamentary system. France experienced the deep cleavages involved in the Dreyfus affair; the clash between church and state which culminated in the Law of Separation of 1905; the class struggles which produced a million socialist votes by 1906. Italy, although lagging in industrialization, presented the familiar problem of progress and poverty; the typical responses—a trade union movement and a socialist party—and a unique response too: the promulgation by Pope Leo XIII of social doctrines designed to alleviate the lot of the masses while saving them from the sins of socialism.

Little of this ferment reaches us through Rhodes, either in his correspondence or in his published work. His interests were those of the cultivated tourist rather than those of the student. He and Mrs. Rhodes visited Egypt, Athens, Florence, Rome, London, Oxford, Stratford-on-Avon.[9] Egypt he found less interesting than the European cities but enjoyable in contemplation of its past with the aid of Herodotus, "one of the historians we all take our hats off to in that he was sincere, honest and readable." [10]

A visit to Stratford-on-Avon prompted him to repeat a favorite observation that Shakespeare and Homer were the world's greatest historians.[11] Oxford, he thought, was incomparable: "Nowhere else do I enjoy myself so well and from no other place do I carry away such enjoyable memories." [12] Indeed, he humorously suggested to Charles Harding Firth that America might well profit from an exchange: "you might trade us Oxford and its architecture for a few of our Steel Works. We would work up the tradition if we could get the buildings." [13] He met the three men whom he most desired to see—Gardiner, Lecky and Bryce—and in addition he made acquaintance with the historians, A. V. Dicey, Sir Spencer Walpole, Charles Harding Firth, C. W. C. Oman and Sir George Otto Trevelyan.[14] He also met Frederic Harrison, the literary critic and social reformer, and Henry James.

Of such men, Rhodes' comments were few and generally couched in generalities: Spencer Walpole, for example, was described simply as a "delightful gentleman." [15] Years later, Rhodes recalled that Henry James

> was more egotistical in his writing than in his conversation. I did not meet him personally until late in his life and I have no hesitation in pronouncing him a good fellow. He was however a terrible Anglomaniac and it was better to keep off the subject of the relative merits of England and America. But in ability he was, . . . , no comparison to William James, who was a towering genius; . . .[16]

He also remembered

> the rather doleful confidence Mr. Lecky indulged in to me at the time of the South African war. As a member of the House [of Commons] he said I feel obliged to vote all of Lord Salisbury's measures, the intent of which is to carry on the war but at home my wife who sympathizes with the Boers criticizes my action.[17]

Rhodes' avoidance of the centers of political and social tension is even more marked in his trip of 1906–1907, when he was presumably seeking some enlightenment on that very tension. Rather, his itinerary took him to the resorts of the wealthy and the haunts of the medievalist: Chartres, Blois, Amiens, Tours, Vichy, Geneva, the Black Forest, Baden-Baden, Interlaken. When he did find himself in cities where contemporary history was being made —Rome, Paris, Lyons, Florence, Coblentz—he was interested only in their past. As he wrote from Rome, he was content to read and see the sights.[18] His correspondence during the trip dealt largely with scenery, castles, and cathedrals; the quality of board and lodging (the inns of Southern France he found "dirty, filthy and vile") and appraisal of wines (Moselle wines "seemed to have a gently stimulating quality, grateful to gods and men.").[19]

Rhodes himself felt a little apologetic about his preoccupation with personal tastes. "You may think," he wrote to Barrett Wendell, "we only go around to resorts where the hotels are excellent and the 'vintages' good," and to another friend he wrote from Rome, "I am supposing myself getting light on American history by reading furiously Roman." [20]

But for all his realization that he was not learning much about the social problems that vexed Europe he insulated himself still further from contact with the workaday European. Instead of using public transportation, in which one can hardly fail to pick up something about the lives and problems of a people, he resorted to the private automobile.[21] In pre-war Europe he could hardly have found a better way to isolate himself from the common run of humanity.

Even his reading in Europe was such as to shed little light on the continent's contemporary troubles. Voltaire, Tacitus, Cicero, Goethe, Lord Acton, Leslie Stephen, Ferrero and Boisseau, provocative and significant though they might be, were hardly the sources to provide a 20th century American with insight into 20th century Europe.[22] Apart from Jean Jaurès' *Histoire Socialiste de la Révolution Française* he read little of relevance to the problems he was supposedly exploring.[23] A perceptive man, he might have found value in a study of the work of Balzac which he undertook on the basis of Brunetière's observation that the novelist presented, in Rhodes' paraphrase, "a perfect historical picture of French moeurs and otherwise of great historical value from 1815 to 1850." [24] But Rhodes, no longer the daring translator of *The Abbess of Jouarre*, was offended by the "lubricity" of *La Cousine*

Bette and concluded that "tested by any true historic judgment, Brunetière and Henry James have said a lot of nonsense about Balzac." [25] The book, he wrote, reminded him of "Carlyle's unjust but expressive remark that French literature was given over to Phallus-worship." [26]

Incidentally, Balzac was not the only French author to incur his displeasure. He sent Barrett Wendell, a sympathetic student of French culture, a copy of a work by Henri Lavedan, a French Academician who had made a reputation with amusing and often risqué plays and novelettes, together with a note:

> I believe in your conclusions about French society but such a book as this, written by a member of the French Academy and going through twenty-two editions is hard to reconcile with them. Whether you read the book or not do what you will with it. It ought to go on to your library fire in the end. Had I not thought you might want to look into it I should have thrown it into the sea . . . as I threw Jude the Obscure into the sea at Seal Harbor . . .[27]

In the few observations he did make about contemporary Europe he expressed admiration for the cultural interests of French small towns, confidence in the Third Republic, doubt about a war between England and Germany, and fear of English decline. Writing from France he was

> much interested . . . in seeing the theatres and reading the programs of theatrical and operatic attractions [in small towns in France] . . . I like to think of the high class of operatic and theatrical entertainment offered to the dwellers of these provincial cities, . . .[28]

The Third Republic, he believed, was

> the best government France has ever had since Louis XVI. It has endured thirty-five years and not had a war of any account —two important facts. . . . There is a good deal of corruption . . . but I doubt if the percentage of stealing is greater than it was under Napoleon III or Louis Philippe; and as between now and the Ancien Régime, the commonalty gets a chance at the pickings and the princes and nobles do not. . . .[29]

Rhodes was not impressed with the talk of inevitable war between Germany and England, nor with English talk about the virtues of preventive war against Germany. "I shall not believe in this much predicted war until it comes," he wrote.[30] Those who strove against war of any kind had his warm support:

> The more I study war the more I detest it [he wrote to Frederic Harrison] and I think that most wars nowadays might be avoided; however, as human nature is what it is, it seems to me that the cause of peace will advance slowly. All honor, however, to gentlemen like yourselves who advocate peace without ceasing.[31]

He was disturbed, however, by evidences of the decline of England as an economic power:

> In the race of material development among nations no nation can afford to go back. Progress therein is the law of life. A government and an administration carried on by men of the best intellectual training will avail little unless the people governed are kept at work and are well fed. . . .[32]

Part of the English problem, he thought, was that "labor had England by the throat," and discouraged individual initiative. He conceded that in political and social morality England might be ahead of the United States, but held the reverse was true as to commercial morality. He was also struck painfully by the obsequiousness of English tradesmen and storekeepers.[33]

On the other hand, he thought England a more conscientious guardian of civil liberties in times of stress than was the United States:

> I do not believe that in England [during the Boer War] the suggestion was seriously made to bring any direct power of the government towards any interference . . . with free speaking or free writing. But the indirect influences were enormous. . . . trade, society, political and church preferment were all brought to bear on the side of the government, . . . In my opinion the indirect method . . . is better than to do it by arbitrary acts of the government, or by stringent laws effectually enforced against sedition; . . .[34]

Two conclusions Rhodes did draw from his visits to Europe. First, that if he were an Englishman he would probably be a good Tory.[35] Second, that the United States, in all things that really mattered, was superior to Europe.

His old friend, Mrs. C. H. Toy, wrote expressing some doubt as to the future of the United States, to which Rhodes replied:

> Your pessimistic mood is not unnatural. The pessimists in the United States are people of large intelligence and high ideals and they are pessimistic because the country falls short of their aspirations for it. For a cure of it, I know nothing better than to spend

twelve months in Europe; and if one be generally pessimistic regarding the nineteenth and twentieth centuries, let him study the history of the past, I care not what past, and he will have cause to rejoice that his lot is cast in the present.[36]

To Theodore Roosevelt he wrote:

> During my stay abroad I have come to have a higher opinion of our rich men. . . . I am quite willing to agree . . . that few large fortunes are made honestly. But that will apply to Europe and to ancient Rome as well as to our own country, and comes from a defect in human nature and not from an American failing. But where in my judgment our rich men are the best rich men who have ever lived is that when they get this immense amount of money they do not give themselves up to a life of calculated luxury and unbridled sensuality.

Wealthy Americans, he believed, were "superior" men

> who give their surplus to universities, to education and to libraries and to the relief of the sick and unfortunate, and who lead simple lives.
>
> It is a pretty good country, I think, where popular sentiment exacts such results.[37]

Even in the matter of weather, America was preferable. Rome, he wrote, was a most satisfactory place to spend the winter—"next to Boston." [38]

Rhodes himself needed no trip to Europe to sharpen his appreciation of his native land; indeed, as a close friend of that prince of President-makers, Mark Hanna, he was privy to many of the political secrets of the day and in a position to exchange views with Presidents and Senators. As early as 1888, apparently, he was aware of Hanna's plans for McKinley and cherished an ambition to be rewarded with a diplomatic post should the latter become President. After the election of 1896 Frederic Bancroft urged him to press for redemption of what Bancroft regarded as a promise by McKinley to appoint Rhodes:

> Now is your time to put in your claim for a foreign mission, which McKinley promised you at the Arlington [Hotel] on or about Dec. 29, 1888. . . .
>
> P. S. It occurred to me that it might be interesting to know what McKinley did say. Here is a copy of what I wrote in my note-book within a day or two of the time it occurred. "R. now and then said: 'When you become our next President,' etc., etc. Each time McKinley turned the remark into a laugh by some

bright non-committal . . . reply. R. several times showed that he really believed that McKinley would be in the White House in four years, . . . The 'Major' would be an ideal president; he would be progressive and have ideas of his own; he would send men of ability abroad.—'Certainly, certainly, my dear fellow, where would you like to go?' interjected McKinley with a flash of wit."[39]

By 1897 Rhodes was tasting literary glory, and it may be that he had lost some of his enthusiasm about the lawyer from Canton, for there is no indication that he sounded out McKinley on any governmental post. In 1904, however, he wrote to Theodore Roosevelt with a coyness which suggests that he was "available." He had no intention of leaving his work on the *History*, he said, "unless I could be of some service to you which of course is unthinkable."[40] One may well speculate on what might have happened to the volumes on Reconstruction had the President decided that it was not "unthinkable" that Rhodes could be of service.

Personal participation in governmental service was denied him, but he played a significant role in the politics that centered on Mark Hanna. In December, 1896, for instance, Rhodes discussed with Hanna the appointment as secretary of state of John Sherman, whom McKinley was loath to appoint lest he dominate the administration. "I said [noted Rhodes] no man in the country was so well fitted for the position as he."[41] Hanna also asked Rhodes "who was the best man for ambassador to England. I said at once, John Hay."[42] The fact that both men were appointed need not argue the decisive influence of Rhodes, but Hanna's discussion of such matters with his brother-in-law is some indication of the politician's regard for the opinions of the historian.

Hanna also confided to Rhodes the plan of the new administration to rescind an order of Grover Cleveland expanding the civil service just before he left the White House. "He [Hanna] thought it was unfair in Cleveland just as he was going out to tie up the offices thus," noted Rhodes.[43] McKinley himself talked over with the historian such matters as the resignation of John Sherman; the gold standard; civil service; and the ambassadorial reports of John Hay—which had a great deal to say about the evils of bimetallism and little about the diplomatic issues at stake between the United States and Great Britain.[44] McKinley also discussed with Rhodes his problem in finding a capable man to send as ambassador to Spain just prior to the Spanish-American War.[45]

Perhaps because he was so close to the machinery of politics,

Rhodes, despite his Republican faith, was far from being a zealot. During the bitter election of 1896 his moderation vexed some of his friends. Barrett Wendell wrote to him that since McKinley stood for financial stability, his election was "the most desirable political result which has been possible in my voting life . . . public interest demands the judicious use of every known engine of electioneering." [46] Edward L. Pierce, the scholarly biographer of Sumner, believed the election to be "a great struggle for civilization. . . . The election has passed the domain of ordinary politics and has become a contest between social forces. If . . . Bryan and his gang win, it would be the saddest day this country has ever had." [47] Rhodes' own son, Daniel, found his father's position exasperating. Daniel, in a letter to his mother, wrote:

> I have read Father's letter . . . on the subject of the election . . . Regarding Father's ideas . . . , I wish you would say to Father that his judicial method of viewing historical questions has led him to a point where he stands in terror of entertaining an extensive opinion on any topic. When he feels an opinion growing within him . . . , he must forthwith spend all his energies in the effort to controvert it or, at least, to reduce it to harmless proportions. What he says about the election is very true: what I object to is his improper consideration of the facts . . . , also his comparison between this campaign and previous campaigns. I do not see . . . any reason for such comparison nor for the consolation which Father draws out of them.[48]

Moderate in campaign spirit though he might be, Rhodes was a warm partisan of the McKinley administration. Before the outbreak of the Spanish-American War he praised the administration in unusually enthusiastic terms:

> the President is doing admirably. I know of no country in the world that has as good a lot of men at the head of it as we have now in our national government. . . . of the sincerity, honesty, and integrity of the President and his cabinet I have absolutely no question. . . .[49]

Opposed to the war and to annexation of the Philippines, he was nevertheless in favor of McKinley in the election of 1900. Bryan, he felt, lacked the ability and judgment required of a president.[50] As if to underline the fact that his own anti-imperialism did not alienate him from the administration he deplored Carl Schurz's support of Bryan on that issue. "What twists do get into the brains of good people," he observed.[51] John Hay, then secretary of state, was grateful for Rhodes' support during the campaign, for, as he expressed it:

> It is a great deliverance. For the first time in our history a candidate for the presidency has made his canvass exclusively on an appeal to the sentiments of hatred and envy among the less fortunate classes.[52]

Rhodes' feelings on imperialism, however, were far from superficial. The only discoverable occasion on which he made a donation to a "cause" was twenty-five dollars to the Anti-Imperialist League.[53] His utterances were such as to persuade a sympathetic clergyman that they were in agreement "in condemning the imperialist craze." [54] Later, Rhodes wrote that McKinley was forced into the war by Congress and "I suppose Congress was backed by popular sentiment; . . . We have had our war and I hope we shall never have another." [55]

Certainly, Rhodes must have had some doubts as to how deep the war sentiment went. In April, 1898, before war was declared, he had queried a friend in Cleveland about war sentiment in Ohio and received this reply:

> the great mass of the conservative thinking people are with McKinley in his efforts to bring about a reasonable adjustment of differences without going to war. There are of course yellow journals and hot heads who make a great deal of war talk, but the businessmen are universally peace men if peace can be had on any fair and honorable basis. Of course everybody believes that Spain is responsible for the . . . Maine though probably indirectly. . . . if they [Spain] would pay reasonable indemnity it would seem better than to sacrifice thousands of lives more and untold millions for war for simple revenge . . . men of good judgment feel that Congress is making a great mistake in not standing by the President whose plan was evidently to force Spain to give Cuba a government similar to that of Canada and on the other hand [to force] the Cubans to accept such a government. . . .[56]

As time passed Rhodes felt less charitable in appraising McKinley's role in the war. In his notebooks he compared the President's course with those of Lords Aberdeen and Salisbury who let Great Britain stumble into the Crimean and South African wars respectively.[57] In a letter to George Myers he confirmed

> the impression I have long had that if Mr. Hanna had been President, the Spanish-American war wd (sic) not have occurred.

> The Spaniards wd (sic) have been negotiated out of Cuba and we should not now have the "gold brick," the Philippines.[58]

If McKinley proved a disappointment, Theodore Roosevelt was all that Rhodes could desire in a President. Roosevelt, in turn, thought highly of the *History*, visited the author in Boston and was happy to have him at the White House.[59] After one such visit with the President the historian wrote to him with all the fervor of an adolescent addressing his first love:

> I returned to my desk yesterday with renewed zest . . . arising in this case I am sure from contact with a vigorous personality, who is rendering a great service in the cause of political righteousness.
>
> I hardly expected to see in my own day a President who would so thoroughly carry out the ideas that I have embraced from my life of affairs and study. . . . To evolve these ideas from solitary thought in a library is not difficult. To carry them out as you are doing with physical and moral courage and with persistence requires rare qualities of the highest order. . . .
>
> This tremendous energy, this power of doing things falls so often to men of low political ideals that it is a constant cause for rejoicing that one of our own kind possesses it, who is in a position to give it free exercise.[60]

Rhodes' admiration extended to some members of the cabinet. "No country in Europe has three such able men at the head of affairs as are the President, and Secretaries Root and Taft," he wrote.[61]

Of Roosevelt's policies, three in particular earned Rhodes' outspoken approval. The war on the trusts frustrated the socialists and would show eventually, he believed, that Roosevelt was "the best of friends to honest wealth." [62] Rhodes defended the President's course in Panama so stoutly that John Hay thanked him "for breaking an occasional lance for us in the headquarters of Mugwumpery [Boston]." [63] The historian also endorsed Roosevelt's encouragement of "the Booker Washington kind of negroes," while leaving the white South free to handle the race problem in its own way.[64] In this way, Roosevelt's influence was exerted "to draw the South and the North nearer together." [65]

In private conversations Rhodes urged the President to continue this policy. The level of some of these discussions may be gauged from Rhodes' report of Roosevelt's comments after the President had returned from a visit to the South:

> The negroes change about their wives. Real animal jealousy when with a new woman. The negroes have little respect for property, about on a level with brutes. The negroes, the President said, are 200,000 years behind (I suggested a million, an amendment which he accepted). . . .[66]

In view of their utter agreement on such matters it is little wonder that Rhodes held that "no President since Lincoln has, on the whole, been so great a benefactor to the country."[67]

Rhodes' prejudices were not confined to Negroes, however. He also entertained low opinions of certain white peoples, largely because he deemed them willing to intermarry with Negroes. To an old friend who had assisted some Italians to come to the United States he wrote:

> It would have been a good idea if you had sent the Italians you brought over to the cotton and rice fields of the South, where . . . they are suited to the climate and the kind of work. Booker Washington and men of his kind are the only ones who can save the negro from being forced to the wall in competition with the whites. The remedy of [miscegenation, suggested by H. G. Wells and John Graham Brooks] . . . would be too horrible to think of if it were not ridiculous and showed an entire lack of knowledge of the problem and the antagonism of race between the Anglo-Saxon and the negro.
>
> It just occurs to me that as the French, Spanish and Portuguese mix with the negro, did these political philosophers mean that the Italians who are now emigrating to the South might do likewise? There may be something in that but the Anglo-Saxon never.[68]

That there were mulattoes in the South could not be denied, of course, but Rhodes comforted himself with the anti-Semitic observation that their number had declined since the Civil War and that in his day only Jews were guilty of intercourse with Negro women.[69]

Biased though he may have been in such matters—and it must be remembered that such scarcely-credible opinions were widely shared—Rhodes was by no means the reactionary that espousal of such views would classify him today. Nowhere is this more apparent than in his defense of academic freedom. The occasion for this was an attempt by clergymen and some members of the Board of Overseers of Harvard College to remove George Santayana, assistant professor of philosophy, for the materialist beliefs expressed in his recently published work, *The Life of Reason.*

Rhodes was in Europe when the controversy broke out, but he made his opinions known to Mrs. C. H. Toy, who in turn was a friend of President Charles W. Eliot. Wrote Rhodes:

> the professors of a university should have absolute freedom of speech, and no book should affect a man's standing or promotion, provided his views are expressed with decorum; . . . Of course I know little about philosophy but I supposed that, for two or three centuries at least, philosophers had been doubting the existence of a personal God. If that is Mr. Santayana's whole offense, it does not seem to me a grave one, and if the book is, as Dr. James says, the most notable book published since Emerson, Mr. Santayana not only deserves promotion but the highest honors of the university. I cannot believe he will be asked to resign. . . .

Rhodes' belief proved correct: Santayana was not dismissed, but neither was he given an expected promotion.[70]

Devoted as he was to the *History*, and engrossed in politics as he might be, Rhodes never lost sight of his business interests: an iron concern in Sharpsville, Pa.; street railways in Cleveland; real estate in what is now Lakewood and Rocky River, Ohio.[71] Over the years he liquidated these interests, seeking advice for new fields of investment from such friends as Henry Lee Higginson, the investment banker. Higginson recommended to him a favorite source of much Brahmin wealth, the Calumet copper mine at Calumet, Michigan. Shares in that enterprise, said Higginson, were

> cheaper at $1000 than anything else within my knowledge. Since Dec. 1869 the Calumet mine has been paying dividends, and it has never owed any money. It has always had the best machinery, explored its territory far, far ahead, and has now acquired a lot of very valuable new territory . . . All these new and old things have been paid for out of earnings, and one hundred million dollars have been paid in dividends,—the only capital ever paid in being six hundred thousand dollars. I have never known so satisfactory and comfortable an investment as that mine, . . .[72]

Whether Rhodes participated in that bonanza is not known from the available records. At any rate, whatever the sources of his income, he lived well the part of the gentleman of culture, playing the gracious host to the famous of both his own and foreign lands, traveling the fashionable orbit of Beacon Street, Seal Harbor and Europe. As he sat on the porch of Ravenscleft, with Mrs. Rhodes by his side, watching the moon shimmer on the Atlantic, he could well reflect on how far he had come since that distant day in 1888 when he had embarked on the writing of the *History*.

Then unknown, now famous on two continents; then a man who had never finished college, now the holder of a host of honorary degrees; then the Western "good fellow," now the Proper Bostonian; then a citizen who shrank from politics, now the confidant of Presidents. And, as he himself thought, life had yielded something finer than riches, fame and influence:

> When [I consider] . . . the acquaintances I have made, the friends I have gained by my History, . . . my book has a large amount to its credit. Had I continued in business, I should have been rich by this time and I should be roaming around Europe in a fast automobile, restless, living high, drinking '89 champagne, while now I am leading the simple life and having a delightful time, . . .[73]

NOTES

[1] "Carl Schurz, 1829– ," in Charles Dudley Warner (ed.), *Library of the World's Best Literature* (New York, 1902), XXIII, 12976–12977. Schurz was delighted that Rhodes had been chosen to write the introductory essay to selections of his work. "I may congratulate myself upon the good fortune which put the introductory notice into hands so competent and so friendly," he wrote to Rhodes, June 18, 1897. Rhodes Papers.

[2] M. A. D. Howe, *Rhodes*, pp. 220–221.

[3] Charles W. Eliot to Rhodes, Nov. 16, 1904; James F. Bryce to Rhodes, Sept. 27, 1901, Sept. 16, 1904; Rhodes to Charles H. Firth, Jan. 15, 1905, photostat fragment. Rhodes Papers. Text of the lecture delivered to the students, "The Profession of Historian," may be found in *Historical Essays*, pp. 49–79.

[4] Rhodes to Charles H. Firth, Jan. 15, 1905, photostat fragment. Letters to Rhodes from H. E. von Holst, June 13, 1894; Albert B. Hart, July 11, 1894; Jan. 26, 1900; J. D. Cox, July 17, 1895; Mrs. Mark Hanna, n.d. Rhodes Papers.

[5] Mrs. Bertha H. Rhodes, interview.

[6] Rhodes to Frederic Bancroft [1895], in M. A. D. Howe, *Rhodes*, p. 91.

[7] Mrs. Bertha H. Rhodes, interview.

[8] Rhodes to Theodore Roosevelt, May 8, 1906. Rhodes Papers.

[9] Rhodes to Mrs. C. H. Toy, Sept. 3 [?], photostat fragment, Rhodes Papers.

[10] Rhodes to Frederic Bancroft, Dec. 31, 1894, in M. A. D. Howe, *Rhodes*, p. 88; Edward G. Bourne to Rhodes, Jan. 13, 1895. Rhodes Papers.

[11] Rhodes to Frederic Bancroft, Sept. 18, 1894, in M. A. D. Howe, *Rhodes*, p. 87.

[12] Rhodes to Charles H. Firth, April 30, 1906. Rhodes Papers.

[13] Rhodes to Charles H. Firth, June 28, 1904. Rhodes Papers.

[14] Rhodes to Frederic Bancroft, in M. A. D. Howe, *Rhodes*, p. 91. Rhodes to Barrett Wendell, May 7, 1907; letters to Rhodes from Mrs. John R. Green, Aug. 13, 1900; C. W. C. Oman, May 25, 1900; W. T. Ashley, Oct. 20, 1894; Charles H. Firth, April 11, 1900. Rhodes Papers.

[15] Rhodes to Barrett Wendell, May 7, 1907. Rhodes Papers.

[16] Rhodes to William R. Thayer, Sept. 3, 1920. Rhodes Papers.

[17] Rhodes to Sir George Otto Trevelyan, July 16, 1920. Rhodes Papers.

[18] Rhodes to Barrett Wendell, Jan. 25, 1907. Rhodes Papers.

[19] Rhodes to Barrett Wendell, June 9, 1906; Aug. 22, 1906; Oct. 5, 1906; April 7, 1907. Rhodes Papers.

[20] Rhodes to Barrett Wendell, Nov. 4, 1906; to Mrs. C. H. Toy, Jan. 10, 1907, photostat fragment. Rhodes Papers.

[21] Rhodes to Charles Francis Adams, Aug. 11, 1906, photostat fragment. Rhodes Papers.

[22] *Ibid.;* also Rhodes to Charles Francis Adams, Dec. 9, 1906; to Mrs. C. H. Toy, May 13, 1907, in M. A. D. Howe, *Rhodes*, pp. 142, 156–158. Rhodes wrote to Barrett Wendell, Jan. 25, 1907, that Ferrero's work on the Roman Empire was "superficial, . . . conceited and partial." Rhodes Papers.

[23] Rhodes to Barrett Wendell, April 7, 1907. Rhodes Papers.

[24] Rhodes to Charles Francis Adams, Aug. 11, 1906, photostat fragment. Rhodes Papers.

[25] Rhodes to Mrs. C. H. Toy, Aug. 7, 1906, in M. A. D. Howe, *Rhodes*, pp. 133–134.

[26] Rhodes to Barrett Wendell, Aug. 6, 1906. Rhodes Papers.

[27] Rhodes to Barrett Wendell, Nov. 4, 1906. Rhodes Papers. The title of the book is not mentioned in the correspondence.

[28] Rhodes to Barrett Wendell, Nov. 4, 1906. Rhodes Papers.

[29] Rhodes to Barrett Wendell, Sept. 1, 1906. Rhodes Papers.

[30] Rhodes to Mrs. C. H. Toy, May 13, 1907, in M. A. D. Howe, *Rhodes*, p. 158.

[31] Rhodes to Frederic Harrison, May 8, 1901, in M. A. D. Howe, *Rhodes*, p. 109.

[32] "Some Recent Impressions of England," *Proceedings, Massachusetts Historical Society*, Second Series, XIV (1900–1901), 316.

[33] *Ibid.*, pp. 305, 306, 316, 317.

[34] *Ibid.*, pp. 311–312.

[35] Rhodes to Mrs. C. H. Toy, May 13, 1907, in M. A. D. Howe, *Rhodes*, p. 156.

[36] *Ibid.*, p. 157.

[37] Rhodes to Theodore Roosevelt, March 16, 1907, in M. A. D. Howe, *Rhodes*, pp. 147–148.

[38] Rhodes to Frederick Shattuck, M.D., Jan. 18, 1907. Rhodes Papers.

[39] Frederic Bancroft to Rhodes, Nov. 9, 1896. Rhodes Papers.

[40] Rhodes to Theodore Roosevelt, Nov. 15, 1904. Rhodes Papers.

[41] Rhodes Papers, XI, Ha. Rhodes noted: "This was written down May 31, 1908."

[42] *Ibid.*, p. aH. This, too, was noted May 31, 1908.

[43] *Ibid.*, p. eH. This, too, was noted May 31, 1908.

[44] *Ibid.*, pp. aH, eH. These were noted May 31, 1908.

[45] *Ibid.*, p. Sa.

[46] Barrett Wendell to Rhodes, July 30, 1896. Rhodes Papers.

[47] Edward L. Pierce to Rhodes, Aug. 4, 1896. Rhodes Papers.

[48] Daniel P. Rhodes to Mrs. James Ford Rhodes, Nov. 11, 1896. Rhodes Papers.

[49] James Ford Rhodes to Frederic Bancroft, Jan. 10, 1898, in M. A. D. Howe, *Rhodes*, p. 94.

[50] Rhodes to Frederic Bancroft, Oct. 10, 1900, in M. A. D. Howe, *Rhodes*, p. 108.

[51] *Ibid.*

[52] John Hay to Rhodes, Nov. 9, 1900. Rhodes Papers.

[53] Rhodes to Edward Atkinson, Dec. 4, 1898. Atkinson Papers, Houghton Library, Harvard University.

[54] Rev. Hale Harrison, St. John's Church, Ellicott City, Md., to Rhodes, Nov. 1, 1899, Rhodes Papers.

[55] Rhodes to Frederic Bancroft, May 18, 1901, in M. A. D. Howe, *Rhodes*, p. 109.

[56] H. R. Newcomb, secretary-treasurer, The Savings and Trust Company, Cleveland, Ohio, to Rhodes, April 14, 1898. Rhodes Papers.

[57] Rhodes Papers, XI, Sa.

[58] Rhodes to George A. Myers, Aug. 26, 1916, in John A. Garraty (ed.), "Correspondence," *Ohio Historical Quarterly*, LXIV (1955), 158.

[59] Rhodes was a guest at the White House in 1902, 1904, 1905 and 1908. Roosevelt was Rhodes' guest in Boston in 1910 and 1911. Rhodes Papers, XII, inside front cover.

[60] Rhodes to Theodore Roosevelt, Nov. 19, 1905, in M. A. D. Howe, *Rhodes*, pp. 117–118.

[61] *Ibid.*

[62] Rhodes to Mrs. C. H. Toy, Aug. 27, 1906, in M. A. D. Howe, *Rhodes*, pp. 135–136.

[63] John Hay to Rhodes, Dec. 8, 1903, in William R. Thayer, *The Life and Letters of John Hay* (Boston, 1915), II, 325.

[64] Rhodes Papers, XII, unlettered page.

[65] Rhodes to Theodore Roosevelt, Feb. 17, 1905. Rhodes Papers.

[66] The conversation took place at a dinner at the White House, Nov. 16, 1905. Topics covered a wide range of both domestic and foreign affairs, with Roosevelt doing most of the talking. Rhodes Papers, XII, unlettered page towards end of volume. A partial text of Rhodes' report, omitting the section cited here, may be found in M. A. D. Howe, *Rhodes*, pp. 119–124.

[67] Rhodes to Mrs. C. H. Toy, Aug. 27, 1906, in M. A. D. Howe, *Rhodes*, pp. 135–136.

[68] Rhodes to Mrs. C. H. Toy, May 6, 1906, photostat fragment. Rhodes Papers.

[69] Rhodes to Mrs. C. H. Toy, May 13 [1906?], photostat fragment. Rhodes Papers.

[70] Rhodes to Mrs. C. H. Toy, Aug. 27, 1906, in M. A. D. Howe, *Rhodes*, pp. 134–135. Mrs. Toy to Rhodes, Oct. 20, 1906. Rhodes Papers.

[71] Simon Perkins to Rhodes, Feb. 15, 1894; Dec. 6, 1906; Mark Hanna to Rhodes, Feb. 12, 1899; April 29, 1899; H. R. Newcomb to Rhodes, April 14, 1898; June 5, 1906; June 14, 1906. Rhodes Papers.

[72] Henry Lee Higginson to Rhodes, Dec. 27, 1906. Rhodes Papers.

[73] Rhodes to Charles Francis Adams, Dec. 9, 1906, in M. A. D. Howe, *Rhodes*, p. 141.

Chapter 10

RHODES AND HIS AMERICA, 1907–1914

RHODES returned from Europe in 1907, glad to be back to "the Tavern Club and all the other good things of Boston." [1] So tired was he of travel that he thought of the future strictly in terms of Beacon Street: "I want to spend the rest of my life reading and writing, going to Boston clubs and societies, with an occasional dinner, and I shall be quite happy enough." [2] There was also, of course, Ravenscleft, that comfortable 12-room house at Seal Harbor rising sheer from the granite of Mount Desert Island, a place of cool delight of sunlit summer days, a cosy refuge when storms blew in from the Atlantic. There he could write in the mornings, there he could entertain such neighbors as Charles W. Eliot, A. Lawrence Lowell and the Rockefellers. From there he could take leisurely walks through the meadows and hills of the island, discussing with his companions politics and scenery, literature and history. To be sure, this was Beacon Hill transplanted down East—but what of that? Rhodes, in friendship as in other things, was not a man of catholic tastes: to him Boston society was peerless.[3]

The America to which he returned was not quite that which he had left, but to Rhodes it was home—and a home being put in order as he wanted it to be, under the direction of Theodore Roosevelt. In one significant aspect, however, the domestic arrangements were unsatisfactory. In March, 1907, a stock market slump marked the beginning of the financial panic of that year, and like many other investors, Rhodes suffered considerably. So disturbed was he that on occasion he betrayed those symptoms of financial anxiety which even gentlemen may share with the *hoi polloi*. He explained ruefully to Barrett Wendell how he had badgered Jacob Schiff, the aging partner of Kuhn, Loeb and Company, during a walking trip on Mount Desert Island:

> I wanted to talk with Schiff about the financial outlook, while he preferred to talk of the unique walk we were taking amongst rocks and trees. Being somewhat persistent and seeming very much so, because Schiff is deaf and I had to shout . . . I re-

> ceived a mild rebuke when we reached the top of Gorham Mountain . . . I said, "Mr. Schiff, this is a more pleasing outlook than Wall Street." "Well," was the reply, "I guess you have Wall Street more on the brain than I have.". . .[4]

The historian, faithful football fan though he was, confessed that he and others had little spirit for the Harvard-Yale game of that year because they were too upset by the slump.[5] He counselled his niece not to sell on the falling market: "On no account touch the principal but spend the income before Tom Johnson or some other Socialist gets hold of it." [6] Whatever his losses may have been, they failed to alter Rhodes' optimistic temper—a temper which, of course, was justified in the outcome. The country worked its way up and out of the collapse, the stock market rose again and investors were happy. By 1911 Rhodes noted complacently that his life had been "attended with good luck" [7] and he lectured the pessimistic Barrett Wendell on the virtues of "constructive optimism." [8]

Apart from this state of affairs, Rhodes had ample personal grounds for satisfaction. His popularity and prestige were even higher than before. The Macmillan Company, impressed by sales of his work and his national, even international, fame, eagerly printed a collection of his essays and lectures as *Historical Essays* (1909) and the lectures he delivered at Oxford University in 1912 as *Lectures on the American Civil War* (1913), and pressed him to begin work on the history after 1877.[9] His works sold relatively well, earning him the following royalties: 1907, $2748.00; 1908, $1621.50; 1909, $2003.65; 1910, $1511.36; 1911, $1309.75; 1912, $1252.86.[10]

Personal tributes continued to flow in on him. Bradley Gilman, a biographer of Robert E. Lee, used the *History* as one of his major sources.[11] Professor James K. Hosmer, the Civil War veteran who wrote the volumes on that war for *The American Nation* series, drew heavily from Rhodes' volumes: "They were for me a pathbreaker. I often tested your references, and found your accuracy unfailing. In general, as to judgment and spirit, I was fully in accord with you." [12] Oswald Garrison Villard sent Rhodes a copy of his biography of John Brown with the note: "No one in the field of historical writing today but must acknowledge his indebtedness to you. My own is very great—there exists but one history of the United States since 1850 for me." [13]

S. Weir Mitchell, the neurologist and novelist, thanked the historian for providing "the material out of which the political history of my new novel has been constructed." [14] Andrew D. White, president of Cornell University, apologized for omitting the *History* from a list of "great books" he had compiled for young men. A new list was being issued, he wrote,

> showing the importance of your work, the admirable way in which it has been done, and its claims upon the careful attention of young men who really wish to be informed and to think justly and clearly regarding the most important epoch in the history of our country . . .[15]

Englishmen were, if anything, more effusive than Americans. Sir George Otto Trevelyan thought the *History* "certainly is among the great histories of the world."[16] A. V. Dicey, after re-reading the first five volumes, considered them "the fairest . . . written by a contemporary with the events he records."[17] H. E. Egerton, writing in the *English Historical Review*, felt that Rhodes had maintained such standards of research and judgment "as shall elicit the utmost of truth."[18]

Such was Rhodes' fame that magazine editors were eager to print anything he cared to write, at fees which would be substantial even in our day.[19] Rhodes, on his part, was less reluctant than formerly to comply with these requests. The pressure of writing the *History* was now relaxed; many of the essays he submitted were simply early drafts of chapters for the continuation of the *History*, and the fees were welcome, especially after the scare of the Panic of 1907.[20] Besides, Rhodes was in an enviable position: he did not have to cater to the demands of editors—they came to him, not he to them. As a result, as he put it, he did not have to "yield to the cry of the ordinary magazine editor . . . to make your articles popular, or even striking, if not sensational . . . truth is not to be won by that method."[21] His work never appeared in the "popular" magazines, but the *Atlantic Monthly*, *Scribner's*, and the *Century* published a variety of articles, ranging in subject from the work of Edward Gibbon to the railroad strikes of 1877.[22]

His work was much sought after by other editors and publishers, but Rhodes yielded only once. He wrote an introduction to *The Abolition Crusade and Its Consequences* by Hilary A. Herbert, former soldier in the Confederate army, Democratic Congressman and Secretary of the Navy in the second Cleveland administration. The book was a plea for the white South to be let alone in handling the race issue, which, said the author, it had been doing successfully since the end of Reconstruction. In his introduction Rhodes barely alluded to this message, confining himself to the historical aspects of the problem:

> the question over which they [North and South] fought for four years had two sides; . . . all the right was not on one side, all the wrong on the other. The North should welcome, therefore, accounts of the conflict written by candid Southern men.[23]

Another significance of the book was not expressed, although it was much in the minds of both men. The book appeared in 1912, in the midst of the bitter political battle of that year, when Theodore Roosevelt had alarmed conservatives with his demand for the recall of federal judicial decisions. Rhodes, for all his admiration of Roosevelt, was appalled at such a proposal; to him, as to other conservatives, it was laying profane hands on the holy of holies, the Constitution. He believed, apparently, that Hilary's book, with its eloquent description of how abolitionists and lynchers alike flouted the Constitution, might demonstrate the necessity of adhering strictly to the limitations of that instrument:

> To my mind [wrote Herbert to Rhodes] the story related in my book is, as you indicated in your letter to me, a protest against all this modern craze against constitutional limitations, which Mr. Roosevelt is contending should be swept away because they are obstacles to the people's will. . . .[24]

Rhodes was also in demand as a lecturer, even by such a distinguished body as the International Congress of Historical Studies. Usually he declined, pleading pressure of work and an "utter deficiency in the art of lecturing," but eventually he accepted invitations from Harvard, Yale and Oxford.[25] In 1908 he delivered the Godkin lectures at Harvard, discussing Godkin, Gibbon and "The Profession of Historian." President Charles W. Eliot, who was absent when the lectures were given, wrote that the reports he heard indicated the talks had been a decided success.[26] Professor Max Farrand's comments on Rhodes' lecture at Yale also belie Rhodes' poor opinion of his lecturing talent: "everyone here is still speaking enthusiastically of your visit. . . . Those . . . fortunate enough to hear your paper cannot say enough in its praise." [27]

The invitation to speak at Oxford came as a result of the establishment there of a new lectureship in American History and Institutions, part of that Anglo-American *rapprochement* which characterized the pre–World War I era. Rhodes was loath to go: he was at work on the continuation of his *History;* there were magazine articles to write; and he was not eager to leave the United States.[28] Besides, there was a question of gentlemanly ethics involved: he understood that Oxford had proffered the invitation to

Albert Bushnell Hart and that invitation he loyally endorsed: "Professor Hart, your first selection, is an excellent lecturer, an untiring worker, faithful friend and good companion . . . his lectures will be illuminating." [29] Even after Arthur T. Hadley, president of Yale University and a member of the American advisory committee on the lectureship, had informed him that he misunderstood the situation and even after the official invitation came from Oxford, Rhodes was still reluctant.[30]

He yielded only after President Nicholas Murray Butler of Columbia University, President A. Lawrence Lowell of Harvard University and Whitelaw Reid, United States Ambassador in London, joined Hadley in urging his acceptance.[31] Professor Charles Harding Firth, in welcoming the announcement, cautioned Rhodes: "I should like to hear what you think of saying. Oxford is accessible to certain truths but not to all." [32] There need have been no occasion for anxiety. Rhodes' natural caution and geniality would have prevented him from voicing unwelcome "truths."

In fact, the lectures turned out to be a diluted version of some sections of the *History* adapted for reading. They were marked by apologies for such blunders as the *Trent* affair and the virtual expulsion from the United States of William H. Russell, the correspondent of the London *Times;* discreet criticism of the behavior of the British government in the *Alabama* and *Florida* cases; and praise for its actions on the ironclad rams and on non-intervention.[33] He was lionized by the university; he made new friends, including Sir William Osler, and renewed association with older friends; and his lectures proved successful: "I had a distinguished audience and am well satisfied with the result [he wrote]. I am therefore glad I came here this year, although I left Boston . . . with bitter regret." [34]

Formal honors continued to be showered on him. In 1911 the British Academy elected him a corresponding member; five years later he was asked to join the Royal Historical Society.[35] In 1910 the American Philosophical Society elected him to membership and that same year the National Institute of Arts and Letters awarded him its gold medal.[36] Universities pressed honorary degrees upon him: New York University (1908), Princeton (1916), Brown (1914), California (1916), Oxford (1909).[37]

Of these, Rhodes probably valued most the Oxford degree. When the subject was first broached he responded with the eagerness of a child: "I will go to Oxford any time for the sake of the degree," he informed an Englishman who had a hand in the matter.[38] While there Rhodes helped to dedicate a tablet to the English historian, John R. Green. Not only did he extol Green as a man who had shaped American thought "more than any writers of history except . . . Gibbon, Macaulay and Carlyle," but he also paid tribute to the English in what seems extravagant terms:

> the development of the English nation is one of the most wonderful things, if not the most wonderful thing, which history records. That history before James I is our own, . . . It was our ancestors who preserved liberty, maintained order, set the train moving toward religious toleration, and wrought out that language and literature which we are proud of, as well as you.[39]

Under the shower of honors, Rhodes' geniality blossomed. Not only his own countrymen but also foreigners commented on the warmth of his personality.[40] A. V. Dicey wanted him to write an autobiography, for he had led "the most interesting and valuable of lives." [41] André Tardieu was delighted with the hospitality shown him by Rhodes, as was Guigliemo Ferrero, who wrote to Rhodes after a visit to his home: "*vous êtes un des plus charmantes personnes qui j'ai vu ici. Il m'a semble que vous aviez, pour moi historien, une éspèce d'affection paternelle.*" [42] Eduard Meyer, the German historian, in appreciation of Rhodes' work and hospitality, dedicated a book of essays jointly to him and to A. Lawrence Lowell.[43]

Rhodes' friendliness, however, consisted in more than playing the generous host. To his old barber and friendly critic, George A. Myers, he sent discarded neckties and on occasion some of Rhodes' treasured Moselle wine.[44] To the widow of Grover Cleveland he sent a book made up of the articles on the administrations of her husband which had appeared in *Scribner's Magazine*.[45] Rhodes proposed to Harvard that Barrett Wendell be given an honorary degree and to the Nobel Prize Committee that an award be conferred upon Henry James.[46] He tried to persuade President Wilson to retain William Cameron Forbes, of the Boston mercantile dynasty, as governor-general of the Philippines.[47]

Some authors received the benefit of his careful criticism: Winston Churchill the novelist; Lawrence Shaw Mayo, the biographer of Jeffrey Amherst; and Herbert Croly, the biographer of Mark Hanna.[48] Others received unstinted praise: Owen Wister for *The Virginian;* Frederic Bancroft for his work on Carl Schurz; André Tardieu for *Notes Sur Les États-Unis;* Frederic L. Paxson for his book on the Civil War; George Otto Trevelyan for his history of the American Revolutionary War, which, wrote Rhodes, "will be for us an everlasting possession; it has not been approached and cannot be superseded."[49]

This made up the good life for Rhodes. He was writing his *History* again; he was not without honor, in his own as well as in foreign lands; he enjoyed the friendship of "choice spirits in an easy hospitable way";[50] he gladly did the deeds of friendship; and after the recovery from 1907, his financial prospects were bright. As he told Charles Francis Adams, he was "entirely satisfied."[51]

Rhodes' expression of euphoria was written early in 1912, before the outbreak of the political wars of that year, which upset him considerably. Until that occurrence, however, his satisfaction stemmed not only from personal considerations but also from his conviction that the destiny of his country was safe in the hands of Theodore Roosevelt and that the world itself might be saved from the supreme folly of war by the work of Roosevelt's successor, William Howard Taft.

In Rhodes' view, the prime danger to his own country lay in the rise of socialism, symbolized in the agitations of the Industrial Workers of the World and in the growing voting strength of the Socialist Party, from 95,000 in 1900 to 402,000 in 1904. As he saw it, anarchy was in the air.[52] The prime virtue of Roosevelt consisted in his program of social reform, which, ameliorating many of the more obvious social abuses, frustrated radical solutions. He himself, Rhodes explained,

> would have been satisfied with a continuance of the Cleveland-McKinley regime, but I now recognize that was impossible with due regard to the safety of the State and the question for us Conservatives is, was it not better to have the reform made by a man who is sound on the fundamentals than by a ruthless or shifty hand? . . .[53]

Roosevelt's social reforms, thought Rhodes, would constitute a major achievement which would "impress posterity":

> you have emphasized [he wrote to Roosevelt] the position of our government as being neither a government for the rich nor for the poor, but an arbiter endeavoring to deal out exact justice to both. Until the 19th century most governments were apt to be under the sway of one class or the other, more generally the rich, . . . In the immense communities of nations now it is disastrous to have the rich and the government synonymous, for resentment and indignation at their selfishness is apt to turn into an attack on the nation's life. I consider therefore the policy you have identified yourself with a boon for the country; and those

> who are eager that we shall deal properly with the different questions that arise must congratulate ourselves that a man sound in fundamental economic doctrines who is not a socialist should have the opportunity to grapple with this grave issue. It is yet impossible to measure the result of your policy, but it seems to me so essentially just and right that I believe its benefits must be enduring.[54]

When Roosevelt was assailed by wealthy Bostonians for his attacks upon the trusts, Rhodes came to his defense, explaining the process of curbing wealth in the interest of society was only what was to be expected:

> up to . . . the French Revolution the rich and influential had steadily preyed upon the weak and poor. "Now," said he [Rhodes], "we must expect for the next few generations that the poor will—as they have already begun to do—prey by the help of laws of their own enacting upon property."[55]

This view Rhodes expressed more positively in a letter to Barrett Wendell, in which the historian criticized Wendell's book, *The Privileged Classes*, for its "lack of sympathy with democracy":

> I know [wrote Rhodes] that you say reaction is impossible and that we must submit to the rule of the many. This is nothing but a logical development. The few had their chance and exploited the many; now the many are exploiting the few; and I think the latter condition means happiness for the greatest number. Either condition may oppress the moderately well-to-do, who want to hand on the torch of enlightenment and at the same time enjoy the good things of life. . . . As between the whim of the absolute monarch or his mistress and the dictum of fifteen million voters, I prefer the latter.[56]

Rhodes conceded that Roosevelt made mistakes, "but the essential thing is that in his weighty policies and well-matured acts he is (in my judgment) absolutely right."[57] It is not surprising, then, that Rhodes continued to be a welcome guest of the President. Rhodes, for his part, enjoyed the talk and ebullience of his host; he noted that a luncheon at the White House was "the merriest luncheon I have ever shared."[58]

The talk, of course, was largely by Roosevelt. He criticized Rhodes for being too sympathetic to the South in his treatment of Reconstruction, feeling that the historian had neglected to explain the behavior of the South which had made Reconstruction necessary. He deplored the tendency of nearly all historians to dwell on characters dear to the East, like Carl Schurz, while neglecting Western men, such as Oliver Morton. He bemoaned his lack of support from the cultivated classes but comforted himself with the backing of the "one-suspender men." He was pleased with what he had done in Cuba and the Philippines; happy that his sending the fleet around the world had "stopped the Jap talk of war" against the United States; and convinced that the Japanese must be excluded from this country.

J. P. Morgan, proclaimed Roosevelt, was "not a good financial adviser" while James J. Hill was "very good"—even though he had to "keep a lookout . . . that the latter [Hill] has not an especial eye to his own interest." When Rhodes expressed fear that governmental corruption might be worse in the United States than in England Roosevelt assured him that much of it was merely newspaper talk. The President also ridiculed gossip that he was both an alocholic and an opium fiend; his guest solemnly commented: "I wish to record here that there is absolutely no foundation for any of these statements." [59]

The friendship between the two continued after Roosevelt's departure from the White House. On his return from Europe in 1910 the former president had breakfast with Rhodes and other friends in Boston and regaled them with his observations:

> Roosevelt full of his European kings. The only man of real ability he saw among the crowned heads was the German Emperor and he is superficial in his intelligence but has real executive ability. . . .
>
> [Roosevelt] Disappointed in English women, impressed with Hungarian women. German admiral at head of navy impressed with voyage of fleet around the world . . . Europeans impressed with our naval trip . . . and with our construction of Panama Canal.
>
> We are entitled to open door in Manchuria but to him [Roosevelt] Manchuria is Japan's life. Better to concede that than to claim what we cannot enforce. The Japanese government earnestly in favor of peace. [Philander] Knox a splendid Attorney-general but runs the State Department as an attorney runs a lawsuit.
>
> Norway with a king as funny as Vermont would be with a king. No nobility in Norway and little culture in our sense or in the sense of Oxford and Cambridge. . . .[60]

A year later, when Roosevelt was a guest of Rhodes, he assured his host that he had no intention of seeking the Presidential nomination in 1912, criticized Taft's foreign policy, and expatiated on his attitude towards Germany and Japan:

> Theodore Roosevelt arrived in Boston at 3 P.M. on Tuesday, Dec. 12, and remained with me until Thursday, Dec. 14. . . . He does not want the nomination for the presidency and is doing nothing to secure it. . . . The matter of waiting until 1916 had of course occurred to him. Thinks if the Democrats win in 1912 it will be easy for a Republican in 1916. But some governor or senator or someone may come up to attract public attention. . . . he does not feel friendly to Pres. Taft nor has he a hearty liking for LaFollette.
>
> He is opposed to the arbitration treaties [proposed by Pres. Taft]. No use. Look at the Ho. of Reps. (sic) abrogating the Russian treaty. . . .
>
> He is not friendly to Germany. . . . They are not capable of a broad humanitarian impulse like the English, Americans or French. . . . I think Mr. Roosevelt appreciates the seriousness of war. . . . he would not want to go to war unless he thought he had a good chance of winning at the first go-off. If we went to war with Japan and lost the Philippines we could not get them back. He would like to get rid of the Philippines honorably but we must not let them be taken from us. . . .[61]

Doubtless Roosevelt's endorsement as well as Rhodes' traditional Republican sympathies led to Rhodes' support of Taft in the election of 1908. Indeed, Rhodes appeared to look on the outcome as a personal triumph for his idol. "It is another triumph for you," he wrote to Roosevelt after the election, "I believe that history will do you as full justice as did the American people yesterday."[62] But, for all his idolatry, Rhodes was unwilling to follow Roosevelt when the latter broke with Taft. Rhodes continued to support the President despite his approval of the Payne-Aldrich tariff (which Rhodes opposed) and his veto of Senator Lodge's bill for a literacy test for immigrants (which Rhodes approved).[63] He was specially enthusiastic about Taft's policies on Canadian reciprocity and arbitration treaties. When the Senate ratified the proposed Canadian reciprocity treaty, Rhodes wrote to the President:

> Reciprocity went through and you are the hero of it. If Canada adopts it, the results . . . will be so beneficial to both countries, that the work of the men who have had a hand in it will be gratefully appreciated. If the teaching of history and economics is worth anything our country has reached a point where every wise and careful reduction of the tariff will redound to the good of the greatest number.[64]

On another occasion he assured the President that the reciprocity measure would glorify the administration.[65]

In similar tone he lauded the President's attempts to negotiate arbitration treaties with foreign nations. "War is so horrible and now so useless," he wrote to Taft, "that the ruler who outlines a policy to make it highly improbable between civilized nations will reach a high fame." [66] As for the administration generally, he agreed with George A. Myers that Taft was "one of our best Presidents and that the softening influence of time will bring him complete vindication." [67]

Then, in 1912, came an event which shook Rhodes both personally and politically. Theodore Roosevelt, despite his protestations to the contrary, became an active candidate for the presidency. And, what was worse from the viewpoint of conservatives, he picked up and trumpeted the rallying cries of the reformers: initiative, referendum and recall, even recall of judicial decisions, although in the popular mind this was identified with recall of judges. Confusion on this point, Judge Grant wrote to Rhodes (who was in Europe at the time), had thrown "the property owning class and all reverers of our constitutions into pink fits." Grant, who was not pleased that Roosevelt had chosen his home to make public announcement of his candidacy, explained that the candidate had told him

> that he [Roosevelt] believed the most important questions today were the human one and economic problems, and intimated that the will of the people had been thwarted . . . , especially by the courts on constitutional grounds, and that reforms were urgent.

The judge was clear that Roosevelt had made "a great mistake,—an unnecessary and possibly fatal blunder," but, as he pointed out, Roosevelt had

> the reputation of being the most far-sighted politician in the country, and he unquestionably believes that we are on the eve of an economic revolution, and that it is better for the country that the Republican Party should point the way rather than the Socialists. . . .[68]

Rhodes, despite his previous attachment to this view, was not to be beguiled this time. He felt that he had been deceived. During Roosevelt's stay with Rhodes in December, 1911, they had talked confidentially of this very matter, wrote Rhodes to Henry Cabot Lodge, and he had concluded that Roosevelt would not

> announce his candidacy . . . unless there was an unmistakable drift of popular sentiment toward him. . . . As far as I could, in my timid and unobtrusive way I advised him to put any aspirations for the presidency in 1912 behind him . . . I had hoped that he would come out mildly in favor of President Taft. . . .[69]

Rhodes was opposed to Roosevelt's personal ambition and to his new policies: "His attacks on the decisions of the Supreme Court and the New York Court of Appeals are mischievous and savor of the demagogue rather than of the statesman. It is an infinite pity." [70] Roosevelt's policies, he felt, had as their final objective "the recall of the United States judges, those of the Supreme Court included." [71] To Barrett Wendell he spoke with unwonted feeling:

> For myself I see an idol shattered . . . I have had no such political grief since Senator Hanna died, . . . to fight for the nomination in a vulgar way as Senator LaFollette and Mr. Wilson are doing means a tremendous fall, and I never thought he would do it.
>
> Mr. Roosevelt is fascinating at his best, cultivated, courteous, considerate, thoroughly at home with those of his birth, breeding and education, and it is a pity to see him appealing to a mob. When he visited me last December one of the books he read on the train was Boissier's "Conspiracy of Catiline." Was he thinking then whether he might and how he could sway the mass? . . .[72]

In the heat of the moment he pledged allegiance to the Old Guard Republicanism of Henry Cabot Lodge. Lodge, who fancied himself as the High Priest of the Constitution, had little use for the reformers—even when they included his friend, Theodore Roosevelt. In an address delivered at Raleigh, N. C., he rallied the faithful against the infidels. Among them, he conceded, there were many "excellent persons" but he left little doubt that in his opinion most of them were envious malcontents, chronic reformers "of other people's mideeds," raw demagogues and noisy agitators. Initiative and referendum, said Lodge, would destroy representative government and restore direct government by the people, a system which had been tried in Greece and Rome and established a "dark record of disorder and failure." Even these, however, were not as dangerous as the proposals for recall of judges. These would end the independent judiciary, "the corner-stone of all liberty," and make judges the creatures of both popular majorities and the rich.[73] After reading this address, and a similar speech given at Princeton, N. J., Rhodes wrote to Lodge:

> I agree with all that you say. I applaud your reverence for the makers of our Constitution. I think that you have drawn candidly and fearlessly wise lessons from history and I am willing to take these two addresses as the chart of my political faith. . . .[74]

His preference, then, lay with Taft in the prospective campaign. Roosevelt and Wilson, he believed, could "thrive only on calamity"; [75] and while he had little respect for Roosevelt under the circumstances he also had none for Wilson, against whom he made the extraordinary accusation of having "little or no idea of the right of private property, and . . . [of believing] that private property is mainly robbery." Wilson, said he, was a politician with a "feverish craving for the presidency." [76] This attitude is the more astonishing in view of the warm praise with which Rhodes had greeted Wilson's work as governor of New Jersey. At that time Rhodes had written to Wilson:

> I marvel at your courage and persistence, instead of taking the primrose path which would have been so easy. When I have known personally a man like yourself it is no wonder that I like to write American history; but it is lucky that I live in cold critical Boston or I should indulge in a spread-eagle strain. . . .[77]

Rhodes returned to the United States that spring, and, once more on home grounds, his views began to moderate. To be sure, he found the pre-convention campaigns of Taft and Roosevelt "abominable" but the platforms adopted by both major parties reassured him on such issues as initiative, referendum and recall while that of the Democrats pleased him with its call for tariff reduction.[78] By September he had gone a long way: he found Wilson's conduct since his nomination "exemplary" and was "tempted" to vote for the Democrats—they had "shown courage in putting the tariff question to the fore, for I am not sure that tariff reduction is wholly popular." [79] He was also tempted because of the prospect of William Jennings Bryan as secretary of state. He had a poor opinion of Bryan's ability,

> but he is a strong advocate for peace, which will counterbalance his deficiencies. In my renewed study of our Civil War I am led to the belief that nothing worse can happen to us than a foreign war. And it is the easiest thing in the world to keep out of one.[80]

Eventually, Rhodes did return to the political faith of his father, and when his support was inadvertently questioned after the election he retorted with some heat:

> you are egregiously mistaken in supposing that I voted for President Taft . . . On the contrary, I not only voted for Mr. Wilson, but after August 15 I told everybody who asked me that I was going to do so. . . . It was sufficient that the issue of tariff reduction was plainly made. I have favored that for more than twenty years, and believing in it, I voted for it with enthusiasm. . . .[81]

Rhodes had changed his views about Wilson—but not about the Roosevelt Republicans. Approached to help the Progressive cause he told the solicitor: "I shall do all possible in my limited way to defeat the movement." [82]

With Roosevelt himself Rhodes found it impossible to remain angry; however much he might detest Roosevelt's new policies he could not resist the personal charm of the man. A few weeks after the election he met Roosevelt and had a "very agreeable" talk with him on non-political matters; as of old, Rhodes found the former president "courteous and dignified," "a wonderful man." [83] They had another friendly conversation at the meeting of the American Historical Association in Boston in December of that year. Rhodes termed "interesting and excellent" Roosevelt's address on "History as Literature." [84]

Soon, indeed, the two were on such terms that Roosevelt was once again a guest at the house on Beacon Street.

> I had two long talks with him [wrote Rhodes] in which the subject of present politics was not referred to. Truly he is a wonderful man and the more I see of him the more I regret his work in breaking up our grand old party, when by patient waiting he might have been the nominee four years hence.[85]

As the memories of the campaign faded, Rhodes mellowed even further:

> The longer I think of it, the more convinced am I that on the whole Mr. Roosevelt made a very good President. . . . like many great men before, he allowed his ambition to get the better of his judgment and the counsel of his best friends. . . . he is a fascinating man . . .[86]

Towards Wilson, Rhodes' attitude was based on agreement with policy rather than personal affection. He was agreeably surprised by Wilson's political talents but it was the President's fight for tariff reduction which won his enthusiastic support, even though the income tax provision of the Underwood tariff cost him considerably. He was so convinced of the virtues of both tariff reduction and the income tax that he was willing to defend both against the excoriations of his fellow club-men in Boston. As he put it:

> I believe in the [tariff] reduction and I hope that the greatest good of the greatest number will be so apparent that further reduction may be made within a decade. For that, however, the Democratic Party must keep in power. . . .[87]

Rhodes also supported the Administration in the controversy over the Federal Reserve Act; [88] and he backed Wilson in his stand that in the operation of the Panama Canal there should be no discrimination against shipping of other nations. Even before this became a political issue Rhodes felt it was "a pity that this most splendid work of our nation . . . should be marred by anything savoring of sharp commercial practice, . . ." [89]

Other aspects of the Administration he found less pleasing. The Newlands Act, providing for federal mediation of railroad labor disputes, he thought provided higher wages for workers without permitting a corresponding increase in railroad rates, a development he attributed to the recent trend of the "poor . . . exploiting the rich." He wondered, somewhat pessimistically, "Whether they [the poor] will show the same measure and consideration" as the rich had shown when they exploited the poor.[90] Regulation of business practices by government he believed to be persecution of "corporations and business men who are trying to make an honest penny." [91] William Jennings Bryan, he thought, was "thoroughly incompetent"; in his role as "Apostle of Peace" Bryan was "unstable as water" and had degraded his office by public lecturing to eke out his salary.[92]

Such failings, however, were little compared to the great virtues demonstrated by Wilson when war broke out in Europe. To Rhodes, self-styled "preacher of peace," the conduct of the President was ideal. When George Otto Trevelyan sharply questioned the validity of American neutrality Rhodes replied with a warm defense of the President's course:

> Mr. Wilson has amazed his friends by his political sagacity, and, so far, he has guided his country with wonderful skill through the difficulties brought on by the . . . war. He has the confidence of the whole community in foreign matters . . .[93]

His letters of commendation to the President himself were such as to elicit Wilson's thanks for "generous words of approval." [94]

NOTES

[1] Rhodes to Barrett Wendell, April 7, 1907. Rhodes Papers.

[2] Rhodes to Barrett Wendell, May 7, 1907, in M. A. D. Howe, *Rhodes*, p. 154.

[3] Rhodes to Charles Francis Adams, in M. A. D. Howe, *Rhodes*, p. 210. Barrett Wendell remarked to Rhodes, with some exaggeration, "You can't think of a friend who is not a railroad president." Charles K. Bolton, *Notebook, 1914–1917*, p. 242 (Oct. 23, 1916).

[4] Rhodes to Barrett Wendell, Aug. 30, 1907, in M. A. D. Howe, *Rhodes*, pp. 162–163.

[5] Rhodes to Mrs. Lucia McBride, Oct. 27, 1907. Letter in possession of Mrs. McBride.

[6] Rhodes to Mrs. Lucia McBride, Aug. 28, 1907. Letter in possession of Mrs. McBride.

[7] Rhodes to Charles H. Firth, Feb. 8, 1911. Rhodes Papers.

[8] Rhodes to Barrett Wendell, June 5, 1911, quoted in letter from Wendell to Rhodes, June 28, 1911. Rhodes Papers.

[9] George P. Brett to Rhodes, Oct. 21, 1907. Rhodes Papers. Rhodes began work on the new volume Oct. 29, 1908. This was the work entitled *History of the United States from Hayes to McKinley, 1877–1896*. Rhodes Papers, XI, unlettered page.

[10] Royalty statements, Macmillan Company to Rhodes, 1908, 1909, 1910, 1911, 1912 and 1913. These are dated April 30 of each year and cover the fiscal year prior to that date. Rhodes Papers.

[11] Bradley Gilman to Rhodes, Oct. 8, 1914. Rhodes Papers.

[12] James K. Hosmer to Rhodes, Feb. 14, 1912. Rhodes Papers.

[13] Oswald Garrison Villard to Rhodes, Oct. 10, 1910. Rhodes Papers.

[14] S. Weir Mitchell to Rhodes, March 27, 1913. Rhodes Papers.

[15] Andrew D. White to Rhodes, Nov. 1, 1915. Rhodes Papers.

[16] Sir George Otto Trevelyan to Rhodes, Aug. 7, 1910. Rhodes Papers.

[17] A. V. Dicey to Rhodes, May 18, 1912. Rhodes Papers.

[18] XXIII (1908), 395.

[19] For his articles in *Scribner's* Rhodes was paid fees ranging from $250 to $500 each. E. L. Burlingame, *Scribner's Magazine*, to Rhodes, Dec. 30, 1910. Rhodes Papers.

[20] For example, see "Cleveland's Administrations," *Scribner's Magazine*, L (1911), 496–504; 602–612; "A Review of President Hayes' Administration in the Light of Thirty Years," *Century Magazine*, LXVIII (1909), 883–891.

[21] Rhodes to Gamaliel Bradford, April 16, 1914. Rhodes Papers.

[22] *Infra*, pp. 280–281.

[23] In Hilary A. Herbert, *The Abolition Crusade and Its Consequences: Four Periods of American History* (New York, 1912), viii.

[24] Hilary A. Herbert to Rhodes, May 27, 1912. Rhodes Papers.

[25] Rhodes, quoted in M. A. D. Howe, *Rhodes*, p. 165. For lecture invitations see letters to Rhodes from Evart B. Greene, University of Illinois, Nov. 3, 1908; Brander Matthews and A. H. Thorndike, Columbia University, June 16 and June 19, 1909; Harold W. Temperly, secretary, section IV, International Congress of Historical Studies, dated only 1913; A. M. Dobie, University of Virginia, June 6, 1913; Samuel B. Platner, Western Reserve University, March 14, 1914; William S. Pierce, Kenyon College, April 8, 1914. Rhodes Papers.

[26] Charles W. Eliot to Rhodes, May 6, 1908. In agreeing to lecture, Feb. 28, 1908, Rhodes stipulated: "I do not desire any compensation for

them, . . . I am glad to offer them in partial return for the indirect benefits I have received from Harvard University." Rhodes Papers.

[27] Max Farrand to Rhodes, April 26, 1909. Rhodes Papers.

[28] Rhodes to Charles H. Firth, Feb. 12, 1911. Rhodes Papers. Rhodes to John T. Morse, Jr., May 22, 1912, in M. A. D. Howe, *Rhodes*, p. 222.

[29] Rhodes to Charles H. Firth, Feb. 8, 1911. Rhodes Papers.

[30] C. B. Heberden, vice-chancellor, Brasenose College, Oxford University, to Rhodes, Feb. 1, 1911; Arthur T. Hadley to Rhodes, Feb. 11, 1911. Rhodes Papers.

[31] Nicholas Murray Butler to Rhodes, Feb. 10, 1911; Arthur T. Hadley to Rhodes, Feb. 11, 1911. Rhodes to Paul Elmer More, *The Nation*, June 9, 1913. Rhodes Papers.

[32] Charles H. Firth to Rhodes, Aug. 13, 1911. Rhodes Papers.

[33] James Ford Rhodes, *Lectures on the American Civil War, Delivered Before the University of Oxford in Easter and Trinity Terms, 1912* (New York, 1913), pp. 157–170, 180–181.

[34] Rhodes to John T. Morse, Jr., May 22, 1912, in M. A. D. Howe, *Rhodes*, pp. 221–222.

[35] I. Gollancz, secretary, British Academy, to Rhodes, July 8, 1911; George W. Prothero to Rhodes, July 5, 1911; Royal Historical Society, to Rhodes, Nov. 23, 1916. Rhodes Papers.

[36] J. M. Hays, secretary, American Philosophical Society, to Rhodes, April 23, 1910; Harrison S. Norris, secretary, National Institute of Arts and Letters, to Rhodes, Dec. 6, 1910. Rhodes Papers. Rhodes had been active in the affairs of the institute since its organization in 1900.

[37] Letters to Rhodes from I. C. Pierson, New York University, April 28, 1908; Benjamin Ida Wheeler, University of California, April 21, 1916; C. Lendesdorf, Oxford University, May 29, 1909; citation for LL.D., Princeton University, Commencement, 1916. Rhodes Papers. M. A. D. Howe, *Rhodes*, p. 224.

[38] Rhodes to Harry Johnson, pencilled draft on letter from Johnson to Rhodes, April 17, 1907. Rhodes Papers. Harry Johnson was a brother of Rhodes' daughter-in-law, Bertha H. Rhodes.

[39] Text of the address, "John Richard Green," will be found in *Historical Essays*, pp. 169–173.

[40] Admiral Alfred T. Mahan sponsored Rhodes as a member of the University Club of New York, Barrett Wendell as a member of the Somerset Club of Boston. Mahan to Rhodes, April 8, April 11, July 4, 1908; Rhodes to Wendell, Oct. 4, 1912. Rhodes Papers.

[41] A. V. Dicey to Rhodes, Sept. 27, 1910. Rhodes Papers.

[42] André Tardieu to Rhodes, Jan. 1 [1909?]. Rhodes Papers. Guigliemo Ferrero to Rhodes, in M. A. D. Howe, *Rhodes*, p. 181.

[43] Eduard Meyer to Rhodes, Jan. 29, 1910. Rhodes Papers.

[44] George A. Myers to Rhodes, Oct. 10, 1910. Rhodes Papers. Also, Myers to Rhodes, Sept. 30, 1910; May 29, 1913; Sept. 20, 1913, in John A. Garraty (ed.), "Correspondence," *Ohio Historical Quarterly*, LXIV (1955), 14, 128, 132.

[45] Rhodes to Mrs. Frances F. Cleveland, May 16, 1912. Rhodes Papers.

[46] A. Lawrence Lowell to Rhodes, Aug. 17, 1909; Edith Wharton to Rhodes, July 16, 1911. Rhodes Papers.

[47] Woodrow Wilson to Rhodes, Aug. 15, 1913. Rhodes Papers.

[48] Winston Churchill to Rhodes, Feb. 2, 1907; Lawrence S. Mayo to Rhodes, July 6, 1916. Rhodes to George P. Brett, Macmillan Company, regarding Croly's *Marcus Alonzo Hanna*, undated pencilled draft. Rhodes Papers.

[49] Rhodes to Sir George Otto Trevelyan, June 29, 1910; Frederic L.

Paxson, Feb. 9, 1912; Frederic Bancroft, Dec. 18, 1908; André Tardieu, pencilled draft, March, 1908. Owen Wister to Rhodes, Aug. 31, 1902. Rhodes Papers.

[50] Rhodes to Charles Francis Adams, Feb. 9, 1912, in M. A. D. Howe, *Rhodes*, p. 210.

[51] *Ibid.*

[52] Rhodes to Henry Cabot Lodge, Jan. 7, 1907, in M. A. D. Howe, *Rhodes*, p. 144; Rhodes Papers, XII, So.

[53] Rhodes to Theodore Roosevelt, May 18, 1908, in M. A. D. Howe, *Rhodes*, p. 174.

[54] Rhodes to Theodore Roosevelt, March 16, 1907, in M. A. D. Howe, *Rhodes*, pp. 146–147.

[55] Charles K. Bolton, *Notebook, 1886–1914*, p. 131 (Feb. 3, 1908).

[56] Rhodes to Barrett Wendell, Dec. 16, 1908, in M. A. D. Howe, *Rhodes*, p. 179.

[57] Rhodes to Henry Cabot Lodge, Jan. 7, 1907, in M. A. D. Howe, *Rhodes*, p. 144.

[58] White House place card, dated Dec. 29, 1908. Rhodes Papers.

[59] Rhodes Papers, XII, Xa, eX, aY, Ye, eY. These notes deal with Rhodes' visit to the White House, May 15, 1908.

[60] Rhodes Papers, XII, oR.

[61] Rhodes Papers, XII, aS, uR.

[62] Rhodes to Theodore Roosevelt, Nov. 4, 1908, in M. A. D. Howe, *Rhodes*, pp. 178–179.

[63] William Howard Taft to Rhodes, April 3, 1909; Rep. S. W. McCall of Massachusetts to Rhodes, Oct. 8, 1909; Rhodes to Henry Cabot Lodge, Feb. 1, 1913, photostat fragment. Rhodes Papers.

[64] Rhodes to William Howard Taft, undated pencilled draft. Rhodes Papers.

[65] Rhodes to William Howard Taft, March 7, 1911, in Henry F. Pringle, *The Life and Times of William Howard Taft* (New York, 1939), II, 590.

[66] Rhodes to William Howard Taft, undated pencilled draft. Taft replied gratefully, Sept. 5, 1911. Rhodes Papers.

[67] George A. Myers to Rhodes, Sept. 24, 1912; Rhodes to Myers, Oct. 7, 1912; in John A. Garraty (ed.), "Correspondence," *Ohio Historical Quarterly*, LXIV (1955), 21, 24.

[68] Robert Grant to Rhodes, March 22, 1912. Rhodes Papers.

[69] Rhodes to Henry Cabot Lodge, April 13, 1912. Rhodes Papers.

[70] Rhodes to Robert Grant, April 11, 1912. Rhodes Papers.

[71] *Ibid.*

[72] Rhodes to Barrett Wendell, April 12, 1912, in M. A. D. Howe, *Rhodes*, pp. 216–217.

[73] Henry Cabot Lodge, "The Constitution and Its Makers," in *The Democracy of the Constitution and Other Addresses and Essays* (New York, 1915), pp. 35–36, 54, 59–60, 70–77.

[74] Rhodes to Henry Cabot Lodge, April 13 [1912?]. Rhodes Papers.

[75] Rhodes to Robert Grant, April 11, 1912. Rhodes Papers.

[76] Rhodes to Mrs. C. H. Toy, April 28, 1912, in M. A. D. Howe, *Rhodes*, p. 217. Nowhere does Rhodes offer evidence in support of his accusation.

[77] Rhodes to Woodrow Wilson, Dec. 11, 1910, in M. A. D. Howe, *Rhodes*, p. 193.

[78] Rhodes to William R. Thayer, July 14, 1912, in M. A. D. Howe, *Rhodes*, pp. 226–227.

[79] Rhodes to William R. Thayer, Sept. 1, 1912, in M. A. D. Howe, *Rhodes*, p. 227.

[80] *Ibid.*

[81] Rhodes to Frederic Bancroft, Sept. 4, 1913, in M. A. D. Howe, *Rhodes*, p. 238.

[82] Rhodes to Sir George Otto Trevelyan, Jan. 19, 1913. Rhodes Papers.

[83] Rhodes to Sir George Otto Trevelyan, Dec. 9, 1912. Rhodes Papers.

[84] Rhodes to Sir George Otto Trevelyan, Jan. 19, 1913. Rhodes Papers.

[85] Rhodes to George A. Myers, Jan. 17, 1913, in John A. Garraty (ed.), "Correspondence," *Ohio Historical Quarterly*, LXIV (1955), 125.

[86] Rhodes to Frederic Bancroft, Sept. 4, 1913, in M. A. D. Howe, *Rhodes*, p. 240.

[87] Rhodes to Sir George Otto Trevelyan, May 25, 1913. Rhodes Papers. Rhodes Papers, X, Io. Rhodes to Frederic Bancroft, Sept. 4, 1913, in M. A. D. Howe, *Rhodes*, p. 238.

[88] U. S. Senator John W. Weeks to Rhodes, Dec. 27, 1913. Rhodes Papers.

[89] Rhodes to Mrs. C. H. Toy, Sept. 24, 1912, photostat fragment. Rhodes Papers.

[90] Rhodes to Sir George Otto Trevelyan, Sept. 12, 1913. Rhodes Papers.

[91] Rhodes to Mrs. C. H. Toy, Dec. 25, 1913, in M. A. D. Howe, *Rhodes*, p. 241.

[92] Rhodes to Mrs. C. H. Toy, Sept. 4, 1913, in M. A. D. Howe, *Rhodes*, p. 239.

[93] Rhodes to Sir George Otto Trevelyan, Nov. 30, 1914. Rhodes Papers.

[94] Woodrow Wilson to Rhodes, Nov. 18, 1914. Rhodes Papers.

Chapter 11

BEGINNINGS OF PESSIMISM

THE COURSE of his own life and the course of his country's development help explain in part Rhodes' deep feeling of satisfaction with life in America. There was yet another factor—the trend of affairs in Europe. He had always been a fervent admirer of France and England, but during his visits in 1909, 1911–12, and 1914 he found that Europe, too, was changing—and changing in a direction he found unpalatable. Socialism, no longer a spectre, sat embodied in parliaments. The lower classes, no longer suffering in decent anonymity, were in a ferment of revolt. There was talk of war—which the historian refused to take seriously—and finally, incomprehensible and terrifying, there was war itself, trapping him in France, sending him scurrying across the Channel, across the ocean, to the calm haven of his native land.

For the most part, Rhodes and his wife travelled as during previous visits. They used an automobile to visit "the proper places and [admire] the proper things." [1] They sought to alleviate their ailments with the waters of Baden-Baden, Aix-les-Bains and Evian-les-Bains. Rhodes sought inspiration from St. Francis at Assisi; from Goethe at Weimar; from Shakespeare at Stratford-on-Avon; from Gibbon at Rome.[2] He had little to do with Continental scholars, but he renewed old friendships and made new acquaintances with those of England: Sir George Otto Trevelyan, J. B. Bury, Andrew Lang, Charles Harding Firth, among others.[3] Indeed, Rhodes was a kind of unofficial ambassador of his country to his own kind in Europe: he bore with him official letters of introduction from the State Department, and he was an honored guest of the American ambassadors in London and Rome.[4]

At first, Rhodes tried to temper his reactions to the changing state of Europe. After a month in France he observed ironically

> we are ready with profound thoughts on the state of the country, which will be about as valuable as similar ideas which foreigners express about our own country from superficial observations. . . .[5]

As of old, he was impressed by the industry and frugality of the French, and the brilliance of their intellectual life, but he was less hopeful of the country's future. Once he had thought the Third Republic gave the French the best government they had had since Louis XIV. Now he was not so certain:

> Ever since my first trip to France in 1867 [he wrote] I have loved France and the French but I do not feel sure that they are retaining their proper place in the progress of the world. I am inclined to think that parliamentary government in France is a failure and that its operation has been attended with much corruption.[6]

He found it "sad to see this highly civilized nation without a rallying point. No King, Church, Constitution, Parliament or Congress which can inspire the people in a stress."[7] During the critical summer of 1914, however, he was inclined to doubt his own appraisal. Using the yardstick of the businessman, he thought oversubscription of a government bond issue "may well make one pause before asserting that France is on the downgrade."[8]

England provided his keenest disappointment. That country he regarded as "our old home"; he delighted in its quiet countryside, its rich historical tradition, and its serene and ordered social life.[9] Now all those were challenged. Lloyd George's "Land Tax" budget of 1909 had struck at the privileges of the landed aristocracy. That had been followed by the bitter political struggles, which, culminating in the passage of the Parliament Act of 1911, had shattered the power of the House of Lords. In that year, seamen, longshoremen and railwaymen went on strike, paralyzing the English economy; Liverpool, the port from which Rhodes expected to sail on his return to the United States, was for a few days in a state of siege.[10]

Rhodes, on the continent, was distressed. His departure, he wrote, "depends upon the men who are running the labor unions in England. . . . England has had a dreadful summer between the political agitation and the labor troubles."[11] The strikes, in his view, were like those in America: "outbreaks of savagery where the worst elements of the community come to the front."[12] Later he revised that opinion: American strikers were not as bad as English:

> I am happy in our comparative calm serenity [he wrote]. The strikes in England seemed to me much more alarming than our own contests between capital and labor. Blatant talk about revolution and forcible division of property is not pleasant to hear in the country we have so long regarded as our old home.[13]

In addition, the English suffragists appalled him. To him, even their demands were execrable—as a youth he had lost some of his admiration for John Stuart Mill after he discovered Mill's views on women's rights—but their methods, which included smashing windows, burning mail boxes, and assaulting members of Parliament, smacked too much of revolution. He wrote soberly: "I certainly do not like the encroachments of the proletariat and the women in England. It would grieve me much should England suffer any misfortune." [14]

There was, however, one facet of English life which impressed him favorably:

> the average Englishman in an international dispute always takes the part zealously of his own country and finds arguments to sanction his position. He would not want to say, "My country, right or wrong," because he always believes his country to be right in a matter of diplomacy. The position has merit.[15]

Perhaps because of new trends, perhaps because of his own age, he was less beguiled than formerly with good wine and medieval cathedrals; there was a new acerbity in his observations. Europeans, he wrote, "outside of a small set in England, . . . look upon us as half-barbarian and they do not believe that we can teach them anything." [16] From Florence he wrote that nothing appealed to him

> so much as American history and politics. It does not show culture to say so, but the Middle Ages and the Renaissance and their glorious products pale with me in comparison. . . . the manner in which we are working out our social problems in comparison with England, Germany, France and Italy seems to me more important than to measure the contribution of the Middle Ages to civilization, . . . I feel sure that we are coming out all right with neither the sacrifice of liberty nor order and with the results of civilization intact.[17]

When Frederic Bancroft wrote that he could not blame the English for lack of interest in American history, Rhodes retorted: "I suspect that they could learn considerable from us as to how to run a democracy . . . , they seem to be making a mess of it." [18] He conceded that had he gone to live at Oxford when he was thirty he might have been happy, but "now no place outside the United States could be endurable for a period of years." [19]

Vexed though he might be with Europe, Rhodes was yet unwilling to agree with his friend, Barrett Wendell, who, from the vantage point of Peking, hailed the superiority of the Oriental way of life to that of the West:

> These people [wrote Wendell] are really civilized, with a civilization in many respects deeper and more stable than our own. . . . It solves the conflict between means and ends by reducing desire and demand to the lowest terms compatible with industrious, orderly, healthy existence. . . . The contrast with the malignant and malicious discontent . . . of revolutionary and socialistic Europe or America is not in our favor. . . .[20]

To which Rhodes replied:

> Germany, the United States and England . . . must be excepted from your generalizations. I believe the mass of the human race have never had so good a time as they are now having in the United States, and that, take it all in all, materialistic conditions were never so good. . . . Dirt and filth [the existence of which in China Wendell had conceded] . . . do not accompany the highest civilization.
>
> And you quite left out of account Christianity. . . .[21]

Two days later he sent Wendell a clipping from *The Nation* reporting attacks by Chinese pirates on wrecked ships. "Could that have happened on the English, German or American coasts?" he asked, "Are not the Orientals entirely deficient in humanity?" He added, with a touch of humor, "I do not want to 'crow' but I gathered from one of your books that, . . . the United States was the best of all countries." [22]

In his reply Wendell called attention to the piratical conduct of coast-dwellers in both England and America in fairly recent times and expressed doubt whether Christianity "is half so efficacious for human happiness as the more nearly indigenous religions of Asia." The masses of the West, he agreed, were better off materially than those of the Orient, but they were less contented, less happy, less virtuous. "In brief," he concluded, "they begin to display the vices, without the graces and the self-mastery, of the smaller ruling classes in the past." [23]

Rhodes, feeling, perhaps, that the correspondence was drifting into controversy, ended the exchange with a batch of clippings showing the seamy side of Chinese civilization and a quotation from Goethe which emphasized the kinship, rather than the differences, between East and West:

"The Chinamen think, act, and feel almost exactly like us; we soon find that we are perfectly like them, excepting that all they do is more clear, more pure, and decorous than with us. With them, all is orderly, citizen-like, without great passion or poetic flight.". . .[24]

However much Rhodes' enthusiasm for Europe may have dimmed, he could not believe it capable of the folly of war. At the height of the Moroccan crisis of 1911 he dismissed the possibility of conflict: England was not anxious for war, the Kaiser had "always been for peace." [25] Even in July, 1914, Rhodes was apparently unimpressed by the military preparations taking place on the Continent. He wrote from France only that he was "a bit tired of the Continent" and was looking forward to visiting England.[26] When the unbelievable did happen, he hastened to the relative safety of England, enlisting the aid of the American Ambassador in Paris, Myron T. Herrick, an old personal acquaintance from Cleveland, to get his private automobile shipped from Dieppe to England.[27] Once in England he importuned his friends, James Bryce, and Walter Hines Page, the American Ambassador, to obtain for him early passage to the United States. As it turned out, they were able to do little for him: he returned on the voyage of the *Mauretania* which he had planned to take before he left Boston.[28]

On Rhodes, the impact of the war was decisive. It shattered the basic assumption on which his genial optimism was based: namely, that life in general was steadily improving, thanks to inexorable laws of economics and history, one manifestation of which was that reasonableness of Western man which would make another great war between Western nations impossible. Europe, which he had regarded as the very heart of civilization, had betrayed him. The war in itself would have basically changed his attitudes, but it was only one—albeit a major one—of many sorrows which combined to suffuse a pall of pessimism which darkened the rest of his life.

The state of his health contributed no little to this development. Indeed, the noted physician, Dr. Harvey Cushing, was of the opinion that Rhodes' change in attitude derived largely from developing arteriosclerosis.[29] After Rhodes passed his sixtieth birthday the spells of ill-health became more frequent, recovery more slow and difficult, and he himself became somewhat of a hypochondriac. He refused to handle books from the public library lest he become contaminated by germs; he kept careful records of ocular and physical examinations.[30] These seem to indicate reassuring reports from his physicians, but his correspondence tells quite another story.

In 1909 he fell prey to illness in the digestive system; a recurrence in 1910 was serious enough to require surgery. After recuperation at Lakewood, N. J., a haven for the well-to-do in those pre-war years, he returned to Boston and suffered a relapse so severe that he was glad to take advantage of Woodrow Wilson's offer to postpone the granting to him of the honorary degree by Princeton University.[31]

The experience left him weak. He declined an invitation from his native city to be guest of honor at a civic celebration, explaining: "Since my operation three and a half years ago, I am easily subject to fatigue, . . . I could not undertake a journey to Cleveland with the fatigue and excitement of the celebration without undergoing a considerable risk." [32] In 1915 he was ill frequently, apparently from infection of the digestive tract. One such attack, in the winter, was quite serious, for he wrote later: "I think the poison must have gone to my brain as I have forgotten many things during these months. I did practically no work during that time . . . I was a miserable being." [33]

Early in 1916 he fled to California, partly in order to receive an honorary degree from the University of California, partly in the hope of recovery in the climate. In this latter he was disappointed. He was laid low by another attack: "not a severe one," wrote his son, "but one so unexpected as to leave him constantly apprehensive and rather disheartened." [34] The aging historian must have felt even more disheartened after his return to New England, for by September of 1916 he was ill once more.[35]

To the gloom which he felt about his own health was added concern about that of his wife. Never well, she had become increasingly frail with the passage of the years; the trips to the watering places of Europe had produced little improvement in her health, although she remained as calm and cheerful as ever.[36]

Upon chronic physical pain was imposed emotional distress as death took many of those who were closest to him. In 1907 he hastened to his mother, in time for that final greeting: "She recognized me: her death was painless and peaceful." [37] Seven years later the passing of a nephew moved him to unwonted expression of feeling:

> Most of us cannot be here a great while longer and there is one comfort when we go, we shall end the struggle against adverse

> circumstances and conditions. For many times it seems as if life was not worth living.[38]

He was even more upset by the death of his only brother, Robert, a wealthy businessman of Cleveland. The brothers had drifted apart during the years, for aside from the family tie they had little in common, but the circumstances of Robert's death caused James grief and anger. James, himself far from well, was on his way to California when informed of Robert's illness. He thought it a minor ailment, but expressed willingness to stop at Cleveland if the family thought it advisable; repeated telegrams from them, however, assured him that all was well. He was dismayed, upon arrival in California, to learn that Robert had died.

He was angered to hear later that gossip in Cleveland condemned him for passing through the city while his brother lay dying. There was little he could do, save to explain to his old friend, George A. Myers, that both telegrams and gossip had a common origin in a friend of the family who had not the courage to admit he had misled James—adding, "Had I known his [Robert's] serious condition I should have gone to Cleveland at once whatever happened to me." [39] This was little solace to a man of Rhodes' strict standards of propriety. He felt he had failed his own brother, and there was wrung from him that bitter regret which death so often occasions:

> I wish now that I had made a point of seeing more of him recently but during the past nine months, I have been swayed by the feeling of an invalid and I thought there were influences wh. (sic) I was not strong enough to overcome. And so it has happened that I have not done thoroughly what I ought to have done . . .[40]

Ill health and the death of close relatives—these were sorrows enough for a man in his sixties: but worse was to come. In 1913, "the Gibraltar of Yankee financial strength," [41] the New York, New Haven and Hartford railroad, in which Rhodes, like most wealthy New Englanders, had made heavy investments, collapsed. Hearings before the Interstate Commerce Commission disclosed that the creation of a railroad empire in New England by J. P. Morgan had been attended by fraud and corruption and that the financial condition of the New Haven road was dismal. Stock of the railroad fell from 142 in April, 1912, to 102 in May, 1913.[42] In December, 1913, the road, which had never failed to pay dividends of at least eight per cent since 1872, passed its dividend—a practice which, continued until 1927, accelerated decline of the stock. By June, 1914, New Haven stock sold for 63.[43]

Nor, in that year, could hapless investors look elsewhere for relief. The country as a whole was slipping into the recession which lasted until war orders from Europe revived the economy; between 1912 and 1914 stock market prices as a whole declined 15.4%.[44] Rhodes was far from being wiped out financially, as some New England families were, but his losses were severe.

> My optimism was too great [he wrote] . . . There has been a great drop in . . . railroad shares and a reduction on dividends on gilt-edged securities so that in this community there is a feeling of real distress, so widely distributed are the shares of New Haven, Boston and Maine and Boston Elevated. . . .[45]

"Not since the summer of 1907 have I been so much disturbed by my private finances," he wrote to George A. Myers, but, as he explained to George Otto Trevelyan, he dared not let go:

> I have suffered much from the decline in railroad stocks, especially the New York, New Haven and Hartford, but unless I see something to change decidedly my course I am going to hold on in the hope of better times. . . .[46]

Although such a course gave him anxiety, he pursued it until March, 1914, when, at last persuaded that better times were not in the offing, he sold his New Haven holdings at a loss.[47]

Although Rhodes complained that he was confronted with increased expenses while his income declined, there is little indication that his reverses caused significant changes in his living standards. In the fall of 1913, for example, he purchased for cash a Pierce-Arrow automobile at a cost of five thousand dollars.[48] In the spring of 1914 he departed for a prolonged stay in Europe, where, as he said, he put behind him "private financial losses and the general financial outlook." [49] His club life, his hospitality at Beacon Street and Seal Harbor, suffered no diminution.

Also, as time went on, he may well have recouped much of his loss by appreciation of other investments. Sale of real estate on the west side of Cleveland, during the war boom, as well as the sale of mineral lands in Tuscarawas County, Ohio, must have been quite profitable.[50] How profitable we may guess from a letter written to Rhodes by his friend in Cleveland, S. W. Croxton. Reporting that some time previously he had been tempted to sell holdings in the Cleveland Furnace Company, Croxton went on,

> luckily I did not do it and now I am ashamed to tell you how much profit this concern is making as it verges on Grand Larceny, but we will get the other end of it . . . when they get all tired out of fighting on the other side of the Globe. . . .[51]

Whatever may have been the immediate financial significance of the New Haven affair there is no doubt of its protracted psychological importance. First, Rhodes was compelled to confront one of his prejudices—a bias against Louis Brandeis, which he shared with most of Proper Boston [52]—and to admit that he was wrong; a change in attitude no less basic because it forced him to change his evaluation of that good Christian financier, J. P. Morgan.

In 1912 and in 1913 he had joined in campaigns to keep Brandeis out of the cabinet of President-elect Wilson and out of the American Academy of Arts and Letters.[53] In 1916 he took quite a different tack. He was still far from liking the Jewish crusader, but, as he pointed out to John T. Morse, Jr.,

> the trouble with our position is that Brandeis is a better man than our great representative of "la haute finance," J. P. Morgan, Sr. I speak feelingly, as I lost a great lot of money in New Haven from over-weening confidence in J. P. M. (sic) who seems to me to have been a fraud of the first water. I wonder if [in] his high church and low church Episcopal heaven he can hear the sobs and the wailings of the widows and orphans of Massachusetts and Connecticut. If I had followed Brandeis instead of Morgan I shd (sic) have been better off financially and not looked irritated every time that some one asked me for a benevolent or charitable contribution. . . .[54]

Secondly, Rhodes' confidence in his own business acumen was shaken. The New Haven debacle showed him that his 19th century business experience was of little value in the new day of predatory finance, that his unvarying optimism about business might well betray him. Thereafter he had little to say about business prospects: as he explained to Dr. Frederick Shattuck in the grim winter of 1913, "I have made such a failure at prophecy that I have abandoned the business and I now confine myself to the records of the past." [55]

Even those very traits which had made him so popular in Proper Boston involved him in situations which helped cast a pall over these years. His friendships were many, including men of diverse and often of contradictory views. Rhodes, who disliked controversy even on the level of scholarship, long contrived to stay out of the personal feuds which raged even in the rarefied atmospheres of

Harvard and Beacon Street, but eventually he found himself drawn into the vortex of one of the most bitter.[56]

The issue arose in 1915, when the death of Charles Francis Adams left vacant the presidency of the Massachusetts Historical Society, and the antagonists, ancient enemies, were men whom Rhodes liked and admired: Charles W. Eliot and Henry Cabot Lodge. Lodge's enemies in the society immediately proposed Rhodes for the presidency—a proposal which Lodge shrewdly endorsed.[57]

Rhodes was not enthusiastic. He felt, probably not without reason, that at least some Brahmins would resent an "outsider" becoming president of their hallowed society.[58] Besides, he found the duties of the presidency distasteful and he was of the opinion that Adams had expressed a preference for Lodge—a preference which Rhodes shared. He himself, therefore, nominated Lodge.[59]

Eliot was vexed. Rhodes' attitude, he wrote, was "unjust to the Society; because [it] would deprive it [the Society] of its first chance to have a professional historian as President." [60] Failing to persuade Rhodes on that ground, he passed on to attacks on Lodge:

> It is too bad that the Historical Society should drop to Henry Cabot Lodge as President when they have the chance to make a real historian President. Lodge is not an historian at all, . . . , but only an opportunist politician, who has always been a bigoted protectionist and a hater of England. I want to enter a protest . . .[61]

Nor was Eliot convinced that Rhodes had understood Adams correctly. "You were certainly Mr. Adams' first choice," he wrote, adding:

> I confess to having been keenly disappointed in Lodge as a public servant. I thought that, having been a student and teacher of History at Harvard, he would turn out to be peculiarly high-minded and serviceable in public office. On the contrary, he turned out to be a skilful boss, a compromiser on moral questions, and a promoter of suspicion and distrust between the United States and Great Britain. . . .[62]

Since Rhodes had never shared the Brahmin hostility to Lodge, which dated back to Lodge's support for James G. Blaine in the presidential election of 1884, such arguments made little headway with him. With Rhodes' backing, Lodge was elected, and Rhodes continued to be friends with both Eliot and the Senator. To a man of Rhodes' feelings, however, the entire affair must have been displeasing: he abhorred such naked displays of animosity.[63]

The shadows were beginning to gather around the historian. Failing health, the emotional distress arising from the passing of dear friends and relatives, financial anxiety, his involvement in personal feuds, his loss of faith in Europe—all these combined to change the happy optimist to a disillusioned old man.

NOTES

[1] Rhodes to Barrett Wendell, April 12, 1912. Rhodes Papers.

[2] Rhodes to Frederick C. Shattuck, M.D., Aug. 12, 1909; Charles H. Firth, Aug. 18, 1911, Jan. 13, 1912; Robert Grant, April 11, 1912; Barrett Wendell, June 28, 1914; Sir George Otto Trevelyan, July 21, 1914, Feb. 18, 1916. Rhodes Papers.

[3] Rhodes to Sir George Otto Trevelyan, March 6, 1911; Charles H. Firth, Aug. 18, 1911. Trevelyan to Rhodes, Nov. 4, 1909; J. B. Bury to Rhodes, March 23 [1908?]. Rhodes Papers. Rhodes to Mrs. C. H. Toy, April 28, 1912, in M. A. D. Howe, *Rhodes*, pp. 218–219.

[4] Rhodes to Barrett Wendell, April 12, 1912. Philander C. Knox, secretary of state, to Rhodes, May 4, 1909; Whitelaw Reid, U. S. ambassador to Great Britain, to Rhodes, May 20, 1909. Rhodes Papers.

[5] Rhodes to Mrs. C. H. Toy, July 31, 1909, in M. A. D. Howe, *Rhodes*, p. 187.

[6] Rhodes to Henry Cabot Lodge, April 13, 1912; Sir George Otto Trevelyan, July 21, 1914; Frederick C. Shattuck, M.D., Aug. 12, 1909. Rhodes Papers.

[7] Rhodes to Mrs. C. H. Toy, July 31, 1909, in M. A. D. Howe, *Rhodes*, pp. 187–188.

[8] Rhodes to Barrett Wendell, July 8, 1914. Rhodes Papers.

[9] Rhodes to William R. Thayer, July 14, 1912. Rhodes Papers.

[10] G. D. H. Cole and Raymond Postgate, *The British People, 1746–1946* (New York, 1947), p. 410.

[11] Rhodes to Barrett Wendell, Aug. 26, 1911. Rhodes Papers.

[12] Rhodes to Mrs. C. H. Toy, Sept. 3, 1911, in M. A. D. Howe, *Rhodes*, p. 208.

[13] Rhodes to William R. Thayer, July 14, 1912. Rhodes Papers.

[14] Rhodes to Barrett Wendell, June 28, 1914. Rhodes Papers.

[15] Rhodes to Mrs. C. H. Toy, Sept. 24, 1912, photostat fragment. Rhodes Papers.

[16] Rhodes to William R. Thayer, Feb. 24, 1911. Rhodes Papers.

[17] Rhodes to Mrs. C. H. Toy, March 31, 1912, in M. A. D. Howe, *Rhodes*, p. 211.

[18] Rhodes to Frederic Bancroft, Sept. 4, 1913, in *ibid.*, p. 240.

[19] Rhodes to William R. Thayer, July 14, 1912. Rhodes Papers.

[20] Barrett Wendell to Rhodes, May 19, 1911. Rhodes Papers.

[21] Rhodes to Barrett Wendell, June 5, 1911. Rhodes Papers.

[22] Rhodes to Barrett Wendell, June 7, 1911. Rhodes Papers.

[23] Barrett Wendell to Rhodes, June 28, 1911. Rhodes Papers.

[24] Rhodes to Barrett Wendell, Aug. 25, 1911. Rhodes Papers.

[25] Rhodes to Mrs. C. H. Toy, Sept. 3, 1911, in M. A. D. Howe, *Rhodes*, p. 208.

[26] Rhodes to Sir George Otto Trevelyan, July 21, 1914. Rhodes Papers.

[27] Charles K. Bolton, *Notebook, 1914–1917*, p. 23 (Oct. 5, 1914).

[28] Rhodes to Sir George Otto Trevelyan, July 21, 1914, Aug. 30, 1914,

and Sept. 13, 1914; Walter Hines Page to Rhodes, Aug. 11, 1914; James Bryce to Rhodes, Aug. 11, 1914. Rhodes Papers.

[29] Harvey Cushing, M.D., "James Ford Rhodes," in M. A. D. Howe (ed.) *Later Years of the Saturday Club*, p. 354.

[30] Mrs. Bertha H. Rhodes, interview; Rhodes Papers, XI, inside front and back covers.

[31] Rhodes to Woodrow Wilson, June 1, 1910. Letters to Rhodes from Henry S. Pritchett, Feb. 19, 1909; Frederic Bancroft, Feb. 14, 1910; Moorfield Storey, Jan. 23, 1910; Frederick C. Shattuck, M.D., April 13, 1910. Rhodes Papers.

[32] Rhodes to George A. Myers, Oct. 10, 1913, in John A. Garraty (ed.), "Correspondence," *Ohio Historical Quarterly*, LXIV (1955), 131.

[33] Rhodes to George A. Myers, Aug. 26, 1916, in *ibid.*, p. 158. Rhodes to John T. Morse, Jr., May 26, 1915. Morse Papers. Rhodes to Barrett Wendell, May 25, 1915; Sir George Otto Trevelyan to Rhodes, July 5, 1915. Rhodes Papers.

[34] Rhodes to Sir George Otto Trevelyan, April 20, 1916; Daniel P. Rhodes to Barrett Wendell, May 4, 1916. Rhodes Papers.

[35] William M. Sloane to Rhodes, Sept. 9, 1916. Rhodes Papers.

[36] Henry Lee Higginson to Rhodes, Jan. 2, 1909. Rhodes to Sir George Otto Trevelyan, Aug. 1, 1911. Rhodes Papers.

[37] Rhodes to Barrett Wendell, Aug. 30, 1907. Rhodes Papers.

[38] Rhodes to George A. Myers, Feb. 13, 1914, in John A. Garraty (ed.), "Correspondence," *Ohio Historical Quarterly*, LXIV (1955), 135.

[39] Rhodes to George A. Myers, May 2, 1916, in *ibid.*, p. 150.

[40] Rhodes to George A. Myers, March 23, 1916; April 19, 1916; May 2, 1916; and June 14, 1916, in *ibid.*, pp. 146–147, 150, 151. Myra S. Rhodes to James Ford Rhodes, Feb. 24, 1916, wrote that Robert's operation had proved successful and the patient was recovering. Rhodes Papers.

[41] Alpheus T. Mason, *Brandeis*, p. 185.

[42] *Commercial and Financial Chronicle* (New York), XCVI (1913), 1607.

[43] *Ibid.*, XCVIII (1914), 1978; Alpheus T. Mason, *Brandeis*, pp. 205–206, 211–213.

[44] Richard B. Morris (ed.), *Encyclopedia of American History*, p. 511.

[45] Rhodes to Sir George Otto Trevelyan, May 25, 1913. Rhodes Papers.

[46] Rhodes to George A. Myers, Sept. 17, 1913, in John A. Garraty (ed.), "Correspondence," *Ohio Historical Quarterly*, LXIV (1955), 131. Rhodes to Sir George Otto Trevelyan, Sept. 12, 1913. Rhodes Papers.

[47] Henry Lee Higginson to Rhodes, March 13, 1914. Rhodes Papers.

[48] J. W. Maguire Company, Boston, Mass., to Rhodes, Sept. 26, 1913. Rhodes Papers.

[49] Rhodes to Harvey Cushing, M.D., May 24, 1914, in M. A. D. Howe, *Rhodes*, p. 242.

[50] Letters to Rhodes from W. M. Baldwin, treasurer, Citizens Savings and Trust Company, Cleveland, Ohio, Aug. 20, 1915; Aug. 1, 1916; Samuel Rea, president, Pennsylvania Railroad Company, Jan. 29, 1915; S. W. Croxton, secretary, Tuscarawas Mineral Land Company, Cleveland, Ohio, May 17, 1916; May 24, 1916; and June 7, 1916. Rhodes Papers.

[51] S. W. Croxton to Rhodes, May 24, 1916. Rhodes Papers. Capitalization as in original.

[52] Alpheus T. Mason, *Brandeis*, pp. 203–204.

[53] Rhodes to Woodrow Wilson, Dec. 19, 1912, typewritten fragment, Rhodes Papers. Text of the note may be found in Ray Stannard Baker, *Woodrow Wilson: Life and Letters* (Garden City, N. Y., 1931), III, 450. A. Lawrence Lowell to Rhodes, Feb. 24, 1913. Rhodes Papers.

[54] Rhodes to John T. Morse, Jr., Aug. 21, 1916. Morse Papers.

[55] Rhodes to Frederick C. Shattuck, M.D., July 2, 1913. Rhodes Papers.

[56] For instance, Rhodes courteously declined to be drawn into the quarrel between Barrett Wendell and President Charles W. Eliot of Harvard, whom Wendell thought "a force almost purely destructive." Wendell to Rhodes, June 28, 1911; Rhodes to Wendell, Oct. 29, 1909; June 5, 1911. Rhodes Papers.

[57] William R. Thayer to Rhodes, March 24, 1915; Henry Cabot Lodge to Rhodes, April 3, 1915. Rhodes Papers.

[58] Mrs. Bertha H. Rhodes, interview.

[59] William R. Thayer to Rhodes, March 24, 1915; Henry Cabot Lodge to Rhodes, April 3, 1915, April 20, 1915. Rhodes Papers.

[60] Charles W. Eliot to Rhodes, March 31, 1915. Rhodes Papers.

[61] Charles W. Eliot to Rhodes, April 5, 1915. Rhodes Papers.

[62] Charles W. Eliot to Rhodes, April 7, 1915. Rhodes Papers.

[63] Mrs. Bertha H. Rhodes, interview.

Chapter 12

RHODES AND WORLD WAR I

Above all, however, it was World War I which leached out Rhodes' genial optimism. He had cherished the belief that the cause of civilization was safe in the hands of the Anglo-Saxon nations and of France; war was such obvious folly that none of the Great Powers would resort to it against each other. Now he wrote, "My blindness was thorough," and he was not happy that his eyes had been opened: "I wish they were not and I could think this is a holy war." [1] If the war lasted two years, he thought, "it will end our civilization." [2] To the patriotic pleas of Sir George Otto Trevelyan for American support of the Allied cause, Rhodes replied that he could see "no result that will compensate for the misery and distress in Europe . . ." [3] Small wonder, then, that he approached the Christmas season of 1914 with despondency: "Why anyone should make merry for the incoming of 1915 passes my comprehension," he wrote.[4] As the war went on, he lost faith in patriotism and despaired of mankind.[5]

One hope remained: American neutrality. He wrote so frequently to the President, expressing approval of the President's policy of neutrality that early in 1916 the secretary of war, Newton D. Baker, wrote to thank the historian for his "steady and reasoned . . . approval . . . of the President's course." [6] The old geniality of Rhodes appears rarely in the correspondence which he maintained with Wilson's critics. When that old unreconstructed Republican, George A. Myers, suggested that Wilson's successes were due more to luck than to judgment, Rhodes retorted sharply:

> The President is wearing out his brain and nervous system to keep out of this horrible war, and he should have the praise of every business man. He is enabling you to take in your daily shekels and, what is better, to keep the fine young men who resort to your shop from going to the front to be food for powder . . . You should thank Heaven morning and night that Mr. Wilson is in the White House instead of others that I might name.[7]

With George Otto Trevelyan, Rhodes was equally firm, if not quite so sharp. As early as November, 1914, Trevelyan expressed the wish that American sympathy with the Allies

> could be reflected in the action of the American Government. A State . . . so powerful, so independent, so admirably intelligent, might . . . step outside the conventions of diplomacy, and openly and sternly express its views on the murder of Belgium and the defiance of neutral rights. . . .

Rhodes was not moved.

> It is much better to my mind [he wrote] that instead of any formal statement regarding any incident of the war, which might militate against our perfect neutrality, we should send food and clothing and Christmas presents by the ship-load to the suffering Belgians and Frenchmen. . . .[8]

The Englishman became increasingly critical of American policy, and in the summer of 1915 blamed American neutrality for the plight in which Allies found themselves:

> It [the war] is very serious indeed. The strength of Germany, Hungary, Austria and Turkey—all lying together, all long ago organized for war, all absolutely disposed of, for one common purpose,—by the German General Staff, is enormous. There is, to my view, another aspect vastly important, and to me personally far more painful. The effect of the American Government having carefully abstained from any clear expression with regard to the rights and wrongs of the war is showing itself fatally in every direction. . . .

Rhodes affirmed his support of American policy in a lengthy reply:

> I am grieved beyond measure at [your] attitude . . . But I must not conceal from you the fact that I have some very intelligent friends who share the same opinion. I think however they are wrong, as they fail to see that it would be useless for our government to make such a protest as they desire without following it up by an ultimatum and probably a declaration of war against Germany.

Trevelyan should remember, Rhodes continued, that the United States, while strong in defensive wars, was poor in offensive; her entry into the war would prove little help to the Allies. Also, said he, America was no longer an Anglo-Saxon nation: there were about 22,500,000 foreign-born residents of the United States. And, he added, with an emphasis that was new to Rhodes: "Many of these . . . are citizens voting and paying taxes, supporters of our government, having a voice in it and a right to have a voice." He contrasted American behavior in this war with that of Great Britain in the Civil War, for to Britain the United States had extended "generous sympathy" and "an honest, yea a friendly neutrality." He concluded with emphatic support of the President: "We approve thoroughly of the President's action . . . he has been President of the whole American people while his bias is for the Allies." [9]

Trevelyan responded angrily that he would

> never again . . . recur to this question. But once for all I must put on record that in this struggle for freedom and humanity, and this deliberate effort to make the Anglo-Saxon go down before the German, it had been my ideal that Anglo-Saxons, . . . , all the world over, would be together as the Germans are together. That was my ideal; but it is the business of the Americans, and not ours. . . .[10]

Later, perhaps in an effort to mollify Trevelyan, Rhodes adduced yet another reason for American neutrality. From California he wrote to the Englishman that

> the President and the War Dept (sic) have confidential information that the Japanese are awaiting an opportunity to make a descent upon the Pacific coast and capture California, Oregon and Washington. It is not surprising that they should covet this fertile country. . . .[11]

Whether Trevelyan believed this tale or not is unknown, but another correspondent in whom Rhodes confided replied: "We don't—with all respect to the greatest American historian—believe a word about Japanese hostile intentions *in re* the Pacific Coast. . . . no more does Pres. [C. W.] Eliot." [12]

Had Trevelyan known Rhodes' opinions about English war guilt he would have been shocked, as were the few intimate friends to whom Rhodes revealed his unconventional views. Proper Boston, of course, was convinced that England was fighting that "holy war" for civilization in which Rhodes wished he could believe. In his view, however, England had herself to blame for many of her difficulties: she had isolated Germany diplomatically; had bound herself to Germany's enemy, France; and war was the inevitable outcome. England's "asinine" policy was all the more reprehensible because it had its origin in the playboy proclivities of Edward VII.[13]

In explaining his position to John T. Morse, Jr., Rhodes recalled a conversation he had had in 1906 with Mrs. John R. Green, widow of the famous English historian:

> She said Sir Edward Grey and King Edward VII are getting us into a lot of trouble by their foreign policy. They are wrong to tie to France and isolate Germany. . . . It will get us into difficulty with Germany. . . . I felt that she must be wrong but now I am struck with her foresight. . . .

Further, Morse should not forget that Edward's attitude toward France was influenced by "the attractions of the green rooms and 'girls' of Paris. Is it not terrible to reflect what we are all coming to due to such influences?" [14] Morse, indignant over such "very indelicate allusions," reiterated the popular argument that had England not joined with France and Russia she and the others would have been destroyed by Germany, one by one.[15]

Rhodes, wearied, and perhaps worried by the trend of the discussion, replied:

> you, Tom Perry and the majority of the people who side with the Allies are against me and I must refrain from speaking my opinion. If you read the *Atlantic*, as all good Bostonians are supposed to do, read the two citations in Lowes Dickinson's article in the August number. One from the London *Times* of Nov. 23, 1912, the other from the London *Standard* of Aug. 3, 1914. They express thoroughly my sentiments.[16]

The quotation from the *Times* began with a question, "Who, then, makes war?" and continued:

> The answer is to be found in the Chancellories of Europe, among the men who have too long played with human lives as pawns . . . , who have become so enmeshed in formulae and the jargon of diplomacy that they have ceased to be conscious of the poignant realities with which they trifle. And thus war will continue to be made, until the great masses . . . say the word which shall bring, not eternal peace, for that is impossible, but a determination that war should be fought only on a just and righteous and vital cause.

The quotation from the *Standard* was in a similar strain:

> Europe went to war in 1914 without passion or hatred or malice — . . . people set out to slaughter one another in a fatalistic way merely because the diplomatists had arranged things so . . . The Powers of Europe are at each other's throats in obedience to a barren diplomatic formula.[17]

There was no "holy war" then: the conflict grew out of the bankrupt diplomacy which characterized *all* the European powers. When Morse pointed out that Dickinson's article upheld the war as "just and righteous and vital" Rhodes retorted that he had read only the quotations. Then, in a querulous vein which would have astounded his English friends, he added:

> The strictures of Dickinson and the other Englishmen, who write in the modern style, so different from that in wh (sic) we were brought up, on the United States come from unadulterated envy, and it is not a high class envy. They envy us our broad acres, rich yield, our knack at making money, our desire for peace, our wealth and power, . . . the English do not like to see anyone making money except themselves.
>
> While this is all true my heart and soul is (sic) with England in this conflict and my grief at her probable downfall is heartfelt. Of course I expect the allies will win the war.[18]

In calmer mood, he summed up his position briefly:

> If I were an Englishman or a Frenchman, I would not be a pacifist. As an American . . . I am for peace and lament bitterly the struggle in Europe, but of course my hearty sympathy is with the Allies. I feel sure that Europe is going to the devil. I hope that the United States will be spared such a fate, but I am not certain of it. . . .[19]

But however much we might have hearty sympathy with the Allies, he wrote George A. Myers, "we are not called upon to send our best young men to battle for what England and France are fighting for." [20] This pacifist approach colored his public utterances, albeit in restrained fashion. He lectured to the Harvard chapter of Phi Beta Kappa in 1915 on Lincoln and the Civil War, but he carefully refrained from aligning himself with the popular Boston view that the World War was another war for liberty; indeed such implications as there were in the lecture tended to an anti-war position.[21] His book, *History of the Civil War*, which appeared in 1917, reasserted Rhodes' belief that "we are but poorly equipped for making war. The genius of the American Commonwealth lies in peace." [22]

So much seems clear. Rhodes thought World War I a real threat to civilization but he did not believe that the Allies were waging a war on behalf of civilization; he supported American neutrality, and resented English criticism of that policy. But in his correspondence with Englishmen Rhodes sounded other themes which appear inconsistent with such views: namely, that Germany was responsible for the war and that her conduct put her beyond the pale of humanity. In the first month of the war, while he was still in England, he wrote:

> The war grows more terrible . . . I never thought that a civilized nation would burn a city like Louvain. The German army there has put itself in the same class as the Communists of 1871 who tried to burn the Louvre. . . .[23]

On the eve of his departure for the United States in 1914 he expressed the view that the Kaiser was either insane or criminal and avowed his intention of demonstrating sympathy for the Allies when he reached home. After his arrival he reiterated his views and said he had not met a person whose sympathies were not with Britain and her allies.[24]

By 1915 Rhodes' aversion to the Kaiser had spread to German scholars. "I looked upon them as cosmopolitans in the world of learning," he explained to Trevelyan, "But I am disillusioned and the process has been painful. I would not have believed that Harnack, Eduard Meyer and Eucken would have set their hands to what they have written." [25] Before the war, Rhodes said, he had believed Harnack

> to be an honest man. But the brutality of his utterances at the commencement of the war has lost him the confidence of all of his American friends and admirers. Still I can hardly believe that he would allow the Emperor to use him to throw dust in our eyes; more than likely he has himself been deceived.[26]

In that summer of 1916 when Rhodes was privately expressing such bitter opinions of English motives he also wrote to Englishmen saying that England had developed the highest type of civilization, that it was shameful that the Kaiser should have endangered civilization by starting the war, and that he himself had been misled as to the character of the German people.[27]

How is one to explain such apparent contradictions? While solution of the problems of personality thus revealed may be beyond the competence of the historian, some factors may be suggested in partial explanation.

First, Rhodes lived by the code of the 19th century gentleman. No gentleman would find fault with a friend's country in time of war; rather he would conceive it his duty to express such sympathy and understanding as he might without compromising his views as to the role his own country should play. That the expression of such sympathy should lead him to denunciation of the Germans is understandable in view of the fact that Rhodes' associations with the English scholars were intimate, those with continental scholars, formal. By that same code of the gentleman Rhodes was constrained to be frank with other gentlemen of his own country: to them the truth must be told, unpalatable though it might be.

Second, Rhodes was an old man in ill health—and an old man who had just seen the foundations of his beliefs and hopes washed away, an old man who feared that even his own beloved land might be swept by the storm. From fear come erratic judgments, and regrets for such judgments. The correspondence of the period reflects such fluctuating moods.

Third, Rhodes may not have felt any contradictions. The war was not a holy war; England and Germany were both to blame; with clear conscience he could inveigh against Germany to his English friends, against England to American friends. The future of civilization rested, not in Europe, but in America, based on American neutrality. On that issue he made no compromises, uttered no equivocal judgments. Perhaps, then, there was an inner consistency in his views which belies the outward appearance.

Shortly, however, even the comfort of American neutrality was denied him; and like many Americans of his day, he was swept headlong by the flood of hate. He could "see no result but the downfall of our civilization," [28] but he held Germany responsible for it all:

> No doubt can exist [he wrote] that we were forced into the war, as, if the German government had not shown an asininity passing comprehension, it might have preserved the peace with us. Different from a good many good people here, I see with regret our country in the war, but really we had no option, as Germany forced the war upon us.
>
> It is difficult to understand the German state of mind. Why the Germans should have shown so great a lack of humanity and such brutality is almost incomprehensible. Tacitus wrote centuries ago that the Germans were barbarians, and apparently their contact with the French, English and Italians has given them only a veneer of civilization. Their assumption of superior knowledge and culture has been a sort of bluff that imposed upon me and perhaps on many others. . . .[29]

Soon he was writing that the cause of civilization depended upon the defeat of Germany; that the Allies were waging, not a war of conquest, but one of emancipation; that it was regrettable that the United States did not enter the war earlier.[30] At the behest of Walter Hines Page, the American Ambassador in London, he helped welcome the Archbishop of York to Boston when that dignitary made a propaganda visit.[31] He acknowledged to Trevelyan that his appraisal of the Germans had been incorrect:

> how the world has changed [since 1914] . . . due, more than all else, to the ambition and unscrupulousness of William II. The devotion of his people to him passes my comprehension; but indeed in many ways I have had to revise my opinion of the German people which I began forming before 1866 . . . the germ of cruelty must have been in them. . . .[32]

This was also the attitude adopted by Rhodes in discussing the war with Americans: Anglophiles could find no fault with him now. Count Bernstorff, the German ambassador, Rhodes thought a liar of such proportions that he would never get past the Pearly Gates.[33] He chided John Spencer Bassett, the eminent historian at Smith College, for what Rhodes conceived to be a comparison between Jefferson Davis and the Kaiser.[34] To the diners gathered to celebrate his 70th birthday he made one of his infrequent addresses, charging that

> Germany, whom ten or twenty years ago we regarded as an exponent of light and learning, has thrown down the gauntlet to the civilized world and by undreamed of tactics is endeavoring to accomplish her end. Her eventual defeat is certain . . . the man who defies the universal opinion of mankind cannot succeed . . . the right cause will triumph in the end. . . .[35]

When Henry Lee Higginson asked him to intercede with the Department of Justice on behalf of Dr. Carl Muck, German-born director of the Boston Symphony Orchestra, who was the victim of a press campaign demanding his imprisonment, Rhodes complied in a cautious letter reporting the views of others without committing himself. Wrote Rhodes: "Based on talks with many music lovers, all strongly pro-allies, I am decidedly of the opinion that the continuance of the symphony concerts and the retention of Dr. Muck are strongly desired." [36] Indeed, he was far from disturbed by Muck's later imprisonment; with an insensitivity unusual in him, he joked about it.

> It is a pity that Mr. Higginson should have been so disturbed over Muck [he wrote]. I heard last spring that he had been shot and then a lady who visited Chattanooga told my wife that he was interned near there and suffering from the heat (of this world) . . .[37]

And yet, such was the temper of the time, that even Rhodes' attitude seems the very stuff of moderation. Proper Boston's emotions had at last found acceptable outlet in almost pathological hatred for Germans. G. W. Chadwick, director of the New England Conservatory of Music, helped celebrate Rhodes' 70th birthday by voicing the hope that the historian would live long enough to "record the part of the United States against the greatest egotist, tyrant, robber and butcher of all time." [38] W. T. Sedgwick of the Department of Biology and Public Health at Massachusetts Institute of Technology thought the occasion called for denunciation of "the insane or, worse, the devilish Germans!" [39] Even the amiable Morse wrote to Rhodes:

> If I could take the place, for a brief period, of the Omnipotent Ruler, it wld (sic) be hard, after my abdication, to find even one German to be put in a Dime Museum as a curiosity. I would *extirpate the whole boche race.* What a pity that there is no chance of my having the opportunity.[40]

Rhodes, swept along by such a tide, nevertheless contrived to maintain a semblance of judgment. He drew a line between rulers and ruled in Germany, telling Morse that he shared his sentiments only so far as they related to the Kaiser and his advisors.[41] When peace was in sight, Rhodes took a stand against a "hard" peace, even though his political mentor, Henry Cabot Lodge, declared the peace should be dictated after Germany had been beaten to her knees on German soil.[42] Such a course, believed Rhodes, was neither wise nor expedient. As he told Lodge:

> I take exception to your statement that we must go to Berlin and there dictate the peace. It seems to me that as good terms as we ought to ask may be dictated on the Rhine. The Rhine will be a difficult river to cross and the passage will cost an enormous number of men. . . .[43]

To Trevelyan he was more explicit:

> the allies should not be actuated by revenge in the settlement. . . . doubt may well exist whether the Germans should be goaded to desperation. It is not so much what they deserve as what it will be policy to inflict upon them. . . .[44]

Even in relation to Russia Rhodes tried to keep a balance. The collapse of the Russian war effort in 1917 he thought tragic; it was not pleasant "to think that her keeping in the right course depends upon Kerensky, who has lost one kidney and has tuberculosis in the other." [45] Reports of the displacement of Kerensky did not disturb him:

> Kerensky appears to be a man of ability and force but it is a pity that he has not robust health [he wrote]. . . . It is a pity

> that so much should depend on one man. But I despair in no way should he be removed, although I do not think the harm of the defection of Russia can be exaggerated. But when the Germans get into Russia they will have to experience the hatred of the Slav which will count for much and perhaps they will not get the coveted depots of grain. . . .[46]

But the armistice at Brest-Litovsk was something else again. He refused to accept the "astounding news that Russia was going to back out of the conflict: this . . . I shall not believe until it is confirmed but her course has been a bitter disappointment."[47]

Rhodes may have been swept away by the Germanophobia of Proper Boston, but he held fast to his moorings in the tide of what Mrs. C. H. Toy called the "virulent" anti-Wilson sentiment in Boston.[48] Rhodes parted company politically with Wilson in the election of 1916 but he would not allow partisanship to dim his appreciation of the President's conduct of the war. Wilson, wrote Rhodes, was a man of such outstanding ability that only Theodore Roosevelt surpassed him; his conduct of the war had been excellent.[49]

As to some of the cabinet officers and some of the President's specific policies—that was another matter. Josephus Daniels, the secretary of the navy, incurred Rhodes' wrath for his order prohibiting the use of liquor in the Navy. When he had to concede that the Navy was well conducted he added testily, "no thanks to the Secretary, however."[50] He doubted the competency of William G. MacAdoo, secretary of the treasury, and of Newton D. Baker, secretary of war; and lamented that Wilson had not appointed businessmen to the cabinet, despite their willingness to serve.[51] The cabinet officer, he wrote, "is an autocrat and if you have a despot, it is desirable to have a wise one."[52] An appointment which met with his wholehearted approval was that of Herbert Hoover as food director.[53] Rhodes, the disciple of Spencer, could only condemn Wilson and Baker for their "mania for fixing prices" and even Hoover came under the ban for "too arbitrary" setting of the price of wheat, although Rhodes conceded that in his case there were extenuating circumstances:

> food is now so important, . . . , that the power of the government might be properly exercised in fixing a price for it, but great care should be taken not in any way to limit the production. . . . apart from food I believe that supply and demand should regulate the price of everything.[54]

Indeed, an aspect of the war which distressed Rhodes most was management of the economy in violation of the basic economic principles he had learned at college.[55] The war, he feared, had accelerated realization of the dire predictions of Malthus, which, as he saw them, simply reflected "the constant working of an economic law." [56] Despite all mistakes and weaknesses, however, he thought it better that war had come under a Democratic administration:

> It is on the whole a good thing that the war has come with a Democratic administration as it has had more influence with the Southern States and the Irish Catholics than a Republican Adm (sic) could have had; and the majority of the Republicans, outside of the German Americans, are all right anyway. . . .[57]

Rhodes' pessimism, deepened by the war, was colored strongly by his feelings about what the war was doing to his country. Not the assaults upon free speech, free press, and free political organization; not the danger to the American tradition represented by the hysteria directed against a significant section of the American people because of their ancestry; not the attacks upon academic freedom in the name of patriotism—these hardly bothered him, to judge from the available evidence. What did distress him were the trends in political and economic affairs which to him portended the coming of socialism, trends centered in the domestic policies of the Wilson administration.

After 1913, for example, United States Senators were directly elected by the voters, a process which in Rhodes' view, provided a poorer grade of Senator.[58] Also, there was such popular pressure for women's suffrage that the Republican candidate in 1916, Charles Evans Hughes, endorsed it—a serious error on Hughes' part, thought Rhodes. Women, he believed, would help make easier passage of prohibition, and in matters of finance and economics the judgment of women was inferior to that of men.[59]

More to the point, early in 1915 the administration proposed that the government take over ownership of alien shipping in American harbors, a proposal which Henry Cabot Lodge instantly denounced as socialistic. Rhodes applauded Lodge's attitude, and he praised the opposition of Senator John W. Weeks to the measure.[60] In view of the war, however, he continued to support Wilson, whose policy of neutrality he likened to that of Washington, and whose acceptance of William Jennings Bryan's resignation as secretary of state he endorsed.[61]

Hughes, on the other hand, was unsound on votes for women; was "reactionary" on the tariff; and was belaboring Wilson's Mexican policy for purely partisan purposes while neglecting the dangerous issues arising from the European war.[62] Rhodes' sense of propriety, too, was offended: "Mr. Hughes made a mistake in accepting the Republican nomination. He should have remained on the Supreme Bench." [63] It was "a dangerous precedent going to the Supreme Bench for a candidate." [64] And while he was persuaded of Hughes' own patriotism he was disturbed by the support given Hughes by German-American organizations.[65]

Nevertheless, Rhodes' heart still belonged to the Grand Old Party. Hughes, he thought, might make a good President, like Rutherford B. Hayes. And, he added wistfully, "I should indeed like to get back into the Republican Party, but I am not sure whether I shall not be prevented from returning to the fold by its unfairness and partisanship." [66]

The Wilson Administration soon made easy the return to the fold. In response to demands from the operating railroad brotherhoods for an eight-hour day, Congress on Sept. 3, 1916, passed the Adamson act. To Rhodes, the issue was now clear: America must ignobly yield to the tyranny of organized labor or fight for its traditional freedom under the banner of the Republican party:

> a real issue has projected itself into our political canvass [he wrote to Trevelyan]. President Wilson and Congress have made an ignoble surrender to the four Brotherhoods, who with astuteness had disguised their demands for an advance in wages as a desire for a labor day of eight hours. Governor Hughes at once attacked the action of the President and Congress and made a virtual attack upon the tyrannical hold-up by organized labor. . . .[67]

Agreeing with editorial comment branding the act as a disgraceful surrender to labor, Rhodes wrote to Bryce that in denouncing the measure

> Mr. Hughes showed wonderful courage and . . . , political character of a high order. It had to be tested whether organized labor was to rule, and perhaps now is as good a time as any to have it out at the polls.[68]

To George A. Myers he announced his return to the Republican party—with some reservations:

> I am for Hughes, but I am sorry he is putting the protection argument so to the fore. . . . the Democratic tariff bill is on the whole the best revenue bill that has passed since the Civil War and the imposition of the income tax (although it hits me harshly) progress in the right direction. Legislation shd (sic) be

for the greatest good of the greatest number. To my mind the President let his foot slip in siding with the Brotherhoods. I do not suspect his motive, and he is probably more long-headed than I am, but I do not like the idea of the President and Congress of the great United States surrendering to a threat. Mr. Hughes showed great courage in attacking the Adamson Act and the action of the President right on the eve of the Maine election, and Mr. Roosevelt spoke solid truth at Wilkesbarre. I cannot longer stay out of a party led by such courageous men, although as evidence of my not full conversion, I must write it with small letters, g.o.p.

So impressed was Rhodes with Hughes' stand that he was willing to overlook all other questions:

> I do not quite understand why the Germans and the Catholics [are] for Hughes. We certainly do not want a pro-German president, but since Mr. Hughes came out so courageously in Maine, I am ready to trust him in every respect.[69]

The election results left Rhodes a saddened man: the Republican campaign, in his view, had been a series of blunders; the country was now skidding down the slippery slide of socialism. He poured out his feelings to Myers, complaining that the Republicans had made a great mistake in taking Hughes off the bench and that Hughes had compounded the error by "stepping down from his dignified place into the arena of politics"; that the campaigning, especially in California, had been badly managed and that Hughes' conduct in that state (where he had miffed Hiram Johnson, one of the Republican powers) was that of an infant.

Wilson, on the contrary, had proved to be "a very great man, abler than Hughes, stronger than his party, and received his reward for keeping the country out of the war." Rhodes consoled himself with the reflection that "the two great personalities politically are Roosevelt and Wilson, both men of education, culture and ability. It is a great country to have two such men at the head of the two great parties!" What was a man to do under such circumstances?

> I see nothing for us to do but to be at the back of the President in all foreign matters and to criticize him fully in matters domestic. His surrender to the labor unions was fraught with mischief, but it is idle now to say how the thing will turn out; it seems to me, however, that the President inclines to Socialism, and that his work will tend in that direction. The appointments of [Louis] Brandeis and [John H.] Clarke [to the Supreme

Court] would seem an indication, and it is a cruel thought that our sacred Supreme Bench will be filled with men who will incline to the labor unions and Socialism. . . .[70]

To Trevelyan he expressed the same foreboding:

> Anatole France said that after the present war there would be either Socialism or Chaos. It may be that the President believes this and desires the United States to become gradually under the form of law Socialistic. This I thought when I voted for Hughes. . . .[71]

Neither at home nor abroad was there balm for an old man's despair; the genial Rhodes who had expatiated on the virtues of "constructive optimism" had become a Rhodes who wrote sadly: "I don't know what is going to happen to the world. The outlook is certainly dreary." [72]

This pessimistic mood was manifested in a withdrawal from many of the activities in which he had once found delight and in a growing querulousness. He sought to be relieved from his light responsibilities as senior vice-president of the Massachusetts Historical Society; and, even more striking, he resigned from active membership in some of his clubs. "When one fails to have the flow of gastric juice inspired by American food and French wine it is time to step out," he explained to Barrett Wendell.[73] He resented the invasion of Mount Desert island by the plebeians of Maine:

> For a long while, we kept motor-cars out . . . , but now they are here and every Saturday and Sunday the butcher, the baker and candlestick maker of Bar Harbor and Bangor invade our quiet precincts with their horrid machines. . . .[74]

There were reviewers, too, who proved just as vexing as the autoists from Bangor. His *Lectures on the American Civil War*, which appeared in 1913, received the usual accolades, but some reviewers expressed reservations.[75] *The Nation*, for example, thought that while the book might prove useful for English readers American readers would find it disappointing because there was nothing new in it. The reviewer also noted that Rhodes' style was not adapted for "limited space; and its effectiveness is not enhanced by a punctuation which at times is extraordinary." [76]

Rhodes complained to Paul Elmer More, the editor, that the reviewer had sneered at his attitude toward England and made baseless reflections upon his punctuation. More replied that he had

> hardly appreciated the fact that there was a covert sneer in what we said about your attitude towards England. I certainly should not feel personally like sneering at any work of yours, nor should I wish any of my reviewers to do so. Your letter was evidently not meant for publication; but if you care to have that part of it printed which corrects our misstatement in regard to your punctuation, I should of course be quite ready to do this.[77]

Rhodes' answer was almost childish: he would not argue about punctuation; his letter was not meant for publication; he had not wanted to give the lectures at Oxford; he had done so only under pressure from his own friends at Oxford and from the American Ambassador in London; he had spent six months preparing the lectures and another six preparing them for publication. In view of all this,

> when I saw your notice I was hurt and it seemed almost spiteful. As the Nation had been so appreciative of all of my work since 1892 it seemed to me that if it could not say a good word for what at all events was honest and pains-taking labor on my part it ought to have kept silence.[78]

Rhodes found cause for complaint, too, in the treatment given the *Lectures* by the *American Historical Review*. E. L. C. Morse, the reviewer, credited Rhodes with impartiality but pointed out that Rhodes neglected both recent contributions to the study of the Civil War and the significance of economic factors in the *antebellum* period.[79] Rhodes protested to J. Franklin Jameson, editor of the *Review*, that these observations were unjust, but Jameson was not impressed:

> I am deeply sorry [he wrote to Rhodes] that the review of your book is not such as to meet in a better manner your desires and your belief as to what is just. . . . The review . . . seems to me more nearly such as might gratify an author . . . it often happens that reviews which seemed harsh or unamiable to the author . . . seem to me much less so, or not at all, and that I am prone to believe that the general public sees them more as I do. . . .[80]

Rhodes, however, apparently felt himself ill-used. When William R. Thayer suggested that he submit for publication his address to the Harvard chapter of Phi Beta Kappa in 1915 he replied that such a project would be futile: "There is almost no chance that any magazine would want the address as there is not at present any wordly (sic) demand for my literary wares." [81]

In fact, there was considerable demand for his wares, although it may well be that Rhodes, feeling out of touch with so many of his fellows on matters of war and domestic policy, was reluctant to commit himself to publication which might entail controversy or which might lead to exploitation of his name for ends of which he did not approve. Finley Peter Dunne of *Collier's*, for example, importuned him during 1916 and 1917 to contribute articles to bolster the morale of Americans. In Dunne's view,

> Our people are hopelessly bewildered. . . . They don't know what to expect. You might do much to raise their spirits by picturing what happened after our Civil War, as a guide to what is likely to occur after this war.
>
> I speak not as an editor but as despondent citizen when I say that something from your sane and tolerant reflections ought to be given to the public at this moment, . . .[82]

On scholarly levels, W. P. Trent asked Rhodes to write a chapter on Harriet Beecher Stowe, Abraham Lincoln and American publicists during the period 1850–1865 for the *Cambridge History of English Literature;* and Allen Johnson requested him to prepare the volume on the Lincoln Administration for the *Chronicles of America* series.[83] Harvard once again called for his services, offering him the Godkin lectureship in 1918 on "Essentials of Free Government and the Duties of the Citizen."[84]

Certainly, the awarding to him in 1917 of the Pulitzer Prize demonstrated that his work was far from lacking appreciation. But even in expressing gratitude for the honor Rhodes displayed an attitude which the fastidious Barrett Wendell must have found disconcerting in his old friend. Wendell had been one of the judges who made the award, based on Rhodes' *History of the Civil War*, and in sending him thanks Rhodes commented:

> As a matter of fact the money as well as the honor is grateful for (as Mr. Brett and I delude ourselves) owing to the war the History of the Civil War did not sell as well as we expected. Consequently I shall in my mind put this sum [$2000.00] to the credit of that volume. What with investments in Liberty Bonds and the Red Cross, I find my bank a/c (sic) depleted and I will not sell Liberty bonds.[85]

Even more bluntly he wrote to John T. Morse, Jr., that with the exception of university degrees he was not interested in honors, since they would not survive the war; rather would he have the money.[86]

Rhodes' pessimism, however, beclouded for him the reality of his continued appeal to the American public, both lay and professional. To be sure, the *Historical Essays* and the *Lectures on the Civil War* were not publishers' delights, but the other works enjoyed steady sale. The *History*, for example, had been on the market for almost a decade, and yet in the five years, 1913–1917 inclusive, a total of 8676 of the various volumes were sold; and in its first year *History of the Civil War* sold 1934 copies. Total royalties for that period amounted to $5,483.88—no small sum considering the age of the *History* and the limited appeal of the book on the Civil War.[87]

On that work, too, he received praise which might have flattered even Rhodes, accustomed though he was to adulation. The *American Historical Review* and the *American Political Science Review* warmly recommended it.[88] Moorfield Storey read it "with great interest and admiration, but not with pleasure. It carried me back so completely to the days that we lived through . . . that it opened old wounds afresh." [89] Justice Oliver Wendell Holmes "became so absorbed that I looked at nothing else . . . This in spite of the fact that in general I hate to read about those times. . . . [It is] the work of an artist." [90] Barrett Wendell thought the book, "The best example of classical thinking since Thucydides. His [Rhodes'] style is not perfect but in grasp of his subject and choice of material he has a touch of genius." [91]

In addition to such open expression of esteem there was the more subtle tribute paid Rhodes by men like George A. Myers, who believed that were the historian to change his evaluation of the Negro a great advance would be made in racial understanding. Myers set out to convert Rhodes by sending him a copy of an article by Kelly Miller, a conservative Negro leader and professor at Howard University.

The article was a plea for admitting the Negro to full political rights on the grounds that the Negro could not be "effectually ignored as a governmental factor by any section . . . without accumulating serious peril, not only for that section but for the nation at large." In his discussion Miller challenged the claim of Negro racial inferiority, pointed out that Anglo-Saxon peoples never thought colored peoples capable of self-government, and asserted that Negro political ability had been shown in Haiti, Liberia and in the South during Reconstruction. The Reconstruction governments, wrote Miller, were genuinely democratic, as demonstrated by their constitutions and their establishment of free public education for the first time in Southern states.[92]

Rhodes was not impressed. Miller's style he liked, but

> For the matter, I cannot say so much. Like all controversialists he sees his side of the question so thoroughly that he cannot see the other side. At times I noted a lack of candour and specious reasoning. I shall not go into these matters in detail, for you or he might join issue with me and Kelly Miller is too earnest and thorough a controversialist for me to desire to break lances with him.[93]

Neither was Myers impressed with Rhodes' position. He quoted Rhodes on the narrowness of the controversialist back to him and commented:

> if I was (sic) inclined to be a critic I might with equal grace apply [it] to some portions of your recital of the history of the Reconstruction period so far as the Negro is concerned . . .[94]

But Myers was not discouraged. Some years later he sent Rhodes a copy of a new book by John R. Lynch, a Negro Republican who had played an active part in the Reconstruction politics of Mississippi.[95] The book, basically an autobiography, presented considerable data on Reconstruction in that state which raised serious questions about the validity of some of Rhodes' generalizations on that era. Rhodes replied that he was too busy to read the work carefully, adding, "I never expect to tackle the subject of Reconstruction again."[96]

Myers was not to be put off, however. He proposed that Rhodes revise his work so as to give full credit to the Negro troops who helped save the Union.

> Such a statement from you [he wrote] would establish the negroes (sic) place in history beyond the peradventure of a doubt and help to dissipate this damnable prejudice in the future, that we as a people have to contend with now. You cannot understand this because you have not been discriminated against. . . .[97]

Rhodes cited his long footnote on page 333 of Volume IV of the *History* to show that he had recognized the worth and valor of the Negro soldiers, but Myers thought this insufficient:

> What I . . . am still after, is, . . . to have you give them full credit for their valor and bravery, . . . It is not the amount of what is said, but who says it that counts. Negro historians

> might write until their hands palsied and . . . would not be given the credence of one chapter in your history. . . . it makes a difference in who says it. . . .[98]

Rhodes showed little interest, and Myers then returned to the subject of Reconstruction: Rhodes and Lynch should meet and discuss their different approaches to that era, he suggested. Again Rhodes was cold:

> I note carefully what you say about Mr. Lynch for whose character and ability I have profound respect and admiration. It does not surprise me that he thinks I am inaccurate, unjust and unfair for he was a severely partisan actor at the time while I, an earnest seeker after truth, am trying to hold a judicial balance and to tell the story without fear, favor or prejudice. Please do not make any arrangement for me to see Mr. Lynch before next autumn or winter . . . Why does not Mr. Lynch write a magazine article and show up mistakes and inaccuracies and injustice?[99]

So far as the evidence shows, Rhodes never did meet Lynch. Indeed, the only influential Negro with whom Rhodes had any contact was Booker T. Washington, whom he met while the Negro was lecturing in Boston. The only notes he kept of that occasion were anecdotes told about his own people by Washington—the kind of thing Washington would tell a white audience from whom he was soliciting funds.[100]

Rhodes, then, reflected in his historical approach to problems involving Negroes the racial feeling which had been his since childhood. In this, of course, Rhodes was merely human—and yet, had he been less rigid in this attitude, as well as in others, he might not have felt so utterly lost in the new America which emerged from the war.

NOTES

[1] Rhodes to William R. Thayer, Oct. 13, 1917; Robert Grant, undated but apparently written in 1916. Rhodes Papers.

[2] Rhodes to Robert Grant, Oct. 20, 1914. Rhodes Papers.

[3] Rhodes to Sir George Otto Trevelyan, Nov. 30, 1914. Rhodes Papers.

[4] Rhodes to John T. Morse, Jr., Dec. 20, 1914. Morse Papers.

[5] Rhodes to Mrs. C. H. Toy, April 16, 1916, in M. A. D. Howe, *Rhodes*, p. 260.

[6] Newton D. Baker to Rhodes, March 14, 1916; Woodrow Wilson to Rhodes, April 26, 1915; May 12, 1915; Oct. 16, 1915; Nov. 9, 1915; Joseph P. Tumulty to Rhodes, July 27, 1915. Rhodes Papers.

[7] Rhodes to George A. Myers, Sept. 20, 1915, in M. A. D. Howe, *Rhodes*, p. 254.

[8] Sir George Otto Trevelyan to Rhodes, Nov. 11, 1914; Rhodes to Trevelyan, Nov. 30, 1914. Rhodes Papers.

[9] Sir George Otto Trevelyan to Rhodes, July 5, 1915; Rhodes to Trevelyan, July 25, 1915. Rhodes Papers.

[10] Sir George Otto Trevelyan to Rhodes, undated. Rhodes Papers.

[11] Rhodes to Sir George Otto Trevelyan, April 20, 1916. Rhodes Papers.

[12] Mrs. C. H. Toy to Rhodes, May 4, 1916. Rhodes Papers.

[13] Rhodes to Thomas S. Perry, quoted in letter from Perry to Rhodes, July 15, 1916. Rhodes Papers.

[14] Rhodes to John T. Morse, Jr., June 11, 1916. Morse Papers.

[15] John T. Morse, Jr., to Rhodes, July 15, 1916. Rhodes Papers.

[16] Rhodes to John T. Morse, Jr., Aug. 12, 1916. Morse Papers. The reference is to G. Lowes Dickinson, "Democratic Control of Foreign Policy," *Atlantic Monthly*, CXVIII (1916), 145–152. At the time, Rhodes was also engaged in a controversy with Thomas S. Perry on this issue. Perry was particularly annoyed with Rhodes' "boast that you are one of the judicious minority, but . . . a good deal depends on what the minority thinks. There is a minority holding the view that the earth is flat. . . . You see, being in a minority is not always a convincing proof that one is right. Even the minority, if it is really judicious, will grant this." Perry to Rhodes, July 6, 1916. See also his letters to Rhodes, June 11, 1916, and July 1, 1916. Rhodes Papers.

[17] In G. Lowes Dickinson, "Democratic Control of Foreign Policy," *Atlantic Monthly*, CXVIII (1916), 145.

[18] Rhodes to John T. Morse, Jr., Aug. 21, 1916. Morse Papers.

[19] Rhodes to William R. Thayer, Sept. 7, 1916, in M. A. D. Howe, *Rhodes*, p. 268.

[20] Rhodes to George A. Myers, Aug. 12, 1915, in M. A. D. Howe, *Rhodes*, p. 254.

[21] "Lincoln in Some Phases of the Civil War," *Harvard Graduates' Magazine*, XXIV (1915), 5, 18.

[22] *History of the Civil War, 1861–1865* (New York, 1917), p. 364.

[23] Rhodes to Sir George Otto Trevelyan, Aug. 30, 1914. Rhodes Papers.

[24] Rhodes to Sir George Otto Trevelyan, Sept. 13, 1914; Nov. 2, 1914. Rhodes Papers.

[25] Rhodes to Sir George Otto Trevelyan, April 18, 1915. Adolf von Harnack was a church historian and theologian; Eduard Meyer an authority on ancient history; Rudolf C. Eucken a philosopher. Rhodes apparently objected to their justification of Germany's course. He himself received such a message from Meyer. The German nation was united behind the government, wrote Meyer, and "we feel sure that we shall save the cause of civilization and humanity." The letter continued: "It is England which has raised this war and has done everything to destroy the civilization of Europe and to deliver it to the Muscovite barbarians. But we in alliance with the great Austro-Hungarian monarchy shall save the cause of freedom and of human development." He asked Rhodes not to believe atrocity tales directed against the Germans: "Our enemies have given to the war . . . a character of brutality and cruelty which was foreign to the wars of the 19th century, and we are forced to defend ourselves . . . But our army is immensely superior to theirs in humanity and in moral piety; for it is the nation in arms, and in the breast of every one of our soldiers lives a consciousness of the ideals for which they are fighting, and a high moral feeling, which would never sink to the low standard of our enemies." Meyer to Rhodes, Sept. 23 [?]. Rhodes Papers. Meyer's letter is in English.

[26] Rhodes to Sir George Otto Trevelyan, Aug. 29, 1915. Rhodes Papers.

[27] Rhodes to Sir George Otto Trevelyan, Aug. 20, 1916; Sept. 30, 1916. Rhodes Papers. Rhodes to James Bryce, Sept. 28, 1916, in M. A. D. Howe, *Rhodes*, p. 269.

[28] Rhodes to Worthington C. Ford, Aug. 1, 1917, photostat fragment. Rhodes Papers.

[29] Rhodes to George A. Myers, April 17, 1917, in M. A. D. Howe, *Rhodes*, pp. 276–277.

[30] Rhodes to Charles H. Firth, July 31, 1917; Sir George Otto Trevelyan, March 31, 1918. G. W. Prothero to Rhodes, July 18, 1917. Rhodes Papers.

[31] Walter Hines Page to Rhodes, Jan. 16, 1918. Rhodes to Sir George Otto Trevelyan, March 13, 1918. Rhodes Papers.

[32] Rhodes to Sir George Otto Trevelyan, Aug. 1, 1918. Rhodes Papers.

[33] Charles K. Bolton, *Notebook, 1914–1917*, p. 292 (Feb. 5, 1917).

[34] John S. Bassett to Rhodes, June 21, 1918. Rhodes Papers.

[35] Rhodes quoted this part of his address in letter to Sir George Otto Trevelyan, April 28, 1918. Rhodes Papers.

[36] Pencilled draft of letter to Department of Justice on letter to Rhodes from Henry Lee Higginson, Nov. 20, 1917. Rhodes Papers.

[37] Rhodes to John T. Morse, Jr., Aug. 29, 1918. Rhodes Papers.

[38] G. W. Chadwick to Rhodes, May 1, 1918. Rhodes Papers.

[39] W. T. Sedgwick to Rhodes, May 1, 1918. Rhodes Papers.

[40] John T. Morse, Jr., to Rhodes, Aug. 25, 1918. Rhodes Papers. Underlining in original.

[41] Rhodes to John T. Morse, Jr., Aug. 29, 1918. Morse Papers.

[42] Henry Cabot Lodge to Rhodes, Sept. 11, 1918. Rhodes Papers.

[43] Rhodes to Henry Cabot Lodge, Sept. 7, 1918, in M. A. D. Howe, *Rhodes*, p. 300.

[44] Rhodes to Sir George Otto Trevelyan, Oct. 31, 1918. Rhodes Papers.

[45] Rhodes to Mrs. C. H. Toy, Aug. 10, 1917, in M. A. D. Howe, *Rhodes*, p. 284.

[46] Rhodes to Sir George Otto Trevelyan, Aug. 16, 1917. Rhodes Papers.

[47] Rhodes to Sir George Otto Trevelyan, Nov. 2, 1917. Rhodes Papers.

[48] Mrs. C. H. Toy to Mrs. James Ford Rhodes, June 22, 1918. Rhodes Papers. John T. Morse, Jr., also commented on this feeling in a letter to Rhodes, Aug. 25, 1918. Rhodes Papers.

[49] Rhodes to Mrs. C. H. Toy, July 9, 1917; Sir George Otto Trevelyan, Jan. 31, 1918. Rhodes Papers.

[50] Rhodes to Charles H. Firth, July 31, 1917. Rhodes Papers. Rhodes to Sir George Otto Trevelyan, Jan. 31, 1918, March 13, 1918, in M. A. D. Howe, *Rhodes*, pp. 287, 297.

[51] Rhodes to Sir George Otto Trevelyan, May 22, 1917, Aug. 16, 1917. Rhodes Papers. Rhodes to Mrs. C. H. Toy, Aug. 10, 1917, in M. A. D. Howe, *Rhodes*, pp. 283–284. Rhodes to George A. Myers, Aug. 26, 1916, in John A. Garraty (ed.), "Correspondence," *Ohio Historical Quarterly*, LXIV (1955), 159.

[52] Rhodes to Charles H. Firth, July 31, 1917; Sir George Otto Trevelyan, Aug. 16, 1917. Rhodes Papers.

[53] Rhodes to Sir George Otto Trevelyan, March 13, 1918. Rhodes Papers.

[54] Rhodes to Sir George Otto Trevelyan, Jan. 31, 1918. Rhodes Papers.

[55] Rhodes to Sir George Otto Trevelyan, March 13, 1918. Rhodes Papers.

[56] Rhodes to Sir George Otto Trevelyan, May 22, 1917. Rhodes Papers.

[57] Rhodes to Sir George Otto Trevelyan, Sept. 18, 1917. Rhodes Papers.

[58] Rhodes to Sir George Otto Trevelyan, Aug. 20, 1916. Rhodes Papers.

[59] Rhodes to James Bryce, Sept. 28, 1916, in M. A. D. Howe, *Rhodes*, p. 271.

[60] Letters to Rhodes from Henry Cabot Lodge, Jan. 25, 1915; John W. Weeks, Jan. 25, 1915; Theodore Burton, Jan. 28, 1915; Elihu Root, Feb. 5, 1915; Andrew J. Peters, Jan. 27, 1915. Rhodes Papers.

[61] Rhodes to Sir George Otto Trevelyan, June 17, 1915. Rhodes Papers. Rhodes to John T. Morse, Jr., Aug. 12, 1916. Morse Papers. Rhodes to George A. Myers, Jan. 6, 1916, in M. A. D. Howe, *Rhodes*, p. 257.

[62] Rhodes to George A. Myers, Aug. 3, 1916, in John A. Garraty (ed.), "Correspondence," *Ohio Historical Quarterly*, LXIV (1955), 153–154.

[63] Rhodes to Sir George Otto Trevelyan, Aug. 20, 1916. Rhodes Papers.

[64] Rhodes to George A. Myers, June 11, 1916, in M. A. D. Howe, *Rhodes*, pp. 263–264.

[65] Rhodes to George A. Myers, Aug. 3, 1916, in John A. Garraty (ed.), "Correspondence," *Ohio Historical Quarterly*, LXIV (1955), 154.

[66] *Ibid.*, pp. 154–155.

[67] Rhodes to Sir George Otto Trevelyan, Sept. 30, 1916. Rhodes Papers.

[68] Rhodes to James Bryce, Sept. 28, 1916, in M. A. D. Howe, *Rhodes*, p. 271.

[69] Rhodes to George A. Myers, Oct. 18, 1916, in John A. Garraty (ed.), "Correspondence," *Ohio Historical Quarterly*, LXIV (1955), 161–162. Myers replied with mellow humor, Oct. 26, 1916: "I am exceedingly glad to learn that you are again 'on the Lord's side.' . . . Like our 'Father's Mansion' in the skies, there is always room in the Grand Old Party for all and the vilest sinner is ever welcome to return." Rhodes Papers.

[70] Rhodes to George A. Myers, Nov. 20, 1916, in M. A. D. Howe, *Rhodes*, pp. 275–276.

[71] Rhodes to Sir George Otto Trevelyan, Nov. 19, 1916, in M. A. D. Howe, *Rhodes*, p. 274. See also Rhodes to Trevelyan, Jan. 3, 1917. Rhodes Papers.

[72] Rhodes to George A. Myers, Nov. 20, 1916, in John A. Garraty (ed.), "Correspondence," *Ohio Historical Quarterly*, LXIV (1955), 166.

[73] Rhodes to William R. Thayer, Sept. 30, 1917; Barrett Wendell, June 22, 1918. Holden Abbott to Rhodes, March 2, 1917, April 9, 1917. Rhodes Papers.

[74] Rhodes to John T. Morse, Jr., Aug. 12, 1916, in M. A. D. Howe, *Rhodes*, p. 265.

[75] Letters to Rhodes from William R. Thayer, March 17, 1913; Lawrence F. Abbott, editor, *The Outlook*, June 11, 1913; Charles H. Firth, March 5, 1913; Mrs. John R. Green, March 11, 1913. Rhodes Papers.

[76] XCVI (1913), 446–447.

[77] Paul Elmer More to Rhodes, June 9, 1913. Rhodes Papers.

[78] Rhodes to Paul Elmer More, pencilled draft, undated. Rhodes Papers. The formal draft was apparently dated June 11, 1913, for More acknowledged receipt of such a letter, June 16, 1913. Rhodes Papers.

[79] XVIII (1912–1913), 844–845.

[80] J. Franklin Jameson to Rhodes, July 18, 1913. Rhodes Papers.

[81] Rhodes to William R. Thayer, Feb. 6, 1915. Rhodes Papers. In fact, Rhodes' address was published: "Lincoln in Some Phases of the Civil War," *Harvard Graduates' Magazine*, XXIV (1915), 1–19.

[82] Finley Peter Dunne to Rhodes, Dec. 20, 1917. Also Dunne to Rhodes, Jan. 18, 1916. Rhodes Papers.

[83] W. P. Trent to Rhodes, Feb. 13, 1914; Allen Johnson to Rhodes, June 24, 1916. Rhodes Papers.

[84] A. Lawrence Lowell to Rhodes, Dec. 14, 1917. Rhodes Papers.

[85] Rhodes to Barrett Wendell, June 6, 1918. Rhodes Papers.

[86] Rhodes to John T. Morse, Jr., Aug. 29, 1918. Morse Papers.

[87] Annual statements of royalty accounts, Macmillan Company, to Rhodes, for fiscal years ending April 30 of the years 1914–1918 inclusive. Rhodes Papers.

[88] *American Historical Review*, XXIV (1919), 520–521; *American Political Science Review*, XII (1918), 158.

[89] Moorfield Storey to Rhodes, June 10, 1918. Rhodes Papers.

[90] Oliver Wendell Holmes, Jr., to Mrs. Mark Hanna, March 31, 1919. Rhodes Papers.

[91] Quoted in Charles K. Bolton, *Notebook, 1917–1920*, p. 189 (Dec. 28, 1918).

[92] "The American Negro as a Political Factor," *Nineteenth Century and After*, LXVIII (1910), 286–291.

[93] Rhodes to George A. Myers, Oct. 7, 1910, in John A. Garraty (ed.), "Correspondence," *Ohio Historical Quarterly*, LXIV (1955), 16–17.

[94] George A. Myers to Rhodes, Oct. 10, 1910. Rhodes Papers.

[95] John R. Lynch, *The Facts of Reconstruction* (New York, 1914).

[96] Rhodes to George A. Myers, March 29, 1914, in John A. Garraty (ed.), "Correspondence," *Ohio Historical Quarterly*, LXIV (1955), 135–136.

[97] George A. Myers to Rhodes, Sept. 23, 1915. Rhodes Papers.

[98] George A. Myers to Rhodes, Oct. 14, 1915. Rhodes Papers.

[99] Rhodes to George A. Myers, April 19, 1916, in John A. Garraty (ed.), "Correspondence," *Ohio Historical Quarterly*, LXIV (1955), 148. Lynch wrote two such articles: "Some Historical Errors of James Ford Rhodes" and "More About the Historical Errors of James Ford Rhodes," *Journal of Negro History*, II (1917), 345–368; III (1918), 139–157.

[100] Rhodes Papers, X, aW. The reference is to a visit to Boston by Washington, Nov. 16, 1895.

Chapter 13

AN ALIEN IN HIS OWN LAND

POST-WAR AMERICA was shockingly new to men of Rhodes' generation. The age which had borne and shaped them had been one permeated with Victorian notions of status and gentility. Workers, Negroes, foreign-born, women—each of these subordinate groups knew and generally accepted its assigned status in society, just as the governing classes of the wealthy, the cultured, the gentlemen, knew and accepted their places. It was, socially, an orderly society, in which scholarship often tended to identify the search for truth with the accepted order of society; and history in particular often was not so much a scientific inquiry into man's past as an exercise in patriotism.

There was order, too, in that world beyond the senses: laws of religion and morality, of economics and sociology, were as immutable as those of physics and biology. From this sense of order flowed a serene optimism—not a crass and cultivated cheerfulness masking basic cynicism but a genuine belief that however much life might present on the surface aspects of hardship and injustice it was, in all matters of importance, good, and, in accord with basic laws of the universe, moving toward even better things.

In the America which confronted Rhodes after the war this was gone: order, faith, optimism—all were gone. The ideas let loose by Marx, Freud and Einstein, the forces let slip by war, were solvents, dissolving the old order but powerless to create a new one—or at any rate, a new one acceptable to the men of the Victorian age. To them there was not only chaos in thought but also a frightening disorder in conduct. As Rhodes himself put it, "there is an unquiet, restless feeling abroad which is disturbing." [1]

Evidences of it were not far to seek. Women, now enjoying the right to vote, flaunted their new freedom in short skirts and short hair, in talk of sex and birth control, in almost casual violation of the Victorian conventions. The flapper, not the Gibson girl, now symbolized American womanhood. Labor, with equal abandon, consorted with radicalism: a general strike in Seattle, a police strike in Boston, a national strike in the steel mills, and, in 1924, a bold attempt, in collaboration with discontented farmers, to capture the Presidency—these were some of the disturbing offspring of the union. Negroes, flooding into the Northern cities, were no longer suppliants of white charity, no longer persuaded of the truth of Anglo-Saxon supremacy. Led by W. E. B. DuBois, they struggled for first-class citizenship, and in that struggle developed their own writers, sociologists, historians—even establishing a *Journal of Negro History*, which, symbolically, devoted considerable space to discussion of "Some Historical Errors of James Ford Rhodes." [2]

In the realm of scholarship, too, the new spirit dominated. Concepts of evolution and relativism supplanted those of absolutes; man, no longer the captain of his soul, was seen as the creature of impersonal, sometimes irrational, forces: the society in which he lived, the economic system in which he functioned, and the vast depths of the unconscious. The sanctions of the physical sciences were applied to the traditional disciplines: moral judgments were irrelevant, the end was objective truth. In Rhodes' own field, and to the distress of many of his generation, this new approach found outlet in the cult of the "debunker," who stripped the heroes of the past of their haloes and in the name of making them "human" contrived to make them incapable of any thought or deed without mean and sordid motives.

Such cynicism was typical of the spirit of the postwar generation, represented in such diverse forms as the political isolationism which covered unilateral forays in foreign affairs; the uninhibited pursuit of the bitch goddess, Success, which saw no blasphemy in claiming Jesus Christ as the model of the Successful Salesman; the unabashed contempt for law which made a national hero out of the hoodlum; the trail of corruption which wound through the national life from Comiskey Field to the White House. It was, to use T. S. Eliot's words, the age of "the hollow men, . . . the stuffed men, Leaning together, Headpiece filled with straw." [3] Small wonder that the aging Rhodes sought refuge from "the gloom and sadness of present days" in the contemplation of the years of Victoria, happier times than those in which he now lived.[4]

The melancholy present even obtruded itself into his home. The servants were not as efficient as they used to be, although they were good Irish Catholics who showed real attachment to Mrs. Rhodes.[5] His grandsons brought home from school so much slang that he could barely understand them, and his attempts to discourage it were as futile as his efforts to stop young women smoking cigarettes.[6] He was offended by the "nastiness" of the novels of the day. And, "The way women and misses say 'damned' and smoke and drink whiskey" made him shudder and "wish for the older time." [7]

He even gave up a favorite means of entertainment, the theatre. "The bad air and uncomfortable seats, the liability of getting the influenza in the winter have made me forego the new interpretations of the drama," he explained to Trevelyan, adding that in Boston the popular trend was toward comic opera and movies. The latter he saw as "a symptom of the degeneracy of the times as since the Great War we have been going down hill morally as well as politically." The theatre and its followers in these days, he wrote, were a far cry from those great days in Cleveland when he and Mark Hanna had counted the receipts of the Euclid Avenue Opera House and "ascertained that the best drawing play was Hamlet, which filled the galleries as well as more expensive parts of the theatre." [8]

Eventually, Rhodes' cherished house on Beacon Street had to be sacrificed to the new age. All around him arose flashy new apartment houses, crowding out the stately homes of Proper Boston, dispersing their residents to such opulent suburbs as Newton and Brookline. He himself, confronted with the steadily rising cost of maintaining an old-fashioned establishment with its retinue of servants in the face of continued financial difficulties, found the house too expensive to maintain. In 1924 it was sold, and the family moved to Brookline, having first sold the library of 5700 books which Rhodes had accumulated through the years. He was not distressed, apparently, by the sale of his books—"I am no preserver of books," he told Charles K. Bolton—but he must have appreciated the irony in the report that his house, together with its neighbors, was to be replaced by an apartment house financed by two men of business, one of whom, wrote John T. Morse, Jr., was a successful bootlegger.[9]

There were, of course, some refuges from the all-too-present present. There was Europe, to which he and Mrs. Rhodes returned in 1922, 1925 and 1926 for long visits. In the milder climes of France and Switzerland he could escape the bitter Boston winters, enjoy good cooking and good wine, let his mind lie fallow (as he put it), and pass the time with such popular fiction as *The Enchanted April* and *Elizabeth and Her German Garden* and with classics he had long neglected, such as *Travels with a Donkey* and the works of Samuel Butler.[10] But even in Europe gnawed the canker of the times:

> each morning as you take up the newspaper you are afraid of war somewhere and would fain be in a country which with all of its faults is a peace-loving country. . . . I am tired of Europe and would like to go home. . . .[11]

Boston, for all its inclement weather, still was closest to Rhodes' heart: "the more I wander on *this earth's* surface the more does my heart incline to Boston." [12] Only there, after all, could he relax before a blazing fire of cannel coal in his library while he browsed through his treasured volumes of Tacitus and Macaulay and Henry Adams or read approvingly the latest works of his friends, Robert Grant and Gamaliel Bradford.[13] Only in Boston could he have his portrait done by John Singer Sargent, a charcoal head showing Rhodes as a mellow, shrewd, bearded man with a twinkle in his eye which verged on the mischievous—the genial Rhodes of old.[14]

And only in Boston was the Athenaeum, that private library and cultural refuge of Proper Boston. Behind its massive and blackened walls was an oasis of quiet and seclusion in the very midst of Business Boston. There, day after day, he could work on the new volumes of the *History* or pass the time in conversation with other members or with Charles K. Bolton, the librarian, or lose himself in the books of all kinds which the library afforded. To Rhodes it was a delightful retreat; he regretted "That the days are not longer, so agreeable a place is it to linger—that is, if you are fond of books." [15] Even this refuge, however, became less accessible after the move to Brookline. From his house on Beacon Street it was but a few minutes' walk; from the suburb it was a long journey, not lightly undertaken by a septuagenarian in poor health.

His most lasting refuge, however, was the continuation of the *History*. He had begun work on it in 1907, but the writing had gone slowly, with many interruptions: the *Lectures on the American Civil War*, the *History of the Civil War*, the World War itself, frequent illness. Now, in these dismal times, he found a measure of consolation in re-creating what were to him the better days of the recent past. The volume dealing with the years 1877–1896 finally appeared in 1919, and that on the administrations of McKinley and Theodore Roosevelt in 1922.[16] While he was at work on the earlier volume during the war, he wrote to Charles W. Eliot, "Gloom must more or less be present now, but the scholar has some comfort in his work and in his belief that good results may come from this terrible upheaval." [17] Even this comfort was not unalloyed with pain. After the war was over he wrote that he found it hard to keep up his work: "when you feel that probably everything is going to ruin you have little incentive to tell the story of the past." [18]

Everything was going to ruin! That he believed! That he laid to the war, and the war to the Germans. The war had destroyed civilization; it was the greatest of evils; and in particular was not a business for the United States.[19] Books about the war he avoided because it was "all too sad for me." [20] As to American participation in the war, he was, as before, of two minds. Sometimes he thought the United States was lucky in getting into it so late; at others, he believed the United States should have entered the war after the sinking of the *Lusitania*.[21] The letters of Walter Hines Page, he wrote, persuaded him that "we should have gone to war on the destruction of the Lusitania, that is, we should have seized the German passenger ships then in our harbors and so forced Germany to declare war upon us." [22] On occasion he went even further. To James Bryce he expressed the view that if the war had to come it would have been better had it come in 1905 during the Moroccan crisis of that year, for at that time Germany would have been less well prepared than in 1914.[23] As to responsibility for the war, he had doubts no longer: "the German Emperor might have stopped the war and he did not." [24]

Indeed, the virulence with which Rhodes pursued the Germans long after the war was over seems remarkable. He refused to read German books, shunning even his favorite, Goethe, because he was German! [25] Even more astonishing in a man of his gentle nature was his opposition to relief measures on behalf of hungry German children. He put it bluntly himself:

> I am one of those who wish that the Great War had never occurred and I cannot forget that Germany and Wilhelm II were the chief promoters of it. It worries me to the quick to see a certain rapproachement between the United States and Germany, such as helping the suffering German children. . . .[26]

The Germans, he now believed, had proved poor fighters in the Union army during the Civil War; outside of their own country, where they were honest and clever, they were cowards and plunderers, traits which he thought they demonstrated again during the World War.[27] As to how to deal with a Germany struggling under the burdens of Versailles, he was uncertain. He thought John Maynard Keynes foolhardy in the proposals advanced in what Rhodes conceded to be his "thoughtful" book, *The Economic Consequences of the Peace*, but he was impressed with Keynes' position that Germany could not possibly pay the reparations demanded of her. "The question arises," he wrote to Trevelyan, "shall Germany be utterly crushed or shall we try to live along with her in some possible way? Verily the times are out of joint." [28]

There was no uncertainty in his mind, however, as to American policy toward naval disarmament, Japanese immigration and the League of Nations. He favored the Washington Conference on naval armaments, feeling that since nations must economize there was no way so easy as to stop building warships.[29] He opposed the Japanese Exclusion Act of 1924, believing that the United States was adequately protected under the old "Gentleman's Agreement" with Japan. Senator Lodge, he thought, made a grave mistake in supporting the measure, "in view of the appalling catastrophe Japan met last autumn." [30]

The senator was mistaken, too, Rhodes believed, in his opposition to the League of Nations. Lodge's objections seemed to Rhodes petty compared to the alternative of war.[31] The Republicans, in their attacks upon the League, were guilty of putting up purely destructive opposition, and, besides, their arguments were out-of-date:

> The cogency of the Republican objections might be sound were things as they were thirty years ago but with aeroplanes, dirigibles, poisonous gases and bombs, the Republicans do not take account sufficiently of the dreadful alternative to a non-ratification of the treaty [of Versailles] and to the adoption of a League of Nations.[32]

At first, Rhodes was in favor of the Treaty and the Covenant as they stood: they were "as good, all things considered, as could have been secured." [33] As the struggle in the Senate developed and it became apparent that this was not possible he favored acceptance of the reservations offered by Elihu Root and the "interpretations" proposed by William Howard Taft.[34] But Lodge, who, in Rhodes' words, hated Wilson "as the devil hates holy water," was not to be appeased.[35] Rhodes, ironically impressed with the fact that during the bitter struggle Wilson collapsed physically while Lodge gained weight, concluded that if anything were to be salvaged it would have to be on Lodge's terms:

> Senator Lodge is a very able man. The contest has been between him and the President. The President has had a stroke of paralysis; the Senator has gained ten pounds. Naturally any man who comprehends the game should be on the side of the Senator;

> therefore the ratification of the treaty and the League of Nations with the Lodge reservations should be the platform of men who hope to save civilization from the wreck which threatens it.[36]

By October, 1920, Rhodes had given up all hope. The Senate had defeated American membership in the League, and in Rhodes' estimate neither of the Presidential candidates really favored it: "Cox will 'shake' the League if elected. He cares no more for it than Harding does." [37]

Despite this blow, Rhodes felt no ire toward Lodge. When Charles W. Eliot suggested that the senator's activities made him *persona non grata* for the Saturday Club, Rhodes replied: "While the position of Senator Lodge may be deprecated it does not, it seems to me, invalidate a membership in the Saturday Club for him. He is a gentleman, clubbable, and distinctly devoted to letters." [38] He resented George A. Myers' comment that Lodge was too susceptible to "the plutocracy influence." "I do not understand what you mean," he replied sharply, ". . . I am on excellent terms with Senator Lodge, whose towering ability I cannot help but admire." [39] Even during the height of the controversy over the League he had affirmed his confidence in Lodge: "nothing else could be expected from the leader of an opposing party. Had I his ability, leadership, power of work and expression, I should probably have done what he has done." [40]

Apart from the League, Rhodes thought that American foreign policy should be based on friendship with Great Britain—a policy which was having heavy going at the time because of the war raging in Ireland between the Republicans and the "Black and Tans." The Irish in the United States, aided and abetted by Rhodes' hero, Senator Lodge, were striving to influence American policy against the British. Rhodes, on the contrary, thought American policy "ought to be plain; not to encourage either the Irish or the Ulster party but to do everything to promote a good feeling between Great Britain and the United States." [41] He would have liked to see Britain settle the Irish question but he was not optimistic about the possibility:

> is it not a characteristic of the English to see their own side firmly and not the other side? And is it not that quality which has made the English supremely great and enabled them to make their history and literature the greatest in the world? . . . Of course it has had one bad side. The English have failed to comprehend Ireland, . . .[42]

As for the Irish themselves, Rhodes confessed himself baffled. Personally, he found them loyal and honest; collectively, they joined secret societies and endorsed terrorism:

> It is a curious phase in the Celtic character [he wrote]. All of our servants . . . are Irish and Roman Catholic. We trust them implicitly, never lock up anything, and the cook and head waitress have the key to my wine cellar. They never take a drop for themselves or for their friends, and that in our day of Prohibition is evidence of rare virtue. But their acquaintances join such societies as the "Invincibles." I simply cannot understand the inconsistencies in their character. . . .[43]

On one aspect of foreign affairs Rhodes had surprisingly little to say, in view of the controversies which raged around it. Russia figures little in his correspondence, except for a brief comment indicating that he had read Norman Hapgood's book, *The Advancing Hour*, and was glad to learn from it "that the Marx tenets have proved a failure in Russia." [44]

Domestic politics offered Rhodes as little hope as international. The era of "normalcy" was upon the country, and while Rhodes had now little use for the ailing Wilson he had to confess that the presidential candidates chosen by the major parties in 1920—James B. Cox and Warren G. Harding—were mediocre. He himself would have preferred Herbert Hoover.[45] The vice-presidential nominees, Franklin D. Roosevelt and Calvin Coolidge, he thought, were "considerably above the ability of the average man in public life." [46] Pleased with the conservative character of both party platforms, he was impressed by the Democrats' rejection of the demands of organized labor. He hoped this indicated a conservative reaction but feared it was too good to believe.[47] He thought that Harding might turn out to be another Rutherford B. Hayes: "not so able as McKinley but very respectable." [48] Regarding himself as a "quasi-Republican," he voted for Harding with the explanation: "Our civilization is of course declining but I hope for a Republican administration of eight years so that in the decline of my life I shall have a little solace as I gaze upon a little check to the dying world." [49]

Some solace he did find. He thought that in the first six months of his administration Harding had done remarkably well, in contrast to affairs in Europe, which went from bad to worse:

> nothing seems to go aright and those will be nearest the truth who regard the world as going to the demnition bow-wows. But if anything can save us it will be such a Republican adminis-

> tration as we now have which seems to hit it right in nearly every respect.[50]

He continued to be as satisfied with Republican "normalcy" as were most of his fellow-citizens. He was disturbed by the Senate struggle over the seating of Senator-elect Truman H. Newberry of Michigan—not because of the corruption involved, but because Newberry was

> a gentleman . . . [who] was badly deceived and [whose] eagerness to be Senator caused him to make an awkward use of money. Nevertheless, he is a great burden for the party to carry, and I could wish we did not have it.[51]

As for Harding himself, Rhodes' only criticism was of the trip to Alaska on which the President died:

> Harding's death seems to me a useless sacrifice. . . . Mr. Harding made a great mistake in taking the Alaskan trip . . . If he had remained in Washington or gone to a dignified seaside place as did Roosevelt, he would have been living now.[52]

Given his high standards of public morality, Rhodes was no doubt shocked by the revelations of corruption in the Harding Administration, although there is no reference to them in his correspondence. He was not distressed enough, however, to vote Democratic in 1924: the nominee of that party, John W. Davis, the Wall Street lawyer, was, in Rhodes' opinion, "too good for his party and his running mate [Charles W. Bryan of Nebraska, brother of William Jennings Bryan]." [53]

In one election contest Rhodes felt constrained to take part, albeit in a negative way. In 1922 Senator Lodge was faced with an unprecedented battle for re-election. Liberal Republicans in Massachusetts revolted against his domination of the party, giving their support to the Prohibition party candidate, John F. Nicholls. The Democrats, sensing victory for the first time in years, nominated a Brahmin, William A. Gaston.[54] Rhodes' last volume was scheduled for publication in the midst of this political contest—and in that volume Rhodes extolled the Senator for his role in opposition to federal regulation of railroad rates during the debate over the Hepburn bill.[55]

To bring such information to public attention during the heated campaign would, Rhodes feared, cost Lodge votes. He therefore held up publication of the volume until after the election. "I feared that the Proletariat that casts the great majority of the votes would not agree with him," he explained.[56] Lodge defeated Gaston by a mere 7000 votes, while the Prohibition party candidate polled 25,000, indicating that Lodge's day was drawing to a close.[57] But Rhodes was pleased; he believed that "as long as he [Lodge] is content to stay in public life the people of Massachusetts ought to keep him there." [58]

The political issue which irked Rhodes most was prohibition. To him it was a "project of making men good by legislation," which had destroyed the promising wine industry of California and practically killed dinner parties in Boston.[59] It was, in addition, futile. When George A. Myers complained that his private stocks were running low, Rhodes reminded him that Myers had supported prohibition on the grounds that it would instill sobriety among employes. Added Rhodes:

> Prohibition has turned out as I expected. You remember when you and your brother capitalists favored it because you thought you could have enough to drink for yourselves, who used it in moderation, and yet cut off the supply from your employees who were inclined to use alcoholic drink to excess. You now find that will not work. Your private stock is nearly exhausted and you feel the pangs of thirst. You ought to have remembered that the saloon is the club of the proletariat and it would not do to abolish the saloon and allow capitalists, like yourself, all that you wanted to drink. You have tried to make men good by act of Congress and have failed. . . .[60]

While he hoped that the "Prohibition spasm" would pass, he had few illusions about its early repeal.[61] Rather, he attempted to persuade his friends in and out of Congress that funds should be as generously appropriated for enforcement of the 14th and 15th amendments as for the 18th. Drastic enforcement of all three, he reasoned, would diminish the enthusiasm of white Southerners for prohibition, with the result that the prohibition amendment would become as little effective as those protecting the rights of Negroes. As he explained it to Barrett Wendell:

> I do not want the negroes to vote any more than you do but I do want to be able to have a bottle of wine at the Somerset or Tavern and to replenish my wine cellar. I am working in a quiet way on the principle do not enforce the XVIII and we shall not insist upon the enforcement of the XV and the second section of the XIV.[62]

He even besought the aid of George A. Myers, who was influential politically in the Negro community of Cleveland: "it is silly to enforce the XVIII amendment while the second section of the XIV and the XV remain a dead letter. Keep harping on that string and line up all of the colored voters."[63] Myers was favorably impressed,[64] but apart from him Rhodes' "quiet" campaign made little progress. Senator Lodge agreed that all amendments should be equally enforced but made no commitments, and Rhodes' Congressman, George H. Tinkham, contented himself with a pledge to call for equal enforcement of the laws when the matter of reapportionment of seats came before the house after the 1920 census.[65]

Prohibition itself made little change in Rhodes' habits. He continued to drink wine and champagne so long as that was possible; after which he was willing to take to cocktails and liquor.[66] Generous as he had been in pre-Volstead days, he offered some of his choicest wines to help friends play the role of proper host to visitors from Europe.[67] When George A. Myers commented that Rhodes would welcome crossing the three-mile limit on his way to Europe, Rhodes replied:

> There will be no difference in my drinking habits when I cross the three mile limit except that I shall imbibe milder fluids. I shall be glad to get a whack again at my favorite wines and leave off spirits and mineral water.[68]

Prohibition, in general, added to his pessimism about the times:

> Morality seems to be going down hill fast and we must give to the fanatics sincerity in the attempt to check the tendency by Prohibition. Did they think straight and see clear they would know that their darling prohibition only accelerated the pace. I suspect our civilization will go. It is so based on European that any attempt to revive it will be hopeless. So stick to your John Barley Corn . . .[69]

On social problems, Rhodes continued to reflect the old outlook of his class. He applauded Mayor Ole Hanson for crushing the general strike in Seattle in 1919 and approved the deportation of some of its leaders.[70] He conceded, however, that strikes, for all their evils, were "far preferable to war than which no evil is so great. . . . the strikers . . . will listen to a little reason and . . . can be argued with."[71] And American strikes, he thought, were not as bitter as those of Europe, a fact which he attributed to American workers being better off.[72]

For American workers as a class, however, he had little admiration. John T. Morse, Jr., in discussing the labor problem, suggested it was "nonsense" to rely on the beneficence of the wealthy as a solution:

> what basis is there for hoping ever to see any infusion of humane and Christian feeling invade the hearts of our multi-millionaires? [he asked] Not much, i' faith. If the people could only learn to separate the abstract system of capitalism (which is of course vitally essential to any form of social existence) from the concrete class of capitalists, their hostility to the latter might be unobjectionable. As a class, our capitalists are a bad lot; and those who are capitalist by inheritance are as evil a gang as has ever been seen in the world. Let the people hate them as much as they will. If the Bolsheviki should hang up a few coal-barons, I would stand smilingly by with my hands in my pockets, indifferent if not sympathetic. . . .[73]

To which Rhodes replied:

> I do not wonder that you are disgusted with the capitalists, but really they are a lot sight better than the proletariat. Their work is not as bad, the benefits they confer on mankind are greater. When the hanging begins it will not stop with the coal barons and the like. It will hit the "damn littery fellers" who do not do an honest day's work but only sit in a study and write. That you are disgusted with mankind in general shows that your heart is in the right place. . . .[74]

The historian, in short, had lived beyond his time. Unable to adapt himself to the rapidly changing society about him, he was an increasingly lonely and despondent figure among a generation that knew him not. The bitterness of this he was to drink to the full in the reception accorded his last work.

NOTES

[1] Rhodes to Sir George Otto Trevelyan, Jan. 17, 1920. Rhodes Papers.

[2] John R. Lynch, "Some Historical Errors of James Ford Rhodes," *Journal of Negro History*, II (1917), 345–363; "More About the Historical Errors of James Ford Rhodes," *ibid.*, III (1918), 139–157.

[3] The mood of the Twenties may be recaptured in Mark Sullivan, *Our Times: The United States, 1900–1925* (New York, 1925), VI, *passim;* Frederick L. Allen, *Only Yesterday: An Informal History of the Nineteen Twenties* (New York, 1931); Lloyd Morris, *Postscript to Yesterday: America, The Last Fifty Years* (New York, 1947).

[4] Rhodes to Sir George Otto Trevelyan, Jan. 17, 1920. Rhodes Papers. Rhodes to Trevelyan, Nov. 12, 1922, in M. A. D. Howe, *Rhodes*, pp. 331, 346.

[5] Rhodes to Sir George Otto Trevelyan, July 17, 1924. Rhodes Papers.

[6] Rhodes to Sir George Otto Trevelyan, May 11, 1924. Rhodes Papers.

[7] Rhodes to Robert Grant, Dec. 2, 1922; March 23, 1925. Rhodes Papers.

[8] Rhodes to Sir George Otto Trevelyan, May 12, 1920. Rhodes Papers.

[9] John T. Morse, Jr., to Rhodes, Feb. 27, 1925; Rhodes to Robert Grant, April 2, 1922; Lady Marion Bryce, April 2, 1922; Sir George Otto Trevelyan, Oct. 28, 1924. Rhodes Papers. This last letter is dated 1904 but the text clearly indicates it was written in 1924. Charles K. Bolton, *Notebook, 1922–1925*, pp. 232, 236 (Oct. 8, 1924, Oct. 17, 1924).

[10] Rhodes to Sir George Otto Trevelyan, Nov. 12, 1922; Jan. 9, 1923; William M. Sloane, Sept. 18, 1925. Rhodes Papers. Rhodes to John T. Morse, Jr., July 15, 1922, in M. A. D. Howe, *Rhodes*, p. 326.

[11] Rhodes to John T. Morse, Jr., March 15, 1923; Robert Grant, Sept. 24, 1922. Rhodes Papers.

[12] Rhodes to Frederick C. Shattuck, M.D., Dec. 15, 1922. Rhodes Papers.

[13] Rhodes to Robert Grant, March 23, 1925. Rhodes Papers. Rhodes to Mrs. C. H. Toy, Sept. 16, 1922, and to Gamaliel Bradford, Jan. 1, 1926, in M. A. D. Howe, *Rhodes*, pp. 329, 349–350.

[14] Rhodes had been reluctant to have the drawing made because of Sargent's reputation for charging high prices. It actually cost him $400. John Singer Sargent to Rhodes, April 21, 1919; Rhodes to Sir George Otto Trevelyan, Feb. 8, 1924. Rhodes Papers. Charles K. Bolton, *Notebook, 1920–1922*, pp. 8, 12 (April 1, 1920, April 12, 1920). The drawing now hangs in the building of the Massachusetts Historical Society.

[15] Rhodes to Sir George Otto Trevelyan, March 23, 1921. Rhodes Papers.

[16] *History of the United States from Hayes to McKinley, 1877–1896* (New York, 1919); *The McKinley and Roosevelt Administrations, 1897–1909* (New York, 1922).

[17] Rhodes to Charles W. Eliot, May 15, 1918, in M. A. D. Howe, *Rhodes*, p. 298.

[18] Rhodes to Charles H. Firth, Feb. 14, 1919. Rhodes Papers.

[19] Charles K. Bolton, *Notebook, 1925–1928*, p. 176 (Feb. 2, 1927). Rhodes to James Bryce, Dec. 9, 1921, in M. A. D. Howe, *Rhodes*, pp. 324–325. Rhodes to Sir George Otto Trevelyan, Jan. 20, 1921. Rhodes Papers.

[20] Rhodes to Sir George Otto Trevelyan, Aug. 18, 1920. Rhodes Papers.

[21] Rhodes to Sir George Otto Trevelyan, Feb. 17, 1919; Aug. 19, 1924. Rhodes Papers.

[22] Rhodes to Worthington C. Ford, Dec. 2, 1922, in M. A. D. Howe, *Rhodes*, p. 332.

[23] Rhodes to James Bryce, March 11, 1921, in M. A. D. Howe, *Rhodes* pp. 320–321.

[24] Rhodes to Sir George Otto Trevelyan, Aug. 18, 1920. Rhodes Papers.

[25] Rhodes to Sir George Otto Trevelyan, May 11, 1924. Rhodes Papers.

[26] Rhodes to Sir George Otto Trevelyan, July 17, 1924. Rhodes Papers.

[27] Rhodes to Sir George Otto Trevelyan, Dec. 18, 1923. Rhodes Papers. Trevelyan entered a demurrer: "Good Lord, how those Germans fought at the Somme, . . . and your own Armageddon, the Argonne." Trevelyan to Rhodes, Jan. 1, 1924. Rhodes Papers.

[28] Rhodes to Sir George Otto Trevelyan, Feb. 24, 1920. Rhodes Papers.

[29] Rhodes to James Bryce, Dec. 9, 1921, in M. A. D. Howe, *Rhodes*, pp. 324–325.

[30] Rhodes to Sir George Otto Trevelyan, May 11, 1924. Rhodes Papers. The reference is to the earthquake which shook Japan in 1923.

[31] Rhodes to Charles W. Eliot, July 6, 1919. Rhodes Papers.

[32] Rhodes to Sir George Otto Trevelyan, April 1, 1919; July 25, 1919, in M. A. D. Howe, *Rhodes*, pp. 303, 305–306.

[33] Rhodes to Charles W. Eliot, July 6, 1919. Rhodes Papers.

[34] Rhodes to David M. Matteson, Aug. 3, 1919, in M. A. D. Howe, *Rhodes*, pp. 306–307.

[35] Rhodes to George A. Myers, May 22, 1920, in M. A. D. Howe, *Rhodes*, p. 313.

[36] *Ibid.*

[37] Rhodes, quoted in conversation with Charles K. Bolton in M. A. D. Howe, *Rhodes*, p. 314.

[38] Rhodes to Charles W. Eliot, July 6, 1919. Rhodes Papers.

[39] Rhodes to George A. Myers, May 22, 1920, in M. A. D. Howe, *Rhodes*, p. 313.

[40] Rhodes to Robert Grant, March 11, [?], in M. A. D. Howe, *Rhodes*, p. 302.

[41] Rhodes to Sir George Otto Trevelyan, April 11, 1920. Rhodes Papers.

[42] Rhodes to Sir George Otto Trevelyan, Dec. 16, 1918; Mrs. C. H. Toy, undated photostat fragment in response to letter from Mrs. Toy, Aug. 2, 1920. Rhodes Papers.

[43] Rhodes to Sir George Otto Trevelyan, March 6, 1920. Rhodes Papers.

[44] Rhodes to Mrs. C. H. Toy, Sept. 2, 1920, in M. A. D. Howe, *Rhodes*, p. 319.

[45] Rhodes to Sir George Otto Trevelyan, Jan. 17, 1920; July 16, 1920. Rhodes Papers. Rhodes to George A. Myers, May 11, 1919; March 26, 1920, in John A. Garraty (ed.), "Correspondence," *Ohio Historical Quarterly*, LXIV (1955), 273, 280.

[46] Rhodes to Sir George Otto Trevelyan, July 16, 1920. Rhodes Papers.

[47] *Ibid.*

[48] Charles K. Bolton, *Notebook, 1920–1922*, p. 55 (Oct. 21, 1920).

[49] Rhodes to George A. Myers, Sept. 18, 1920, in John A. Garraty (ed.), "Correspondence," *Ohio Historical Quarterly* LXIV (1955), 371.

[50] Rhodes to George A. Myers, Sept. 24, 1921, in *ibid.*, pp. 387–388.

[51] Rhodes to George A. Myers, May 6, 1922, in *ibid.*, p. 397.

[52] Rhodes to John T. Morse, Jr., Aug. 11, 1923, in M. A. D. Howe, *Rhodes*, p. 345.

[53] Rhodes to Frederick C. Shattuck, M.D., Aug. 18, 1924. Rhodes Papers.

[54] John A. Garraty, *Henry Cabot Lodge: A Biography* (New York, 1953), p. 413.

[55] *The McKinley and Roosevelt Administrations*, p. 329.

[56] Rhodes to Robert Grant, Dec. 21, 1922, in M. A. D. Howe, *Rhodes*, p. 333.

[57] John A. Garraty, *Henry Cabot Lodge*, p. 414.

[58] Rhodes to Frederick C. Shattuck, M.D., Dec. 15, 1922. Rhodes Papers.

[59] Rhodes to Sir George Otto Trevelyan, Jan. 22, 1919; Feb. 24, 1920. Rhodes Papers.

[60] George A. Myers to Rhodes, March 21, 1919. Rhodes Papers. Myers to Rhodes, Aug. 31, 1920; Rhodes to Myers, Sept. 18, 1920, in John A. Garraty (ed.), "Correspondence," *Ohio Historical Quarterly*, LXIV (1955), 369–370.

[61] Rhodes to Barrett Wendell, Feb. 3, 1920. Rhodes Papers.

[62] Rhodes to Barrett Wendell, Nov. 15, 1920. Rhodes Papers.

[63] Rhodes to George A. Myers, May 6, 1922, in John A. Garraty (ed.), "Correspondence," *Ohio Historical Quarterly*, LXIV (1955), 397.

[64] George A. Myers to Rhodes, May 22, 1922, in *ibid.*, p. 398.

[65] Henry Cabot Lodge to Rhodes, March 28, 1921; July 11, 1921; George H. Tinkham to Rhodes, Nov. 19, 1920. Rhodes Papers.

[66] Rhodes to Robert Grant, April 24, 1922; June 30, 1923. Rhodes Papers.

[67] Rhodes to Robert Grant, April 24, 1922. Rhodes Papers.

[68] Rhodes to George A. Myers, May 6, 1922, in John A. Garraty (ed.), "Correspondence," *Ohio Historical Quarterly*, LXIV (1955), 396–398.

[69] Rhodes to George A. Myers, May 6, 1922, in *ibid.*, p. 398.

[70] Rhodes to Sir George Otto Trevelyan, Feb. 27, 1919. Rhodes Papers.

[71] Rhodes to Sir George Otto Trevelyan, Aug. 28, 1919. Rhodes Papers.

[72] Rhodes to Sir George Otto Trevelyan, Feb. 27, 1919. Rhodes Papers.

[73] John T. Morse, Jr., to Rhodes, Aug. 5, 1923. Rhodes Papers.

[74] Rhodes to John T. Morse, Jr., Aug. 11, 1923, in M. A. D. Howe, *Rhodes*, p. 345.

Chapter 14

THE BITTERNESS OF REJECTION

THE ESSENTIAL sadness of the fate of Rhodes' last work lies in the fact that what he believed to be honest historical presentation was judged to be shoddy work by that professional public whose opinions he valued most. This was due, more than to changes in Rhodes' approach, to the substantial changes in the outlook of that public itself. That which had seemed objective truth in the '90's now appeared the most obvious of prejudices; extolling of the old bourgeois virtues amused a generation nurtured on Babbitt; sanctification of Mark Hanna and Theodore Roosevelt offended a generation of young historians trained in scientific method and attitudes. For the first time in his experience, Rhodes lacked *rapport* with his audience. To understand this, it is necessary to examine in some detail the two volumes.

As has been noted, work on *From Hayes to McKinley*, begun in 1907, was not completed until after World War I, although some of the work appeared as magazine articles in the pre-war years. Hampered as he was by ill-health, Rhodes found the work exhausting. It left him "neither brains nor eyes for aught else." [1] At its conclusion he was indifferent whether he published any more or not, but he felt compelled to go on because of his admiration for Theodore Roosevelt:

> It is my purpose to continue my history . . . so that I shall have two administrations of Theodore Roosevelt. Mr. Roosevelt was to me a great administrator. How one man could do so much will ever be a mystery! . . . he made a mistake in . . . 1912 and afterwards for heading the progressive movement but . . . who am I to criticize a very great man! [2]

He was also haunted by Trevelyan's observation that no serious worthwhile work in the English language had been done by anyone past the age of seventy, but, as he explained to Trevelyan: "I was personally acquainted so well with Roosevelt, Hanna, Hay and had [such] a fairly good acquaintance with Lodge, Taft and Root that I deemed it on the whole wise to continue." [3] This last volume,

The McKinley and Roosevelt Administrations, he completed fairly quickly, although he complained about the delays caused by his inability to come to a verdict about Rockefeller, Carnegie, and J. P. Morgan; it was difficult to decide "whether such large fortunes are an evil or not; whether the good the first two have done does not overbalance their excessive profits?" [4] He finished the writing in December, 1921, with a feeling of relief:

> I shall write no more. I began my literary life in 1885 and . . . have had thirty-seven years of it. . . . Sir George Otto Trevelyan wrote . . . that he knew of no good serious book written in English after the writer had passed seventy, and I am following pretty nearly his advice. . . .[5]

Both of the last volumes bear the marks of age and fatigue. The organization of material is almost mechanically chronological; the literary style is stiff and awkward; eulogies of deceased leaders are quoted as if they constituted historical evidence; arid wastes of political oratory stretch over page after page; and much of the material is personal reminiscence. Indeed, the books are far less history than a recollection of historical events as viewed by one who lived through them and knew the active participants.

The books' failure as history is emphasized by Rhodes' failure to grasp the essential factors which provided the basic unity of the years between 1877 and 1909: industrialization, urbanization, disappearance of the frontier, the rise of finance capital, and the efforts made by various elements of the American people to solve the problems arising from these phenomena. The first seven volumes of the *History* possessed an internal unity: organized around the central theme of slavery as the cause of the Civil War they carried it through, in all its variations, until it was exhausted in Reconstruction. As a result, these volumes have all the sweep and impact of drama, however much one might disagree with their historical interpretations. The last two volumes, lacking such unity, present only a maundering chronicle of the times, interspersed with essays in which Rhodes gave vent to his feelings against organized labor, foreign-born Americans, Populists, William Jennings Bryan and others who did not conform to his gentlemanly standards.

How far Rhodes allowed himself to be beguiled by surface manifestations of profound social developments, how far he permitted his writing to become the vehicle of personal opinion, may be gathered from some examples. The railroad strikes of 1877 are dealt with almost entirely in the light of the violent incidents which accompanied them.[6] Rhodes saw them as almost a social uprising in which leadership was snatched from honest American workingmen by "the tramps, communists, criminals and outcasts,—the dregs of society." [7] In New York, "where the dangerous classes abounded," the fashionable Seventh Regiment was mobilized, and, wrote Rhodes,

> some of the communists, . . . , got a look into this armory, and, seeing the best young citizens of New York lying on their arms with the determined look of men who are out on grave duty, felt their courage for the attempt to overturn society ooze away. . . .[8]

He solemnly conceded that the strikes were really not as menacing as the French Revolution or the Paris Commune, but they were serious enough, for they seemed to threaten the foundations of social order.[9] In putting down the strike through the use of federal troops, President Hayes earned the praise of the historian, just as he had won the approval of businessmen at the time:

> there was much thoughtful and earnest discussion of the riots in private gatherings and many a grateful word was said of the quiet unassuming man in the White House who saw his duty clearly and never faltered in its performance. It was seen that the federal government with a resolute President at its head was a tower of strength in the event of a social uprising. The number of outcasts and the prevalence of the mob spirit, disclosed by the events of July, made thoughtful men shudder as they reckoned what might have happened had not the disputed presidency of a few months earlier been peacefully settled. . . .[10]

Pointing out the lessons to be learned from such an experience Rhodes counselled employers to make common cause with their skilled workers in explaining the problems of management to the unskilled. Had such a course been followed in 1877, "Employers and employed might then have stood shoulder to shoulder in an honest endeavor to cope with a deplorable state of affairs." [11] Unions, for their part, should join hands with management against "outcasts and communists," and as part of such a program, should abandon the "system" of persuasion, threats and terror which, he claimed, the unions had developed since 1877. In addition, organized labor should give up its hostility to the use of federal troops in strikes.[12]

Should labor fail to heed such advice, Rhodes urged that in place of the Regular Army there should be employed during strikes selected elements of the National Guard:

> there are points of superiority in a first class militia regiment like the Seventh [New York]. Made up of men of good physique, character and social standing, owners of property and presumably inheritors of it, such a body, . . . , has behind it, in dealing with an insurrection, an invincible moral force. . . .[13]

Indeed, this method of handling labor disputes exercised a certain fascination for Rhodes. In his discussion of the strike on the Gould Southwest railroad system in 1886 he lauded Senator Joseph R. Hawley of Connecticut for a speech in which the Senator said if he had the power to do so he would "call out the old Seventh Regiment and shoot the defiant wrong-doers down." [14]

The historian found little excuse for the strikes he discussed. The strike of 1886, for example,

> was not a strike for an advance of wages or against a reduction, or for the redress of grievances, but . . . a contest for power, to determine whether the railroad company or the Knights of Labor should have control, . . .[15]

The leader of the strike, Martin Irons, was a "vulgar labor agitator" while the leading railroad executive, H. M. Hoxie, was "able, straightforward and humane." [16] The Homestead strike of 1892 again was "probably a contest for dominion," with the unionists prepared to enforce their rules by violence.[17]

The Pullman strike of 1894, to be sure, had its origin in a wage reduction, but this was due to the depression which followed the Panic of 1893, and in any event the strike quickly "had become a riot" with strikers interfering with the movement of the United States mails.[18] "Anarchy was threatened," not only by the strikers, but also by Governor Altgeld of Illinois, who, in Rhodes' view, was aptly called "the friend and champion of disorder." [19] Fortunately, President Cleveland, who "had the true instincts of a gentleman," used federal troops to crush the strike, and Eugene V. Debs, its leader, "allowed himself to be imprisoned as a martyr." For these developments Rhodes had high praise for Cleveland and his attorney-general, Richard P. Olney:

> The action of Cleveland in repressing this alarming disturbance is on a par with the best work of this kind accomplished by our Presidents. In the precedent that it established, it amounts to something more. Olney furnished Cleveland with a powerful weapon in the new use of the injunction . . .[20]

As for the Haymarket affair, the strike for the eight-hour day which started at the McCormick works on May 1, 1886, speedily became "a contest between the anarchists . . . and society." With never an expression of doubt, Rhodes reported that "an anarchist threw a dynamite bomb" at the fateful meeting in Haymarket Square; and the action of the police thereafter was "an exhibition of nerve and courage that forms an heroic chapter in the annals of the American police." Nor was Rhodes in doubt as to the justice meted out to the victims:

> There can be no question that the punishment meted out to the anarchists was legally just. . . .
>
> The historical judgment confirms the legal. The anarchists attacked Society and Society defended itself under due forms of law. . . . All thoughtful citizens must have been interested to note that six out of the eight who stood trial were Germans, as was also the thrower of the bomb. . . .
>
> When the Germans came to America they translated liberty into license; . . .[21]

A chapter devoted to the Molly Maguires displays the same approach. Little is said to explain the emergence of such an organization, much is made of murder and terror. The typical Molly, wrote Rhodes, assassinated "to satisfy the revengeful spirit of the Molly Maguires," and "true to his Irish Roman Catholic blood, he hated the capitalist and had a profound contempt for the law." The Mollies were "arrogant in their success, drunk with deeds of violence and thirsting for blood." [22] By way of contrast, the Pinkerton detective who brought about their destruction, James McParlan, was "accurate and truthful, . . . excelled as a witness as he had as a detective." [23] When the Mollies were hanged, "the majesty of the law had a triumph." [24]

In his discussion of national financial problems during the latter decades of the 19th century he demonstrated again the hard-money outlook of the earlier volumes. Hayes' unsuccessful veto of the Bland-Allison Act, he wrote, was admirable. The resistance of Hayes, and his secretary of the treasury, John Sherman, to expansion of the currency was "to [their] lasting merit . . . they, with cool heads and unshaken faith, kept the country in the path of financial safety and honor despite bitter opposition and clamorous abuse." [25] Compromise on slavery, as in 1850, was justifiable, but no compromise was possible on the issue of money. On this subject, Rhodes gave thanks for the Republican Party: "The brightest page in the history of the Republican Party since the Civil War tells of its work in the cause of sound finance . . . The Republican Party was sounder than the Democratic . . . in the advocacy of a correct money standard." [26]

As in his previous volumes, Rhodes expressed satisfaction with his countrymen and their institutions; no hint of his personal doubts and questioning appears. Americans, he wrote, probably showed less greed than citizens of other nations.[27] The Presidency was "well worth the ambitions of the best and ablest men" and the American people generally had shown, in their political behavior, love of order and rare good sense.[28] Congressional government was superior to parliamentary, for it subjected partisan considerations to the interests of the nation, while the parliamentary form emphasized the ascendancy of party.[29] Some actions of Congress were singled out for specific approval. Passage of civil service reform was a great work of righteousness. The McKinley tariff was good because it developed the manufacture of tin plate in the United States and the Wilson-Gorman tariff because it provided for an income tax which favored "many of the intellectual class, . . . who should be fostered by the State." While the treatment of Chinese by Californians was to be deplored, exclusion of the Chinese by Congress was an act of statesmanship: "An overcrowded country with 350 millions . . . could not fail to look covetously upon the fair land of California." [30]

As for the American system in general, Rhodes agreed with the observation of President Benjamin Harrison in his inaugural address, that "No other people have a government more worthy of their respect and love, a land so magnificent in extent, . . . so full of generous suggestion to enterprise and labor." [31]

Rhodes' last volume, *The McKinley and Roosevelt Administrations*, reads better than the work just summarized. It was written in a much shorter period of time (three years, as compared to twelve), it covers a much shorter period (twelve years, as compared with twenty), and it deals with the administrations of only two presidents, as compared with five. Like its predecessor it suffers from lack of analysis of the basic forces at work in the period, but the fact that it covers only two administrations does provide it with more unity than the earlier volume. Besides, this last volume contains unique elements of interest. Much of it is personal reminiscence of leading personalities, such as Mark Hanna and Theodore Roosevelt. Not only is this of the usual biographical interest, but its effect is heightened by Rhodes' desire to portray Hanna as a misunderstood patriot and Roosevelt as a knight in shining armor.

In addition, much of the book is polemic, however much Rhodes might try to disguise it as history. It was written, it will be remembered, during the years 1919–1921, a period marked by great labor unrest, the "red scare," the spread of such "socialist" doctrines as that of government ownership of railroads, an upsurge of criticism of the role of the United States in Latin America, and the renewal of the Filipino campaign for independence. Rhodes had opinions on these matters, and the fact that the opinions are expressed positively, even dogmatically, carries the reader into that reciprocal relationship with the author which often results from good polemics.

Symbolically, the work opens with a long character sketch of Mark Hanna—and also, perhaps symbolically, Rhodes never mentions that Hanna was his brother-in-law and friend. To Rhodes, Hanna was

> a severely moral man . . . Loving the society of refined and well-bred women, he might be looked upon as a model of chastity. Passionately fond of cards, he preferred whist or bridge without a money stake; . . . He had a pure mind, rarely told a smutty story . . . He gravitated toward the society of the best men. . . .

Indeed, as a politician Hanna's fault lay in his being too honest about the uses of money in campaigns; he "stood in need of a certain hypocrisy which was lacking in his character." Actually, said Rhodes, Hanna looked upon the raising of funds for the Republican Party as a kind of religious exercise needing no justification:

> Collecting money for a political party must be regarded differently from getting means for the support of a church, . . . But many voters looked upon the Republican Party as something sacred, whose control was necessary to the well-being and perpetuity of the Republic. The man who raised money in order to insure its continuance in power was looked upon by them as doing holy work. Some such idea must have passed through Hanna's mind when without concealment he continually preached the use of money to save the party.[32]

Hanna's character was manifested in his capacity for disinterested friendship, his failure to make demands on McKinley because Hanna had saved McKinley from bankruptcy, and in his refusal to permit use of corrupt methods in getting the nomination for McKinley in 1896. In that year, it was well for "the financial honor of the country" that its defense was entrusted to Hanna and McKinley. The lavish expenditure of funds was essential:

> Hanna early perceived that this was to be a campaign of education. Six hundred thousand dollars were spent for documents . . . Innumerable speakers . . . presented the case against free silver. Men in every county of the pivotal Western states were supplied with sound money literature; and, as they could not give their time for nothing, they were hired to read and explain the pamphlets . . .[33]

Hanna himself was greater than McKinley. A man of towering ability, he would have made an admirable secretary of the treasury; as President he would have had the "nerve and power to resist the pressure for war. . . . there would have been no war with Spain." As Senator he wrought for his country's good, particularly in his single-handed campaign to persuade the Senate to vote for the Panama instead of the Nicaraguan route of the projected isthmian canal.[34]

As businessman, Hanna had yet another contribution to make. From his own experience, which convinced him that negotiation with labor was preferable to strikes, he helped bring about a settlement of the anthracite strike in 1902 on a basis favorable to labor. Thereafter Hanna preached the doctrine of settling labor disputes through collective bargaining, believing that labor unions would prove a boon to the country, and that cooperation between capital and labor would contribute to the prosperity of the nation.[35]

To be sure, Hanna was not in good repute among some elements of the population, but once they met him in the flesh they saw how badly they had misjudged him:

> Westerners beyond Ohio had the idea that he was a "bloated millionaire," and when they came to see a man of easy bearing, of democratic ways, placing himself on a par with the common man and hear his rough speech adapted to their easy comprehension, they were converted to the Hanna cult. . . .

In his death, the nation lost a man of "ability, honor and unselfishness," the last representative of an order that had passed away before a new order, the symbol of which was Theodore Roosevelt.[36]

Roosevelt was "a man of . . . capacious brain, equal in action and study to that of three men!" No other man so impressed Rhodes with his ability; when the historian saw the President at a meeting of state governors in 1908 Rhodes was reminded of "the Homeric Council at which Agamemnon, King of Men, was at the head. Verily Roosevelt was in this assemblage 'King of Men.'" In his approach to the social problems of his time, particularly in his war upon the trusts, Roosevelt enunciated truths showing that he was activated by sound principles. Standing midway between rich and poor, the President "upheld without ceasing the right of private property; he was bitterly opposed to socialism." [37]

The character of Roosevelt was such that if he had been President in 1914 the Kaiser would have been so impressed that "the Great War would not have occurred during his occupancy of the White House." The President's talent as "a rare judge of men" was exemplified in his appointment to the cabinet of such men as John Hay, "the refined gentleman from the West," Elihu Root, the Wall Street lawyer who "regarded the United States as the greatest of his clients"; and William Howard Taft, who repeatedly sacrificed his personal ambitions to serve his country.[38]

In discussing the significant developments during Roosevelt's administration Rhodes' treatment is, for the most part, encomium. The President's course in the anthracite coal strike assured labor peace in the mines for years to come. In the Northern Securities case, despite the fact that James J. Hill, "as honest a man as ever lived," had formed the company in a statesmanlike project to protect investors, the President was right in his opposition, for had this merger been approved, "a few men, by successive steps might have controlled the railroad system of the country." [39]

On the other hand, Roosevelt was also right when he permitted the United States Steel Corporation to take over the Tennessee Coal and Iron Company during the Panic of 1907. Roosevelt was right again when he ordered the dishonorable discharge of Negro troops following the Brownsville affair. He was "supremely right" when he urged rapid expansion of the navy, and "we peace lovers . . . were wrong" in opposing him.[40]

In sending Marines to Santo Domingo, Roosevelt "acted simply as a policeman" at the request of that country's government but in so doing he made it possible for that country to fare better than ever before. The President's action in remitting part of the indemnity levied against China for the Boxer Rebellion showed his magnanimity of soul. It was due to his tact and influence that the Russians and Japanese finally reached agreement at Portsmouth, and it was further due to Roosevelt's talents that the dispute over Japanese immigration was resolved peacefully:

> It was fortunate that in the presidential chair was a man of culture who appreciated the Japanese civilization and at the same time was a true American full of sympathy for the West and who understood the view of the Californians.[41]

Of some actions of Roosevelt Rhodes did not entirely approve. His inviting Booker T. Washington to the White House was a mischief, for it encouraged Negroes to think the President was going to "raise them to social equality." The President, too, would have done better to avoid interference in the Moroccan crisis of 1905, but, "As long as a different view obtained, Roosevelt's action was wise and just." On Panama, Roosevelt should have "exercised the virtue of patience, as he was so advised by Senator Hanna. Many things might have happened without the secession of Panama." On the other hand, the refusal of Colombia to cede the canal territory on the terms offered "was blackmail and aroused all the fighting qualities in Roosevelt's nature." As to the building of the canal itself, Rhodes agreed with James Bryce: "There is something in the magnitude and the methods of this enterprise which a poet might take as his theme." [42]

Compared with such luminaries as Hanna and Roosevelt, McKinley was a pale star indeed. Rhodes was impressed with McKinley's devotion to his wife, his Methodist sincerity, and his willingness to modify his protectionist views once he saw the problem from the vantage point of the White House. But McKinley was weak, and his weakness helped bring on the "unnecessary war" with Spain. Further, although McKinley had said forcible annexation of Spanish territories would be "criminal aggression," he did acquire the Philippines through forcible annexation. Nor was the President forced into this policy: his hold upon the country was so great that any peace policy he recommended would have carried. Rhodes acquitted McKinley of hypocrisy, however; "President McKinley was a conscientious Methodist, and he fully believed that in the Philippines the white man's burden was laid upon the United States." Rhodes added, however, that McKinley's desire for "personal fame doubtless was bound up in his action." [43]

McKinley's conduct may have left something to be desired, but not that of American soldiers and sailors. At Santiago, "American seamen fought like gentlemen and not like brutes. Exactly the same may be said of the American soldiers who contended before Santiago." The battle of Manila Bay was among the great naval engagements of history, thanks to Admiral Dewey, "long headed as well as daring," and to his seamen, most of whom were native-born Americans. The attack on San Juan Hill, "as gallant a deed as was ever done," was made by troops of the regular army: "No word of praise can be too high for the work of the soldiers that day." [44]

The war may have been unnecessary, but with most of its consequences Rhodes was pleased. American policy in Cuba in respect to observing the Teller amendment constituted a "glorious page" in history, while the Platt amendment was wise. In Puerto Rico, the American record was creditable; if the United States had erred, it was in granting too much, not too little, autonomy. Even in regard to the Philippines, Rhodes had words of approval. He paid tribute to the anti-imperialists for "taking the part of the inferior" peoples, but in making his estimate of American policy he preferred to take, out of "the maze of contradictions" offered by officials and observers, the word of "the man, who, more than any other one, is responsible for our policy—Elihu Root." [45]

On the basis of such testimony, he concluded that American rule in the islands furnished an example of "wise administration of colonial possessions on a new and original plan." There was "absolutely no exploitation," Rhodes affirmed. If American troops had been less than gentlemanly during the Filipino rebellion it should be remembered that they used the "water cure" only to get information, and, in any case, "While very painful this torture was seldom fatal nor permanently damaging." Besides, the troops operated under intolerable conditions and were subject to outrageous provocation.[46] As to the disposition of the islands, Rhodes recommended the "sound and complete" answer given by Theodore Roosevelt in 1913:

> "We are governing and have been governing the islands in the interests of the Filipinos themselves. If, after due time, the Filipinos themselves decide that they do not wish to be thus governed, then I trust that we will leave; but when we do leave it must be distinctly understood that . . . we are absolutely quit of responsibility for them of every kind and description." [47]

However much Rhodes modified his anti-imperialist beliefs, he held fast to the economic and social faith of the 19th century. Indeed, in the last volume his opinions on such matters have an acerbity and shrillness lacking in the earlier volumes. That the masses were aroused against the classes in 1896 was due to "Bryan's oratory more than to any other one cause." For an analysis of that election written with "a comparative lack of bias" he offered the commentary of Goldwin Smith, "a keen observer from England":

> the organization of the Democratic party [has been] captured by Anarchism and Repudiation. Bimetallism . . . is the least part of the matter; even Repudiation is not the greatest. The

> greatest is the uprising of disorder, . . . against the institutions of the Republic. . . . Bryanism is a vast cave of Adullam, in which are combined all the distressed, all the discontented, all who have nothing to lose and may hope to gain by a general overturn. . . . In November the Republic of the Fathers will be fighting for its life.

The Hepburn bill of 1905, he charged, was based on the principle, "Resolved, That we don't like railroads and wish we knew some way to bang 'em good.' " Such evils as there may have been in railroad operation should have been left to the correction of "the natural working of economic forces." Natural forces, too, explained economic depressions, which were phenomena inseparable from progress and civilization:

> In making a study of the panic of 1857 I wrote, "The reason of panics lies deep in the human heart." Passing through the panic of 1873 as a business man, those of 1893 and 1907 as an investor, I have seen no reason to change this opinion. . . . the cause is always the same. If men were always wise, if they themselves or corporations in which they held stock never ran into debt, if there were never fluctuations in the prices of produce—in short, if all business was done for cash, if men never incurred obligations which they could not at once meet, if they did not spread out with the idea that every extension, every conversion of liquid into fixed capital meant a larger income from their enterprise, financial panics would never occur. But a society of that kind would lack commercial energy, would cease its material progress, and, in fact, would be impossible in one based on European civilization.[48]

Rhodes' judgments of business leaders embodied such assumptions. John D. Rockefeller was compared to Napoleon; he was an organizing genius who "acted in accordance with the conditions of his time," was "fair to all of his stockholders and gentle to competing refineries who would work with him on his own terms, which in every case turned out advantageously for those manufacturers." The Standard Oil Company performed a service in stabilizing prices, and these "could not have been excessive or it would have lacked candid defenders." [49]

The critics of Rockefeller he dismissed rather summarily. Ida Tarbell's work, *The History of the Standard Oil Company*, was tailored to fit the prejudices of the author; Henry Demarest Lloyd's *Wealth Against Commonwealth* reflected its author's socialist beliefs and besides, his accusations against the Standard Oil Company were so extreme as to warrant disbelief.[50]

Andrew Carnegie, too, was portrayed as a great man whose "faults were those of many self-made men and lay on the surface." His foibles were apparent but "he was ahead of his age in his devotion to 'gentle Peace.' . . . No wonder then that the great war of 1914 broke his heart." Carnegie's career prompted Rhodes to allude to the advantages of poverty in childhood and to raise the question:

> Is it well for the State to have such huge fortunes as those of Rockefeller and Carnegie accumulate in a lifetime? It must be said in their defense that they accomplished the difficult art of giving, that their benefactions were noble and that they set a pattern for other rich men, whose gifts and bequests have been on the side of civilization. . . . That their gifts made for the good of civilization, however, will fail to convince the mass of voters, who cannot see that fine pictures, well-collected libraries, endowed universities, cure of disease and prophylactic treatment compensate them for a deprivation of their share of the cake in favor of Rockefeller, Carnegie and others.[51]

About J. P. Morgan Rhodes was not quite so certain. To be sure, Morgan's reorganization of the railroads after 1899 was really marvelous: he substituted "excellent business management and the proper payment of interest and dividends" for "a cut-throat competition that did no one, except perhaps speculators, any good." In his financing of the United States Steel Corporation, however, Morgan was far from marvelous:

> the whole amount of cash in the flotation of the United States Steel Corporation was twenty-five millions; the rest was faith in Morgan. . . . was it worth while to abuse that faith and put upon the market . . . more than five hundred and fifty millions of "water"? True, Morgan's friends argued that the capitalization was based upon earnings and not upon the value of the property; but what consolation was that to "widows and orphans" who had invested in Steel Common at from 38 to 55 because it paid four per cent, when the Corporation suspended dividends on the Common and the stock went below 10 as it did in 1903? . . .

Rhodes concluded that "the United States Steel Corporation has never been the asset for the country that the Carnegie Steel Company was or might have been."[52]

This, then, was Rhodes' final message to his readers: The United States was the finest country in the world, possessing a citizenry worthy of such a country, except for labor agitators, radical reformers and some foreign-born elements; its government had proved a blessing not only to its own people but also to peoples in the Caribbean and the Philippines; its economic system was sound, operating in accord with economic law, providing not only direct material benefits to the masses but also great indirect benefactions through the philanthropy of the wealthy; the major dangers to this happy state arose from attempts to interfere with the natural laws of economics and to weaken the gold standard; but such attempts would come to naught provided the voters kept the Republican Party in power and so long as that party produced leaders of the calibre of Mark Hanna and Theodore Roosevelt.

To readers of Rhodes' own generation this made sense. John T. Morse, Jr., in commenting on *From Hayes to McKinley*, likened Rhodes' combination of kindliness, mercy and justice to that of God.[53] Senator Lodge read the book with interest and admiration.[54] William R. Thayer thought it "must stand as the chief product in American history during our half-century."[55] Charles Harding Firth said it was "of the greatest value to foreign students" and James Bryce praised Rhodes' "constant sense of impartiality and the preference of truth to effect."[56] Comments on *The McKinley and Roosevelt Administrations* were in the same vein. Albert J. Beveridge found this volume admirably done, Rhodes' discussion of Hanna being "quite the best thing that has been done on that subject."[57] Albert Bushnell Hart, while disagreeing with some of Rhodes' estimates, praised the book as

> the most individual of all your books. No one else would have written it because it embodies personal contacts and observations, and participations which no other historian has had. It is a very interesting and important period of American history viewed from the inside. . . .[58]

Some reviewers echoed these sentiments. L. E. Robinson in *The Bookman* praised *From Hayes to McKinley* because of its cogent application to current events. The book, said he, "furnishes a strikingly suggestive background for a sane and constructive study of contemporary social and economic disquietude." Rhodes' discussion of the Molly Maguires, wrote Robinson, "reminds one of the sad vacancy in the thought of the day in respect to ideals and methods of Americanizing . . . foreign labor in industries essential to the support of those finer human products of our civilization."[59] The *Review of Reviews* opined that

> Mr. Rhodes displays in this volume the same qualities that have given him very high rank as an historian. . . . His care in the

> use of documentary materials and the abundant foot-note references . . . enable the reader to know just what is behind his every statement . . .[60]

The *New York Times Book Review* gave page one position to a review by Brander Matthews, the noted literary critic, in which he lavished praise on a "good job well done. . . . His [Rhodes'] dominating quality is integrity; his main desire is to see the thing as it is and to set it forth as naked as the truth itself."[61]

Reviewers also found much to commend in *The McKinley and Roosevelt Administrations*. The *Review of Reviews* briefly noted:

> The quality of Mr. Rhodes' historical writing has been fully tested and never found wanting. . . . In the present volume Mr. Rhodes is writing about men whom he knew personally, . . . At the same time, the trained historian's sense of perspective gives to each personality its due place . . . the author has had access to the personal and official sources of information, and has made wise use of his materials.[62]

The Bookman recommended it as providing "a delightful way of reviewing events so recent as with difficulty to appear already historical."[63] The *New York Times Book Review* was especially flattering. The front page was devoted to a review which, together with an additional column and a half on an inside page, seemed to indicate that Rhodes' work was little short of perfect:

> When a historian who has shown the master's touch as often as Rhodes has shown it deals with conditions as late as those of 1909, we are almost startled at the picture which he presents. Figures that strutted importantly before the eyes of many of us, . . . are paraded in a steady searching light approaching that of permanent judgment.

While the anonymous reviewer thought the book of uniform excellence he was impressed particularly by Rhodes' treatment of the leaders of business. Not only did Rhodes do much to remove the dollar mark from the reputation of Mark Hanna, but he also discussed John D. Rockefeller in such a way as to "inspire confidence [in Rockefeller] on the part of the reader." The reviewer then went on to praise Rhodes for his balance and fairness:

> Let us observe with gratitude that the sanity and impartiality which Rhodes has brought to the study of our national life are abundantly in evidence in his new volume. . . .
>
> Rhodes is the apostle of perspective, the foe of slant. He

> actually teaches us to think well of men whose opinions were not his own or ours, . . . In his quest of truth he is tireless, and usually finds it. He assembles and weighs all the evidence, . . . , and then with a happy faculty—even a marvelous gift when he is at his best—delivers his dictum free from the unessential, the distracting, the distorted, . . . He is no propagandist for any cause and he is not afraid to be original.[64]

There were sufficient numbers of readers of Rhodes' own generation, too, to provide appreciation for his work and a market for his newer volumes. During these years, as during his heyday, readers whom Rhodes never saw wrote to him expressing commendation for his work. His volumes, they wrote, recreated old times; awakened renewed interest in history; provided fair accounts of controversial developments; and led to their being better citizens.[65] They continued to buy the older volumes of the *History* and they also purchased the newer books. *From Hayes to McKinley* ($2.75) sold nearly 3400 copies in the first year of publication; *The McKinley and Roosevelt Administrations* ($4.00) more than 3000 within five months after its appearance. Also impressive were sales of an eight-volume set placed on the market in 1920: these amounted to 1044 in three years.[66] Rhodes, however, was not pleased. The Macmillan Company, he felt, was not advertising his books aggressively enough. He was not persuaded by the company's explanation that his works had been given special attention in its sales campaigns but that the public was not in a mood to buy great numbers of books of a serious nature.[67]

What proved distressing to Rhodes was the reception accorded by scholars to the two volumes. *The Nation* dismissed *From Hayes to McKinley* in a brief notice saying the book was "far from constituting a satisfactory history." [68] David Y. Thomas, writing in the *Mississippi Valley Historical Review*, found the volume enjoyable but disappointing. Rhodes, he noted, discussed the Molly Maguires and the Knights of Labor without alluding to the factors which produced them, a failing which the historian repeated in his treatment of the silver issue and the Interstate Commerce Commission Act. The movements of population and the settlement of the West were not even mentioned, he pointed out.[69]

Frederic L. Paxson made somewhat the same criticism, adding that Rhodes neglected social and economic factors almost entirely. He then struck at Rhodes' extensive use of assistants in research:

> the result of such historical method is unlikely to . . . reveal unity of historical construction or the ripe judgments . . . that

> come only to the writer who has done his own selecting and discarding among the sources. . . .
>
> Rarely do the related facts in this volume appear to have meaning or to be parts of a coherent structure. . . .[70]

Charles A. Beard used a review of the work to challenge Rhodes' reputation for fairness and impartiality:

> Mr. Rhodes is widely celebrated . . . as just, impartial, punctilious and fair. The text before us speaks for itself. Is it fair to give nearly one hundred pages to the disorders (real and alleged) ascribed to labor and scarcely a line to labor organizations, programs, . . . and unendurable labor conditions? Is it fair to cite Judge J. E. Gary on the Chicago trial of 1887 and not allow the reader to know Governor Altgeld's reasons for issuing his celebrated pardons? Are Agnes Repplier, *The Nation*, and President Cleveland our chief reliable authorities on the Pullman strike? . . . Does the office of the impartial historian require that Mr. Bryan be dismissed as "specious" and Mr. Cleveland suffocated with repetitious praise: . . . ?

To this, Beard added the charge that Rhodes was remiss in his research: "Careful reading . . . fails to reveal a single capital idea or fact that cannot be found in the books available in any Carnegie library of fair proportions." Rhodes, indeed, was completely out of touch with the period on which he wrote:

> Henry Adams . . . came to the conclusion that the most significant thing . . . between the Compromise of 1850 and the campaign of 1896 was the triumph of capitalism over the "agrarians," . . . Mr. Rhodes sees in the same period a great military drama followed by the dullest play that could be imagined. Though of Henry Adams' epoch he has written a phantom history of twenty years in which wooden characters come upon the stage like marionettes, wave their arms, deliver orations on the rectitude of their intentions, are challenged, and retire (usually) to oblivion. . . . Mr. Rhodes has seen America a part of the time through the windows of a country house and the remainder of the time through the windows of the Centennial Club.[71]

The reception given *From Hayes to McKinley*, however, was mild compared to that accorded *The McKinley and Roosevelt Administrations*. A brief note in the *Mississippi Valley Historical Review* suggested that

> if the reader can suppress the uncomfortable feeling that what he is perusing purports to be history, and settle down to gather

> the reactions of an amiable gentleman on certain past and gone events, all is well.[72]

Professor Charles R. Lingley of Dartmouth College, writing in the *American Political Science Review*, described the volume as "excellent raw material"; to him Rhodes' judgments of the Democratic party and William Jennings Bryan seemed "surprisingly superficial in these days when we have seen so much of the Bryan platform of 1896 put into operation by both great parties." [73]

Frederic L. Paxson thought this volume, like its predecessor, lacked treatment of social and economic matters. It was political history of a high order, Paxson conceded, but even so it only provided "the materials that some future historian will need to use." He criticized Rhodes' uncritical use of biography and autobiography as sources as well as his failure to appreciate that there had been a change in American thought and standards as well as in behavior: "We have had a revolution in ethics as well as in manners, but he does not show it." [74]

Frederic A. Ogg, the distinguished political scientist, agreed with other reviewers that the book was "rather the raw material of history than history itself." He, too, pointed out the lack of a unifying theme, and continued:

> one cannot repress the feeling that if Mr. Rhodes had been less content to move along easily with the surface drift of party politics and diplomacy and had probed resolutely into the social and economic phenomena of the period . . . he would have given us a richer, more colorful, and permanently useful book. . . .[75]

Oswald Garrison Villard, an old admirer of Rhodes, reviewed the book for *The Nation* (of which he was now editor), under the heading "Near Journalistic History."

> It illustrates well the danger of writing the chronicles of a period that one has himself lived through [wrote Villard]. It is, like all his writing, easy and delightful reading, but smacks neither of the diligent research nor of the shrewd, penetrating judgments which made the fame of his first volumes so far-reaching and so secure. . . . It is, moreover, far more of a study of Mark Hanna, McKinley and Roosevelt than a thorough study of their times and the deep underlying currents. . . .

Villard suggested that Rhodes' relationship to Hanna made his work difficult; he wondered whether Rhodes would have been opposed to the Spanish-American War had Hanna favored it; he felt

Rhodes had been sketchy and one-sided in his treatment of the Boxer Rebellion and of American relations with Santo Domingo. But, he went on,

> the great weakness of this history is that it accepts the existing economic order as hardly worth treatment, that it skims the surface of the labor problems, and contains no independent judgments upon the labor and economic happenings of the times. The name of Samuel Gompers appears but once, . . . ; that of Eugene Debs not at all. . . .[76]

Perhaps the most devastating analysis came from Harry Elmer Barnes. Having conceded that Rhodes was an historian of "unquestionable integrity and honesty of purpose, a powerful intellect, dignity of expression, and, an extensive personal knowledge of the events and figures described," Barnes went on to say that Rhodes lacked training in the methods and content of historiography, concentrated on political history based on personalities and episodes imperfectly placed in their social setting, failed to grasp the "sweeping economic transformation which completely revolutionized American industry" since 1865, and made neither analysis nor synthesis of American society and culture in the period covered.

Rhodes' reputation for impartiality, he said, rested on his work on Reconstruction, but in his treatment of the period since 1876,

> His work has been constructed on the basis of as definite an economic philosophy and as fixed a set of social preconceptions as [socialist writings]. Mr. Rhodes writes from the standpoint of a Cleveland Democrat, with the social philosophy of Herbert Spencer and William Graham Sumner, and the economic doctrines of Cobden. He apparently believes with Henry Cabot Lodge in the efficacy of "natural forces" as the solution of modern economic and social problems. This outlook, in at least a subconscious manner, colors all his judgments on such matters, and, to no small extent, has determined his selection of material. Further, impartiality is not objectivity. Mr. Rhodes is not objective, but . . . [passes] severe moral judgments upon his characters.

These may be interesting, Barnes concluded, but Rhodes wrote as if he expected "that St. Peter will rely in no small degree upon these judgments at the 'Great Assize.' "[77]

Such criticism deeply disturbed Rhodes. To John T. Morse, Jr., he tried to dismiss it lightly as being "socialistic," or, in the case of the *American Historical Review*, as being the product of reviewers who begrudged giving authors proper credit for their work.[78] But the depth of his hurt is indicated by the letters he wrote to unfavorable reviewers. To the reviewer of the Boston *Evening Transcript*, who wrote that *The McKinley and Roosevelt Administrations* was "absolutely barren" in "illuminating detail," and that the volume was "one that would not be a credit to a lesser man," Rhodes retorted that he had possessed a mass of such detail but had refrained from using it because he did not want to waste time discussing "a lot of subjects no one cares anything about." He pointedly reminded the reviewer that the New York *Times* reviewer thought Rhodes had chosen wisely out of the mass of material before him.[79] To Frederic A. Ogg Rhodes complained that his review had been unkind; to Charles A. Beard that his had been sarcastic. Ogg returned a soft answer,[80] but Beard snapped back:

> I am sorry that you think my criticism was "sarcastic." I meant it to be frank and honest difference of opinion on questions of proportion and methods of treatment. I have read with interest your statements about your familiarity with the writings of Governor Altgeld and H. D. Lloyd. I can only say that I am surprised that they did not exercise a greater influence upon the formulation of your historical opinions.
>
> I agree with you that matters of proportion are difficult, and perhaps had better rest our case in agreeing with Goethe that after all we see what we see, and nothing more.[81]

Hostile criticism of his work certainly disturbed Rhodes, but there were other, and more personal, factors which contributed to what Charles W. Eliot told him was his "very unhappy state of mind." [82] Financial anxieties, family problems, his wife's and his own declining health—all these contributed, along with the scholarly reception of his last volumes, to the deepening gloom.

Financial worries, symbolized by the sale of the house on Beacon Street, had their roots in unfortunate investments. These investments declined in value during the depression in the immediate postwar years, a decline which Rhodes felt so keenly that he sharply curtailed his purchases of books.[83]

His anxiety was accentuated by the fact that the burden of caring for his son's family was almost entirely on his shoulders—a family that now numbered seven children. Daniel, who had been marked out for a literary career by his father, never fulfilled his father's ambition; neither was he successful in his attempts at a business career. He married an Englishwoman, Bertha Johnson, assisted his father in the literary revision of much of James' work, and himself wrote several books of a philosophical nature, none of which made an impression. Much of his time was spent on the Continent, where he was noted as a mountain climber and tennis player. Given James' puritan conscience, the responsibility for Daniel's family was one he could not take lightly.[84]

The historian, of course, was far from that want which overtook so many of his fellow-Americans in their old age, but one fate he shared in common with even the poorest: the growing sense of loneliness as those closest to him slipped away in death. Charles Francis Adams, Walter Hines Page, James Bryce, Henry Lee Higginson, Dr. Ian Maclaurin, president of the Massachusetts Institute of Technology, whose "quiet humor and . . . eagerness to get at the bottom of things" so pleased Rhodes, and Barrett Wendell, his closest friend—they all passed, leaving Rhodes a bitter residue of grief.[85]

He was moved most deeply by the deaths of Theodore Roosevelt and of Mrs. Augusta Hanna, his sister and widow of Mark Hanna. "I cannot tell you how I sorrow at his [Roosevelt's] loss," Rhodes wrote to Trevelyan. "He was a warm friend, and to him and to Mark Hanna I am more deeply indebted than to any other men."[86]

Mrs. Hanna died in November, 1921. Rhodes wished to attend her funeral, but he dared not:

> I have lost my sister Mrs. Hanna to whom I was devotedly attached and of whom I have seen much during the past years. Her death has affected me profoundly . . . [It] was unexpected to me as I had had cheering indications . . . and the sad news itself I read in the newspaper . . . I commenced immediately to go to the funeral in Cleveland when Lucia McBride [his niece] came in and insisted persistently that I should not go to which were joined the entreaties of my wife lest I should take cold in the sleeping-car and have another attack of bronchitis. Much to my grief I gave up the project as I would have liked to pay the last rites to her whom I loved so much.[87]

Rhodes, brooding over his loss, a prey to insomnia, once more journeyed to Europe with his wife, hopeful that the change of scene would distract and soothe him. But the trip only helped to bring to the fore another source of distress, the failing health of Mrs. Rhodes. Never sturdy, now she was obviously declining. In 1924 she was completely prostrated by paralysis.[88]

To such strain was added the steady impairment of his own constitution; he wrote wistfully echoing the wish of Robert G. Ingersoll "that when the world was made good health ought to have been made catching instead of disease." [89] To the usual ailments of throat and stomach was added a new one, unknown to him if not to his doctors—arteriosclerosis.[90] In 1923 he noted that his penmanship bore the mark of age and that his eyesight was failing. Within two years the condition of his eyes was such that he had to give up reading, one of his greatest pleasures; his writing became so feeble that he had to resort to a typist for his correspondence.[91]

He was vexed by his own failings. He wrote to Trevelyan that it "does not seem creditable to me when I think that I am ten years younger than you, but some way or other, decay has set in with me earlier." [92] When Rhodes returned from Europe in the fall of 1926 Charles K. Bolton was shocked to notice that he "looked shrunken and wasted away." [93] On Jan. 22, 1927, he died. His ashes were sent to Riverside Cemetery in Cleveland, to rest with those of the members of his family.

So passed into history a man who, after middle age, had wrought so mightily in the writing of history that he had helped shape the thoughts and attitudes of generations, at home and abroad, not only in such historical matters as the Civil War and Reconstruction but also in the broader issues of race, international amity, relations of capital and labor, and the basic social virtues. That he faltered in his declining years does not detract from the significance of his contribution. A study of that contribution is now in order. To do so, it may be of value to summarize, first, Rhodes' overall interpretation of American history, and, second, the commentaries of historical critics upon his work.

NOTES

[1] Rhodes to William R. Thayer, Nov. 21, 1918; Nov. 22, 1918. Rhodes Papers.

[2] Rhodes to Charles H. Firth, April 17, 1919, in M. A. D. Howe, *Rhodes*, p. 303; Rhodes to Robert Grant, Nov. 6, 1919. Rhodes Papers.

[3] Rhodes to Sir George Otto Trevelyan, July 13, 1921. Rhodes Papers.

[4] Rhodes to Barrett Wendell, Feb. 27, 1920. Rhodes Papers.

[5] Rhodes to George A. Myers, Dec. 27, 1921, in M. A. D. Howe, *Rhodes*, p. 325.

[6] *From Hayes to McKinley*, pp. 19–51.

[7] *Ibid.*, pp. 13, 32–33.

[8] *Ibid.*, p. 41.

[9] *Ibid.*, pp. 46–47.

[10] *Ibid.*, p. 48.

[11] *Ibid.*, p. 19.

[12] *Ibid.*, pp. 25–26, 48–49.

[13] *Ibid.*, p. 50. Rhodes thought it worth noting that mess for the fashionable Seventh Regiment was supplied by Delmonico's. *Ibid.*, p. 51.
[14] *Ibid.*, p. 278.
[15] *Ibid.*, p. 270.
[16] *Ibid.* The characterization of Hoxie is attributed to the economist, F. W. Taussig.
[17] *Ibid.*, p. 386.
[18] *Ibid.*, pp. 424–425.
[19] *Ibid.*, p. 426. The reference to Altgeld is cited from *The Nation*, July 12, 1894.
[20] *From Hayes to McKinley*, pp. 394, 426–428. During the Pullman strike Rhodes commended U. S. District Judge Augustus R. Ricks for issuing an injunction against the strikers in Cleveland, Ohio. Ricks to Rhodes, Aug. 21, 1894. Rhodes Papers.
[21] *From Hayes to McKinley*, pp. 278, 281, 283–284.
[22] *Ibid.*, pp. 55, 64, 70. Rhodes noted later that the Roman Catholic church "was, as has always been the case in the United States . . . on the side of law and order." *Ibid.*, p. 86.
[23] *Ibid.*, p. 81. Rhodes mentioned the common belief that McParlan was a provocateur but did not discuss it. *Ibid.*, p. 79.
[24] *Ibid.*, p. 84.
[25] *Ibid.*, pp. 95, 99.
[26] *Ibid.*, p. 357 n.
[27] *Ibid.*, p. 296.
[28] *Ibid.*, pp. 230–231.
[29] *Ibid.*, pp. 268–269.
[30] *Ibid.*, pp. 167, 191, 196, 348, 423.
[31] *Ibid.*, pp. 328–329.
[32] *The McKinley and Roosevelt Administrations*, pp. 7, 8.
[33] *Ibid.*, pp. 10–12, 23–24.
[34] *Ibid.*, pp. 1, 30, 61, 264–265.
[35] *Ibid.*, pp. 237–246, 280. It is interesting to note that in discussing the anthracite strike Rhodes showed none of that harshness which marked his treatment of other strikes.
[36] *Ibid.*, pp. 140, 290–291.
[37] *Ibid.*, pp. 230, 234, 299, 361, 389, 395.
[38] *Ibid.*, pp. 184, 208–212, 310, 311, 318.
[39] *Ibid.*, pp. 221, 226, 247.
[40] *Ibid.*, pp. 341, 350, 368.
[41] *Ibid.*, pp. 307, 318–319, 373.
[42] *Ibid.*, pp. 229, 267, 271, 277, 312. Rhodes remarked of Washington: "his clear comprehension and unselfish advocacy made you forget his color." *Ibid.*, p. 228.
[43] *Ibid.*, pp. 10, 55, 61, 64, 67, 107–108, 173, 184, 187.
[44] *Ibid.*, pp. 74–75, 86, 95.
[45] *Ibid.*, pp. 99, 176–177, 181, 183, 188, 190.
[46] *Ibid.*, pp. 201, 203–204, 213.
[47] Quoted in *ibid.*, pp. 216–217.
[48] *Ibid.*, pp. 27–28, 323, 329, 344.
[49] *Ibid.*, pp. 158–161, 165.
[50] *Ibid.*, pp. 165–166.
[51] *Ibid.*, pp. 146, 148, 153–154, 168.
[52] *Ibid.*, pp. 115–116, 153, 156.
[53] John T. Morse, Jr., to Rhodes, Feb. 7, 1920. Rhodes Papers.
[54] Henry Cabot Lodge to Rhodes, Feb. 5, 1920. Rhodes Papers.
[55] William R. Thayer to Rhodes, Oct. 30, 1919. Rhodes Papers.

[56] Charles H. Firth to Rhodes, Nov. 20, 1919; James Bryce to Rhodes, Dec. 6, 1919. Rhodes Papers.

[57] Albert J. Beveridge to Rhodes, Jan. 16, 1923. Rhodes Papers.

[58] Albert B. Hart to Rhodes, Jan. 1, 1924. Rhodes Papers.

[59] L (1920), 611–612.

[60] LXI (1920), 107.

[61] "From Hayes to McKinley in America," *New York Times Book Review*, Dec. 28, 1919, p. 1.

[62] LXVII (1923), 110.

[63] LVII (1923), 99.

[64] Dec. 3, 1922, pp. 1, 27. Somewhat similar were the comments of William Lyon Phelps, the popular literary critic of the day. See his column, "As I Like It," *Scribner's Magazine*, LXXIII (1923), 369.

[65] A sampling of such letters include those to Rhodes from Edmund Pechin, July 19, 1918; Jan. 29, 1920; Richard Henry Dana, Dec. 20, 1923; Julian Street, Aug. 9, 1923; Theodore L. Van Norden, Jan. 10, 1923; John T. Edsall, Dec. 28, 1920; William E. Endicott, Sept. 3, 1919; Harold G. Black, Jan. 17, 1922. Rhodes Papers.

[66] Statements of royalties, Macmillan Company to Rhodes, July 31, 1920; July 29, 1921; July 30, 1923; July 29, 1924. No report is available for fiscal year 1921–1922. Total royalties for four years indicated were $8,916.69. Rhodes Papers.

[67] George P. Brett, president, Macmillan Company, to Rhodes, Feb. 8, 1921; Aug. 23, 1921. Rhodes Papers.

[68] CX (1920), 805.

[69] VII (1920), 84–85.

[70] *American Historical Review*, XXV (1920), 525–526.

[71] *New Republic*, XXI (1919), 82.

[72] X (1923), 200.

[73] XVII (1923), 318–319.

[74] *American Historical Review*, XXVIII (1923), 565–566.

[75] *Yale Review*, New series, XIII (1924), 602.

[76] *The Nation*, CXVI (1923), 550–551.

[77] *New Republic*, XXXIV (1923), 23–24.

[78] Rhodes to John T. Morse, Jr., Feb. 10, 1920; July 21, 1920. Morse Papers.

[79] Boston *Evening Transcript*, Dec. 6, 1922, p. 9, quoted in *Book Review Digest*, XVIII (1923), 452. Rhodes to Sherwin L. Book, Dec. 22, 1922, in M. A. D. Howe, *Rhodes*, pp. 334–335.

[80] Frederick A. Ogg to Rhodes, April 1, 1924. Rhodes Papers. Wrote Ogg: "I am deeply sorry if my comment seemed unkind. It was not meant so."

[81] Charles A. Beard to Rhodes, Jan. 5, 1920. Rhodes Papers.

[82] Charles W. Eliot to Rhodes, Jan. 31, 1921. Rhodes Papers.

[83] Rhodes to Robert Grant, Nov. 2, 1919; Sir George Otto Trevelyan, Feb. 25, 1921. Rhodes Papers. Rhodes to George A. Myers, Sept. 24, 1921, in John A. Garraty (ed.), "Correspondence," *Ohio Historical Quarterly*, LXIV (1955), 388. Myers to Rhodes, April 15, 1921; W. M. Baldwin, Citizens Savings and Trust Company, Cleveland, Ohio, to Rhodes, June 26, 1918. Rhodes Papers.

[84] Interviews, Mrs. Bertha H. Rhodes, Mrs. Lucia McBride. Charles K. Bolton, *Notebook, 1886–1914*, p. 97 (Nov. 2, 1899). Rhodes to Paul L. Ford, Aug. 6, 1898; Daniel P. Rhodes to Rhodes, Oct. 26, 1896; April 1, 1897; June 22, 1900; Mark Hanna to Rhodes, Jan. 2, 1896. Rhodes Papers. The books written by Daniel were *A Pleasure Book of Grundenwald* (1903); *The Great Resolve: An Essay on the European War and the Possible Settlement Thereof* (n.d.); *The Philosophy of Change* (1909);

and *Our Immortality* (1919). Publication of the last two by the Macmillan Company was financed by James; sales were far short of meeting expenses. Statements, Macmillan Company to Rhodes, Sept. 15, 1910; April 30, 1920; July 31, 1920. Rhodes Papers. Daniel died in Switzerland, May, 1949. *New York Times*, May 9, 1949.

[85] Rhodes to Sir George Otto Trevelyan, Jan. 17, 1920; Worthington C. Ford, Feb. 24, 1922, in M. A. D. Howe, *Rhodes*, pp. 311, 328. Rhodes to Trevelyan, Nov. 12, 1922; Feb. 8, 1924; Frederick C. Shattuck, M.D., March 7, 1925; Lady Marion Bryce, April 2, 1922. Ida A. Higginson to Rhodes, Nov. 23, 1919; Nov. 9, 1921; William Sloane to Rhodes, Nov. 13, 1921. Rhodes Papers.

[86] Rhodes to Sir George Otto Trevelyan, Jan. 22, 1919, in M. A. D. Howe, *Rhodes*, p. 301.

[87] B. L. Hardin, M.D., to Rhodes, Nov. 19, 1921. Rhodes Papers. Rhodes to George A. Myers, Dec. 27, 1921, in John A. Garraty (ed.), "Correspondence," *Ohio Historical Quarterly*, LXIV (1955), 390–391.

[88] Moorfield Storey to Rhodes, Jan. 16, 1922; Rhodes to Gamaliel Bradford, June 2, 1924; F. C. Shattuck, M.D., Aug. 18, 1924. Rhodes Papers. Mrs. Rhodes died May 27, 1929. For a biographical sketch see Cleveland *Town Topics*, June 1, 1929.

[89] Rhodes to William R. Thayer, Dec. 26, 1919. Rhodes Papers.

[90] Harvey Cushing, M.D., "James Ford Rhodes," in M. A. D. Howe (ed.), *Later Years of the Saturday Club*, p. 354.

[91] Rhodes to Sir George Otto Trevelyan, April 28, 1923; Dec. 18, 1923; Robert Grant, Sept. 25, 1925. Rhodes Papers.

[92] Rhodes to Sir George Otto Trevelyan, Jan. 16, 1925. Rhodes Papers.

[93] Charles K. Bolton, *Notebook, 1925–1928*, p. 154 (Oct. 26, 1926).

Chapter 15

RHODES' INTERPRETATION OF AMERICAN HISTORY

STUDY of Rhodes' work, the salient points of which have already been covered in previous chapters, shows that his interpretation of the period, 1850–1909, was as follows:

The American people had produced a superior type of society because of their Anglo-Saxon heritage, their lofty standards of business and sexual morality, their sound character (derived largely from the Puritans), their capacity for hard work, and the disinterested generosity of their wealthy fellows. The Civil War was essentially a moral struggle over slavery, and while the North was on the side of the angels the South fought nobly for what it believed to be right. Reconstruction was basically an immoral process, subverting the order of nature by giving an inferior race power over a superior. Eventually, the good sense of Anglo-Saxons in both North and South prevailed in restoring "home rule" to the South, a development which represented a victory for "righteousness."

That there were defects in the American character, Rhodes conceded, filing a plea in extenuation, however, that they were largely attributable to Americans of recent foreign antecedents, with special allusion to Americans of Jewish descent. He also granted weaknesses in American society, noting that they were largely due to the activities of labor organizations, ignorance of the basic beneficence of "hard money," and existence of the protective tariff, misguided concern for the plight of the Negro, and too wide an extension of the franchise.

Fortunately, during critical times leadership of the country was in the hands of the Republican party. During its early years the party was a symbol of morality in politics; in its youth it gave Abraham Lincoln to the world and wiped out the stain of slavery; and if it erred in Reconstruction it redeemed itself nobly by upholding the standard of "honest money" and by asserting the national authority against the subversive elements which dominated the railroad strikes of 1877.

The country was fortunate, too, in possessing a matured Democratic party. The Northern wing, conducting itself as an Anglo-

Saxon party, gave loyal if critical support to Lincoln; and the Southern wing, purged of the sin of slavery, restored morality and order to the South. Grover Cleveland was a credit to his country: he fought "free silver," he resisted the temptations of imperialism, and he, like the Republican, Hayes, put down a challenge to governmental authority from labor agitators.

This Northern middle-class approach is developed in the one essay in which Rhodes attempted an interpretation of American history as a whole: "The Presidential Office," which first appeared in 1903.[1] Its theses were, first, the near-perfection of the American Constitution, and, second, the high level of the conduct of American government. As to the Constitution,

> it may be said that in the main it is rigid in those matters which should not be submitted to the decision of a legislature or to a popular vote without checks which secure reflection and a chance for the sober second thought, and that it has proved flexible in its adaptation to the growth of the country and to the development of the 19th century.[2]

As to government,

> An American may judge his own country best from European soil, . . . During the natural process of comparison, when one must recognize in many things the distinct superiority of England, Germany and France, . . . I have never had any reason to feel that the conduct of our national government has been inferior to that of any one of these highly civilized powers.[3]

In proof, Rhodes offered his appraisal of the various occupants of the White House. Of Washington:

> Never did a country begin a new enterprise with so wise a ruler. An admirable polity had been adopted, but much depended upon getting it to work, and the man who was selected to start the government was the man of all men for the task.[4]

Washington erred, apparently, in making Thomas Jefferson secretary of state, for Rhodes omitted mention of that, while emphasizing, "In domestic affairs he [Washington] showed discernment in selecting as his confidential adviser, Alexander Hamilton, a man who had great constructive talent." [5] Perhaps his slighting of Jefferson arose from his feeling that Jefferson was too democratic: "I wish Jefferson had not had that great faith in 'The People,' but he could not foresee our vast foreign immigration and the stimulus to large cities from our commercial and manufacturing expansion." [6]

At any rate, Adams, Jefferson and Madison were fairly good presidents, "inasmuch as they either maintained the power of the executive or increased its influence. Despite their many mistakes they somehow overcame . . . great difficulties." [7]

The country erred in not availing itself of a second term for John Quincy Adams, a man of sturdy Americanism and excellent training. This left it at the mercy of Andrew Jackson, who, "uneducated and with little experience in civil life, showed what power might be exercised by an arbitrary, unreasonable man who had the people at his back." [8] Jackson ushered in an "era of vulgarity in national politics" through the spoils system, and

> The evil which Jackson did lived after him; indeed, only a man as powerful for the good as he had been for the bad could have restored the civil service to the merit system which had prevailed before he occupied the White House. . . .[9]

Tyler and Polk, thought Rhodes, had suffered in their reputations because the histories of their administrations had been written by anti-slavery historians; he thought they merited approbation for the acquisition of Texas and the Mexican territories just as Jefferson did for acquiring Louisiana.[10]

Lincoln was significant in the growth of the presidential office because he so extended its powers as to establish, in effect, a dictatorship, a development which was possible only because Congress and the people supported him:

> Lincoln could not have persisted in his arbitrary acts had a majority of Congress definitely opposed them, and his real strength lay in the fact that he had the people at his back. . . . This is the safety of a dictatorship as long as the same intelligence obtains among the voters as now; for the people will not support a ruler in the exercise of extra-legal powers unless he be honest and patriotic. . . .[11]

Andrew Johnson, "by habits, manners, mind and character, was unfit for the presidential office, and whatever may have been the merit of his policy, a policy devised by angels could never have been carried on by such an advocate." [12] On the other hand, Grant "will be treated with charity by those who write about his presidential terms, because he meant well although he did not know how to do well." Grant, indeed, was to be praised for two achievements: his treaties of arbitration with Great Britain and his veto of the currency inflation measure of 1873. In the case of the latter:

> The wisdom of the framers of the Constitution in giving the President the veto power was exemplified. . . . His [Grant's] action demonstrated what a President may do in resisting by his constitutional authority some transitory wave of popular opinion, . . .[13]

Under Hayes the office not only gained in "force and dignity" but life in the White House itself was restored to the high moral atmosphere of the typical American home.[14] Grover Cleveland's administrations "made for righteousness." He strove for extension of the civil service; and, in using federal troops in the Pullman strike Cleveland "accomplished a fresh extension of executive power without an infraction of the Constitution." Also, in affirming the gold standard, Cleveland "served his country at the expense of his party,"[15] but it was well for the country in 1896 that the Republicans possessed an

> able and adroit manager [who] was quick to see, . . . , the force of the principle of sound money and started a remarkable campaign of education . . . the strength of the Republican canvass lay in the fact that the speakers and writers who made it believed sincerely that the gold standard would conduce to the greatest good of the greatest number. It was an inspiring canvass. The honest advocacy of sound principle won.[16]

McKinley, Rhodes wrote, represented one phase of Lincoln's genius: "The controlling idea of McKinley probably was that as he was elected by the people he should represent them. . . . it was his duty to carry out their will." Opinions might differ as to McKinley's impress, he conceded, but, "It is the judgment of two men of large knowledge of American history and present affairs that no President since Jefferson has been so successful in getting Congress to adopt the positive measures he desired."[17]

Of Theodore Roosevelt, of course, Rhodes could write only in superlatives:

> His birth, breeding, education and social advantages have been of the best. . . . As an American citizen we are all proud of him, . . . His transparent honesty and sincerity are winning qualities, . . . especially important in him who is the ruler of a nation. . . .

Roosevelt, in fact, possessed all the qualities listed essential by Justice Story: elevated talents, ripe virtue, incorruptible integrity, true patriotism.[18]

Thus, in his analysis of the presidential office, Rhodes accepted without reservation the New England Federalist interpretation of American constitutional development. The executive had served as a beneficent check on popular excess and as a positive check to public disorder, but despite its great power it had never succumbed to corruption or dictatorship: "From dangers of this sort the political virtue which we inherited from our English ancestors has preserved us."[19] The Presidency had been at its best when it saw and fulfilled this function, at its worst when it catered to popular feeling. The great Presidents had been Washington, John Quincy Adams, Lincoln, Grover Cleveland and Theodore Roosevelt; the worst, Andrew Jackson and Andrew Johnson. In these estimates, of course, Rhodes walked firmly in the footsteps of the traditional New England historians.

Now we may review what historical critics have said about Rhodes' work.

NOTES

[1] *Scribner's Magazine*, XXIII (1903), 157–173, reprinted in *Historical Essays*, pp. 203–241.

[2] *Historical Essays*, p. 203.

[3] *Ibid.*, p. 241.

[4] *Ibid.*, p. 205. Rhodes' reverence for Washington was such that he found it difficult to concede that Washington might have had weaknesses. He wrote to Mrs. C. H. Toy, Aug. 7, 1906, "it has never seemed a reason to me that because Webster and Napoleon and William III had vices that Washington must necessarily have." Rhodes Papers.

[5] *Historical Essays*, p. 207.

[6] Rhodes to John T. Morse, Jr., June 21, 1908. Morse Papers.

[7] *Historical Essays*, p. 207.

[8] *Ibid.*, pp. 209–210.

[9] *Ibid.*, pp. 209, 211.

[10] *Ibid.*, p. 212.

[11] *Ibid.*, pp. 215–216.

[12] *Ibid.*, p. 217.

[13] *Ibid.*, pp. 218, 219.

[14] *Ibid.*, p. 221.

[15] *Ibid.*, pp. 224–225, 226.

[16] *Ibid.*, pp. 228–229.

[17] *Ibid.*, p. 232, 234. Rhodes did not name the two men.

[18] *Ibid.*, p. 235.

[19] *Ibid.*, p. 240.

Chapter 16

SOME APPRAISALS OF RHODES

WHILE no exhaustive study of Rhodes' work has been made so far, significant commentaries have been written which call for attention.

The first such appraisal came, appropriately, from the Negro, John R. Lynch, whose views on Reconstruction George A. Myers had tried in vain to impress upon Rhodes. The *History*, insofar as it related to Reconstruction, wrote Lynch, was "not only inaccurate and unreliable but . . . biased, partisan and prejudiced," based upon partial, partisan and prejudiced sources.[1] Rhodes had minimized the mistakes of Southern Democrats while magnifying those of Southern Republicans.[2] In portraying white Republicans in the South as men of little property and character he ignored evidence showing that many leading white men of the South did in fact become leaders of the Republican party and were active in the Reconstruction governments.[3] The authenticity of some of Rhodes' examples of Negro corruption and incompetency was challenged, with the observation that even if true they were not sufficient to prove Rhodes' conclusions about the Negro in politics.[4] Rhodes, too, suppressed evidence of corruption in the "home rule" governments while he ignored the records made by Negroes who had distinguished themselves in political life.

The *History*, commented Lynch, was "remarkable, not only for what it says, but for what it leaves unsaid."[5] This was part of a pattern in which Rhodes tailored the facts to harmonize with his own view of Reconstruction and the Negro.[6] The very use of the term "home rule" was misleading, for in fact the South, except for brief periods of military rule, had never been ruled by foreigners, and the Reconstruction governments had been the only governments in the South genuinely republican in form.[7] Rhodes' portrayal of Reconstruction as a failure was false: "that policy was a grand and brilliant success."[8]

In more scholarly vein Professor Lester B. Shippee reviewed Rhodes' work as a whole upon the occasion of publication of the *History* in eight volumes, said to be a revised edition of the old

History plus the volume, *From Hayes to McKinley.*[9] Shippee conceded that the original seven-volume *History* would "always retain its place as a foremost exposition of that fateful era," 1850–1877, but he dismissed the claim that it had been seriously revised in the new edition. Despite the wealth of new materials that had become available since the work first made its appearance between 1893 and 1906 no significant changes were made in the new set; there was no indication that Rhodes had familiarized himself with fresh data and interpretations.[10]

Shippee thought Rhodes' treatment of military matters good; of diplomatic affairs, passable though inadequate; of character studies, interesting.[11] On the other hand, Rhodes was biased in his approach to the Civil War: he believed only an anti-slavery Northerner could write such history; he assumed that the slavery issue explained "practically all the main currents of American national history down to the close of Reconstruction"; he was deeply influenced by von Holst and was careless in handling his sources relating to slavery.[12] Rhodes' discussion of the period was vitiated also because he ignored the Turner thesis, neglecting the role of the West and the significance of public land and railroad legislation.[13] Since his *History* had been centered on slavery his work possessed no unifying factor once that problem was resolved.

Thus, Rhodes failed to grasp the significance of agrarian upheavals; he did not understand the significance of the Fourteenth Amendment, although his sources should have shown him its importance to business; he lacked understanding of economic forces and his chapters on social conditions bore no integral relationship to the body of his work. Rhodes was too preoccupied with political history: "He watches the wheels go round and describes a portion of the machinery; too often, however, the reader is left to guess at the motive forces which supply the power." [14] In addition, Shippee found that Rhodes was unfair to Stephen A. Douglas and Andrew Johnson; devoted too much space to the merely spectacular, such as the Molly Maguires, draft riots and slave rescues; and was superficial in the last volume, covering events from 1876 to 1896.[15]

Even more trenchant criticism came from Professor Raymond C. Miller, for he questioned the very quality on which Rhodes' reputation rested: his impartiality. Rhodes, he pointed out, had little personal knowledge of the South, and depended for his information on sources not beyond suspicion, such as quotations from Southern newspapers in Northern papers and testimony from persons like Fanny Kemble: "No one who knew the South at all and had

Rhodes' earnest desire to serve truth could have written the famous slavery chapter in Volume I." [16]

Absence of Southern material in the North when the early volumes were written might explain such a weakness, but no such explanation was possible for similar defects in the "revised" edition issued in 1921. Ignoring the body of material accumulated since his first writing, Rhodes had modified his position on "no fundamental point on which his findings have been challenged by the work of subsequent students." [17]

Rhodes, influenced by his business background and the scarcity of available sources, was also deeply impressed by the classic historians, whom he took for a model. For that reason he took for subject the Civil War, which could be treated with the synthetic unity characteristic of his masters. Such unity could be attained only by the omission of seemingly irrelevant material, and emphasis upon a central theme occasionally so pronounced that it approached distortion.[18] In his treatment,

> Rhodes was openly and frankly subjective . . . , no one could have the slightest doubt as to where his sympathies lay, or why. His method was deliberately chosen. . . . Rhodes could be judicial; but he followed the practice of the law court, where evidence is presented and weighed in order that judgment may be pronounced.
>
> The sympathies which Rhodes displayed were not those of conscious preconception but were, in his opinion, the result of a very impartial investigation of the facts. Error, he felt, was the result either of deliberate misrepresentation or neglect, and neither of these faults could be charged to him. . . . Although he earnestly desired to tell the truth, he gave no heed to the more subtle psychological factors of importance in every human action. . . .[19]

Rhodes, continued Miller, was biased by patriotic fervor in discussing foreign affairs, constitutional issues, and the American economic system.[20] His work also suffered from deliberate neglect of the West, and from overlooking economic and social forces in the development of the nation, a blindness which led him to misinterpret both the role of the federal navy and the diplomatic struggle during the Civil War and to treat Reconstruction in purely political terms.[21] Miller noted that while Lester B. Shippee, lacking military experience, had thought sound Rhodes' discussion of military matters, Charles Francis Adams, who had served in the Civil War, judged it poor.[22] He himself praised Rhodes' character sketches, but pointed out how unfairly he had portrayed John Brown, Stephen A. Douglas and Andrew Johnson.[23]

The volume covering the years, 1876–1896, Miller described as possessing the faults of the earlier volumes without many of the virtues. Lacking a coherent viewpoint, dominated by a narrow political approach, Rhodes was unable to grasp the essential nature of the problems of that period.[24] Further

> He was in profound sympathy with the social philosophy of the leaders who directed affairs in the last third of the century, and could not find it in his heart to subject them to the criticism he well knew how to use. . . .[25]

In summary, Miller concluded:

> Rhodes' history is not analytical. He was a storyteller rather than a philosopher; and his simple tale of what happened, with slight interest in cause or result, was in accord with the best standards of his day. . . .
>
> Given the age in which Rhodes wrote, the materials which were then available, and the background from which he came, his fairness on most issues is deserving of much praise. As a rule, he made a determined effort to be impartial, and his large measure of success is a tribute to his integrity and sterling resolution. . . .[26]

A significantly different interpretation was offered by Nathaniel W. Stephenson. Writing in 1921 he declared that the hostile critics missed the point by reviewing Rhodes' work as if it had first appeared in that year. As a matter of fact,

> Mr. Rhodes has his permanent place in American historiography, not because he anticipated present-day points of view, but because he summed up and concluded one phase of our interpretation, because he raised that phase out of partisanship into argument, because he released its best self from its mere aberrations.[27]

That phase was the New England federalist interpretation, founded by John Quincy Adams, carried on by the political historians of the '50's and '60's and expounded later by von Holst. It was to Rhodes' credit that he emerged from the "splendid darkness" of that school, but vestiges of it clung to his approach to the problem of slavery; his concentration on military, political and constitutional questions; and his sectional point of view. He was "the last great workman of the school that did not distinguish between nationalism and Northernism," but it must be remembered that historians are usually sectional in their views.[28]

Nor was Rhodes irremediably wedded to his earlier outlook, Stephenson wrote, emphasizing significant changes in emphases between the first two volumes and Volume VI, symbolized by a more mellow evaluation of Jefferson Davis and a harsher estimate of Charles Sumner.[29] Influenced by Woodrow Wilson, William A. Dunning and Dunning's followers, Rhodes had at last come to a genuinely nationalistic position:

> consider in its entirety his [Rhodes'] approach to the Southern problem in 1906 and his approach in 1893. . . . In this volume [VI], . . . his approach is at last nationalistic. In the midst of that congregation of essays and monographs attempting a really nationalistic approach, the sixth volume has its abiding place, the earliest massive achievement of the new day.[30]

A somewhat similar construction has been offered recently by Thomas J. Pressly in his exposition of changing interpretations of the Civil War. Rhodes held to many traditional viewpoints regarding the war, wrote Pressly, but he also embraced some new theses, and "it was his expression of the new attitudes which accounted, in the main, for the impact he made upon his generation as a historian." [31]

Among these were the following: while slavery was the sole cause of the war it in turn was due to the operation of inanimate factors, such as geography, the cotton gin and the cotton economy; the South was not to blame alone for slavery since both England and the North had done much to encourage it; slavery was an evil institution but individual slaveholders, caught in its toils, were more deserving of sympathy than censure; the Southern way of life was in many ways praiseworthy and produced great and good men like Robert E. Lee; both sides deserved praise and blame for their behavior during the war; the Southern attitude toward the war was not the product of a conspiracy but rather an expression of popular sentiment; the war was a civil war rather than a rebellion; in dealing with the Negro the basic element was that of race, which justified neither slavery nor the rights given the Negro during Reconstruction.[32]

In short, Rhodes

> emerged with an over-all judgment [that] . . . the North had been right in the war, while the South had been right in Reconstruction. Rhodes went a step further . . . , and in his volumes most of the blame for what happened was ultimately placed upon inanimate forces. Here was an interpretation of

> the war's causes which went far toward solving the long standing question of war guilt in accord with the new attitudes and points of view developing since the late 1870's. . . .[33]

Apart from his points of view, Rhodes' attitude of fair-minded impartiality, in itself a new thing, made a profound impression upon his contemporaries, winning him acclaim from men of very different backgrounds.[34]

Such have been the more significant commentaries on the work of Rhodes. Let us now examine his work in some detail.

NOTES

1 John R. Lynch, "Some Historical Errors of James Ford Rhodes," *Journal of Negro History*, II (1917), 345–346.

2 *Ibid.*, pp. 351–353.

3 *Ibid.*, pp. 348–349.

4 *Ibid.*, pp. 353–356.

5 *Ibid.*, pp. 357, 360.

6 *Ibid.*, p. 353.

7 *Ibid.*, p. 346.

8 *Ibid.*, p. 364. Rhodes commented that Lynch "found no inaccuracy of importance and the consideration of the article gives me a higher idea of my correctness of statement." Rhodes to George A. Myers, Nov. 22, 1917, in John A. Garraty (ed.), "Correspondence," *Ohio Historical Quarterly*, LXIV (1955), 254.

9 *History of the United States from the Compromise of 1850* (8 vols., New York, 1920).

10 "Rhodes' History of the United States," *Mississippi Valley Historical Review*, VIII (1921), 133–134.

11 *Ibid.*, pp. 141, 143.

12 *Ibid.*, p. 136.

13 *Ibid.*, pp. 136–138.

14 *Ibid.*, pp. 139–140, 142–143, 146.

15 *Ibid.*, pp. 140, 144, 147.

16 Raymond C. Miller, "James Ford Rhodes," in William T. Hutchinson (ed.), *The Marcus W. Jernegan Essays in American Historiography* (Chicago, 1937), pp. 175–176.

17 *Ibid.*, p. 176.

18 *Ibid.*, pp. 176–177.

19 *Ibid.*, pp. 177–178.

20 *Ibid.*, p. 179.

21 *Ibid.*, pp. 181, 182–183.

22 *Ibid.*, pp. 183–184.

23 *Ibid.*, pp. 184–185.

24 *Ibid.*, pp. 186–188.

25 *Ibid.*, p. 188.

26 *Ibid.*, pp. 189–190.

27 Nathaniel W. Stephenson, "Mr. Rhodes as Historian," *Yale Review*, New series, X (1920–1921), 860.

28 *Ibid.*, pp. 860, 861–863.

29 *Ibid.*, p. 864.

30 *Ibid.*

[31] Thomas J. Pressly, *Americans Interpret Their Civil War* (Princeton, N. J., 1954), p. 140.
[32] *Ibid.*, pp. 141–146.
[33] *Ibid.*, p. 146.
[34] *Ibid.*, p. 147.

Chapter 17

RHODES AND THE WRITING OF HISTORY

HAD Rhodes' influence been confined to his own time, a study of the beliefs and attitudes which underlay his work might be of interest purely to the specialist. Such is not the case. Although more than fifty years have elapsed since his major work was completed, and we are separated from him not only by the gulf of years but also by that wider divide which includes a great depression, another world war and a "cold war," his influence still endures, even though he is far from being the dominant figure of a half-century ago.

In the interim his authority has been continuously, if indirectly, pervasive in the acceptance by historians, biographers and other writers of many of his estimates of persons, events and developments; estimates which in turn have been accepted by students and the reading public generally. In this respect, indeed, Rhodes occupied a unique role in American historiography: he was not so much *an* authority as *the* authority, the final arbiter on all matters relating to the Civil War and Reconstruction. In this spirit his findings were cited by such diverse figures as A. M. Simons, the socialist; Washington Gladden, the exponent of the social gospel; David S. Muzzey, the writer of popular history texts for high schools; and the noted historians, James Schouler, William E. Dodd and Frederic L. Paxson.[1] Harry Elmer Barnes, critical though he was of *The McKinley and Roosevelt Administrations*, held that Rhodes' work on the Civil War and Reconstruction was calm, temperate and marked by "objectivity and scholarship." [2] Traces of these appraisals may still be found in some college texts, such as that of Samuel E. Morison and Henry S. Commager, which declares the *History* to be "still the best detailed history of that period although shot full of holes by the research of the last fifty years." They commend Rhodes' discussion of Reconstruction as "notably impartial." [3]

Rhodes has also exercised considerable indirect influence through the work of biographers who drew on him in great measure, including Douglas Southall Freeman (Robert E. Lee),[4] Oswald Garrison

Villard (John Brown),[5] Claude Fuess (Carl Schurz),[6] Paul Revere Frothingham (Edward Everett)[7] and Gamaliel Bradford, who wrote on many souls, damaged and otherwise.[8] Even the novelist, S. Weir Mitchell, found the *History* of great value in writing his story of the Civil War, *The Westways*.[9]

In view of Rhodes' significance, then, it is necessary to examine the basic assumptions, conscious and otherwise, which the historian brought to his work.

It was Rhodes' fond belief, as it was that of his contemporaries, that his work was beyond the reach of personal elements. He conceded that some historians fell into "unconscious partisanship" because of their basic philosophies; that it was impossible for historians to be objective at all times because of their attempts to impress the public or because their "warm sympathies" led them "to color their narratives"; that historians could not remedy the imperfections of poor sources nor wholly escape the influences of "temperament and education."[10] For himself, however, he was persuaded that he was "an earnest seeker after truth, . . . trying to hold a judicial balance and to tell the story without fear, favor or prejudice."[11] He conceived of himself as a "purely narrative historian" who eschewed "philosophic considerations," because, as he explained:

> such is the constitution of the human mind, or at any rate my own, that as I went through the mass of my material I would have seized upon all the facts that made for my theory and marshalled them in its support while those that told against it I would have unconsciously and undoubtedly quite honestly neglected. . . . My aim therefore was to get rid so far as possible of all preconceived notions and theories.[12]

Sometimes he indicated that the problem of historical fairness was really not so difficult after all:

> It is not so difficult as some imagine for a student of history whose work is done in the library to be impartial, provided he has inherited or acquired the desire to be fair and honest, and provided he has the diligence and patience to go through the mass of evidence. His historical material will show him that to every question there are two sides. . . .[13]

In putting the question as he did, however, Rhodes neglected those factors which unconsciously shape one's attitudes, factors which in his own case played a considerable part in molding his approach to historical problems.

One such influence was the Calvinism of his childhood, an outlook which dominated his home and was reinforced at school—but it was the Calvinism of the 19th century, which, while paying tribute to predestination nevertheless insisted on the reality of individual moral responsibility. This influence reflected itself strongly in Rhodes' personal life: his strong sense of propriety, his objections to discussion of sex in literature, his feeling of responsibility for the financial security of his grandchildren.

It also reflected itself in his historical work. As God called men to account in the hereafter, so the historian called them to judgment before the Bar of History. And as the God of Calvin was preoccupied with matters of personal morality, so was the Calvinist historian. It was not enough to discuss the impact of Daniel Webster on the history of the country—the historian must also pass judgment on his financial and sexual morality.[14] James G. Blaine was interpreted not only in the light of his public career but also in the light of his personal honesty (or dishonesty) and his relations with his family.[15] The scales came down heavily in favor of Mark Hanna because he was "a model of chastity." [10] McKinley could be forgiven much because of his devotion to his wife and his Methodist sincerity.[17]

Moral judgments were also applicable to great public issues. The great offense of slavery was that it was a moral evil; of "free silver" that it was dishonest; of labor unions that they were motivated by envy and malice; the historical justification for the concentration of wealth was that it encouraged giving by rich men and did good for society.

The Calvinist influence went further. Even in the watered-down version of the 19th century Calvinism explained the universe as the expression of one supreme will and the fate of man as determined by his one act of disobedience in the Garden of Eden. Life was portrayed as a constant struggle between Good and Evil, the meanings of which were clearly set forth in the Scriptures. It was, in short, a simple interpretation of experience, set forth in terms of blacks and whites. Applied to history by Rhodes, in quite unconscious manner, it led to some naive analyses. Slavery was the sole cause of the Civil War. Race was the sole significant factor in Reconstruction. The period between 1877 and 1909 was one in which good (represented by "hard money," individualism in economics and Republicanism in politics) triumphed over evil (represented by organized labor, free silver and the Democracy of William Jennings Bryan). Consciously, Rhodes recognized that "causes are complex"; [18] in practice, he recognized the principle more in the breach than in the observance.

Another significant influence on Rhodes' outlook was that of his father. The elder Daniel had shaped James' schooling, his political beliefs, his business experience. To him may be traced in considerable degree the historian's preoccupation with political history. To Daniel's experiences during the Civil War may be attributed James' praise for the behavior of Northern Democrats and condemnation of the abrogation of civil liberties during the Civil War.[19] In Daniel's disputes with employes, which he discussed frequently with his family, may be seen the origins of James' hostility to workingmen who disliked industrial paternalism. Indeed, in the combination of Calvinist morality and paternal example one may see the roots of those social attitudes which the historian expounded in his work.

Such influences, however, were so deeply imbedded in his personality as to be beyond the ken of such a non-analytical mind as that of Rhodes. On the conscious level there were other factors which helped develop his attitudes. One of the earliest was the utilitarian humanitarianism of John Stuart Mill. Rhodes himself thought that Mill, to whose thought he was exposed during his college days, shaped many of his views—at least until Rhodes discovered that Mill was a staunch opponent of the subjection of women.[20] Certainly, the spirit of Mill is reflected in the famous chapter on slavery and in the discussion of such issues as the tariff and silver, on which Rhodes passed judgment on the basis of "the greatest good for the greatest number." [21]

Mill, however, was not so significant in Rhodes' thought as Herbert Spencer. Rhodes was exposed to Spencer, too, during his college days; not only did Spencer "take" but the Spencerian influence deepened with the years, partly because it seemed to Rhodes to explain the world in which he lived, partly because it colored the cultural atmosphere in which he lived. Rhodes, it will be remembered, spent years as an active member of the business community during the '70's and '80's, the great years in which Spencer was the Prophet of Individualism. It was Rhodes' belief that he was "emancipated" from Spencer in the early '90's through the influence of James Bryce and *The Nation*,[22] but he forgot to reckon with the fact that during those years and for some time to come he was profoundly affected by the thinking of his collaborator, Edward Gaylord Bourne, himself an ardent disciple of Spencer's American disciple, William Graham Sumner.

It is indeed, easy to detect in Rhodes' work echoes of the English philosopher. Spencer's concept of social evolution, with its emphasis on a struggle for existence, with "survival of the fittest" providing the key to social progress, is imbedded in the *History*, as are the related concepts of immutable economic laws, *laissez-faire* in economics and politics, and Anglo-Saxon supremacy in world affairs. It is interesting to note, too, that Rhodes carried over into his work Spencer's concept of the conflict between militarism and industrialism, insisting that since the United States was primarily an industrial nation warfare "is not for us." [23] Rhodes was so impressed with these viewpoints that he accepted them as "truths"; and thus, in writing history within such a framework, he was writing objectively and dispassionately—or so he thought.

Rhodes' business experience also contributed in no small way to the outlook expressed in the *History*. The firm with which he had been associated was an open-shop employer, and he himself had taken active part in its anti-union activities. It had been intimately associated with the Pennsylvania railroad, one of the key employers in the railroad strikes of 1877. It had also had unfortunate experiences arising from the fluctuating value of United States paper currency. This business background may well explain, at least in part, Rhodes' attitudes towards free silver, labor organizations, and the strikes of 1877. John T. Morse, Jr., who thought Rhodes the embodiment of impartiality, attributed a good deal of Rhodes' method and outlook to this experience.[24]

Yet another factor which shaped Rhodes' views was the cult of the gentleman, particularly as it was practiced in Proper Boston. This cult was, in part, a defensive reaction on the part of the older families to the crude money-making of the Gilded Age; in part, the social expression of that genteel tradition which had dominated for so long the cultural life of New England.[25] The cult was based on the belief, expressed by James Fenimore Cooper, that the class of gentlemen "is the natural repository of the manners, tastes, tone, and, to a certain extent, of the principles of a country." [26] It consisted of such elements as *noblesse oblige*, avoidance of publicity and controversy, deference to the feelings of others, and adherence to the proprieties.

Rhodes accepted this whole-heartedly. His highest praise for a major historian, like Tacitus, or a minor, like Jacob D. Cox, was that they were gentlemen.[27] One of his criticisms of Lincoln was that he lacked the manners of a gentleman.[28] He was fond of quoting John Hay's dictum that the historian must also be a gentleman.[29] Since Rhodes saw himself as gentleman, as historian he found it quite justifiable to destroy documents which might hurt the feelings of a leading Boston family and to withhold material reflecting on the character of a great man unless it were fully authenticated. The concept of gentleman, of course, had its limits: it did not apply to those of inferior race or class. Hearsay and the evidence of his enemies were admissible when discussing the Negro; a nice consideration for the reputations of men did not preclude blackening that of a labor leader like Martin Irons.

A word, finally, about the significance of Boston itself on Rhodes' work. When Rhodes moved to Boston he consummated a spiritual as well as physical abandonment of the section in which he had matured. In his work it meant an exclusion of the West from serious consideration and an embracing of that New England approach to American history which had already outlived its best days. Rhodes' Federalist interpretation of American constitutional development, his concept of the Civil War, his neglect of the West, his preoccupation with the traditional elements of history, his insistence that history was literature—these all mirror that older New England view.

Such seem to have been the basic elements in molding Rhodes' outlook: The Calvinism of his childhood, the abiding influence of his father, the utilitarianism of his youth, the Spencerian economics and sociology of his maturity, the experience of practical business, the cult of the gentleman and the New England approach to history. From this complex of factors arose Rhodes' own outlook on history and the role of the historian.

Rhodes, it will be recalled, wrote during the burgeoning of that "scientific" historiography which followed upon the introduction by Herbert Baxter Adams of the germ-theory of institutional development, which, of course, had its roots in Darwinian evolutionary theory. The major reactions to this school, represented in the work of Frederick Jackson Turner and Henry Adams, differ though they might in interpretation, were also based upon the assumption that the data of history could be processed and interpreted in harmony with the standards of the natural or physical sciences. In view of the impact of Buckle upon his youth, it might be thought that Rhodes would prove hospitable to the tenets of the scientific school. On the contrary, explicitly denying his old master,[30] he harked back to the earlier literary tradition, typified by Parkman and Prescott in the United States and the classical historians abroad, in which history was regarded as a branch of humane letters.

To be sure, he shared some of the characteristics of the new dispensation—its monistic interpretation of phenomena,[31] its emphasis upon the accumulation of data, its belief in the attainment of objective truth through the correct use of sources, its faith that the historian could play the role of disinterested social scientist—but beyond such he placed of greater value the abilities of the literary historians to digest materials, make accurate generalizations, tell interesting stories, and arouse faith in what Rhodes conceived to be sound social values. In his own work he apparently assumed he could combine the better features of both schools. Of the basic problems involved in acceptance of either school's assumptions and values he had no awareness. Indeed, his attitude toward such issues may be judged from his dismissal of "philosophic" history as "parading of trite reflections or . . . rashly broad generalizations." [32]

History, said Rhodes, occupied, at best, a third place in the hierarchy of scholarly pursuits, being inferior to literature and the sciences. The former afforded more insight, in more dramatic form, into the motives and actions of men than did history; the latter assisted men in solving their contemporary problems and thus were of more significance than a study occupied with the problems of the past.[33] The increasing similarity of historical and scientific method did not alter the fact that history itself was basically a branch of literature, comprehended in the narration of past events as they actually happened but including also treatment of the motivations and actions of individuals involved, all of which were linked together in a simple cause-and-effect formula, demonstrated by his own treatment of the Civil War as resulting solely from slavery. Thus, the greatest historians were Homer and Shakespeare; from them the historical student must wrest the secret of narration.[34]

Such a student must not overlook the contributions of the scientific historians, but above all he must bring to history the quality which makes literature. While Rhodes believed there was truth in the views of both literary and scientific historians, he found that the latter overlooked "the importance of digesting materials, of accurate generalizations and method of expression." He doubted, too, whether they produced better history than did Tacitus, Thucydides, Herodotus and Gibbon.[35]

This approach Rhodes emphasized in his advice to college students aspiring to become historians. Mastery of foreign languages, literature, history, fine arts and economics he recommended; mathematics beyond arithmetic and detailed study of the sciences were "of no use to the historian and may be entirely discarded." For basic studies in history he urged the reading of Gibbon and James Bryce's *Holy Roman Empire*. With these must be read Thucydides, Tacitus, Macaulay, Carlyle, Shakespeare and Homer; the scientific historians of Europe; all "eminent American historians"; and Goethe and Sainte-Beuve, the last because

> It is very desirable for us Anglo-Saxons to broaden our minds and soften our prejudices by excursions outside of our own literature and history, and with Goethe for our guide in Germany we can do no better than to accept Sainte-Beuve for France. . . .[36]

After such training, the student who wished to write must select an interesting period in which he can make an original contribution and then evolve his own method "by practice and by comparison with the methods of other historians." He may follow the example of the older historians in assessing praise and blame or that of such scientific historians as Samuel R. Gardiner. If he should choose the latter alternative, he should remember that

> It is well, as the scientific historians warn us, to be suspicious of interesting things, but, on the other hand, every interesting incident is not necessarily untrue. If you have made a conscientious search for historical material and use it with scrupulous honesty, have no fear that you will transgress any reasonable canon of historical writing.[37]

The historians to whom Rhodes himself turned year after year for refreshment and inspiration were those in the classical literary tradition: Herodotus, Thucydides, and Tacitus. In 1899 he extolled Herodotus to the American Historical Association because the Athenian was readable, honest, diligent and possessed an epic unity of plan; in 1921 he was still under the spell, even to the point of being persuaded that the Persian wars had been more significant for civilization than the Napoleonic wars, the American Civil War, World War I or the War of American Independence.[38] Thucydides and Tacitus he admired because both had been men of affairs; wrote practically contemporaneous history; exemplified diligence, accuracy, and objectivity; and had "by long reflection and studious method, . . . digested their materials and compressed their narrative."[39] Tacitus, however, was a favorite—perhaps because Rhodes saw in him a model:

> We approach Tacitus with respect. We rise from reading [him] . . . with reverence. We know that we have been in

the society of a gentleman who had a high standard of morality and honor. We feel that our guide was a serious student, a solid thinker, and a man of the world; that he expressed his opinions and delivered his judgments with a remarkable freedom from prejudice. He draws us to him with sympathy. . . . Tacitus deplores the folly and dissoluteness of the rulers of his nation; he bewails the misfortunes of his country. . . .[40]

In more recent times Rhodes found stimulation in the work of Gibbon; which, said he, constituted "a basis for the study of all other history; it is a mental discipline, and a training for the problems of modern life." [41] Next to Gibbon, Rhodes ranked Macaulay, in whose work Rhodes found more to admire as the years went on.[42] The great Whig might have been prolix and partisan but he possessed the invaluable talent of arousing interest, which Rhodes found lacking in contemporary scientific history. So, too, with Carlyle. He may have lacked the historic sense, but he had "the poetical gift which is a rarer endowment." [43]

Compared with such encomia Rhodes' estimate of scientific historians was lukewarm. He rarely discussed their work in detail; even in a eulogy of Samuel R. Gardiner who represented "fitly the scientific school of historical writers," his greatest tribute was that Gardiner "restores to us the great queen of Shakespeare." [44]

Rhodes' appraisals of American historians were scanty and stemmed from the literary standard he applied to others. At one time he thought John Fiske "the greatest of living historians" and Fiske's *Discovery of America* "the greatest historical work I have ever read by an American except the Rise of the Dutch Republic." [45] He admired Francis Parkman and William Hickling Prescott; found little to praise in George Bancroft.[46] He was "amazed at the depth of . . . intelligence and . . . wisdom" of von Holst, but when he wrote that Henry Adams was "the greatest of us all" he made it clear that this applied to Adams "not as historian but as writer and thinker." [47] James Harvey Robinson he termed "an intelligent, high-minded, witty and ambitious scholar" but there is no evidence that he read Robinson's work.[48] He thought Samuel Eliot Morison "a shining light" but offered no explanation save that he had heard Morison deliver a "well-prepared, well-digested paper at the Massachusetts Historical Society." [49]

Indeed, in view of the ferment taking place in the writing of American history during Rhodes' active years, there is surprisingly little comment about American historians in either his correspondence or his published work, and what little is available indicates that Rhodes was distinctly unsympathetic to the new viewpoints suggested by the younger men. He referred bitingly to the "lot of bright, ambitious and aggressive Northern young men . . . trying to make us believe that slavery was not the cause but only the occasion of the War." [50] He suggested that historical re-interpretations more favorable to Stephen A. Douglas might be attributable to

> the desire to say something novel and sensational . . . I do not believe there will be any lasting change in historical sentiment, unless our young men prove their thesis that slavery was not the cause of the civil war. I am myself glad to be with the old-fashioned thinkers in history, . . .[51]

He showed no understanding at all, either in correspondence or his work, of the epoch-making achievements of Frederick Jackson Turner.

Rhodes' concept of history as a branch of humane letters served to define his thought about the role of the historian. As humane letters historically had been associated with a leisure class, so did Rhodes in the early 20th century limit to such a group the writing of history, for, as he believed, only a leisure class provided the means which made the study and writing of history possible. For those who lacked such means, he recommended a preliminary period in business as a method of accumulating the necessary fortune.[52] It is typical of Rhodes' thought that the idea of bias arising from such class associations never occurred to him.

Backed by financial independence, the historian must show certain attributes:

> diligence, accuracy, love of truth, impartiality, the thorough digestion of his materials by careful selection and long meditating, and the compression of his narrative into the smallest compass consistent with the life of his story. He must also have a power of expression suitable for his purpose. . . .[53]

Significantly, Rhodes laid little emphasis on the need for rigorous professional training, a reflection, perhaps, of the view held by some professional historians that in his case at least the lack of such training was a positive asset.[54]

These attributes were essential because, in Rhodes' view, the historian's role was basically that of judge, not scientist, not even storyteller, although the literary quality was important. Most important for the historian to possess was "the judicial mind," and in its exercise he must be concerned, not with appealing to the public at large but rather to the jury of historical experts:

> Words of approval from them are worth more than any popular recognition, . . . Their criticisms should be respected; . . . No labor should be despised which shall enable one to present things just as they are. Our endeavor should be to think straight and see clear.[55]

Or, as Rhodes put it more bluntly in a letter: "Please the elite; the rest will follow." [56] So far as the public was concerned the historian was "a sort of trustee for his readers. . . . he is bound to assert nothing for which he has not evidence, as much as an executor of a will . . . is obliged to render a correct account of the moneys in his possession." [57]

Given the judicial mind, it was easy to write history, and particularly the history of one's own times. It was this very quality which made the classic historians so superior:

> they wrote what was practically contemporaneous history. . . . It is manifestly easier to describe a life you know than one you must imagine, which is what you must do if you aim to relate events which took place before your own or your father's time. . . . Does not the common rating of Thucydides and Tacitus refute the dictum that history within the memory of men living cannot be written truthfully and fairly? Given then, the judicial mind, how much easier to write it! . . . Not only is no extraordinary ability required to write contemporary history, but the labor of the historian is lightened, and Dryasdust is no longer his sole guide. . . .[58]

The exercise of the judicial function in history, as in society, had a presumably moral end. Rhodes lightly touched upon the controversy between scientific and literary historians as to the place of ethical judgments in the writing of history, but he himself believed with Tacitus, whom he quoted approvingly to the American Historical Association, that "the historian's highest function [is] to let no worthy action be uncommemorated, and to hold out the reprobation of posterity as a terror to evil words and deeds." [59] This standard he applied also to biography: "if the life portrayed is valuable it serves many a good purpose to the young who would fain follow in the path of the distinguished." [60] Thus, the historian was guide as well as judge, a view of the historian which Rhodes had put forth in his earliest historical writings.

As trustee, judge and guide, therefore, the writer of history was obligated to hale before the bar of judgment such miscreants as John C. Calhoun, Jefferson Davis and Stephen A. Douglas; and to lay bare the evils of the protective tariff, government regulation of railroad rates, free silver, and labor unions. He was also obligated, it would seem, to shield his readers from revelations which in his opinion might disturb their judgment. "The great question," he wrote, "is how much should be told?" [61]

On this basis, the historian, in all good faith, could delay publication of some work lest it injure the political career of Senator Lodge; he could describe corruption during the Civil War without hinting (as he did in private correspondence) that the Pennsylvania railroad got "some peculiar payments" from the federal government while one of its officials served as assistant secretary of war; [62] in response to the plea of a friend that historians should show that treatment of federal prisoners of war in the South "was not what the . . . historians and government make it to have been," Rhodes could promise that if his investigations did not lead him to that conclusion, "I do not believe I should treat the subject." [63] In short, Rhodes' view of the role of historian supplemented that of the role of Calvinist censor.

It should be noted, however, that Rhodes never lost sight of the fact that the guide must always keep his audience: not only is the *History* replete with material of little historical but great human interest but Rhodes deliberately excluded treating subjects in which the public had little interest. He advised Gamaliel Bradford not to write about the Beecher-Tilton trial for that reason:

> I can assure you that the public has lost interest [he wrote] . . . I had accumulated a large amount of material and proposed using it on the Trial, but . . . I did not and I doubt whether your book on the subject will sell.[64]

The great end of the historian as American, however, was exaltation of the American way of life—or at least of that way as Rhodes understood it:

> If, like Thucydides and Tacitus, the American historian chooses the history of his own country as his field, he may infuse patriotism into his narrative. He will speak of the broad acres and their products, the splendid industrial development due to the capacity and energy of the captains of industry; but he will like to dwell on the universities and colleges, on the great numbers seeking a higher education, on the morality of the people, their purity of life, their domestic happiness. He will never be weary of referring to Washington and Lincoln, feeling that a country with such exemplars is indeed one to awaken envy, and he will not forget the brave souls who followed where they led.[65]

Would American historians come to rank with the ancients? Rhodes had little doubt as to the answer. American life, it was true, discouraged the habit of long meditation, but Rhodes, believing that Americans shared with the Greeks the ability to think straight and see clear, thought "we may look for as great historians in the future as in the past." [66] Great historians, he once believed, must be men of the world; but in contrasting Samuel R. Gardiner with James Anthony Froude he came to the conclusion that a cloistered scholar could prove superior to the sophisticate: Gardiner, he pointed out, restored Elizabeth to greatness, while the man of the world, Froude, depreciated her.[67]

As Rhodes accepted the traditional view of the literary nature of history so did he practice its view of the content of history as politics, diplomacy, war. He did, indeed, suggest that history might properly concern itself also with economic, social and cultural developments, but for his own work he adhered to the conventional standards.[68] To be sure, he discussed the state of American society between 1850 and 1860,[69] described the institution of slavery in detail, and criticized the tariff, but none of these is integrated into the major elements of his study. They stand isolated, interesting in themselves, but without that relevance which it is the business of the historian to establish. Save for its political aspects, the *ante-bellum* decade, in Rhodes' treatment, seems to have little relationship to the Civil War; slavery is discussed largely as a moral issue; and the tariff appears to have played only a minor role in the struggle between the sections.

Perhaps even more startling is Rhodes' neglect of the West in discussing both *ante* and *post bellum* developments, a neglect all the more astonishing in view of the fact that perceptive discussions of the significance of the Homestead Act appeared in the issues of the *Magazine of Western History* to which Rhodes himself contributed [70]—to say nothing of the fact that long before Rhodes' work was completed the conclusions of Frederick Jackson Turner were known to scholars everywhere. The last two volumes, *From Hayes to McKinley* and *The McKinley and Roosevelt Administrations* do indicate an awareness of the significance of social and economic elements in the nation's history, but again they are treated as isolated factors, not as dynamic forces reflecting the changing nature of American society.

Some explanation for Rhodes' limitations may be found in his belief that the "history of England is the most remarkable and most instructive of all histories," and that American history is "the continuation of a branch of that of England."[71] The English historians were pre-occupied with politics; England had no West, no sectional issues, no obstreperous farmers, no mass immigration, and the very discussion of social issues was associated with such men as Bernard Shaw, for whose "new gospel" Rhodes had little use.[72] How easy it was, then, to overlook such elements in the United States, especially when one's mental as well as physical bounds were set by Beacon and State streets in Boston!

Rhodes, then, while accepting some of the standards set by the scientific historians, was fundamentally a traditionalist in his view of history as a branch of literature and in his limiting of history to politics, statecraft and war. He rejected the role of scientific historian, also, in insisting upon the role of the historian as judge and upon the judicial mind as the prime requisite of the historian. In so doing he permitted himself a rather cavalier attitude toward his sources, although it appears that both he and his public were oblivious to the fact that his use of sources was selective rather than exhaustive. To that problem we may now turn our attention.

NOTES

[1] A. M. Simons, *Social Forces in American History* (New York, 1911), pp. 258, 270, 274, 275, 279, 281, 296, 301. Washington Gladden, *Recollections*, pp. 134, 143, 146–148, 181, 193, 201. David S. Muzzey, *The United States of America* (New York, 1924), II, iii. James Schouler acknowledged his debt to Rhodes in the foreword to *History of the Reconstruction Period, 1865–1877* (New York, 1913); see also Lewis E. Ellis, "James Schouler," in William T. Hutchinson, (ed.), *The Marcus W. Jernegan Essays in American Historiography*, p. 92. William E. Dodd, *Expansion and Conflict* (Boston, 1915), pp. 182, 206, 229, 308. Frederic L. Paxson, *The Civil War* (New York, 1911), p. x.

[2] Harry Elmer Barnes, *A History of Historical Writing* (Norman, Oklahoma, 1938), pp. 261–262.

[3] *The Growth of the American Republic* (4th ed., New York, 1950), I, 780; II, 829. See also John D. Hicks and George E. Mowry, *A Short History of American Democracy* (2nd ed., Boston, 1956), p. 391; and H. J. Carman, H. C. Syrett and B. W. Wishy, *A History of the American People* (New York, 1960), I, 849, 856.

[4] Douglas Southall Freeman to Rhodes, Dec. 1, 1919, wrote that in his work on Lee he had found "no book so lucid and so useful as your history of the Civil War." Rhodes Papers.

[5] Oswald Garrison Villard to Rhodes, Oct. 10, 1910, acknowledged his "very great" indebtedness to Rhodes for his work on John Brown. Rhodes Papers.

[6] Claude Fuess, *Carl Schurz: Reformer, 1829–1906* (New York, 1932), pp. 208, 213, 285, 313, 327, 364.

[7] Paul Revere Frothingham, *Edward Everett: Orator and Statesman* (Boston, 1925), pp. 323, 330, 338.

[8] Gamaliel Bradford wrote to Rhodes, May 18, 1921: "When I begin a portrait, I always turn first to you for the foundations, and when I have examined all the other material as widely as possible, I always return to you for the largest and sanest estimate. . . ." Letter Books of Gamaliel Bradford, Vol. VII. Houghton Library, Harvard University.

[9] S. Weir Mitchell to Rhodes, March 27, 1913. Rhodes Papers.

[10] *The McKinley and Roosevelt Administrations*, p. 123; *Historical Essays*, pp. 43–44. Rhodes to George A. Myers, Jan. 16, 1918, in John A. Garraty (ed.), "Correspondence," *Ohio Historical Quarterly*, LXIV (1955), 256.

[11] Rhodes to George A. Myers, April 19, 1916, in *ibid.*, p. 148.

[12] Rhodes to Charles Francis Adams, March 19, 1907. Rhodes Papers.

[13] *Historical Essays*, p. 179.

[14] *History*, I, 143.

[15] *From Hayes to McKinley*, pp. 157–160, 221.

[16] *The McKinley and Roosevelt Administrations*, p. 8.

[17] *Ibid.*, pp. 10, 187.

[18] Rhodes to Sir George Otto Trevelyan, May 25, 1913. Rhodes Papers.

[19] Harvey Cushing, M.D., a close friend of Rhodes, so attributed Rhodes' treatment of Vallandigham and other Northern Democrats. "James Ford Rhodes," in M. A. D. Howe (ed.), *Later Years of the Saturday Club*, p. 348.

[20] Rhodes wrote to Sir George Otto Trevelyan, Aug. 29, 1915, "to us young men Mill was an apostle until he came out for women's suffrage." Rhodes Papers.

[21] *History*, III, 31–33. Rhodes to Sir George Otto Trevelyan, May 25, 1913; Barrett Wendell, June 5, 1911. Rhodes Papers.

[22] *Historical Essays*, p. 293.

[23] *History*, V, 238; *History of the Civil War*, p. 364; "The First Six Weeks of McClellan's Peninsular Campaign," *Proceedings, Massachusetts Historical Society*, Second series, X (1895–1896), 430.

[24] John T. Morse, Jr., "James Ford Rhodes," *Proceedings, Massachusetts Historical Society*, LX (1927), 181.

[25] Robert Grant, *The Chippendales, passim;* V. L. Parrington, *Main Currents in American Thought* (New York, 1930), III, 53.

[26] *The American Democrat* (New York, 1931), p. 84.

[27] *Historical Essays*, pp. 8, 188.

[28] Rhodes to Barrett Wendell, Sept. 26, 1918. Rhodes Papers.

[29] *The McKinley and Roosevelt Administrations*, p. 123. Rhodes to Sir George Otto Trevelyan, Nov. 2, 1917, in M. A. D. Howe, *Rhodes*, p. 286.

[30] "Quite properly no one reads Buckle now," he wrote in *Historical Essays*, pp. 37–38.

[31] Stow Persons, *American Minds: A History of Ideas* (New York, 1958), p. 323.

[32] *Historical Essays, p.* 154.

[33] *Ibid.*, pp. 1–2.

[34] *Ibid.*, pp. 1, 22, 44. Rhodes to Frederic Bancroft, Sept. 18, 1894, in M. A. D. Howe, *Rhodes*, p. 87. Rhodes to George A. Myers, April 19, 1916, in John A. Garraty (ed.), "Correspondence," *Ohio Historical Quarterly*, LXIV (1955), 148. Rhodes to Charles Francis Adams, March 19, 1907. Rhodes Papers.

[35] *Historical Essays*, pp. 4–5, 39, 103. Rhodes to William R. Thayer, Feb. 14, 1900; July 18, 1915; Barrett Wendell, Oct. 20, 1909. Rhodes Papers.

[36] *Historical Essays*, pp. 49–59, 60, 61–73.

[37] *Ibid.*, pp. 75, 76.

[38] *Ibid.*, pp. 5–6. Rhodes to Sir George Otto Trevelyan, Oct. 4, 1921. Rhodes Papers.

[39] *Historical Essays*, pp. 8, 14, 17.

[40] *Ibid.*, p. 9.

[41] *Ibid.*, pp. 109, 114, 139.

[42] Rhodes to Sir George Otto Trevelyan, Aug. 11, 1921; Oct. 28, 1924. Rhodes Papers.

[43] *Historical Essays*, pp. 37, 38, 41. Rhodes to his wife, Aug. 19 [1892?]. Rhodes Papers.

[44] *Historical Essays*, pp. 143, 149.

[45] Rhodes to Frederic Bancroft, Jan. 10, 1893, photostat fragment. Rhodes Papers.

[46] *Historical Essays*, p. 68. John S. Bassett to Rhodes, March 19, 1917. Rhodes Papers.

[47] Frank Maloy Anderson (ed.), "Letters of James Ford Rhodes to Edward L. Pierce," *American Historical Review*, XXXVI (1931), 780. Rhodes to William R. Thayer, July 18, 1915. Rhodes Papers.

[48] Undated photostat fragment, Rhodes Papers.

[49] Rhodes to Sir George Otto Trevelyan, Jan. 9, 1923, and undated photostat fragment addressed to Trevelyan. Rhodes Papers.

[50] Rhodes to John T. Morse, Jr., May 6 [1893?]. Morse Papers.

[51] Rhodes to Charles Eliot Norton, July 28, 1907, in M. A. D. Howe, *Rhodes*, pp. 158–159.

[52] *Historical Essays*, pp. 78, 79.

[53] *Ibid.*, p. 20.

[54] William Garrott Brown, *American Historical Review*, XI (1905–1906), 182; Claude H. Van Tyne, *ibid.*, XV (1909–1910), 830.

[55] *Historical Essays*, pp. 18, 44.

[56] Rhodes to Frederic Bancroft, Aug. 25, 1898, in M. A. D. Howe, *Rhodes*, p. 94.

[57] *Historical Essays*, p. 32.

[58] *Ibid.*, pp. 17–18.

[59] *Ibid.*, pp. 9, 43, 76. See also *History*, IV, 493; VI, 411, 416.

[60] Rhodes to Sir George Otto Trevelyan, March 3, 1921. Rhodes Papers.

[61] Rhodes to George A. Myers, Feb. 14, 1920, in John A. Garraty (ed.), "Correspondence," *Ohio Historical Quarterly*, LXIV (1955), 276.

[62] Rhodes to Edward L. Pierce, June 25, 1894, in Frank M. Anderson, "Letters . . . to Edward L. Pierce," *American Historical Review*, XXXVI (1931), 784. The railroad official cited was that Thomas A. Scott whom Rhodes extolled in the *History*.

[63] Edward L. Pierce to Rhodes, Oct. 22, 1893, in Rhodes, "Memoir of Edward L. Pierce," *Proceedings*, *Massachusetts Historical Society*, Second series, XVIII (1903–1904), 368. Rhodes to Pierce, June 25, 1894, in Frank M. Anderson, "Letters . . . to Edward L. Pierce," *American Historical Review*, XXXVI (1931), 779.

[64] Rhodes to Gamaliel Bradford, April 20, 1924; Bradford to Rhodes, April 22, 1924. Letter Books of Gamaliel Bradford, Vol. XXII.

[65] *Historical Essays*, p. 22.

[66] *Ibid.*, pp. 21–22.

[67] *Ibid.*, pp. 148–149.

[68] *Ibid.*, p. 22.

[69] *History*, III, ch. XII.

[70] George W. Warvelle, "History and Operation of the Homestead Law," *Magazine of Western History*, I (1884), 300–307; "Precursors of the Homestead Law," *ibid.*, II (1885), 373–375.

[71] *Historical Essays*, pp. 171, 317. Rhodes to Mrs. C. H. Toy, Oct. 17 [1911?]. Rhodes Papers.

[72] Rhodes to Charles Eliot Norton, July 28, 1907, in M. A. D. Howe, *Rhodes*, pp. 158–159.

Chapter 18

RHODES' USE OF SOURCES: THE PROBLEM OF OBJECTIVITY

THE REVIEW of Rhodes' political and social views, together with consideration of the basic influences which shaped his development, his outlook on history and the functions of the historian, indicate that Rhodes was not, and indeed could not have been, the Olympian seeker after truth that he supposed himself. Yet he was acclaimed on both sides of the Atlantic, by scholar and layman alike, for his monumental fairness. Much of this reputation rested on the general belief, which Rhodes himself shared, that he had exhausted the available sources and had used them in accord with the canons of historical criticism. It behooves us, therefore, to examine Rhodes' use of sources in some detail.

In a limited sense, the general belief was founded on fact. Rhodes did indeed use sources correctly and honestly, insofar as citing and quoting them are concerned. A random check of 80 sources cited in Volumes V, VI and VII showed 75 cited accurately and their contents either quoted or summarized correctly; of the remaining five, four were incorrectly cited (which probably arose from errors in transcription or in printing) and only one furnished grounds for possible dispute over Rhodes' interpretation of the material cited.[1] This, no doubt, is a good showing, but it serves also to emphasize more significant weaknesses in the historian's approach to the problems of sources.

These weaknesses stemmed from three major factors. First, Rhodes lacked professional training, which resulted in his not being sufficiently aware of many of the technical problems involved in the critical use of sources.

Second, he relied for much of the work in the sources on his research assistants, particularly David M. Matteson, whom he commissioned eventually not only to gather but also to organize and analyze data.[2] The significance of Matteson's contribution may be gathered from a summary of subjects on which he furnished either facts or "theses": Civil War prisoner issue; Johnson's relations with

Seward; federal troops in the South during Reconstruction; Negro attitude toward freedom; activities of the Ku Klux Klan; role of the Negro in politics; railroad strikes of 1877 and 1886; Republican conventions of 1880, 1884 and 1888; civil service reform; Wilson-Gorman tariff; rehabilitation of the navy under Cleveland. Matteson also furnished "valuable assistance" for *The McKinley and Roosevelt Administrations.*[3] Rhodes, then, used many sources as they were filtered to him through the judgment of others; one wonders whether his treatment of some issues would have been substantially different had he done more work himself in the actual source materials.

A third source of weakness was Rhodes' concept of the historian as judge rather than inquiring scholar. As judge, the historian evaluated the evidence which came before him—and in Rhodes' case this was quite literally true since so much of his research was done by others. Evidence which the judge deemed false or prejudiced, or coming from sources deemed suspect, he rejected. Honest testimony of honest men he accepted. It did not occur to him that such testimony, when rooted in preconceptions as to race or class shared by the judge, might also be tainted.

Further, the historian as judge, unlike the historian as scholar, is under no obligation to scour even the most unlikely places for material, regardless of race, class or creed. The scholar must gather *all* the relevant facts, from whatever source arising, lest his hypotheses suffer from insufficient data. The judge is content to rest his decisions on the basis of valid testimony presented by informed and honest witnesses, so far as the judge appraises such testimony and witnesses. When the judge is convinced, as was Rhodes, that he is an unprejudiced seeker after truth, he may quite honestly exclude testimony favorable to the worker or the Negro for example, without feeling he is doing damage to the canons of historical research and writing.

To Rhodes, the problem of sources was simple: one made a conscientious search for material and used it with scrupulous honesty.[4] We may test the inadequacy of such an approach by first examining Rhodes' use of newspapers as sources.[5] These were valuable, said he, because:

> They are contemporary, and being written without knowledge of the end, cannot bolster any cause without making a plain showing of their intent. Their object is the relation of daily events; and if their relation is colored by honest or dishonest partisanship, this is easily discernible by the critic from the internal

evidence and from an easily acquired knowledge of a few external facts. As the journals themselves say, their aim is to print the news; and much of the news is present politics. Moreover, the newspaper itself, its news and editorial columns, its advertisements, is a graphic picture of society.[6]

Nor need one consult a variety of newspapers or magazines: if one has confidence in a given editor he may rely considerably on the material he presents. As an example, Rhodes cited his own dependence on *The Nation* for his treatment of Reconstruction:

> Frequently its editorials have spoken for the sober sense of the people with amazing success. As a constant reader of *The Nation* since 1866, I have felt that fascination of Godkin, and have been consciously on guard against it. . . . But whatever may be thought of his bias, he had an honest mind, and was incapable of knowingly making a false statement; and this, with his other qualities, makes his journal excellent historical material. . . .

Indeed, his approach to Reconstruction was so thoroughly legislative that he thought newspapers could be dispensed with as sources for that period:

> In the history of Reconstruction the historian may be to a large extent independent of the daily newspaper. For the work of Reconstruction was done by Congress, and Congress had the full support of the Northern people, . . . The debates, the reports, and the acts of Congress are essential, and little else is required except whatever private correspondence may be accessible. . . .

In general, however, newspapers were useful if the historian exercised "care and skepticism." In analyzing a given item,

> the general situation, the surrounding influences, and the individual bias must be taken into account, and, when allowance is made for these circumstances, as well as for the public character of the utterance, it may be used for historical evidence. . . .[7]

But one could exercise care and skepticism, use the material with "scrupulous honesty," and still be wide of the mark of historical accuracy. There were other and more basic questions to be raised in the use of newspapers as historical sources. The primary aim of newspapers, after all, was not "the relation of daily events" but rather the making of profit; reporting of the news was tributary to the business motive. Since the making of profit depended in large measure on circulation it followed that newspapers presented such news in such fashion as would increase circulation: the picture of society so presented might be graphic but not necessarily accurate.

Further, since newspaper publishing generally became a large-scale business enterprise its owners and editors naturally reflected the concerns and interests of the business community of which they were a part. News and editorial columns alike were used to clothe that community with the symbols best calculated to earn it public acceptance and esteem and to discredit those movements and individuals which seemed to present a threat to the business community—a consideration which Rhodes might have recalled from his own experience during the miners' strike of 1876. In short, in the study of those developments in which class interests were involved, newspapers were apt to prove deceptive sources indeed.[8]

Moreover, newspapers were almost entirely white enterprises, mirroring the common white attitude toward Negroes, whether that was the pity or contempt characteristic of the *ante-bellum* years or the impatience and condescension of the post-war period. In neither case could newspapers be relied upon to present an authentic picture of Negro life or to furnish a reasonable account of the Negro point of view. Yet, from such sources, Rhodes drew heavily for his treatment of Negro issues.

Rhodes himself, on occasion, recognized other hazards in the use of newspapers. Sometimes they printed reports which were pure fabrications, as in some of the anti-Negro "outrages" reported in the Northern press during Reconstruction.[9] They pursued vendettas against individuals who incurred their displeasure, as in that of Northern newspapers against General William T. Sherman.[10] They printed hasty and baseless reports, as that in which General Irvin McDowell was pictured as drunk during the first battle of Bull Run.[11] Interested individuals could deliberately use the press for their own ends, as in Secretary of War Edwin Stanton's feud with Sherman.[12]

Despite his recognition of such hazards, however, Rhodes did not always display the caution which such understanding would entail. He accepted without question the press reports that Andrew Johnson was drunk when the President made his famous speech in Cleveland.[13] He thought the newspapers of Richmond valid sources for asserting there was no panic in that city when Union troops approached it in 1862.[14] He termed Jefferson Davis "arrogant" on the basis of a comment by the New York *Tribune*.[15] Most incredible of all, for summaries of opinion in the South he relied often on Southern newspaper comment—as it was filtered through the *Liberator* and other Northern organs.[16]

Rhodes' lack of appreciation of the problems involved in the use of sources is demonstrated also in his treatment of the military aspects of the Civil War. Much of his analysis and description is based on *War of the Rebellion: Compilation of Official Records of the Union and Confederate Armies*, the massive collection of documents edited and published by the United States government. These records Rhodes accepted as authoritative, a unique example of "zeal, intelligence and good judgment." [17] Long after his own work on the Civil War was finished he defended them from criticisms, which, he said, were mere "pin pricks" of a "noble work." [18]

But even while Rhodes was engaged on the Civil War his friend, Jacob D. Cox, who possessed the military experience which Rhodes lacked, pointed out that the *Official Records*, while constituting "the original source and ultimate authority for the history of the period . . . vary in value." They were to be used carefully, he observed:

> National reports need to be compared and checked by the Confederate; the reports of subordinates by the broader summing up of chiefs, and *vice versa*. Personal ambitions, interests, vanities, and prejudices often color the statements of officers. In mishaps and defeats reports will be colored by the desire to cover a fault or to shift a responsibility. In success, the participants are tempted to claim an undue share of credit. . . .[19]

Rhodes might be excused ignorance of such factors: as a civilian he was no doubt awed by military usage and jargon, but as historian he might well have approached this material with some circumspection. The reports were official: their ultimate destinations were Richmond and Washington. In Richmond were centered the bitter internecine quarrels of the Confederate army, and in Washington sat the Joint Committee on the Conduct of the War, investigating the personal and public behavior of Union commanders as well as their thoughts and beliefs. Under such circumstances the reports submitted were likely to be less than candid.

Rhodes' uncritical reliance upon the *Official Records* is matched by his dependence upon testimony adduced before the Joint Committee on the Conduct of the War.[20] It is perhaps significant that nowhere in his work does he deal with the formation, conduct and importance of this committee. Had he done so he probably would have been less prone to accept its testimony at face value. He failed to realize that hearings before an extremely partisan Congressional committee may produce a picture that is partial, misleading and distorted; that even men of integrity, without the checks furnished by cross-examination, may honestly present testimony that is in essence false; and that knaves may use such hearings for purposes of their own.[21]

Rhodes relied on these sources, of course, because he believed them to be reliable. What are we to say of his use of sources that he himself repudiated? James G. Blaine's *Twenty Years of Congress* is frequently cited for detail and interpretation; and in 1903 Rhodes thought it "still the chief source of knowledge on Reconstruction." [22] In the body of his work, however, he dismissed it as "interesting but inaccurate history." [23] Much of his treatment of corruption in the Grant administration is based on *Secrets of the Great Whiskey Ring* by John McDonald; but as Rhodes himself pointed out, McDonald was illiterate, his "statements must . . . be received with caution" and the book "may have been intended" as propaganda against Grant.[24] To make his points against Bryan in the election of 1896 Rhodes cited as an authority "a keen observer from England," Goldwin Smith; but he wrote privately to a friend that he could not recommend Smith as an historian.[25] Rhodes never offered an explanation for his use of sources he deemed suspect; perhaps more significantly, no one else raised the question!

In his use of yet other sources Rhodes showed a cavalier disregard for the canons of historical scholarship. He took at face value the letters of Mrs. George E. Pickett, widow of the general, relative to her husband's role at Gettysburg; Professor William A. Dunning pointed out to him that "they were largely *ex post facto*—the product of the good lady's very lively imagination, reinforced with references to historical writings of a date long subsequent to the battle of Gettysburg." [26] He leaned heavily on *The Diary of a Public Man*, disregarding the warnings of Edward L. Pierce, who anticipated the finding of Frank Maloy Anderson that, "It is not a genuine diary. . . . It is, on the contrary, in part genuine and in part fictitious. . . . ought not to be regarded as a reliable source in any of its details." [27] He conceded that economists held that labor had not shared in the prosperity of the Civil War but went on to interpret domestic problems in the light of second-hand reports that "there must have been many exceptions to the rule. Labourers were in great demand and constantly employed," and his own recollection that it was "a tradition among mechanics [in Cleveland] that times . . . began to be good during the Civil War." [28]

As between the reports of Grant and Carl Schurz on the post-war South he chose to believe Grant because "he possessed one of those minds which often attain to correct judgments without knowing the how and the why." [29] He based much of his treatment of Reconstruction in South Carolina on *The Prostrate State* by James S. Pike, although one might expect a man who cherished moderation to be repelled by Pike's conclusion that, "A large majority of all the voting citizens of the State are habitually guilty of thieving and of concubinage." [30] Also, if Rhodes had been more familiar with his sources, he might have noted that Pike, a year before he ever set foot in South Carolina, wrote for the New York *Tribune* an article which made practically every major assertion later set forth in his famous series of reports, which, of course, purported to be fresh, unbiased first-hand accounts.[31] In any case, Pike was contradicted by General Oliver O. Howard, head of the Freedmen's Bureau and a man of some experience in the South. Rhodes, however, rejected Howard's testimony as "another of these extraordinary apologies for ignorance when covered by a black skin." [32]

In like manner he praised Owen Wister's *Lady Baltimore* for its portrayal of life "as it was" under Reconstruction while he found Albion Tourgée's *A Fool's Errand* "exaggerated and uncritical." [33] In his discussion of the *Report of the Joint Select Committee to Inquire into the Condition of Affairs in the Late Insurrectionary States* [34] (Ku Klux Klan committee) he conceded that both majority and minority reports were partisan,

> but the minority report comes nearer to the truth. At many points the Republican document halts and boggles . . . consciousness of a bad cause may be read between the lines; . . . While the Democrats attempt to prove too much, . . . , they are straightforward and aggressive with the consciousness of a cause based on the eternal principles of nature and justice. . . .[35]

In short, Rhodes was highly selective in his use of sources, and the bases of his selection were hardly those of the scholar: if sources provided interesting material, if they furnished data to fill out Rhodes' already-constructed general framework, he used them; if not, he dismissed them with short shrift.

Disregard of the problems of historical criticism is also reflected in Rhodes' reliance on biased sources. John C. Calhoun is pictured almost entirely on the basis of the unfriendly evidence of Hermann von Holst, James Parton and Thomas Hart Benton.[36] Calhoun's works are not cited, although they had been long available.[37] Daniel Webster, on the other hand, appears through the media of such admirers as Henry Cabot Lodge and George T. Curtis; Webster's own works are referred to frequently.[38] Rhodes, indeed, on the basis of an assertion by Curtis, flatly denied that Webster had been "in the pay of the United States Bank" when even a cursory glance at the relevant documents would have shown that Webster had been both a director and counsel of the bank.[39]

John Brown and Roscoe Conkling also benefitted from Rhodes' reliance on sources friendly to them, while a preponderance of material drawn from hostile sources colored his judgments of John C. Fremont, Andrew Johnson and Stephen A. Douglas.[40] Much of Rhodes' treatment of the background of the Civil War derives from von Holst and from one of von Holst's principal sources, Henry Wilson's *The Rise and Fall of the Slave Power in America;* both of them predicated on the belief, as William MacDonald put it, that slavery was "more an evil to be denounced than an institution to be studied and explained." [41]

The discussion of Reconstruction is, in part, based on the monographs of the Dunning school, but it also draws heavily on sources much less scholarly. Great emphasis is placed, for example, on such journalistic accounts as those of Pike and Nordhoff,[42] and on a work of special pleading by a friend of Rhodes, Hilary A. Herbert's *Why the Solid South? Or Reconstruction and Its Results.*[43] Rhodes also based much of his discussion on reports of state investigating committees appointed after the Democrats regained power; the minority report of the Congressional Ku Klux Klan committee; *The Nation;* and Southern Democratic newspapers.[44]

Sources which tended to discredit the thesis of these materials that Reconstruction had been a monstrous travesty on government were either ignored or belittled.[45] Little of Rhodes' work is based on the use of such sources as Southern Republican newspapers; Negro newspapers; proceedings of the reconstructed state constitutional conventions; white friends of the Negro in Congress and the Negro Congressmen and Senators themselves. In this last connection it may be noted that although Rhodes devoted considerable space to a consideration of the role of the Negro in politics he refrained from mentioning the tribute paid to the integrity of the Negro legislators by James G. Blaine, although in other respects Rhodes uses his work as almost a standard reference.[46] Perhaps a clue to Rhodes' approach to the problems of Reconstruction may be found in his confession that he had not troubled to read all the debates on the Reconstruction Acts—this despite his belief that "little else" was required to write an adequate history of the period.[47]

In the volumes covering the period from 1877 to 1909 the use of biased sources was so common as to be almost typical. The Molly

Maguires, railroad strikes of 1877 and 1886, Haymarket affair, Homestead strike, Pullman strike, Greenbackers, Populists and free-silver Democrats were all interpreted on the basis of hostile testimony.[48] Testimony of a much different order might have been obtained from sources readily available to Rhodes: these he either ignored or listed in his documentation without indication in the body of his writing that he had paid attention to them. These included the New York *Tribune* for background on the Molly Maguires; [49] Terence V. Powderly on the railroad strikes of the Knights of Labor; [50] Governor John P. Altgeld's message on the pardoning of the Chicago anarchists; [51] the reports of the United States Industrial Commission on labor disputes and of the United States Strike Commission on the Pullman strike; [52] and the numerous works by Greenback, Populist and free-silver Democrat leaders.

Another weakness in Rhodes' use of sources was his frequent resort to unconfirmed gossip or reports justified by the use of such vague phrases as "it was said," "it was believed," or "if the tradition be true." Thus, the story that "communists" in New York City in 1877 gave up their plan to foment disorder when they saw the Seventh Regiment in its armory was based on the phrase, "it is said," as was an example of Negro incompetency in governmental affairs.[53] The character sketch of Judah Benjamin noted that he "was by many considered untrustworthy" without further elaboration and that of Clement Vallandigham depended on the qualifying phrase, "if the tradition be true." [54] A partial explanation for Thaddeus Stevens' attitude toward the South rested on "common report." [55]

In some instances Rhodes went beyond such phrases into presumption and conjecture. "We may presume," said Rhodes, that Buchanan endorsed the Ostend Manifesto because he had been shown "the vision of the White House." [56] He conjectured that Charles Francis Adams revealed his instructions relative to possible British recognition of the Confederacy and "that this was the reason why the project of mediation or recognition was so suddenly abandoned." [57] In discussing the adoption of the Thirteenth Amendment he commented, "Money *could probably* have been raised for an attempt to buy [votes] . . . but it is *doubtful* whether any was used for this purpose." [58] Had the iron-clad rams been released to the Confederacy, "they would *undoubtedly* have broken the blockade . . . the harm *would* have been incalculable: the victories even of Gettysburg and Vicksburg *might have been* neutralized." [59]

Early in his career Rhodes had been cautioned by Edward L. Pierce on his indiscriminate use of such phrases, but the warning failed to impress him. He explained to Pierce:

> The "It is said," "It is reported," is all right to make a description of a movement or a state of public opinion and is frequently employed by Macaulay, and by Gardiner, both honest men. But it is quite another matter to use that form of expression to blacken reputations. Nevertheless that does not dispose of the whole matter. A reviewer of Gardiner's History in The Nation expressed the idea I long had and much better . . . "The whole aim of an historian is the discovery and the statement of truth. . . . He must constantly deal not with certainties but with probabilities. . . . The impartiality of the judgment-seat is not the impartiality needed for the discharge of an historian's judicial functions.". . .[60]

A more astonishing feature of Rhodes' use of sources was his failure, in some cases, to supply sources at all. He discussed the motives of Stephen A. Douglas in relation to the Kansas-Nebraska bill on the basis that

> no confidential letters or conversations need be unearthed to arrive at a satisfactory explanation. . . . it may with confidence be affirmed that the action of the Illinois senator was a bid for Southern support in the next Democratic convention. . . .[61]

Rhodes gave no sources for this sweeping conclusion, save for accusations made by enemies of Douglas.

Nor did Rhodes document significant generalizations such as the following: the jury in the Oberlin-Wellington slave rescue trial, although all Democrats, "were willing to give the benefit of the doubt to the accused"; in the Dred Scott case, pressure was used on the Southern members of the court to bring in a pro-slavery decision and the "bait" used to gain Chief Justice Taney was the argument that the court could thus settle the slavery question; Horace Greeley was right when he charged that Douglas borrowed and spent eighty thousand dollars in the election campaign of 1858 and that this debt "remained to harass him out of this mortal life"; the Emancipation Proclamation received the support of a majority of the Northern people in 1862; Negro prisoners of war, "with rare exceptions

. . . were not abused" by the Confederates; the South would have ratified the Fourteenth Amendment had Andrew Johnson advised it; Southerners who cooperated in Congressional Reconstruction were "for the most part shifty men or men of bad character"; the country "was on the verge of civil war" after the Hayes-Tilden election.[62]

One more word needs to be said. Rhodes completed his basic work in the years, 1892 to 1906. Thereafter he published the *Lectures on the American Civil War*, the *History of the Civil War*, and two "new" editions of his entire *History*,[63] one of which appeared after his death. The comments on his basic work apply equally well to these later volumes: there is little indication that he was aware of new interpretations of old materials or of materials made recently available, and there is no sign that he had developed a more critical approach to the sources.

In view of the foregoing we may now properly put the question as to the validity of Rhodes' reputation for fairness. The obvious answer is that the claim lacks validity. Woodrow Wilson pointed this out as early as 1893; and years later Rhodes' friend in the Massachusetts Historical Society, John D. Long, noted that when Rhodes' personal sympathies were aroused he "wrote like a lawyer arguing for a defendant." [64] Such comments, however, explain neither Rhodes' confidence in his impartiality nor that of his contemporaries in his objectivity—a faith so strong that a very Proper Bostonian, John T. Morse, Jr., could write, without trace of embarrassment:

> You are absolutely the most fair-minded man who ever dealt with matters of controversy. . . . Of course you manage to infuse a certain kindliness and gentle mercy into your justice, as we are told that God does—(though I would rather trust you than him).[65]

To discuss this issue adequately we must draw a distinction between, on the one hand, Rhodes' conscious attitudes as historian, and on the other, the assumptions, often unconscious, which he shared with the section of American society of which he was a part.

As to Rhodes' personal and professional integrity there can be little doubt: when he was conscious of problems, of conflicting bodies of data, of rival interpretations, he strove to reach objective judgments. The pages of his notebooks are strewn with notes of readings, conversations, interviews, and suggested revisions in his work, all attesting to his desire to establish his work on a foundation of verified data.[66] When John R. Lynch called his attention to errors of fact in his treatment of Reconstruction he promised correction: "I always correct errors of fact." [67] When Daniel W. Howe, in his book, *Political History of Secession to the Beginning of the American Civil War*,[68] challenged Rhodes' discussion of the Dred Scott case, Rhodes, gravely troubled, pledged himself to present, at least, Howe's view:

> the question is so important that I have not yet arrived at a decision. I fear, however, that I shall have to change my account and I am writing to my publishers asking them what it will cost to break up two pages and have new plates made . . .
>
> * * *
>
> I am a slow thinker and cannot say whether I shall arrive at the opinion you so eloquently express . . . but I shall not allow another edition of my second volume to go to press without, at any rate, presenting your side of the question. . . .[69]

Also, when he was aware that his "historical conclusions" were at variance with his "contemporary opinions" he tried to avoid allowing opinions to color judgments.[70] Thus, privately, he had little liking for Andrew Carnegie; he thought J. P. Morgan little better than a mulcter of widows and orphans; and John D. Rockefeller, Sr., he held to be "an infernal old hypocrite . . . John D., Jr., is a fine earnest man and my friend, but I never tell him what I think of his father. How could John D. make a billion and be honest? It couldn't be done." [71] Conscious of these feelings he strove to counterbalance them, with such success that these men emerge from his pages as benefactors of humanity. If, in striving to be fair he ended with bias, one can at least credit him with the striving.

Such considerations make it difficult to accept the thesis suggested by Professor Frank Hodder and later more positively asserted by George Fort Milton that Rhodes was "unconsciously" biased against Stephen A. Douglas because Rhodes had had to pay $30,000 to Douglas' heirs in settlement of a lawsuit brought against Rhodes' father, Daniel, who had been executor of the Douglas estate.[72] Given Rhodes' sensitivity on matters of money it is hard to believe Rhodes would have been unconscious of such feeling, and granted that he was aware of the prejudice, it is difficult to believe he would allow it to color his historical judgment. If we are to accept Rhodes' own explanation, he came to his conclusions on Douglas with great reluctance. Referring to John W. Burgess' criticism of his treatment of the Senator, he wrote to the reviewer:

> Could the ghost of my Father appear to me he would speak in the words of your review . . . In such wise would he aver that I had misrepresented Douglas . . . I should have been glad to represent Douglas as you intimate . . . It is substantially the defense of him I have heard my Father many times make. When I began my preliminary reading for my history many years ago, I came reluctantly to the conclusion I have expressed of Douglas . . . I should have rejoiced could I have reverted to the opinion of my youth when I learned my political lessons from my father: but I could not honestly do it. . . .[73]

It seems more plausible, in view of Rhodes' confirmed tendency to follow traditional interpretations, to attribute his portrayal of Douglas to the essay in the *North American Review* which had made such a strong impression upon him as a youth; to the influence of John Hay, who abominated Douglas; and to the general tenor of American historiography of the post–Civil War period, which execrated Douglas as a monster of deceit and ambition.[74]

Indeed, so violent were the terms applied to the Senator that a case might well be made that Rhodes introduced corrective elements into the traditional estimate: if Douglas sacrificed the peace of his country for presidential ambition, said Rhodes, he made a noble atonement; Douglas yielded that ambition later on the altar of an unselfish patriotism and his death was a national calamity.[75] This was so exceptional that *The Nation* commented on Rhodes' ascribing to Douglas more sincerity than was usually attributed to him by historians.[76] It is not without significance that a man brought up in staunchly Republican Iowa should thank Rhodes for helping eradicate his prejudices against Douglas.[77]

Granting Rhodes' personal integrity, then, we may attempt to explain his reputation for objective scholarship despite what appear to us to have been violations of the standards of such scholarship.

In the first place, Rhodes did not possess an inquiring mind. As we have seen, he shrank from analyzing the feelings of individuals. In his work also, there was a certain similarity of attitude: Frederic Bancroft, who knew Rhodes and his work well, explained that Rhodes lacked genius and imagination, possessing a mind that, far from being vigorous and resourceful, was sluggish and materialistic, by which latter term he meant that Rhodes' mind had to have "the concrete thing" in view before it could work.[78] With such a mind, then, it is not surprising that Rhodes found it impossible to stand outside his own social frame of reference, to take the long historical perspective toward his own class and race relationships. Rather, his was the type of mind which functioned comfortably within the traditional Northern white middle-class framework, which accepted without question the basic values of his society.

Among these values were white supremacy in race relations, *laissez-faire* in economics and nationalism in politics, just as among the evils were slavery in the *ante-bellum* South and "soft" money and labor unrest in the *post-bellum* North. It must be emphasized that in the America of the late 19th and early 20th centuries these were held not as tentative judgments but as "truths" based on immutable laws laid bare by science. It followed that findings which differed from such "truths" were *ipso facto* based on fallacious premises and therefore beyond the bounds of serious discussion. When one ignored the Negro point of view, dismissed the Southern view of slavery, or treated labor agitation as the result of greed and envy, one was being neither unscholarly nor "unfair"; he was simply confining the discussion to an objective framework of the "facts" of the given problems.

Nowhere was this better expressed than by Rhodes himself in his comment that an accurate history of the Civil War could be written *only* by anti-slavery historians,[79] and in his view that a reasoned presentation of the Southern case for slavery was not within the province of the historian:

> We can only regard with pity these arguments [on behalf of slavery] that were retailed in the select circles of the South and used to persuade willing Northern and English visitors. When we meet them in their balder form, we can only turn away with disgust. . . .[80]

This approach was demonstrated again in an incident which also throws a revealing light on Rhodes' public, showing how clearly both shared certain preconceptions. Charles K. Bolton noted that Rhodes came to the Athenaeum

> to look over some material on the Mollie Maguire trials. . . . As Mr. Rhodes turned from one to another he showed his judicial mind by remarking, "I must read the evidence thoroughly . . . before I convict them and I must convict them before I hang them." [81]

The critic of our day might well argue that Rhodes apparently had made up his mind about the hanging before examining the evidence; to his own generation this was merely an example of the judicial mind.

This supplies us with a clue to Rhodes' reputation for fairness. So far as his public checked his sources, in accord with the scholarly standards of the time, they found Rhodes to be accurate and correct. It did not occur to them—indeed, given their basic assumptions, it would not have seemed proper to them—to raise questions about Rhodes' lack of documentation from labor and Negro sources, for example. As to his careless use of sources or employment of biased sources, Rhodes' judgments seemed so consonant with accepted "truths" that the issue of carelessness or bias rarely arose. We make this point more clear by reference to Rhodes' discussion of Reconstruction.

As we have seen, his case rested largely on *ex parte* sources and is characterized by a complete ignoring of sources favorable to the Negro. To Rhodes' generation, however, believing in the inferiority of the Negro, it was inconceivable that valid testimony could come from the Negro and such material as could come would be "biased" in favor of the Negro view; further, as Rhodes himself said, sources sympathetic to the Negro were tainted either with interest or emotionalism. In short, only the white historian believing in white supremacy could write objective history of the Reconstruction period. This was the view of both historian and his public.

Belief in Rhodes' fairness was strengthened also by his frequent avowal that there was room for difference of interpretation: "all the right is never on one side and all the wrong on the other." [82] Here, too, however, only what seemed to the historian and his public to be *valid* differences in viewpoint were to be considered: and these differences were limited by the preconceptions as to race and class held by the literate public of the day. Thus, Reconstruction could be interpreted only in terms of Radical Republicanism versus White South: a possible Negro view was not even considered. Labor disputes were viewed as struggles between conservatism and social radicalism: pragmatic labor unionism was therefore denied its day in court. The controversy over free silver was treated differently, because in this case both Rhodes and his public were convinced there was only one valid view, that of "hard money." To another generation this may appear a restricted outlook; to Rhodes' generation it was the essence of fair-minded scholarship that he should be willing to concede the right to differ within the intellectual framework of that society.

In summary, Rhodes' public, both lay and scholarly, believed in his objectivity because he conformed to the standards of scholarship they held sound, standards which in turn rested upon a body of assumptions about man, race, class and society held quite uncritically by scholars and laymen predominantly Anglo-Saxon and middle-class in origin and outlook. If we can see Rhodes' failings more clearly than they it is largely because we no longer share the preconceptions which determined the intellectual outlook of his society.

NOTES

[1] *History*, VI, 55, note 4. Rhodes cited *The Nation*, June 14 and June 22, 1866, to support his assertion that Dr. J. J. Craven's *Prison Life of Jefferson Davis* aroused sympathy for Davis in the North. Both issues attacked Craven for *trying* to arouse sympathy for Davis.

[2] Rhodes to Charles H. Firth, Dec. 16, 1902. Rhodes Papers.

[3] *History*, V, 508 n; VI, 70 n, 76 n, 83 n, 85 n, 179 n, 190 n, 317 n, 319 n, 331 n; *From Hayes to McKinley*, pp. 23 n, 45 n, 127 n, 167 n, 186–187, 193 n, 214 n, 275 n, 317 n, 422 n, 438 n; *The McKinley and Roosevelt Administrations*, pp. 297, 399.

[4] *Historical Essays*, p. 76.

[5] The paper, "Newspapers as Historical Sources," was delivered at the meeting of the American Historical Association, 1908. Text may be found in *Historical Essays*, pp. 81–98.

[6] *Ibid.*, p. 83.

[7] *Ibid.*, pp. 94–96.

[8] See, for example, Almont Lindsey, *The Pullman Strike*, ch. XIII; and Robert Cruden, "Representative Cleveland Newspapers and the Pullman Strike, 1894–1895," *passim.*

[9] *History*, VII, 225.

[10] *Ibid.*, V, 25.

[11] Rhodes, "Remarks on General Irvin McDowell," *Proceedings, Massachusetts Historical Society*, XLII (1908–1909), 191.

[12] *History*, V, 171.

[13] *Ibid.*, V, 619. Note Professor Frank Hodder's finding that the evidence is conclusive that Johnson was "a total abstainer from the day of his inauguration as vice-president." "Propaganda as a Source of American History," *Mississippi Valley Historical Review*, IX (1922), 15.

[14] *History*, IV, 28. In discussing the Richmond bread riots, however, Rhodes pointed out that newspapers were subject to influence by the Confederate government. *Ibid.*, V, 365.

[15] *Ibid.*, II, 454.

[16] *Ibid.*, II, 34, 144–145, 151, 204–205, 355. Rhodes employed this device almost universally throughout his work.

[17] *Ibid.*, V, 626 n.

[18] "Tribute to Thomas Leonard Livermore," *Proceedings, Massachusetts Historical Society*, LI (1917–1918), 244.

[19] Jacob D. Cox, "Bibliography of the Civil War Period," in J. N. Larned (ed.), *The Literature of American History: A Bibliographical Guide with Supplement* (Columbus, Ohio, 1953), p. 215. A reprint of the original work which appeared in 1902.

[20] *History*, III, IV, V, *passim.* On one occasion Rhodes noted that a majority of the committee favored John C. Fremont and colored a report accordingly. *Ibid.*, III, 482 n.

[21] William W. Pierson, Jr., "The Committee on the Conduct of the War," *American Historical Review*, XXIII (1918), 550–576; J. G. Randall, *The Civil War and Reconstruction* (Boston, 1953), pp. 367–370.

[22] Quoted in Charles K. Bolton, *Notebook, 1886–1914*, pp. 113–114 (Nov. 23, 1903).

[23] *History*, V, 587.

[24] *Ibid.*, VII, 183–187.

[25] *The McKinley and Roosevelt Administrations*, pp. 27–28. Rhodes to Mrs. C. H. Toy, Oct. 17, 1911. Rhodes Papers.

[26] William A. Dunning to Rhodes, Jan. 17, 1918. Rhodes Papers. The reference is to Mrs. L. C. Pickett, *Pickett and His Men* (Philadelphia, 1913), cited in Rhodes, *History of the Civil War*, pp. 237–243.

[27] Frank Maloy Anderson, *The Mystery of "A Public Man": A Historical Detective Story* (Minneapolis, 1948), pp. 169, 178. Anderson found that Rhodes cited the *Diary* 17 times. *Ibid.*, pp. 69, 146. See also Roy N. Lokken "Has the Mystery of 'A Public Man' Been Solved?," *Mississippi Valley Historical Review*, XL (1953), 419–440.

[28] *History*, V, 203–206.

[29] *Ibid.*, V, 552.

[30] Quoted in *ibid.*, VII, 149.

[31] Robert F. Durden, *James Shepherd Pike: Republicanism and the American Negro* (Durham, N. C., 1957), p. 187.

[32] *History*, VII, 151.

[33] *Ibid.*, VI, vii, 307 n.

[34] U. S. Senate Report 41, 42nd Congress, 2nd session. (13 vols. Washington, 1872).

[35] *History*, VI, 323–324.

[36] *History*, I, 45, 47, 48, 79–85, 127–129. Hermann von Holst, *John C. Calhoun* (Boston, 1882); James Parton, *Life of Andrew Jackson* (New York, 1861); Thomas Hart Benton, *Thirty Years View* (New York, 1854–1856). John S. Jenkins' eulogistic *Life of John Caldwell Calhoun* (Auburn, N. Y., 1852), is cited only incidentally.

[37] Richard K. Cralle (ed.), *Works of John C. Calhoun* (6 vols., New York, 1853–1855).

[38] *History*, I, 42, 50, 72, 77, 78, 91, 98, 137–161. Henry Cabot Lodge, *Daniel Webster* (Boston, 1883); George T. Curtis, *Life of Daniel Webster* (New York, 1870); Josiah Quincy, *Figures of the Past from Leaves of Old Journals* (Boston, 1883).

[39] *History*, I, 143.

[40] *History*, II, 383–409; IV, 11; V, 429–495, 618–621; VI, 422; VII, 26. Hermann von Holst, *John Brown* (Boston, 1889); James Redpath, *Public Life of Captain John Brown* (Boston, 1860); Franklin B. Sanborn (ed.), *Life and Letters of John Brown* (Boston, 1885); A. R. Conkling, *Life and Letters of Roscoe Conkling* (New York, 1889). For testimony on Fremont's command in Missouri Rhodes relied on Francis P. Blair, Jr., who was, said Rhodes, "in spite of their personal quarrel a competent and honest witness." *History*, IV, 11. On Andrew Johnson Rhodes cited such enemies of the President as James Russell Lowell, John Sherman and *The Nation*. On Douglas Rhodes used two campaign biographies by H. M. Flint (New York, 1860) and J. W. Sheahan (New York, 1860), but his major reliance was on newspapers like the New York *Tribune* which he himself admitted were "hostile" to Douglas. *History*, I, 445.

[41] Hermann von Holst, *Constitutional and Political History of the United States* (8 vols., Chicago, 1877–1892); Henry Wilson, *History of the Rise and Fall of the Slave Power in America* (3 vols., Boston, 1872–1877). William MacDonald in J. N. Larned, *The Literature of American History*, p. 203.

[42] *History*, VII, 126, 137, 142, 149. James S. Pike, *The Prostrate State* (New York, 1874); Charles Nordhoff, *The Cotton States in the Spring and Summer of 1875* (New York, 1876).

[43] *History*, VII, 75–79, 84, 97, 140. The book, edited by Herbert, is a series of essays defending Democratic domination of Southern politics. It was published in Baltimore, Md., 1890.

[44] *History*, VI, chs. XXXII, XXXIV, XXXVII; VII, chs. XLI, XLII.

[45] For example, W. E. B. DuBois, "The Freedmen's Bureau," *Atlantic Monthly*, LXXXVII (1901), 354–365. Rhodes cited the article but his discussion showed no consideration of the materials presented by DuBois.

[46] *History*, VII, 168–171. James G. Blaine, *Twenty Years of Congress from Lincoln to Garfield* (Norwich, Conn., 1884–1886), II, 448–449, 515.

[47] "Remarks on Negro Suffrage and Reconstruction," *Proceedings, Massachusetts Historical Society*, Second series, XIX (1905–1906), 35.

[48] *From Hayes to McKinley*, pp. 13–87, 278–284, 351–356, 386–388, 401–408, 424–426; *The McKinley and Roosevelt Administrations*, pp. 18–28, 323–327. A few examples of hostile sources are: F. P. Dewees, *The Molly Maguires* (Philadelphia, 1887); Allen Pinkerton, *Strikers, Communists, Tramps and Detectives* (New York, 1878); F. W. Taussig, "The Southwestern Strike of 1886," *Quarterly Journal of Economics*, I (1887), 184–222; Joseph E. Gary, "The Chicago Anarchists of 1886," *Century Magazine*, XLV (1892–1893), 803–837; Alexander D. Noyes, *Thirty Years of American Finance* (New York, 1898); Harry Thurston Peck, *Twenty Years of the Republic*.

[49] Carl Wittke, *The Irish in America* (Baton Rouge, 1956), p. 221.

[50] T. V. Powderly, *Thirty Years of Labor, 1859–1889* (Columbus, Ohio, 1890). Rhodes listed this as a source but gave little heed to its material. *From Hayes to McKinley*, p. 46.

[51] *Ibid.*, p. 285, indicates this document was available to Rhodes. He made no use of it.

[52] U. S. Industrial Commission, *Reports* (19 vols., Washington, 1900–1902). U. S. Strike Commission, *Report on Chicago Strike*, 53rd Congress, 3rd session, Senate Executive Document No. 7 (Washington, 1895).

[53] *From Hayes to McKinley*, p. 41; *History*, VII, 97.

[54] *History*, IV, 245; V, 63.

[55] *Ibid.*, V, 544.

[56] *Ibid.*, II, 40.

[57] *Ibid.*, IV, 343.

[58] *Ibid.*, V, 50. Italics supplied.

[59] *Ibid.*, IV, 385. Italics supplied.

[60] Rhodes to Edward L. Pierce, May 18, 1894, in Frank M. Anderson, "Letters . . . to Edward L. Pierce," *American Historical Review*, XXXVI (1931), 783.

[61] *History*, I, 429–430.

[62] *Ibid.*, II, 253–254, 338 n, 363; IV, 215; V, 498, 610; VI, 44; VII, 243.

[63] *History of the United States from the Compromise of 1850 to the End of the Roosevelt Administration* (9 vols., New York, 1928).

[64] John D. Long, "On a Reference to W. H. Seward in Carl Schurz's Reminiscences," *Proceedings, Massachusetts Historical Society*, Third series, I (1907–1908), 35.

[65] John T. Morse, Jr., to Rhodes, Feb. 7, 1920. Rhodes Papers.

[66] Rhodes Papers, X, XI, *passim.*

[67] Rhodes to George A. Myers, April 22, 1917, in M. A. D. Howe, *Rhodes*, pp. 277–278.

[68] (New York, 1914).

[69] Rhodes to Daniel W. Howe, Feb. 13, 1915, photostat fragment. Rhodes Papers.

[70] Rhodes to Charles Francis Adams, May 10, 1907, in M. A. D. Howe, *Rhodes*, p. 154.

[71] *Ibid.*, pp. 315–316. Rhodes on Rockefeller quoted in Charles K. Bolton, *Notebook, 1917–1920*, p. 94 (Feb. 9, 1918).

[72] Frank Hodder, "Propaganda as a Source of American History," *Mississippi Valley Historical Review*, IX (1922), 10; George Fort Milton, *The Eve of Conflict*, p. 146.

[73] Rhodes to John W. Burgess, June 5, 1893, in Joseph Borome, "James Ford Rhodes and Historical Scholarship," *New England Quarterly*, XXI (1948), 379–380.

[74] Frank M. Anderson, *Mystery of "A Public Man,"* p. 139. For examples of typical treatment of Douglas see Hermann von Holst, *Constitutional and Political History*, III, 410; V, 278; James Schouler, *History of the United States Under the Constitution* (7 vols., New York, 1880–1913), V, 285, 290, 411; John W. Burgess, *The Middle Period* (New York, 1897), p. 384.

[75] *History*, II, 285, 302, 356; III, 415.

[76] *The Nation*, LV (1893), 499–500.

[77] George F. Parker to Rhodes, Dec. 31, 1919. Rhodes Papers. Parker was the author of *Recollections of Grover Cleveland* (New York, 1909).

[78] Quoted in Jacob E. Cooke, *Frederic Bancroft: Historian* (Norman, Oklahoma, 1957), pp. 48–49.

[79] *History*, II, 502.

[80] *Ibid.*, I, 368–369.

[81] *Notebook, 1886–1914*, p. 144 (March 22, 1909).

[82] *History*, V, 485.

Chapter 19

RHODES' HISTORY: AN APPRAISAL

TO UNDERSTAND Rhodes' place in American historiography we must note that he worked in an era of basic transition: an era in which the literary history typified by Parkman and Prescott and the patriotic history exemplified by Bancroft was giving way to the more rigorous scientific history growing out of the Johns Hopkins seminars of the '80's, represented most strikingly perhaps in the work of Frederick Jackson Turner.

The new approach to the problems of history, originating in the adaptation of the concept of biological evolution to the study of human society, rested on the environmentalist thesis that man was a product of his total environment; to understand man, one must place him in his physical, social, economic and cultural setting; man changed, not spontaneously, not through the influence of great men, not through divine intervention, but because of impersonal factors operating in his environment. History's function was to analyze and explain the nature of such changes; in the words of Herbert Baxter Adams, the pioneer exponent of the new school, "History should not be content with describing effects when it can explain causes." [1]

Such explanation was now thought possible through the accumulation of all relevant data, subjecting them to rigid tests of historical criticism, and interpreting them objectively without intrusion of any personal element on the part of the historian. This last, which may seem naive to a generation brought up on the teachings of modern psychology, was assumed to be attainable if the historian were properly trained and possessed a detached, scientific attitude.

As a fairly consistent Spencerian, Rhodes accepted the postulates of the new school relating to method. That is, he too believed that the historian should consult the relevant sources and test them critically; that it was possible for the historian to interpret his material without injection of personal feeling. This last helped to lead Rhodes astray, as it did others much more severely "scientific" than he. Picturing himself as a disinterested seeker after truth, unaware of those elemental psychic forces which shape the attitudes of men despite their conscious outlooks, unconscious of the manifold ways in which considerations of class and race mold beliefs and behavior, he could quite honestly equate condemnation of the Negro and of labor organization, espousal of the gold standard and free economic competition, with objective historical judgment. And because his public shared this basic illusion as well as his attitudes it accepted his judgments as the last word in historical scholarship.

But Rhodes was much more than Spencerian or Darwinian. On such issues as the nature of man and of society, the function of history and the role of historian he parted company with the scientific school. In part this was due to Rhodes' lack of educational background and professional training which would have enabled him to grapple with the problems raised by the scientific school; in part, also, to the pedestrian nature of his mind, which shied away from analysis and especially from contending with intangibles.

Much more was it due to the Calvinism which colored so much of Rhodes' outlook. Unlike the scientific historians, Rhodes could and did believe in the fundamental nature of man's moral responsibility; man was to be explained less in terms of social and physical environment than in terms of character; free to make choices, man made his own history, for which he was accountable at the bar of judgment. In the writing of history, then, explanation was subordinate to the great end of moral judgment and the supreme function of the historian was didactic. In short, history was designed to elevate the thought and behavior of mankind rather than to provide scientific explanation as to why men had acted as they did. The conflict between the moral judge and the objective historian was resolved through the familiar expedient of identifying what one conceives to be moral good with what Rhodes called "immutable truths."

In Rhodes' view, too, the historian as American had yet another function: to arouse patriotic feeling by calling attention to his country's great resources, the contributions made to its development by captains of industry, its vast educational program, the morality of the people and their domestic happiness. Above all, the historian must remind his countrymen that a nation which produced a Washington and a Lincoln surely excelled all others.

Since history served a fundamentally didactic purpose it followed that the historian must attract and retain those who were to be taught. For this purpose the historian must place his emphasis on narration rather than on scientific inquiry, must emulate Homer and

Shakespeare, Carlyle and Macaulay, rather than Samuel Gardiner or Henry Adams.

Given this set of beliefs, it was perhaps inevitable that Rhodes should identify himself with the literary school of historians, in which the didactic value of history held high place, and in which the lack of professional training appeared no great handicap. It was Rhodes' great advantage, however, that he combined with this literary approach the methods used by the scientific school, and so provided his moral judgments with what appeared to be scientific foundation. This combination helps explain his unique popularity and influence. A brief discussion of that influence may help us understand further Rhodes' place in the writing of American history.

Most obviously, Rhodes secured and kept his audience because he wrote interesting history. His literary talents were meagre. With little command of the varied resources of his native tongue, he had no knack for the well-turned sentence, the apt phrase; he lacked that sense of the comic, the tragic or the ironic which can transform history into literature. But he did write in an easy, simple, unhurried prose which taxed neither the imagination nor the understanding of his readers. Further, he had the good fortune to write, free from the competition of other leading historians, of one of the most dramatic eras in the nation's life—the Civil War and its aftermath—at a time when there was renewed interest in that era arising from the resurgence of nationalism toward the end of the 19th century.

Picturing that conflict in terms of the eternal struggle between vice and virtue so dear to the hearts of the lay public, Rhodes adorned it also with interesting sketches of significant characters and dramatic accounts of epidemics, riots, duels and battles. If critics said that much of this was irrelevant, that it resulted in the ignoring of more historically significant happenings, Rhodes could well retort that his books were widely read and quoted while those of his critics were read only by other historians. To the literary historian that was a matter of prime importance.

But Rhodes' hold on his public is not to be explained alone in terms of literary interest. Rhodes was more than historian. He filled the role of historical judge, in which both he and his public believed. To that role he brought a wealth of scholarship, based on the scientific method of the day, and a remarkably judicial temperament. Most important, the judgments he handed down were those which the American reading public desperately wanted to hear.

The period in which Rhodes wrote his major work (1886–1906) covered two contrasting moods of the middle-class public: one of anxiety, one of optimism. The mood of anxiety grew out of the fears of the middle class that its existence was threatened on the one hand by the growth of economic concentration through Big Business and on the other by the development of militant farmers' and workers' organizations, fears that were given body by the Panic of 1893 and its attendant social disorders. The mood of optimism had its roots in the revived confidence felt as a result of recovery from the Panic, of the victory over Spain, and of America's ability to solve social problems within the traditional social framework, symbolized by the growth of the Progressive spirit.

Rhodes appealed to both moods. For anxiety he offered the balm, for optimism the rational explanation, of a thorough-going Spencerianism, combined with Calvinist morality, as embodied in the lessons of history. From Rhodes one learned that the very experience of mankind itself upon the North American continent had proved the validity of the traditional, conservative middle-class concepts. Given the superior character of the American people, free competition was the key to social progress, and "survival of the fittest" was to be attained through the individualist virtues of hard work, sobriety, thrift, financial probity and sexual morality.

In this framework, labor organization was logically viewed as inimical to social order, attacks upon the gold standard as financial dishonesty, and trusts and the tariff as hostile to the general welfare. In this framework, too, the patriotic historian could quite legitimately emphasize the contributions of the captains of industry while neglecting those of farmers, workers and immigrants.

As it proved the soundness of middle class social concepts, so also did history demonstrate the validity of the traditional belief in the supremacy of the Anglo-Saxon race and the inherent inferiority of the Negro: in the evolutionary struggle for existence the Anglo-Saxon had proved himself the best, the Negro the least, fitted for progress.

It is not surprising, then, that the reading public took Rhodes to its heart, especially since he himself so patently believed in the truth of what he said.

It is against this background of close identity between writer and audience that we must view Rhodes' interpretation of the Civil War. Here again there was an audience waiting, an audience created by the upsurge of national feeling which had grown out of the mellowing of Civil War memories, the emergence of the New South, the feeling of racial identity between Northern and Southern whites, and the expansion of the American economy. There was a sharp revival of interest in the Civil War, an interest showing less sectionalism, more nationalism than that which obtained in the '70's and '80's. Symbolic of the new trend was the interpretation offered by Rhodes.

As might be expected of a man of Rhodes' conservative outlook, he made no sharp break with the past. His basic interpretations were still in the older pattern: slavery was the sole cause of the war; the South, tragically misled by Calhoun and Jefferson Davis, fought for an "unrighteous" cause; the North, under the inspired leadership of Lincoln, represented the conscience of mankind.

Rhodes, however, did introduce some new elements into the accepted picture, growing out of his substitution for the narrowness of Schouler and the harshness of von Holst of a genial fair-mindedness which embraced both South and North. He abandoned, somewhat cautiously, the conspiracy theory of the origins of the war, acknowledging that he was following the example of von Holst and Schouler. In its place he offered the view that secession was the result of a public sentiment so strong that had not Davis and his associates headed the movement, "the people would have found other leaders." [2]

While retaining the palm of virtue for the North he found much to praise in the Southern way of life; extolled leaders whom the South revered, such as Robert E. Lee and "Stonewall" Jackson; held each side equally culpable for the treatment of prisoners of war; described with equal hand corruption in both sections, ascribing much of it to Jews, who were apparently not included in the new dispensation; and in general praised the bravery and behavior of soldiers on both sides, blaming excesses, such as the Fort Pillow massacre and the burning of Columbia, S. C., on forces outside control of the military commanders.[3] In short, Rhodes presented a new synthesis of the war, still favorable to the North but including within it many aspects sympathetic to the South.

There were yet other considerations which Rhodes introduced. He focused favorable attention on the role of businessmen in helping the federal government; he suggested that economic factors, such as an inadequate transportation system and an undeveloped iron industry, played a part in the defeat of the South; and perhaps most significantly he laid the foundation in his first volume of what later became a major element in his discussion, the factor of race.[4]

In the midst of his chapter on slavery, while inveighing against the evils of the institution, he stoutly upheld the Southern white view of the biological inferiority of the Negro as "scientific truth." On that basis he exhorted the North of his own day to exercise the "wisdom of forbearance" while the South must exercise "wisdom of action" in dealing with the "negro question." [5]

Professor Pressly has suggested that Rhodes went much further in his re-interpretation of the Civil War. In Pressly's view, Rhodes explained the origins of the war in terms of "inanimate" causes (cotton and the cotton gin) and thus absolved the South of sole war guilt.[6] It is difficult to accept this view. Such an explanation was too perceptive, too keenly analytical, for Rhodes' rather sluggish mind; too much of a break with the past for a man of his temperament; and it ran counter to his Calvinist conviction of man's moral responsibility for his actions. It is true, of course, that Rhodes alluded to its "being more than probable that the invention of the cotton-gin prevented the peaceful abolition of slavery"; that he pointed out the responsibility of England and the North for the establishment of slavery; that he stated that is was not

> an impossible supposition that if the Puritans had settled Virginia and the Cavaliers had settled Massachusetts, while the question would have remained the same, the Puritans might have fought for slavery and the Cavaliers for liberty.[7]

The difficulty is that Rhodes did not offer these as bases for interpretation, and his work shows no sign of his having used them as such. Rather, it seems, Rhodes threw them out as mere comments or speculations, possessing no integral relation to the body of his material, except as to buttress his main theses by demonstrating familiarity, even sympathy, with some of the extenuating circumstances surrounding the South's behavior. For, he went on to say,

> it does not follow that the Southern men of the generation before the war can plead innocence at the judgment bar of history. . . .
>
> The judgment of posterity is made up: it was an unrighteous case which the South defended by arms; and at the tribunal of modern civilization, Calhoun and Davis must be held accountable for the misery which resulted . . .
>
> Calhoun and Davis were leaders because in them the feelings of the Southern oligarchy found the ablest expression. It is therefore fitting that the judgment which is meted out to the Southern leaders should be shared by their followers . . .[8]

The spirit implicit in these words is inconsistent with an assumption that the war was the product of impersonal forces.[9]

The spirit of sectional reconciliation which pervaded Rhodes' treatment of the Civil War dominated his discussion of Reconstruction, and since it was in this field that Rhodes made his greatest mark on the writing of American history it is necessary to discuss it in some detail, beginning with a brief survey of how Reconstruction had been treated prior to the publication of his volumes.

In the years following the Civil War writers in both sections were more interested in providing briefs for sectional politics and policies than in objective study; since few Southerners were historians, the dominant interpretation was that of Northerners who, emphasizing the constitutional aspects involved, believed Radical Reconstruction necessary to preserve the Union from unregenerate rebels.[10]

The argument ran as follows: Southern states, when they claimed that repeal of the Acts of Secession automatically replaced them "in their original constitutional relations to the Union," indulged in "as emphatic an assertion of State rights as the Secession Acts themselves"; such a challenge to the federal nature of the union required repression; through its policies the Republican party saved "the national interpretation of the Constitution" and proved that "a distinctively free-soil and national policy is practicable and necessary." [11]

It might be conceded by some writers like E. Benjamin Andrews, the president of Brown University, that Radical Reconstruction "occasioned dreadful evils," but, as he went on,

> after all, one cannot see how the giant problem of resuscitating the South could, under the circumstances, have been solved more successfully. The plan proposed by President Johnson had sufficient trial to show that it must have led to ills worse than those actually experienced. A qualified colored suffrage would, as things then were, have been abused. It must be remembered that the war left in the South much less of white loyalty than it found, and Congress was certainly justified in insisting that the revived States should be placed on the most loyal basis possible.
>
> Withal, considering the stupendous upheaval in southern society marked by the erection of bondmen into full citizens, dark days were few. . . .[12]

Another approach, based on the belief that Reconstruction had aided the Negro, was typified by the work of Alexander Johnston, writer of a text that a later critic called, "The best school history of the United States at the time of its publication [1885]." [13] In this work Johnston set forth the view that while Reconstruction had failed to ensure the Negro's right to vote,

> it has been a success in other respects. As a slave, the negro had been only a thing, . . . , without any rights. Reconstruction has given him every right but that of voting; and even this right is being obtained slowly but surely, . . .[14]

A notable Southern view in the '80's was that of Woodrow Wilson, who said he preferred "the damnable cruelty and folly of reconstruction . . . to helpless independency" of the Confederacy.[15] Later, writing of that period, Wilson emphasized the "cruelty and folly," but he also noted modifying features. The Radicals, while dominated by those who sought party mastery and revenge, also included men motivated by humanitarian and statesmanlike concern for the Negro. The Radicals, of course, sought to preserve Republican ascendancy through "safe reconstruction" of the South, but in so doing "they had the pity and the humane feeling of the whole country on their side." Northerners going to the South after the war were not all evil, but "were strangely mixed of good and bad." As Wilson observed, however, there was a dearth of reliable material on which to base discussion of Reconstruction: "All the larger and more systematic histories of the country stop short of times so recent . . . All accounts of a time so recent are contemporary." [16]

Wilson wrote in 1901; within five years Rhodes had filled the need with the first comprehensive and scholarly account of Reconstruction as a whole. The work was notable in two respects. First, it offered a nationalistic synthesis for Reconstruction following the pattern Rhodes had given to the Civil War, but with a significant change: whereas in his treatment of the war Rhodes had made the North the custodian of virtue, in his discussion of Reconstruction this role was assigned to the South. The North, however, was praised for presenting a statesmanlike solution to postwar problems which might well have been adopted had it not been for Andrew Johnson. Second, as the synthesis of the war had been organized around slavery, so that of Reconstruction was based on what Rhodes called "the great fact of race."

The basic issue of Reconstruction, as Rhodes saw it, was that of the place of the Negro freedman in Southern society. Ideally, the Southern states should have been allowed to meet that issue in their own way:

> The higher classes of the South . . . had towards him [the Negro] a feeling of kindness and even gratitude for his conduct during the war. Under the guidance of certain leaders they would eventually have conferred upon the coloured people full civil rights. . . .[17]

This conclusion, he thought, was in no way vitiated by such legislation as the "black codes." These were emergency measures designed to cope with the problems created by bestowing freedom upon "one of the most inferior races of mankind," passed under the "influence of 'the black terror' which was not known and therefore not appreciated at the North." [18]

Unfortunately, this very legislation and outbreaks of racial violence in the South made an ideal policy impossible, but a statesmanlike solution was at hand. Congress, dominated by moderates but under pressure from the Radicals, worked out in 1866 a plan of reconstruction embracing the Freedmen's Bureau, the Civil Rights Act and the Fourteenth Amendment: "altogether . . . a system of constructive legislation which may justly command the admiration of congressional and parliamentary historians." [19] Not so generous as the policy of the President, it was, nevertheless, marked by justice; "compared with the settlement of any other notable civil war by a complete victor, it was magnanimous in a high degree. . . . The Southern states should have taken advantage of the offer eagerly and at once." [20]

But Johnson refused to yield, the South followed his lead, he discredited himself in the North by his "swing around the circle," and thus the way was paved for Radical ascendancy in Congress.[21] For this development responsibility rested squarely on Johnson:

> His quarrel with Congress prevented the readmission into the Union on generous terms of the members of the late Confederacy; and for the quarrel and its unhappy results Johnson's lack of imagination and his inordinate sensitiveness to political gadflies were largely responsible: . . . His pride of opinion, his desire to beat, blinded him to the real welfare of the South and of the whole country.[22]

Radical ascendancy meant passage of the Reconstruction Acts providing for military rule in the South, acts so unjust and dangerous as to merit comparison with the odious Kansas-Nebraska act.[23] The laws were uncalled for, explicable only in terms of misguided humanitarianism, a desire to punish the South and a design to maintain Republican supremacy in government. The trend of legislation in the South, wrote Rhodes, had been favorable to the Negro, and otherwise events in the South were going so well that there was nothing which required the stringent military rule provided for.[24]

Even this was not the worst, however: "Honest government by American soldiers would have been better than negro rule forced on the South at the point of the bayonet, which was the actual result of this legislation."[25] These laws were, in effect, "an attack upon civilization," a turning over of the intelligent and propertied white South to the "ignorant mass of an alien race" which throughout history had shown no capacity for progress.[26] With such a race, plus "carpet-baggers" and Southern "shifty men and men of bad character" the Radicals proposed to reconstruct the South, while destroying leadership based upon "men of brains, character and experience."[27]

For this disaster three men were responsible: "Andrew Johnson by his obstinacy and bad behavior; Thaddeus Stevens by his vindictiveness and parliamentary tyranny; Charles Sumner by his pertinacity in a misguided humanitarianism."[28]

As Rhodes told the story, Reconstruction was stark, unrelieved tragedy: "a sickening tale of extravagance, waste, corruption and fraud."[29] Not only did ignorant and debauched Negroes misrule but propertied classes were also put at the mercy of the propertyless:

> Those who levied taxes did not pay them. Few, if any of the office-holders and members of the legislature, possessed property . . . and they were sustained by the most ignorant and propertyless constituency that ever bore a share of government in our country. . . .[30]

While the Republicans fought only for party interest, the Democrats battled for "the dearest rights of liberty and property." Deprived of their right to carry on legal activity against Negro misrule, they resorted to intimidation and violence. "Whilst regretting some of the means employed, all lovers of good government must rejoice at the redemption" which ensued.[31]

The overthrow of Reconstruction was "a victory of righteousness."[32] No great American policy, Rhodes said, had been "so conspicuous a failure":

> The scheme of Reconstruction pandered to the ignorant negroes, the knavish white natives and the vulturous adventurers who flocked from the North; and these neutralized the work of honest

> Republicans who were officers of State. Intelligence and property stood bound and helpless under negro-carpet-bag rule. . . .[33]

It demoralized the Negro by giving him a taste of power for which he was unfitted and allowing him to fall "to the bottom" again while it alienated his best friends, his old masters.[34] Besides, it gave the South a grievance which often clouded its attitude toward the benefits of emancipation. Finally,

> In that balancing of rights and wrongs, which must be made in a just consideration of a great human transaction, the North at the end of the war could appeal to Europe and to history for the justification of its belief that there was on its side a large credit balance. Some of this it has lost by its repressive, uncivilized and unsuccessful policy of Reconstruction. . . .[35]

Such was Rhodes' sweeping reinterpretation of Reconstruction. It won widespread acceptance, not only in the South, where its vigorous reassertion of the Southern white view made an obvious appeal, but also in the North, for reasons which are not far to seek. It constituted the first comprehensive treatment of that period based on what appeared to be critical use of available sources and carried out according to the existing standards of historical scholarship; its findings corresponded with those of other scholars working in the field; and it was in the spirit of that "genuine reconciliation between South and North" which Rhodes himself had noted so significantly in his preface to Volume VI of the *History*. Most white men at that time were agreed on the folly of admitting the Negro to equality.

The influence of the new interpretation was felt almost immediately. William A. Dunning used Rhodes' work for the final revision of his own manuscript for *Reconstruction, Political and Economic, 1865–1877*, a book which in turn has profoundly affected discussion of Reconstruction down to our own day.[36] Anson Daniel Morse of Amherst College made it the basis for his description of Reconstruction in the eleventh edition of the *Encyclopaedia Britannica*.[37] So generally was it accepted by textbook writers that for several generations of school and college students it provided the standard portrayal of Reconstruction, and thus played no small part in reinforcing, if not shaping, the racial attitudes which have made so difficult a rational approach to a basic national problem.[38] It even played a part in the picture of the United States created for foreign students. The French translation of a widely used American high school text summarized Reconstruction thus: "*ces gouvernments nègres de 1868 ne furent qu'une innomable orgie de gaspillage, de corruption, de revoltante incurie—une sorte de parodie de gouvernment.*" [39]

Despite the caveats of Paul Leland Haworth and W. E. B. DuBois—the latter of whom pointed out some significant contributions of Reconstruction governments as early as 1910 [40]—it was not until the 1930's that a basic reappraisal of the Rhodes interpretation got under way, calling attention to the actual role of the Negro in politics; the significant social, economic and political reforms initiated by the Reconstruction governments; and the place of Southern Reconstruction in a *national* reconstruction dominated by the rise of industrialism and the taking of power by a new social class.[41] How unaware Rhodes was of such problems may be gathered from a letter written in 1902. "I shall not get to the Reconstruction period for over a year yet," he wrote, "but I do not expect to have any trouble with it. . . . after my struggle with [military history] everything else will seem easy." [42]

Rhodes, in his preoccupation with supposed racial characteristics, distorted the picture of Reconstruction, and yet, in seizing upon the key role of race relationships in Southern society he anticipated the later interpretations of Ulrich B. Phillips and Allan Nevins. In effect, he called attention to a factor still largely neglected in overall interpretations of American history: the basic influence of racial beliefs, attitudes and relations on the course of American development.

Examples come readily to mind. Anglo-Saxon hostility to fusion with the Indians, so sharply in contrast to the attitudes of French, Spanish and Portuguese colonists, helped shape our long tragic policy toward the first Americans. Southern opposition to compensated emancipation, as Professor Nevins has pointed out, was based largely on racial fears. White solidarity during Reconstruction proved more potent than class considerations, preventing that unity of Negro and white farmers which might have improved the lot of both. Southern populism, feeding on economic distress, nevertheless made its way by appeals to race pride. Its representatives in Congress, its Tillmans and Watsons, helped to mold the policies of the nation.

Even the international relations of the United States have been affected. American opposition to the Japanese proposal for a statement on racial equality in the covenant of the League of Nations, and our policies of Chinese and Japanese exclusion, are among the more obvious examples. In our own day the struggle for Negro rights has a notable effect on our relations with the emerging nations of Africa and Asia.

It seems rather clear then, that the factor of race relationships deserves consideration as a basic element in any pluralistic interpretation of American history, together with such other elements as the European background, the influence of the frontier, class conflicts, immigration, and the changing nature of the American economy. For calling attention to this factor, albeit in distorted form, Rhodes must be given due credit.

No such claim can be put forward for Rhodes' work covering the period, 1877 to 1909. Far from typical of Rhodes at his best, these volumes were written in his old age when he was plagued by illness and personal misfortune. Because of their intrinsic superficiality as well as their obvious prejudice they have exercised little influence on American historiography, a fate for his work in which Rhodes himself might well concur, for in 1906 he himself penned the most succinct commentary on these volumes:

> To write purely a narrative history from 1877 . . . to 1897 would be to shirk a duty and to miss the significance of the period; and for attacking the social questions involved, I feel . . . a lack of basic knowledge.[43]

Having examined the sources of Rhodes' influence on American historiography, we may now address ourselves to the major elements of weakness in his work.

The lack of professional training is certainly among the more apparent. Few will argue that good history can be written only by professionals, although it should be noted that those amateurs to whom we listen with respect are those who conscientiously apply the canons of historical scholarship. History, even in Rhodes' time, had become a sophisticated discipline requiring critical study in the collection, selection and interpretation of sources; analysis of the fundamental social forces which shape the course of history; and awareness of new insights, new interpretations, furnished by historical scholars. In Rhodes' case, lack of professional training may be seen in his careless use of sources, his failure to comprehend the play of basic social forces, and his indifference to the need of evaluating his data in the light of interpretations suggested by Frederick Jackson Turner and others of the younger generation of historians.

Another element of weakness arose from his adoption of some

of the concepts of the new scientific history, particularly of the notion that the historian could transcend his own *self* to write objective, impartial history. Rhodes believed that he himself was such a historian, seeking only truth. Convinced that he was unbiased, he confused his own assumptions—which he never stopped to analyze—with "immutable truths," and this in turn led to a series of historical judgments colored largely by considerations of class, race and nationality.

Rhodes' work suffered also from his emphasis on history as a branch of literature. In his effort to make his work interesting, if not entertaining,[44] he tended to impose on history a literary pattern, as in supplying to the Civil War and Reconstruction a kind of dramatic unity on the classic model. This gave his history a sweep, simplicity and grandeur which appealed to readers, but it also masked significant defects. Factors which did not fit into the pattern, as for example, the development of the West or the impact of immigration, were excluded. Social and economic developments were treated, not as motive forces in historical development, but as matters for essays on American society—treated as still life.

Rhodes was also led by his fetish into dealing with problems with which he was ill-fitted to cope. Without professional training, he lacked also background in politics, diplomacy, international law and military affairs. Nevertheless, as Charles Francis Adams, Jr., pointed out with some asperity, Rhodes undertook to hand down judgments in all these fields and in so doing committed numerous blunders. He misinterpreted the role of cotton in the South's plans for secession; failed to grasp the key role of cotton in the diplomacy of the period; underestimated the significance of the naval blockade of the South; misunderstood the basic psychological importance of Sherman's March to the Sea; glossed over the outrages committed by Sherman's troops; and blundered in his explanations of the Grant campaigns in Virginia in 1864.[45]

Similar criticism may be made of Rhodes' discussion of the Ostend Manifesto, which he treated as a machination of Pierre Soulé; the French evacuation of Mexico, which he attributed almost entirely to the "cleverness" of Seward; and American relations with Canada, which he viewed largely in the light of Fenianism.[46] As to Rhodes' military judgments, handed down with such sweeping finality, one can only concur with the judgment of his friend, Thomas L. Livermore, that "the competent military critic must have seen actual service."[47]

Finally, Rhodes' conception of the role of historian as judge of and guide for his people adversely affected the quality of much of his work. The historian rendered verdicts when he should have been raising questions; furnished guidance when he should have been engaged in explanation; looked upon his material with an eye (perhaps unconsciously) to its didactic uses when he should have been examining it as a means to the understanding of man.

The concept led Rhodes, quite honestly, to exclude from his historical courtroom witnesses whom he deemed incompetent, such as the Negro, the worker, the farmer, the immigrant. It led him to interpret such testimony as he admitted in the light of basic values which he felt good for his country. And it led him, in combination with his belief in the possibility of the purely objective historian, to identify his personal judgments with those of history itself. Underlying his work was his desire to enhance the moral stature and pride in country of his fellow-Americans, not to help them understand themselves. This made for popularity and influence; it also made for some poor history.

For all that, his work is far from negligible. He helped to develop that re-interpretation of the Civil War which provided a more sympathetic hearing to the Southern case. He presented the first full-scale scholarly presentation of Reconstruction in the South, an account apparently so well-grounded that it endured for decades. In both, he exemplified the new nationalist approach to historical issues, replacing that which had identified the cause of the nation with that of the North and the Republican party. His work, too, represented a fusion of the older tradition of literary history with that of the new scientific history. If, in his emphasis on the element of narration, he went far beyond acceptable limits, nevertheless his words might well be taken to heart by more recent historians who have neglected this vital function of their craft. In addition, his discussion of race, while rooted in prejudice, may well suggest new and fruitful approaches to some problems of American history through further exploration of the role played by race relationships.

Rhodes possesses still another, and perhaps greater, value for the student of our day. Uniquely, he is the symbol of an America that has gone. Imbedded in his work are those expressions of the intangibles, so necessary for the understanding of an era, which still so often escape the historian: expressions of the beliefs, thoughts, attitudes of middle-class America at the turn of the century. Through his work we can envision the mind and heart of that America as it sought, in the midst of a rapidly changing world, to maintain the ancient virtues of hard work, thrift, sobriety, financial and moral responsibility. In recreating that picture for us, Rhodes wrought better than he knew. In that sense, he made of his history what Thucydides made of his: "a possession for all time."

NOTES

[1] Quoted in Stow Persons, *American Minds*, p. 320.

[2] *History*, III, 278.

[3] *History*, V, 513; *Historical Essays*, pp. 301–313.

[4] *History*, III, 397; IV, 508; V, 225, 242, 243, 384–392.

[5] *Ibid.*, I, 370, 383.

[6] Thomas J. Pressly, *Americans Interpret Their Civil War*, p. 146.

[7] *History*, I, 26, 379, 381.

[8] *Ibid.*, I, 379–380.

[9] For comment indicating Rhodes' belief that "the underlying reasons of the war" were far from inanimate, see *ibid.*, III, 149 n.

[10] Howard K. Beale, "On Rewriting Reconstruction History," *American Historical Review*, XLV (1940), 807.

[11] A. D. Heffern, "Republican Party," *Encyclopaedia Britannica* (9th edition, American reprint, Philadelphia, 1886), XX, 906, 908.

[12] *History of the United States from the Earliest Discovery of America to the End of 1902* (New York, 1903), IV, 271, 274–275.

[13] R. C. H. Catterall reviewing Johnston's *History of the United States for Schools* (New York, 1885), in J. N. Larned (ed.), *The Literature of American History*, p. 283.

[14] *History of the United States for Schools*, p. 382.

[15] Quoted in Thomas J. Pressly, *Americans Interpret Their Civil War*, p. 166.

[16] Woodrow Wilson, *A History of the American People* (5 vols., New York, 1902), V, 8, 9, 17, 63–64, 113 n.

[17] *History*, V, 560.

[18] *Ibid.*, pp. 556, 558.

[19] *Ibid.*, pp. 598–599.

[20] *Ibid.*, p. 609.

[21] *Ibid.*, pp. 610–626; VI, 5, 13.

[22] *History*, V, 589.

[23] *History*, VI, 23.

[24] *Ibid.*, pp. 27–28.

[25] *Ibid.*, p. 29.

[26] *Ibid.*, pp. 35, 36–38.

[27] *Ibid.*, pp. 44, 45, 83.

[28] *Ibid.*, p. 47.

[29] *History*, VII, 104. This characterization, applied to Louisiana, summarizes Rhodes' general portrait of Reconstruction.

[30] *Ibid.*, p. 147. The particular reference was to South Carolina.

[31] *History*, VI, 181; VII, 129, 140. The last reference is to Mississippi.

[32] *History*, VI, 309.

[33] *History*, VII, 168.

[34] *Ibid.*, pp. 169–171.

[35] *Ibid.*, p. 171.

[36] William A. Dunning, *Reconstruction, Political and Economic, 1865–1877* (New York, 1907), p. xvi.

[37] "Republican Party," *Encyclopaedia Britannica* (11th ed.), XXIII, 179.

[38] Lawrence D. Reddick, "Racial Attitudes in American History Textbooks of the South," *Journal of Negro History*, XIX (1934), 225–265; Emerson D. Fite, *History of the United States* (New York, 1916), pp. 435–440; Arthur M. Schlesinger, Sr., *Political and Social History of the United States, 1829–1925* (New York, 1925), pp. 242–244, 247–252; Samuel Eliot Morison and Henry S. Commager, *The Growth of the American Republic*, II, 829.

[39] David S. Muzzey, *Histoire des États-Unis d'Amérique*, translated by A. de Lapradelle (Paris, n.d.), p. 502.

[40] W. E. B. DuBois, "Reconstruction and Its Benefits," *American Historical Review*, XV (1910), 781–799.

[41] Howard K. Beale, "On Rewriting Reconstruction History," *American Historical Review*, XLV (1940), 807–827; Francis B. Simkins, "New Viewpoints of Southern Reconstruction," *Journal of Southern History*, V (1939), 49–61; H. M. Bond, "Social and Economic Forces in Alabama Reconstruction," *Journal of Negro History*, XXIII (1938), 290–348; and A. A. Taylor, "The Negro in the Reconstruction of Virginia," *ibid.*, XI (1926), 243–415, 425–537; "The Negro in South Carolina During the Reconstruction," *ibid.*, IX (1924), 241–364, 381–569; "Historians of the Reconstruction," *ibid.*, XXIII (1938), 16–34; *The Negro in Tennessee, 1865–1880* (Washington, D. C., 1941). See also C. Vann Woodward, *Reunion and Reaction* (Boston, 1951), and W. E. B. DuBois, *Black Reconstruction* (New York, 1935).

[42] Rhodes to Charles H. Firth, Feb. 10, 1902. Rhodes Papers.

[43] *History*, VI, vi.

[44] Edward Everett Hale to Rhodes, Nov. 13 [1903?]: "There are two schools of historians;—one wishes to make history dull, and the other wishes to make it entertaining. You belong to the second school, and I am one of the most fervent . . . of your admirers." Rhodes Papers.

[45] "Mr. Rhodes' Fifth Volume," *Proceedings, Massachusetts Historical Society*, Second series, XIX (1905–1906), 314, 324–345.

[46] *History*, II, 40; VI, 207–209, 214–215, 341–343, 354–356, 367–368.

[47] Rhodes, "Tribute to Thomas Leonard Livermore," *Proceedings, Massachusetts Historical Society*, LI (1917–1918), 243. Rhodes himself confessed to a distaste for and incapacity to understand military history. Charles K. Bolton, *Notebook, 1886–1914*, p. 173 (Dec. 14, 1911); Rhodes to John C. Ropes, May 30, 1897, in Joseph Borome, "James Ford Rhodes and Historical Scholarship," *New England Quarterly*, XXI (1948), 381.

Appendix

A COMPLETE BIBLIOGRAPHY OF THE WRITINGS OF JAMES FORD RHODES

PUBLISHED works and manuscripts cited in the course of this study are noted in the appropriate notes at the end of each chapter. Since no complete bibliography of Rhodes' writings is available, it may be of value to students and researchers to present it here.

Published Correspondence

Frank Maloy Anderson (ed.), "Letters of James Ford Rhodes to Edward L. Pierce," *American Historical Review*, XXXVI (1931), 778–785.

Joseph Borome, "James Ford Rhodes and Historical Scholarship," *New England Quarterly*, XXI (1948), 379–383.

John A. Garraty (ed.), "The Correspondence of George A. Myers and James Ford Rhodes, 1910–1923," *Ohio Historical Quarterly*, LXIV (1955), 1–29, 125–167, 239–286, 363–405. Available also in book form as *The Barber and the Historian* (Columbus, Ohio: Ohio Historical Society, 1956).

Mark A. DeWolfe Howe, *James Ford Rhodes: American Historian* (New York: D. Appleton and Company, 1929).

Books
(In chronological order)

History of the United States from the Compromise of 1850. Vol. I, 1850–1854. New York: Harper and Brothers, 1892.

History of the United States from the Compromise of 1850. Vol. II, 1854–1860. New York: Harper and Brothers, 1892.

History of the United States from the Compromise of 1850. Vol. III, 1860–1862. New York: Harper and Brothers, 1895.

History of the United States from the Compromise of 1850. Vol. IV, 1862–1864. New York: Macmillan Company, 1904. (First published by Harper and Brothers, 1899.)

History of the United States from the Compromise of 1850. Vol. V, 1864–1866. New York: Macmillan Company, 1904.

History of the United States from the Compromise of 1850 to the Final Restoration of Home Rule at the South in 1877. Vol. VI, 1866–1872. New York: Macmillan Company, 1906.

History of the United States from the Compromise of 1850 to the Final Restoration of Home Rule at the South in 1877. Vol. VII, 1872–1877. New York: Macmillan Company, 1906. This volume contains a general index for all seven volumes. Set reprinted, 1910.

Historical Essays. New York: Macmillan Company, 1909.

Lectures on the American Civil War, Delivered Before the University of Oxford in Easter and Trinity Terms, 1912. New York: Macmillan Company, 1913.

History of the Civil War, 1861–1865. New York: Macmillan Company, 1917. Reprinted, 1937.

History of the United States from Hayes to McKinley, 1877–1896. New York: Macmillan Company, 1919.

History of the United States from the Compromise of 1850. 8 volumes. New York: Macmillan Company, 1920.

The McKinley and Roosevelt Administrations, 1897–1909. New York: Macmillan Company, 1922.

History of the United States from the Compromise of 1850 to the End of the Roosevelt Administration. 9 volumes. New York: Macmillan Company, 1928.

Essays and Articles
(In chronological order)

"The Coal and Iron Industry of Cleveland," *Magazine of Western History* (Cleveland, Ohio), II (1885), 337–345.

"A Review of the Second Volume of 'McMaster's History of the United States,'" *Magazine of Western History* (Cleveland, Ohio), II (1885), 464–477.

"Wilson's Congressional Government," *Magazine of Western History* (Cleveland, Ohio), III (1885–1886), 15–25.

"Some Lessons of History," *Magazine of Western History* (Cleveland, Ohio), III (1885–1886), 148–157.

"Samuel S. Cox's Three Decades of Federal Legislation," *Magazine of Western History* (Cleveland, Ohio), III (1885–1886), 356–366.

"The First Six Weeks of McClellan's Peninsular Campaign," *Proceedings, Massachusetts Historical Society*, Second series, X (1895–1896), 430–438.

"The First Six Weeks of McClellan's Peninsular Campaign," *American Historical Review*, I (1895–1896), 464–472.

"A New Estimate of Cromwell," *Atlantic Monthly*, LXXXI (1898), 842–845.

"The Battle of Gettysburg," *American Historical Review*, IV (1898–1899), 665–677.

"History," *Annual Report, American Historical Association, 1899*. Vol. I. Washington, 1900.

"History," *Atlantic Monthly*, LXXXV (1900), 158–169.

"Some Recent Impressions of England," *Proceedings, Massachusetts Historical Society*, Second series, XIV (1900–1901), 305–319.

"Sherman's March to the Sea," *American Historical Review*, VI (1900–1901), 466–474.

"Concerning the Writing of History," *Annual Report, American Historical Association, 1900*. Vol. I. Washington, 1901.

"Who Burned Columbia?" *Proceedings, Massachusetts Historical Society*, Second series, XV (1901–1902), 264–274.

"Who Burned Columbia?" *American Historical Review*, VII (1901–1902), 485–493.

"Samuel Rawson Gardiner," *Atlantic Monthly*, LXXXIX (1902), 698–701.

"Carl Schurz, 1829– ," in Charles Dudley Warner, editor, *Library of the World's Best Literature* (New York: J. A. Hill and Company, 1902), XXIII, 12974–12978.

"The Presidential Office," *Scribner's Magazine*, XXXIII (1903), 157–173.

"Negro Carpet-Bag-Rule in South Carolina," *Proceedings, Massachusetts Historical Society*, Second series, XX (1906–1907), 256–257.

"Edwin Lawrence Godkin," *Atlantic Monthly*, CII (1908), 320–334.

"The Molly Maguires in the Anthracite Region of Pennsylvania," *American Historical Review*, XV (1909–1910), 547–561.

"Newspapers as Historical Sources," *Atlantic Monthly*, CIII (1909), 650–657.

"Edward Gibbon," *Scribner's Magazine*, XLV (1909), 724–736.

"A Review of President Hayes' Administration in the Light of Thirty Years," *Century Magazine*, LXXVIII (1909), 883–891.

"The Railroad Riots of 1877," *Scribner's Magazine*, L (1911), 86–96.

"The National Republican Conventions of 1880 and 1884," *Scribner's Magazine*, L (1911), 297–306.

"Cleveland's Administrations," *Scribner's Magazine*, L (1911), 496–504, 602–612.

"Some Humors of American History," *Proceedings*, *American Antiquarian Society*, New series, XXIII (1913), 97–109.

"Lincoln in Some Phases of the Civil War," *Harvard Graduates' Magazine*, XXIV (1915), 1–19.

"Charles Francis Adams," in Mark A. DeWolfe Howe, editor, *Later Years of the Saturday Club, 1870–1920* (Boston: Houghton Mifflin Company, 1927), 174–179.

Tributes, Remarks, Etc.,
(In chronological order)

"Remarks on the Death of Octavius B. Frothingham," *Proceedings, Massachusetts Historical Society*, Second series, X (1895–1896), 367–369.

"Remarks on the Death of Edward L. Pierce," *Proceedings*, *Massachusetts Historical Society*, Second series, XII (1897–1899), 10–14.

"Remarks on the Recent Historical Works of Samuel R. Gardiner," *Proceedings*, *Massachusetts Historical Society*, Second series, XII (1897–1899), 111–113.

"Remarks on the Death of Jacob D. Cox," *Proceedings*, *Massachusetts Historical Society*, Second series, XIV (1900–1901), 284–286.

"Tribute to Herbert B. Adams," *Proceedings*, *Massachusetts Historical Society*, Second series, XV (1901–1902), 198–200. This is essentially the presentation of a paper written by David Coit Gilman.

"Tribute to Samuel R. Gardiner," *Proceedings*, *Massachusetts Historical Society*, Second series, XVI (1902), 3–10.

"Tribute to William E. H. Lecky," *Proceedings*, *Massachusetts Historical Society*, Second series, XVIII (1903–1904), 22–26.

"Memoir of Edward L. Pierce," *Proceedings*, *Massachusetts Historical Society*, Second series, XVIII (1903–1904), 363–369.

"Remarks on the New Orleans Meeting [1903] of the American Historical Association," *Proceedings*, *Massachusetts Historical Society*, Second series, XVIII (1903–1904), 232–237.

"Remarks on Negro Suffrage and Reconstruction," *Proceedings, Massachusetts Historical Society*, Second series, XIX (1905), 34–37.

"Tribute to Sir Spencer Walpole," *Proceedings, Massachusetts Historical Society*, Third series, I (1907–1908), 198–204.

"Tribute to Edward Gaylord Bourne," *Proceedings, Massachusetts Historical Society*, Third series, I (1907–1908), 399–407.

"Remarks on General Irvin McDowell," *Proceedings, Massachusetts Historical Society*, XLII (1908–1909), 191.

"Tribute to Charles Francis Adams," *Proceedings, Massachusetts Historical Society*, XLVIII (1914–1915), 409–413.

"Tribute to Frederic Ward Putnam," *Proceedings, Massachusetts Historical Society*, XLIX (1915–1916), 4.

"Tribute to John Davis Long," *Proceedings, Massachusetts Historical Society*, XLIX (1915–1916), 7.

"Tribute to Samuel Savage Shaw," *Proceedings, Massachusetts Historical Society*, XLIX (1915–1916), 11–12.

"Tribute to Thomas Leonard Livermore," *Proceedings, Massachusetts Historical Society*, LI (1917–1918), 241–244.

"Tribute to Henry Adams," *Proceedings, Massachusetts Historical Society*, LI (1917–1918), 313–317.

"Tribute to William R. Livermore," *Proceedings, Massachusetts Historical Society*, LIII (1919–1920), 5–8.

"Tribute to Rev. Henry Fitch Jenks," *Proceedings, Massachusetts Historical Society*, LIII (1919–1920), 94–95.

"Tribute to Barrett Wendell," *Proceedings, Massachusetts Historical Society*, LIV (1920–1921), 195–198.

"Tribute to Viscount James Bryce," *Proceedings, Massachusetts Historical Society*, LV (1921–1922), 211–214.

"Commemorative Tribute to Barrett Wendell, Prepared for the American Academy of Arts and Letters, 1921." New York: American Academy of Arts and Letters, 1922.

"Tribute to Winslow Warren," *Proceedings, Massachusetts Historical Society*, LVI (1922–1923), 231.

"On Dr. Eliot's Anniversary," *Proceedings, Massachusetts Historical Society*, LVII (1923–1924), 11–13.

"Tribute to Viscount Morley of Blackburn," *Proceedings, Massachusetts Historical Society*, LVII (1923–1924), 77–83.

"Commemorative Tribute to William Roscoe Thayer, Prepared for the American Academy of Arts and Letters, 1924." New York: American Academy of Arts and Letters, 1924.

"Tribute to Charles William Eliot," *Proceedings, Massachusetts Historical Society*, LX (1926–1927), 14–15.

Miscellaneous Writings
(In chronological order)

Circulars of Rhodes and Company in *The Trade Review* (Cleveland, Ohio), XIII–XV (1880–1882); *The Trade Review and Western Machinist* (Cleveland, Ohio), XVI (1883); *Iron Trade Review and Western Machinist* (Cleveland, Ohio), XVII–XVIII (1884–1885).

Translation, in collaboration with Georges Delon, of Ernest Renan, *The Abbess of Jouarre*. New York: G. W. Dillingham, 1888.

"Abstract of Paper on the Emancipation Proclamation of President Lincoln," *Proceedings, Massachusetts Historical Society*, Second series, XI (1896–1897), 239–240.

"Abstract of 'Negro Suffrage and Reconstruction,' " *Proceedings, Massachusetts Historical Society*, Second series, XVIII (1903–1904), 465–467.

"Letters of John Bright to Charles Sumner, 1861–1872," *Proceedings, Massachusetts Historical Society*, XLV (1911–1912), 148–159; XLVI (1912–1913), 93–166.

Preface to Hilary A. Herbert, *The Abolition Crusade and Its Consequences*. New York: Charles Scribner's Sons, 1912.

Letter in *The Nation*, CI (1915), 147, praising the magazine's semicentennial issue.

Introduction to Charles N. Baxter and James M. Dearborn, *Confederate Literature: A List of Books and Newspapers, Maps, Music and Miscellaneous Matter Printed in the South during the Confederacy, Now in the Boston Athenaeum*. Boston: The Athenaeum, 1917.

A picture of James Ford Rhodes may be found as the frontispiece, *Proceedings, Massachusetts Historical Society*, LX (1926–1927).

INDEX